THE ODYSSEY

Johns Hopkins
New Translations
from Antiquity

Homer

THE ODYSSEY

Translated by Edward McCrorie

With an introduction and notes by
Richard P. Martin

The Johns Hopkins University Press
Baltimore and London

© 2004 The Johns Hopkins University Press
All rights reserved. Published 2004
Printed in the United States of America on acid-free paper
9 8 7 6 5 4 3 2 1

Johns Hopkins Paperbacks edition, 2005

The Johns Hopkins University Press
2715 North Charles Street
Baltimore, Maryland 21218-4363
www.press.jhu.edu

The Library of Congress has cataloged the hardcover edition of this book as follows:

Homer.
[Odyssey. English]
    The Odyssey / Homer ; translated by Edward McCrorie ; with an introduction and
notes by Richard P. Martin.
    p. cm — (Johns Hopkins new translations from antiquity)
Includes bibliographical references.
    ISBN 0-8018-6854-8 (hardcover: acid-free paper)
    1. Odysseus (Greek mythology)—Poetry.   2. Epic poetry, Greek—Translations into
English.   I. McCrorie, Edward.   II. Title.   III. Series.
PA4025.A5M43 2004
883'.01—dc22   2003021372

ISBN 0-8018-8267-2 (pbk.: acid-free paper)

A catalog record for this book is available from the British Library.

To Richard Wilbur

Contents

Translator's Preface

The experience of Homer's *Odyssey*, like that of life itself, is one of joy and jitters, wonder and setbacks, the struggle and rewards of a long journey home. An early chapter of my own journey took place in a curious dream some years ago before I began translating Homer. Flying 40,000 feet over the Atlantic I was asked by a woman next to me, "Where are you going?" I answered promptly, "Mycenae."

I woke up thinking that was an alluring destination. In a later chapter of my journey I stood among the excavated ruins of Homer's Mukenai (pronounced by him, roughly, moo-KAY-nai), gazing down at the plain of Argos, still quite green. I touched a circle of shadowy earth where, if Heinrich Schliemann was right, the central hearth-fire of Agamemnon himself had burned. That autumn of 1992 I could not confirm or deny the dream was sent to me by Pallas Athene (PAHL-luhss ah-THAY-nay), but I felt I should pay it some attention. In this Preface, therefore, I'd like to describe one man's *Odyssey* journey, hoping my readers will be as patient and understanding as Homer's Phaiakians. The style and substance of the present translation evolved over a number of years with a great deal of help; some of my critics I think as "godlike" as Homer's swineherd, Eumaios.

In the days following that dream I looked for an old Greek grammar I'd used in college. For some reason I'd never thrown it away. It brought back memories of college teachers roused by Homer, lengthening the Greek vowels and sweating out the perils of Hektor and Odysseus before my eyes. The rugged sound and often harrowing sense of Homer began calling to me; but many hours lay ahead on the distant shore of that grammar. A bevy of hard verbs in particular detained me.

As Odysseus often had a problematical course to map out, right from the start translators have the Greek-into-English *line* to grapple with. Homer often moves rapidly in hexameters with a subtle timbre and texture of vowels and consonants, with varied and dramatic pauses: how to render all that into contemporary English poetry? Having labored through Shelley's style for my doctoral dissertation at Brown and having tried to approximate the music of Virgil in a translation of the *Aeneid*, I wondered if I might adapt that English line for my *Odyssey* work, since the meter of Virgil and Homer is the same—dactylic hexameter. I wanted to avoid, however, a runaway hexameter line like that of Longfellow in *Evangeline*.

The crux, I knew, lay in the dynamics of Homeric verse. It's called "dactylic" but not all six metrical units need be dactyls, scanned / × ×, as in "powerful." Virgil and Homer in fact were obliged to provide a dactyl only in the fifth unit, or "foot." (Even there they don't always obey.) What this means is that both poets enjoyed a wide range of rhythmical flexibility, for example using more dactyls to speed up a line or more spondees to slow it down—two "long" syllables together, the English counterpart scanned / /, as in "great hall"—depending on the emotional and narrative substance of the passage. For the *Aeneid* and then the *Odyssey* I evolved a similar line, using English "accentual" verse. It resembles Homer in that it counts the number of "longs" or stresses but lets the number of "short" or unstressed syllables vary. A famous example is the four-stress line of *Beowulf.* Of course for Homer as for Virgil I needed to extend that line to five and sometimes six stresses. I also decided to end most of my lines, following the ancient epics, with a dactyl-trochee (/ × × / ×) or dactyl-spondee (/ × × / /) combination. Thus in the opening lines of book 2:

> × / × / × / × × / × × / ×
> When newborn Dawn came on with her rose-fingered daylight,

> × / × / × × / × × / × × / ×
> the well-loved son of Odysseus rose in his bedroom

> × / × / × / / × × / ×
> and dressed. He hung a sharp sword from a shoulder,

> / × / × × / × / × × / ×
> strapped two beautiful sandals under his oil-smooth

> / × / × / × / × × / /
> feet and left the room, his face like a great God's.

Style of course does not exist apart from a poet's deepest convictions and feelings. For a firmer grounding in Greek style and experience I thought it wise to travel, to actually sail the seas and walk the lands made famous by Odysseus. I'm grateful to Providence College for a study grant to that end. This time while flying to Athens and gazing down at the Mediterranean I recalled serving as a young man aboard the USS *Leyte,* an aircraft carrier that hunted for nuclear-powered sea-beasts and disgorged rowdy, hubristic sailors on the shores of Piraeos, Krete, and Rhodes. Our skipper slashed no cables or throats of rams but his crewmen relished enough wine and beef, roasted (I liked to imagine) by Odysseus's descendants. Now I sought out Homer in small boats on hazy seas, among gruff men on city streets, proud of their muscle and savvy. I looked through pottery collections in the Athens Archeological Museum and found the *Odyssey*'s women and goddesses in black and red. Along the jade-green Alpheios River, flowing all summer long near Olympia, I saw the spirit of Homer himself sounding out his lines in the Games over 2,700 years ago, strumming his *phorminx*, and garnering the laurels in honor of Zeus. In Patras I discovered the taste of Mavrodaphne, a strong, sweet wine that would brace me before entering the cave of a giant. On the island of Corfu—Kerkyra, the legendary home of Alkinoos and the Phaiakians—a Greek mother and her family extended warm hospitality to a *xeinos*, their stranger-guest from America.

All roads and waves led finally, it seemed, to Ithaka. I stood on a ridge near Mount Aetos with a view so perfect to east and west that I wanted to build a house there. Odysseus did just that, according to Sarantis Syme-onoglou, the archaeologist heading up the Odyssey Project from Washington University in St. Louis. He gestured down one evening to his latest excavation with its "Cyclopean" construction—stones so large that only a giant, supposedly, could place them. Resembling the stones of Mukenai, they clearly established the presence of a people here like Agamemnon's during the Trojan era some 3,300 years ago.

In time my *Odyssey* journey took me back home to America with armfuls of maps, books, conversation notes, and the makings of poems like "Paxos Women," published a few years later in *Columbia*. The journey was often intellectual and cultural in stateside museums with their own collections of ancient Greek artifacts, in essays about Homeric plant life in the Peloponnese, in drawings and photographs of birds and mammals in ancient and modern Hellas. But no doubt visiting or corresponding with other poets and classicists became the keenest pleasure. William Wyatt at Brown, for instance, offered me valuable advice about *over*intellectualizing a translation of Homer—and *in*valuable advice about the danger of using too much Latinate diction. Rely on a forceful English, he would say, stay close to your Anglo-Saxon roots.

Exploring the work of other translators of Homer was another heady and heartening chapter in this *Odyssey* journey. They represented an amazingly broad spectrum of literary assumptions and line-by-line strategies. Grouped at one end of the spectrum were those I began to call *free Homeric spirits*. Chapman and Pope, for example, had paid keen attention to color, drama, and vivacity of style, rendering Homer loosely and imaginatively. Their aim in fact was to generate a kind of love, a passionate devotion to Homer among their contemporaries. So too in the twentieth century, Fitzgerald and Fagles (to name only two) paid less attention to the technicalities of Homeric verse and more to an inventive American style in their mother tongue. Their principal aim, like that of Chapman and Pope, was to arouse new attention and delight in the generation of English readers at hand.

Grouping toward the other end of the spectrum were those I came to think of as *close followers of Homer*. Well-trained in the classics, often lovers of every nuance of the Greek, less concerned with passing styles of English poetry, they worked hard to produce faithful translations of the *Odyssey*. Lattimore's work was a prime example in the twentieth century. He took a bold chance by lengthening the English line for his Homer, aiming at more fidelity to both sense and sound. Many other translators in this group, however, were so concerned about accuracy that they turned to prose. Although they lost nearly all of the *Odyssey*'s music, translators like Murray and Dimock (in the Harvard Loeb edition) did focus on clarity and correctness for their readers.

Might a translation somehow do both? Having aimed at a close approximation to the sound and sense of Virgil's Latin, I initially felt like a member of the second group, the close followers of Homer. I certainly wanted to avoid a free translation that might move in the direction of rewriting the original in what Robert Lowell called "imitation." But I also continued to entertain the possibility of a brisk twenty-first-century English idiom for Homer. When the attainment of both ends, fidelity and freedom, struck me as truly daunting, two eminent forebears gave me hope. William Arrowsmith had written a sly summation of the translator's twofold obligation in his excellent Petronius: devoted to the Latin as though to a wife, he confessed a greater devotion to his English mistress. But exactly how, day by day, can a translator render Homer's Greek faithfully and still remain close to English poetry now? A solution came from my other forebear, Richard Wilbur, who has graciously accepted the dedication of this work. I credit him (though in his modesty he may pass along the credit) for an idea so wonderfully paradoxical that it constantly baffles my poetry students: a close adherence to form may actually have the effect of liberating, not constraining, the poet-translator. At one point Wilbur expressed concern about my trying to stay too close to Homer's orchestration. But I could not resist the model of his Molière. How remarkably devoted to the French and to his own English! Someone has wittily paid him the highest compliment: Molière would insist, if he were alive, that he had beautifully translated Wilbur.

So I aimed at both fidelity to Homer and all the vitality I could muster in English. Perfection was never the goal; I aimed at a good approximation. To that end, since Wilbur's Molière also played so well on the stage and emphasized poetry's performance, the next chapter of my journey took me into recordings and live readings of Homer. They were sadly disappointing. Little or no attention was paid to the Greek metrical patterns; readers generally followed the accent marks, or diacritics, placed in the text after Homer's time. Now of course we'll never know exactly how Homer sang his poetry. But we do know how his meter is scanned and it's unimaginable to me, as a poet, that he largely ignored those rhythmical patterns in oral presentation.

I suspect in fact that he stressed the meter vigorously as a singer (*aoidos*), probably like our contemporary folksingers with their guitars, emphasizing both the words and the beat.

How, then, should the lines in the present translation be performed? Hamlet tells the players not to mouth his lines: no one appreciates a performer who overemphasizes the iambs—da-DUM, da-DUM—in a Shakespeare soliloquy. Some lines in this translation develop an iambic pattern briefly, while others are trochaic (DUM-da, DUM-da); others are a mix of these two or others (like the dactyls noted above, DUM-da-da); in all I tried to orchestrate, as Homer usually does, the mood and pace of the moment. I also took the advice of Donald Hall and tried occasionally to abut strongly accented syllables. A common tactic in English accentual verse, it can prevent the line from overaccelerating. Two fairly simple verses about Penelopeia should illustrate. (I refer the reader to the Glossary for an explanation of the spelling and pronunciation of such names, in this case, following the Greek meter, PAY-neh-law-PAY-uh.) Homer describes her in book 19 (lines 600–601) leaving the great hall of the palace:

```
  / ×     / × | × /     × /   × × / ×
Having spoken she walked upstairs to her glowing

  /   | ×   / ×/  || /   ×   × /     ×
room, and not alone: handmaids had joined her.
```

In the scansion, / represents an accent or stress, × an unaccented syllable, | a short pause (or caesura), and || a longer pause. This English line contains five or six stressed syllables and a varying number of unstressed syllables, approximating Homer's hexameter line with its six "longs" and varying number of "shorts." The rhythm in line 600 is trochaic at first, "HAVING SPOKEN," with a brief caesura, or pause. It rises briefly as the queen ascends, "she WALKED upSTAIRS," and the line ends, like Homer's, with a characteristic dactyl-trochee combination, giving the line a brief acceleration: "STAIRS to her GLOWING." Matthew Arnold was no doubt right to call Homer's line "rapid"—English blank verse or iambic pentameter is definitely slower—but the *Odyssey*'s rhythm often slows down to underscore a somber or tense moment. Here my line 601 has three stressed syllables in a group of four, with a heavy pause as well—"NOT ALONE: HAND-"—suggesting the queen's closeness to and emotional need for her handmaids, their "crowding" together.

Readers will have little trouble with all this, I think, if they don't have high or rigid expectations about the epic line in English *having* to be iambic, dactylic, or something else. This rendering of Homer can be read aloud enjoyably and naturally, though a little help from a *phorminx* or some other tightly strung instrument would help. If only we had recordings of Homer winning the laurels at the first Olympic Games!

In time my frail translator's craft took me more deeply into the caverns of Homeric style. As with Virgil I began paying close attention to Homer's vowels, diphthongs, and consonants. I noticed how often *eta* appears in the *Odyssey*, for example, designating a sound close to our *mare*. On the other hand *iota*, with its long *ee* or short *ih* sound, tends to appear less often, especially in Homer's long syllables. Now all sorts of translation theory and practice flourished in the twentieth century and someone like Rosemary Waldrop might have produced an engagingly musical imitation of Homeric vowels in her English without worrying about literal fidelity—and without failing to produce a strange new Homer. This translation, on the other hand, aimed at both sometimes—the retention of Homer's key vowels and the passage's meaning in English. Thus in the well-known line (2.1 and elsewhere) about the day's beginning—

êmos d' êrigeneia phanê rhododaktulos Êôs—

which in English transcription probably would sound like

HAY-moss DEY-rih-gheh-NAY-uh phuh-NAY rhaw-daw-DAHK-too-
lawss AY-ohss—

four *eta*s appear as "long" syllables and the diphthong, *ei* (*epsilon* and *iota*), has a similar sound. That's a good deal of assonance; no translator could replicate all of it. My version captures two of the *eta*s:

When newborn Dawn *came* on with her rose-fingered *da*ylight—

and I also echoed Homer's *dahk-* with my "on" and his *-ohss* with my "rose." On the other hand I replicated only one of Homer's five *omicron* sounds (as in the second syllable of *êmos*, HAY-moss) with my "Dawn." This sort of thing became possible less frequently with Homer than with Virgil, probably because ancient Greek differs more radically than classical Latin from modern English. When in doubt I let the demands of current English make the final decision. Still it was often exciting, if sometimes overweening, to match Homeric sound and sense to current English music and meaning.

Besides, other real ghosts confronted me soon enough in the caverns of Homeric style. Milman Parry has famously demonstrated how one phrase after another in the epics, whether a personal description, a verb or a noun phrase, fits neatly into the metrical notches of that line. Such diction-and-meter combinations, often names with adjectives or epithets at the end of a line, undoubtedly helped the singer's memory; but for the modern translator they pose considerable problems. Odysseus is often dubbed *polumêtis*, a word suggesting a plenitude of strategies. Should the translator drop the epithet if it has appeared a few lines earlier? Some have seen it as filler in the verse and dropped it altogether; still others have rewritten the phrase to please the modern American ear.

With a good deal of trial and error I began to find that Homer's epithets could move with a certain flow into English. Thus 22.430—

tên d'apameibomenos prosephê polumêtis Odusseus—

might appear in drably literal English: "Then answering her Odysseus, a man of many strategies, said . . ." In this translation:

An answer came from Odysseus, full of the best plans . . .

A fair approximation of Homeric sound and sense, this English also struck me as idiomatic enough. A bigger and harder-looking combination was *polutlas dios Odusseus*. Again I tried to stay close to the Greek's music and meaning without sacrificing current English: "long-suffering, godlike Odysseus." Will some readers have trouble with "godlike"? Not much, I hope: the human and divine often mirrored each other in Homer's world. Poetry readers in fact suspend as much disbelief, surely, encountering Samuel Taylor Coleridge's Ancient Mariner. Another apparently simple adjective has caused both translators and commentators trouble. The word *amumon*, often rendered "flawless" or "noble," links well with a virtuous king or a deathless goddess. But how to link it with Aigisthos, the man who seduced Klutaimnestre and killed her husband, Agamemnon? In a line referring to Zeus's memory (1.29), I chose two other closely related meanings of *amumon*:

His heart recalled the *high-born, handsome* Aigisthos . . .

It was not possible—or wise—to fit all of Homer's epithets into proper metrical notches in English. I experimented for months and settled on choices for many; for others I remain unsure to this day. J. B. Hainsworth's 1968 book with its self-explanatory title, *The Flexibility of the Homeric Formula*, warmly encouraged my experiments and variations—a play with epithets and formulas that Homer himself enjoyed.

As for the syntax, I ran into less trouble and complexity with Homer than with Virgil. Clausal arrangements in the *Odyssey* tend to be direct, marked by that winning plainness that Arnold spoke of. One reason probably was the bardic tradition: since every line must be orally presented, not only the metrical pattern but a certain clarity must have ranked high. Indeed the temptation for many English translators has been to fiddle with things, the formulaic diction as well as the syntax, possibly supposing that a plain Homer is not hardy enough for modernist or postmodernist taste. I too have restructured some of Homer's sentences when the flow of modern

English invited it. I hope I have not strayed too far from the letter and spirit of the Greek. (Actually some of my syntax is plainer than Homer's.) The call of variety—to sail away to some other island—and the insistence of accuracy—to stay close to the Greek home—have both preoccupied my Odyssean journey. I could not have listened to both goddess-like voices without mentors like Arrowsmith and Wilbur.

During revisions of the book I continued traveling, usually by mail, to other poets, friends, and classicists. I hoped each would be a *xeinos amumon*—a noble host. Consistently my excerpts were welcomed and sent off laden with gifts of attention, criticism, and encouragement. If "Nothing is worse for any man than to wander," as Odysseus tells us (15.343), probably nothing is better than to arrive at a place excelling in hospitality like Phaiakia. My thanks go out to all my hosts at least in the form of these acknowledgments. David Konstan at Brown encouraged and discriminated among my earlier efforts closely. Deborah Boedeker at the Center for Hellenic Studies insisted that the hardest question in translating Homer is the metrical one: I value that emphasis. Joseph Tebben at Ohio State, a lover like me of Wilbur's translations of the French, expressed hope for an English Homer both melodic and elegant. I hope my version approximates that ideal. Robert Bly, writing from Moose Lake, Minnesota, welcomed the relaxation in many lines and the tension in others. Richard Janko, writing from Marseille, praised my efforts and warned about spurious lines added to Homer by later writers. I'm grateful to Alan Boegehold at Brown for sending a brisk following wind to a raftlike piece of my translation. Norman Austin at the University of Arizona wisely warned me about false grandeur in English translations of Homer. He also noted that accuracy can result in more, rather then less, vividness. Barry Powell at the University of Wisconsin strongly backed my earliest efforts—*that* took foresight—and emphasized the primacy not of translation theory but of actual practice. William Hansen at Indiana praised the rhythm of my lines and urged me to work harder on the diction; I hope I've complied. William Sale at Washington University in St. Louis advised me to stay in close touch with the Classical tradition in *English* literature while translating Homer.

 I deeply thank Donald Hall, writing from Danbury, New Hampshire, who was distinctly but rightly displeased with much of my early word choice. Peter Green at the University of Texas generously critiqued my versification and Greek translation theory at length. Herbert Howe, writing from retirement in Madison, Wisconsin, expressed particular concern about passages wandering off into non-English idioms. Margaret Graver at Dartmouth recommended, with a stamp of her own enthusiasm, first-rate books about Homeric craft.

I gladly acknowledge a debt, moreover, to those who never saw this work but exercised influence, sometimes enormously, on my tactics. A number of key translators and critics I've noted above; if Pope and Arnold were alive I hope they would both smile on this book. Editors and contributors to commentaries and dictionaries, like Stanford and Autenrieth, have also proved themselves invaluable. Filling out their efforts in a monumental way was the new *Oxford Commentary*. These volumes, arriving in my library at the most opportune moment, solved a myriad of puzzles—or candidly pronounced them unsolvable. I read Heubeck and others at first for their informed judgment; in time, for the sheer beauty of their expertise.

As the nearest help is often the dearest, I hasten to thank my Rhode Island support team, colleagues at Providence College such as Bruce Graver and Rodney Delasanta, always a staunch ally. My principal coach in matters Homeric was often William Wyatt at Brown: his going-away horse-car I would gladly load with a dozen bronze cauldrons, tripods, and silver wine-bowls. My wife, Beatrice, always enthused and encouraging, sounded out the Greek with gusto after I did. She was a *nostos* in herself, a warm home to return to after hours among frail cries of the dead and the living.

I close with a special thanks to you, John Lawless, the only Classicist at our small college. A call or a knock away when I first tangled with Homer's impossible-looking epithets and diphthongs, you were patient and informed especially when I suffered from still another attack of irregular verbs, those one-syllable, virus-looking things beginning with *epsilon*, clearly and maliciously cloning each other. You were my Classics helper par excellence, an Asklepios in my own back yard. Many, many thanks.

Introduction
Richard P. Martin

Plots and Performances

The *Odyssey* charts the end of a voyage, the return home, after twenty years, of a veteran warrior and long-suffering sailor. Odysseus's reentry into life on the island of Ithaka comes just in time. His son Telemakhos is on the verge of full manhood while his patient wife, Penelopeia, is starting to lose hope and contemplating remarriage. It is more difficult to say when this story begins, for the fate of Odysseus is wrapped up with that of the city of Troy. And, from one point of view, Troy's destruction at the hands of avenging Greek troops had been long afoot, reaching back to the origin of the cosmos. We can piece together the story from Greek myths that were most likely known to the audience of the *Odyssey*, while remembering that already in ancient times there existed variant, even contradictory, versions of these events. The sources for these tales include the *Theogony* of Hesiod (roughly contemporary with the rise of Homeric poetry in the eighth century B.C.) and the so-called cyclic epics of the seventh and sixth centuries B.C. (filling out the Trojan "cycle") of which only random citations and a few plot summaries from later sources now survive.

Gaia, the Earth, was one of the first creatures. She arranged for her relentlessly oppressive husband, Ouranos ("sky"), to be overthrown by their son Kronos, who was in turn displaced by her favorite grandson, Zeus, in a family upheaval that had universal consequences. With the advice of his primeval grandmother, Zeus gained the kingship of the heavens by recruiting for his battles against the older generation of gods the monstrous Hundred Handers, who had been imprisoned by the earlier divine tyrants. With her advice as well, he swallowed one of his first wives, Mêtis ("cunning intelligence"), and, thus armed with cautious wisdom, came to ensure that his own reign would never be overthrown. Instead of producing a son stronger than Zeus, as had been predicted, the disempowered Mêtis, tucked safely inside her husband, bore Athene, who sprang full-grown from the chief god's head.

Zeus, therefore, owed Gaia a debt. As time went on and she complained of the increasingly heavy burden of human life, Zeus devised a massive war to decrease world population and lighten the load on the Earth's surface. The conditions for the Trojan War grew out of another averted divine marriage; a hero's wedding; a rape; and an elopement.

Zeus desired the nymph Thetis, one of the fifty daughters of the sea-god

Nereus. But once again, he feared that if he mated with a powerful goddess, any offspring might eventually replace him. So he found reason to marry off Thetis to an unsuspecting mortal, Peleus, as a reward for that hero's pious behavior. It was at their splendid wedding that Strife (Eris), who had not been invited, tossed amid the guests an apple inscribed *"kallistêi"*—"to the fairest." Athene, Here, and Aphrodite each claimed the prize. The father of the gods chose a Trojan, named Paris, to judge. Rejecting the promises of the other two goddesses, he chose Aphrodite and received Helen as his reward.

Her mother Lede had once been taken forcibly by Zeus disguised as a swan. Helen's unusual birth from an egg presaged a remarkable career. By the time she was of marriageable age, she had suitors from every corner of Greece. Menelaos, the son of Atreus, was picked to be her husband, and to avoid further strife, all the suitors bound themselves by an oath that they would rally to retrieve Helen, if ever she might be in need. Odysseus of Ithaka, who had suggested this idea, was in return aided by Helen's mortal father Tundareos, who persuaded his own niece, Helen's first cousin, to marry the young man. Her name was Penelopeia.

Finally the elopement—or abduction, as some preferred—and its aftermath. On a visit to Menelaos at the couple's home in Sparte, Paris found his promised reward for the beauty contest and, with the help of Aphrodite's seductive wiles, persuaded Helen to leave with him for Troy, thus setting in motion the mobilization of Greek forces to punish the eastern transgressor. At the time, Odysseus and Penelopeia had just been blessed with a son— their first child—and the proud father, reluctant to leave Ithaka to retrieve Helen, tried to outfox the recruiting party, led by Agamemnon, brother of the aggrieved husband. Donning a furry cap (although it was summer), he started to plow his field with the ridiculous combination of an ox and a horse. But one of the visitors, Palamedes, refused to believe Odysseus was crazy. Snatching Telemakhos, the infant son of Odysseus, from his nurse's arms, he placed the baby in front of the plow. When Odysseus veered to avoid hurting his child, the charade was exposed. Off he went to war.

The siege of Troy lasted ten years. After the death of Akhilleus and Hektor, the foremost fighters on either side, the Greeks took the advice of Odysseus to insinuate themselves into the city by hiding within the Trojan Horse. In the chaos and slaughter that followed this sneak attack, Troy fell, but Athene's temple within the citadel was desecrated by the invaders. Consequently, her wrath was to hound the Greeks—including Odysseus— on their journey home. The returns of the heroes were narrated in an ancient epic, now lost, called the *Nostoi*. Something like this poem must be the burden of the song of Phemios, the local bard on Ithaka, who sings to the suitors about the homeward journeys of the war-weary Greeks (1.325ff.). Further on within the *Odyssey* itself, we hear about the successful home-coming of Nestor (3.130ff.), how Aias (Ajax) lost his life, the sadly delayed trip of Menelaos, and the fatal return of his brother Agamemnon (all in 4.351ff.). Each of these stories forms a contrast to the overall narrative of Odysseus's voyage. In particular, the cautionary tale of Agamemnon—slain by his wife and her lover soon after his triumphant return—is made into an explicit warning for Odysseus by none other than the victim himself in the underworld (11.441ff.). It is there, too, that Odysseus encounters the great Akhilleus, who chose a short life with glory instead of a long life back in his native place. In another striking contrast with the fate of his former war-comrades, Odysseus manages to have both fame *and* safe return, to obtain glory precisely *through* homecoming. In this, he finally goes one better than his old heroic rival. His return to Ithaka involves one more battle, this time against 108 young men, Penelopeia's arrogant suitors, some of them his fellow islanders. Restored to his rightful place, flanked by his son and father, Odysseus stands as a model of intelligence, care, and perseverance. He is the ultimate survivor.

Even in ancient times, it was recognized that Homeric poetry presented these stories from the Trojan War in a unique manner. In the fourth century B.C., Aristotle in his sketch of literary history and theory, the *Poetics* (1459b), noted that Homer "takes only one portion of the story and makes use of many episodes, such as the Catalogue of Ships and others by means of which he diversifies his poetry. But the others make their poems about one person, one time, one action having many parts, in the way that the com-poser of the *Kupria* and the *Little Iliad* did." In short, Homeric epic had unity, while cyclic epics were just collections.

Thus, the *Iliad* focuses on just a few days in the last year of the war, on the quarrel between Agamemnon and his best warrior, Akhilleus, with its devastating results. By the end of the poem, Akhilleus is still alive, the Horse and the fall of Troy are in the future: the poet has declined to recount the whole saga. Nevertheless, thanks to artful allusions and juxtapositions within the tale, the emotional force of the coming events informs every part of the poem. Through the death of Hektor at the hands of Akhilleus, and Priam's mission to the Greek camp to retrieve his son's body, we feel, at the most personal level, the pathos of a doomed city.

If the *Iliad* is a long saga, brilliantly condensed and intensely focused, the *Odyssey* is rather a simple story told through a complex narrative. The tale of the Trojan War hero starts nearly at the end of his return, uses flashbacks to fill in the previous years, synchronizes several subplots, and presents the major events mostly through the recollections and perspec-

tives of others. In other words, already at the beginning of Western litera-
ture, almost all the devices of the modern film and novel are masterfully put
on display.

The poem's first four "books" (traditional chapter-size divisions) are a
fine example of the *Odyssey*'s indirect tale-telling. We do not meet the hero at
all. Even his name is delayed for a number of lines, as the poem begins with a
generic noun: "The man, my Muse, resourceful, driven a long way . . ."
Instead of simply bringing Odysseus onto the scene from the start, the poet
artfully lets us hear *other* people talking *about* the hero—the gods, his wife
and son, those who miss him, and those who want to replace him. His impact
is made vivid precisely through his absence.

Odysseus's absence, naturally, has the greatest effect on his son, now
twenty years old. Telemakhos has never known his father except by hearsay.
But now he is thrust into action, to go and learn of Odysseus's fate, by a
combination of factors—the gods' plans, the growing impatience of his
mother's suitors, and his own coming of age. The story of his own minia-
ture "odyssey" to visit those heroes who made it back—Nestor and Mene-
laos—and the suitors' plot to murder him, occupy the first four books.
These have been called the "Telemakhy," or story of Telemakhos. A number
of nineteenth-century critics argued that they were part of an extraneous
composition, tacked on inelegantly to the poem. But the few inconsisten-
cies that prompted that criticism are far outnumbered by the rich and
meaningful resonances that emerge when we experience the *Odyssey* in this
way, as the story of a father being gradually learned of by his own son.
Telemakhos, within the poem, is like us outside it, an audience for the
heroic past.

Not only is this poetic strategy compelling and persuasive in terms of
narrative. It is culturally apt as well, since archaic Greek notions of heroic
performance and family history always tied the fame of father and son
closely together. In the best cases, sons continued the fame of their fathers,
or bettered it; fathers promoted the achievements of their sons, and spread
their fame. Odysseus, in the *Iliad*, actually swears oaths with the phrase "as
much as I am the father of Telemakhos"—an assertion that what he says or
does is as true as his paternity. The very name "Telemakhos," which means
"fighting afar," is an adjective applicable to Odysseus, both as an archer and
as one who battled in distant Troy, rather than an epithet befitting his son.
It's as if the son's identity depends on the father's actions. Ironically, the
Odyssey opens with Telemakhos doubting whether Odysseus ever was his
father (1.215–16). A main purpose of the first four books is to show that the
young man deserves to be recognized as Odysseus's son by others and has
the innate qualities that guarantee this paternal bond.

In the next four books of the poem, the center of attention is Odysseus, now on the last leg of his voyage. Even as Telemakhos starts traveling to learn of his lost father, the hero begins moving closer to Ithaka. The fortuitous absence of Poseidon from the gods' company enables Athene, with Zeus's consent, to liberate her favorite from the island of Kalupso, where he has been stranded, increasingly restless although in the company of the beautiful nymph, for seven years. Another shipwreck brings him to the land of the Phaiakians, where Odysseus, revealing his identity, charms the royal family into giving him safe passage home. As the poem makes clear, Odysseus holds his audience enthralled with a performance very much like that of the real poet of the composition: Odysseus takes over as narrator for the next four books, weaving a tale of his previous adventures that includes giant cannibals, seductive witches, sea-monsters, seers, magic, ghosts—the age-old ingredients of folktales, worldwide, worked into an autobiographical narrative. At the same time as it gives us this sailor's tale, the *Odyssey* takes pains to provide a carefully nuanced framework for the story that Odysseus relates. We see him enchant his audience; we hear of their reactions (including the decision to load the teller with more gifts); we can imagine the local bard Demodokos listening to this newly arrived tale-teller with admiration and envy—all of which is surely meant to suggest how *we*, as an audience, might best receive and appreciate the entire Homeric *Odyssey*. More dazzling, still, by posing the "odyssey" of the hero's adventures in this way, the poem teases us with the idea that the whole "autobiography" may itself be largely convenient fiction.

We might notice the sequence and shape of this command performance. The stories that Odysseus relates appear to follow a rhythm of two short episodes, then a long, then two more short, followed by another long one. For example, the Kikones and the Lotos-eaters are described in less than forty lines of verse; they lead up to the Kuklops episode, which takes ten times that many lines to tell. The same happens with the next three stories: Aiolos (short), Laistrugonians (short), and Kirke (long). The effect is nearly tidal. Another subtle pattern emerges if we consider the content of the episodes in social terms. Every place Odysseus describes represents a variation on the conditions of Greek life, if we define those basic conditions as extended family; worship of gods centered on sacrifice; and agriculture. The Kuklops are a negative example: they have no agriculture, no laws, live alone, and call no assembly (deficiencies unthinkable for a Greek community). The Lotos-eaters live, apparently, without cultural memory, and lead others to forget. Kirke and Kalupso—goddesses living alone—embody what is impossible for mortal Greek females. The Phaiakians, on the other hand, look nearly Greek. They worship recognizable gods, enjoy bardic song, and have an appetite for competitive sport. But they are removed from any real conflict, and therefore, from heroism—an unthinkable limitation for "real" ancient communities. In short, Odysseus's tale works like a magnifying glass or measuring stick, clarifying and marking off what it is to be human and Hellenic.

It is perhaps not surprising that allegory-hunters have found fertile ground in these tales. One brand of reading—already current by the second century A.D.—saw Odysseus's journey as the saga of every soul, seduced by worldly goods and concerns, but resisting the Siren-call and enduring to return to its (heavenly) home. More recently, psychoanalytic criticism has discovered oral-narcissistic fantasy or phallic symbolism beneath the text. Ecological thinkers can read these tales as meditations on the use and abuse of natural resources, or celebrations of technology. Such endless flexibility and suggestiveness keeps the story alive. On the cognitive plane, we can trace an arching curve through Odysseus's own recollections, and find a story of education. From his initial savage pirate attack on the Kikones, through his near-fatal boasting to the enraged Kuklops and beyond, to his loss of everything he had, we get the sense that the hero really learns. He is wiser (and makes us wiser) for having seen the cities and grasped the mind of many people.

Although a centerpiece and tour de force within the Odyssey, the adventure story told in books 9 through 12 in the hero's own voice, surprisingly, makes up only one-sixth of the whole poem. Yet it crystalizes and distills all the major themes at work in the rest of the composition. Many of the motifs found in the adventure tale are spun out further in books 13 through 24, spanning the time from Odysseus's arrival back on Ithaka through the reunions with his servants and his son, the fight with the suitors, and the long-awaited meeting with his wife. For example, we learn from his tale how Odysseus constantly encountered unknown lands; then we see him make one more such landfall at his own island. We hear of the power of clever women—Kirke and Kalupso especially—while in the outer story, told by the poet rather than Odysseus himself, such powerful figures recur in the form of Penelopeia, Klutaimnestre, and the Phaiakian queen Arete (perhaps not coincidentally, a member of the audience for Odysseus's story-telling). We are always being reminded of food—a distinct problem in the case of the Lotos-eaters, Kuklops, Kirke, and especially the cattle of the sun-god episodes—while the outer narrative dwells on the insatiable appetite of the suitors. Indeed, the poem is careful to draw a parallel between the unwise crew of Odysseus, who devoured the sun-god's herds, and the arrogant suitors, continually depleting the absent hero's household stocks. Just as the god destroyed the men of Odysseus, so the homecoming warrior will wipe out the intruders. Disguise, cunning intelligence, the clever use of persuasion all occur in the inner tale of books 9 through 12 and find resonances in the larger narrative. And through the episode of the Kuklops—his

behavior, his blinding, the fulfillment of his curse by Poseidon—our atten-
tion is especially drawn to the notion of cosmic justice. This concept (called
dikê) for archaic Greeks included not only the proper functioning of nature
but all kinds of social relations, most prominently the proper treatment of
strangers. It is not accidental that the overall story makes Odysseus into an
avenging revenant, a punisher of the suitors' hubris, a restorer of order, and
a representative of the justice of Zeus on earth. In this light, the continued
performance of the *Odyssey*, within Greek culture, represented not just
enduring entertainment but a constant reassertion of cultural values, of a
society's quest for stability and wholeness. These themes and others will be
highlighted in the running notes to the translation.

Poem and Poet

Where does our *Odyssey* come from? It may help to work backward in time.
Contemporary translators of the epic rely on a fairly standardized Greek
edition of the poem, most often the Oxford Classical Text edited by the
scholar Thomas W. Allen (2d ed., 1917). Allen's Oxford text was the result of
many years of painstaking editorial work. Since this process is crucial for
establishing the text, yet hidden from the view of most general readers, it is
worth outlining the basics here.

   Printed editions of the *Odyssey* have been in circulation since 1488,
when Demetrius Chalcondylas, a Greek living in Florence, first used the
newly invented technology of type to conserve the gem of ancient Greek
literature, Homeric poetry. Until his time, the poems had been transmitted
only in manuscripts laboriously written by hand. For the *Odyssey*, nearly
a hundred such manuscripts still survive. They are stored in libraries
throughout Europe from Moscow, Bratislava, and Vienna to Florence, Ven-
ice, Vatican City, Munich, Paris, and Oxford, and they range in date from the
tenth century A.D. to the sixteenth century, some being produced even after
printing was available. All these copies are based on even earlier manu-
scripts that no longer exist, written by professional Greek scribes, either
monks or laymen, on parchment (or, in later centuries, paper). A scholar
seeking the fullest view of an ancient work cannot rely solely on the earliest
printed editions, but must push back as far as possible toward antiquity.
Therefore, through a combination of personal travel and inspection, and the
use of facsimiles or reports by other scholars, Allen made a "collation," or
systematic word-for-word comparison, of all the manuscripts he could find.

   When there are so many Greek manuscripts—as with Homer, and even
more so, the New Testament—there are inevitably variations from one to
another. This is the result of widespread copying and recopying of a popular
text in the days before printing. Each scribe is liable to make errors, even
when most attentive. Sometimes scribes themselves were collating and

combining the information from several manuscripts at their disposal. Most often, the differences are minor—changes of verb tense, the use of an older or newer form of adjective, varied spellings, and so forth. In several places, the variation does have an impact on plot or characterization, however. Allen printed everything that the manuscripts agreed on, and where they disagreed, chose the best variant based on what is known about Homeric usage, style, meter, and poetic diction. Of course, editors of the *Odyssey*—and there have been scores of them over centuries—never coincide when it comes to such individual choices about the best "reading." Sometimes, in order to make sense of a passage, an editor recommends a Greek word or form that happens not to be attested in any manuscript, a socalled emendation. That is why a scholarly edition, like Allen's, always records at the bottom of each page the variants and a selection of previous editors' speculations.

Two examples might clarify the process:

— When the crew of Odysseus were waiting for the Kuklops to return to his cave, they lit a fire and then "gave gifts to the Gods" (as McCrorie translates the Greek verb *ethusamen*, following Allen's text for *Od.* 9.231). The Oxford editor chose to follow versions in which this verb appears, characterizing the men as ritually observant. But as his notes record, several manuscripts, including an eleventh-century copy in Florence, have a Greek verb meaning merely "remain" instead of "sacrifice" at this line—a minor detail, but one that colors the passage.

— Occasionally, the disputed portion extends to several lines, as at *Od.* 1.93, when Athene is describing how she will inspire Telemakhos to travel for news of his father. The line in all manuscripts reads "I'll send him to Sparte too, and deep-sanded Pulos." However, in one fairly large "family" of related manuscripts, another two lines follow: "And from there to Krete, to Lord Idomeneus, who was second to return from Troy." Obviously, these verses do not correspond to the plot of the poem in the form that it finally reached us, in any manuscript—Telemakhos never goes to Krete. But they tantalize us with the possibility that a more elaborate version of the "Telemakhy" (books 1–4 of the poem) once existed.

Thus far, we have traced the *Odyssey* back to the Middle Ages. It should be remembered that in the period before the Renaissance in Italy, hardly anyone in western Europe knew the poem directly. If people had any idea about Odysseus, it was through the medium of Latin paraphrases from late antiquity, or from the mention of "Ulysses" (the Latin version of his name) in such well-known Roman authors as Virgil, Ovid, Seneca, Horace, and Statius. Dante, who places Ulysses in canto 26 of his *Inferno*, clearly knew (or made up) a version of the hero's fate completely unlike anything in the Greek tradition, one certainly missing from Homer.

From the thirteenth century on, and especially after the fall of Constantinople to the Ottoman Turks in A.D. 1453, a stream of Greek scholars emigrated to Italy and points west. It is to these Byzantine intellectuals and their students that we most likely owe the spread of *Odyssey* manuscripts. The business of copying the poem from generation to generation had extended within Greek-speaking lands all the way back to antiquity. The medieval manuscripts on which McCrorie's translation ultimately depends are an endpoint. But how can we tell that these manuscripts—the earliest of which is from around A.D. 900—preserve with any accuracy what Greeks of the archaic age knew as Homer's *Odyssey*?

The issue is hotly debated even today among Homerists. One sort of control on our text has actually been increasing in the past century—namely, papyri fragments, that is, pieces from ancient scrolls. Papyrus was a cheap and widely available writing material, made from plant fibers, but it rots away in most climates. Fortunately, the dry sands of Egypt, which was a center of Greco-Roman culture, preserve papyrus. Explorers in the nineteenth century uncovered piles of papyri—usually torn into bits in ancient trash heaps, or used to line mummy cases. Along with invaluable documents from antiquity—letters, contracts, deeds, and so on—they found dozens of fragments of Homeric papyri texts. These papyri, of which more are still being discovered by archaeologists every year, usually contain no more than a few lines. But what survives, dated from about 300 B.C. to A.D. 200, is enough to show that the texts inscribed in medieval manuscript books preserve by and large the same verses known to readers of Homer on papyrus rolls in ancient times.

There are a few more turnings in the road, however, before we reach the archaic Greek period, when the *Odyssey* was put down in writing. First, the fact cannot be ignored that a number of early papyri texts contain "extra" lines, compared to the "standard" texts built on full medieval manuscripts. The lines from these so-called wild papyri usually sound like padding—additional descriptions, or elaborated type-scenes, that can usually be paralleled elsewhere in the poem. Where did these lines come from? Most likely, they reflect various traditions of reciting the poem that were current about 300 B.C.

A second factor enters here—namely, ancient scholarship. Shortly after the time of Alexander the Great, who spread Greek culture all the way to India, two great centers of learning arose, one at Pergamum (about seventy-five miles southeast of ancient Troy in what is now Turkey), the other at Alexandria in Egypt. Not only was Homeric poetry Alexander's favorite (he is said to have slept with a copy of the *Iliad* under his pillow). It was a valuable symbol of a shared high Greek culture as well. Fervent, erudite, and competitive Greek scholars at royally supported think tanks wrote about and debated Homeric poetry in every conceivable detail, from the use of pronouns to the diet of the heroes. (It was carefully noted that they never eat fish.) One result of all this scholarly activity by Zenodotus, Aristophanes of Byzantium, and the great Aristarchus, was, apparently, the establishment of a fairly standard ancient text by 150 B.C.—at least, after that date, "extra" lines occur much less often in the papyri. The *Odyssey* and the *Iliad* must have undergone a sort of winnowing process, a standardization that unfortunately must have erased some of the interesting variations that had flourished before.

Some scholars speculate that the *Odyssey* must have been, around 400 B.C., somewhat longer than our version, or quite different—depending on what city you bought your text in, or, more likely, whom you heard perform it. Plato, who was born in 427 B.C., cites as "Homeric" many lines that are either not in our texts or that have quite different wording. As we go further back in time, the *Odyssey* is more and more in the hands of oral performers, like the "rhapsode" ("song-stitcher") named Ion, about whom Plato wrote in a dialogue with that title. This reciter, in Plato's literary account, claims to have encyclopedic knowledge because he knows Homeric poetry so well (and Homer was already considered a universal sage by Plato's time). Apparently this was a common attitude toward the poet in the fifth century B.C., when much of what passed for education was built on extensive learning of the epics.

As a rhapsode, Ion competed against other performers at international festivals. He was in the business, also, of explicating Homer in the intervals of acting out the poems as a dramatic one-man "reading." It is easy to imagine such rhapsodic performers varying, expanding, or highlighting parts of the poem in line with changing audience conditions. There is no evidence that they stuck to an exact text. It is also possible that Odysseus's wanderings were played up by performers who themselves were used to traveling incessantly from one gig to another. (Such an association of fictional hero and actual poet occurs even today among Egyptian epic singers, as the folklorist Dwight Reynolds has shown; see the Bibliography.)

It may not seem far, finally, from the historically attested "rhapsode," a performer claiming to reproduce "Homer's" *Odyssey*, to the phenomenon of a masterly oral poet, who composed in the very act of performance and varied his composition with every new audience, in the way that oral poets (and even rap singers) active today in various cultures still do. But here we finally arrive at the murkiest regions in the search for the *Odyssey*, the realm of the so-called Homeric Question. Did a bard named Homer ever exist? If so, was he the first one to write, or dictate the *Odyssey* and the *Iliad*? And if he was really a practicing oral poet, what motivated him (or her?) to shift technologies?

We know nothing positive about the date, place, or circumstances for the writing down of the *Odyssey*. Most likely, it crystalized within generations of live oral performances and competitions, in the period from about 800 B.C. to 500 B.C. It was probably committed to writing fairly late, perhaps under the patronage of the Peisistratid rulers of Athens (ca. 540–510 B.C.), and in connection with competitive performances of Homeric poetry at festivals (see Nagy, 2002). Nor do we have any reliable information about a poet Homer. He was thought by the Greeks of the classical period to have lived in Ionia (now the west coast of Turkey) about 400 years after the Trojan War (which took place, according to ancient reckoning, around 1150 B.C.). It is completely possible that a great performer named "Homer" existed at the time, but whether he is responsible for our *Odyssey* in its present overall shape is unprovable. Even if he is the "author" in a modern sense—responsible for choosing each word of the poem as we have it—we should not forget that the poem, as its allusions, style, and archaic artificial language show, must also be a highly traditional work. It contains several linguistic layerings that suggest that some elements in the *Odyssey* must have been handed down from the very period that it commemorates—the time of the "heroes" of the Mycenaean age (ca. 1600–1200 B.C.). So there is at least a symbolic truth embedded in one of the many ancient legends that circulated about Homer, according to which he was the son of Telemakhos, son of Odysseus. Whenever the poem was conceived, its composer (thanks to the Muse) felt himself to be almost in immediate contact with its events. The result is the vivid, ageless composition we can still read, hear, and value today.

Homeric Technique

The texture of the *Odyssey* and the *Iliad*, the construction of scenes, speeches, and verses, can best be appreciated in the light of techniques found in traditional orally composed epics of the sort still performed today in parts of the world (especially Central Asia and Africa) and once common throughout Europe. Five interlocking arguments support the idea that Homeric poetry as we have it comes from an art form that did not rely on writing.

First, the poetry itself describes the art of narrating stories about heroes and gods through words related to "song," never mentioning writing or even recitation. For example, the Phaiakian singer Demodokos in book 8 sings three quite different compositions, two of them resembling news flashes for his audience about the Trojan War, while the third relates how the god Hephaistos caught his adulterous wife Aphrodite. Phemios, the Ithakan bard, is shown responding to the whim of his audience (the unruly suitors of Penelopeia) by singing of the disastrous homecomings of the Greeks (including, so the suitors hope, Odysseus). Penelopeia can ask him to change the topic (*Od.* 1.337–44), just as Odysseus can ask Demodokos for a specific performance (*Od.* 8.492). Whether or not the poetry of Homer was composed in this interactive, audience-sensitive way, it at least *wants to imagine* its own roots in such situations. The *Odyssey* is a powerful *story*, a narrative of memory, homecoming, human need, and desire. It is also a finely woven *poem*, with all the power and beauty that arise from precisely used words and images. But above all, it is the result of a centuries-old tradition of audience-tested performance, a tradition that the poetry itself identifies with the singing of tales.

In Homeric Greek, the poet is a singer (*aoidos*) and his craft is song (*aoidê*)—the word that enters English eventually as "ode." The *Odyssey* begins with the poet asking a goddess to tell the story of "the cunning hero." He calls on a Muse (one of the nine daughters of Memory). Not by accident, these tale-telling divinities lend us the word "music." Once again, Homeric poetry presents itself as something beyond ordinary speech, something closer to the special voice of the gods, an art form akin to pure harmonious sound.

The tradition of epic song-making that gave us the *Odyssey* is far from primitive. Instead, Homeric poetry is highly self-conscious about its own medium. The *Odyssey*, even more than the other major surviving epic, the *Iliad*, reflects again and again on the power of narrative song to enshrine the deeds of heroes and transmit them to generations to come. Consequently, in the culture that the poem depicts, singers have a place of high honor. For a would-be hero, not getting into the singer's epic repertoire meant obliteration, as far as future renown. Put another way, the reason we know today about Odysseus and Akhilleus, Helen and Penelopeia, is because epic poetry made good on its proud and ambitious promise of immortality, "unwithering fame." That this entire system of celebratory song depended ultimately on oral performance, rather than writing, is clear from the etymology of the very word for fame in Homeric language. For *kleos*, "fame" or "glory," is literally "what is heard." (The English word "loud" comes from the same shared root.)

Second, archaeological evidence shows that something like the Trojan War took place in the region described in the poems, with bronze weapons like those Homer described, and with resultant destruction and displacement of populations. Furthermore, the traditional ancient dating of the war, in the twelfth century B.C., fits the Homeric account of a final heroic generation. But alphabetic writing to set down either poetic or prose accounts of such a war was not available in Greece until 800 B.C. at the earliest, by the estimation of most scholars, at least another 300 years. Therefore, an oral tradition of some sort must have predated the Homeric texts.

The evidence of Homer's language provides a third confirmation. The

Odyssey's form of Greek was never the spoken language of any one time or region. Multilayered and at times highly conservative, the Homeric "dialect" appeared to have been shaped by and for poets: among other oddities, it contains forms that have no historical basis, on comparison with other related languages, but are metrically convenient. By the same token, it retains a number of forms for a given concept (such as "belonging to me") but only when the forms maintain usefully distinct metrical shapes— somewhat like the use in older English poetry of the synonymous forms "over" and "o'er," which conveniently offer a poet metrical alternatives (the former two syllables, the latter one). In sum, the poetic language is traditional and arches over generations.

The fourth support for an "oral" Homer comes from the evidence of poetic diction. A young Californian, Milman Parry, in his doctoral work on the repeated "formulas" of Homeric poetry in the 1920s and 1930s found an "economy" at work when he meticulously investigated the well-known system of adjectives applied to the important personages of the poems. The characters called "swift-footed Akhilleus" and "Odysseus of much cunning" are at other lines described in the poetry as "shining Akhilleus" or "Odysseus of many devices." When this happens, there is no perceptible shift in the narrative's emphasis. Instead, the phrases involved produce a different metrical shape. Keep in mind that the Homeric verse line consists of six "feet," each of the first five feet being either a "dactyl" (one long plus two short syllables, $-\smile\smile$) or a "spondee" (two long syllables, $--$). The last foot of the six is either a "spondee" or a "trochee" (long + short, $-\smile$, a marked, concluding rhythmic effect that McCrorie's translation brilliantly captures). Now the adjective "swift-footed" with the name "Akhilleus" gives in Greek *podas ôkus Akhilleus*—a phrase that fills out a metrical position occupying two and a half "feet" of the dactylic hexameter line ($\smile\smile-\smile\smile--$). But substitute the adjective "shining" next to the same character's name and you get a short metrical segment, two "feet" long (*dios Akhilleus*, $-\smile\smile--$). Tallying up such phrases, Parry proved that for each and every major heroic and divine figure in Homer there existed one (and almost always *only* one) epithet *per* metrical position and grammatical case (subject, object, possessive, and so forth). Therefore, Homeric poetry once again represents a traditional, multigenerational art form, for the simple reason that no one poet would have the motivation to devise such a thoroughgoing and economical system. It was probably created for the rapid composition of verse while in live performance (as the poetry indeed consistently represents itself).

The fifth argument, that of comparative evidence, is closely related: Parry and his collaborator Albert Lord found through fieldwork in the former Yugoslavia that similar extensive and convenient dictional systems were employed by illiterate performers of traditional Serbo-Croatian heroic poetry. Since their work in the 1930s, fieldworkers have confirmed this tendency in dozens of other oral poetic systems.

Given these indications, we cannot presume to read the *Odyssey* the way one does a written epic, whether Virgil's *Aeneid*, Dante's *Divine Comedy*, or Milton's *Paradise Lost*. Most important, our reading must take into account the resonance of repeated phrases, since we can be certain that most such phrases were already in the poetic tradition, and thus known to an audience listening to Homeric epic performances. A poet like the composer of the *Odyssey* can create meaningful effects by summoning up, at just the right moment, the world of associations built into a single phrase that has been used over generations in many other poems, with a range of significations his audience would appreciate. John Miles Foley (see Bibliography) has named the resulting poetry "immanent art," for in this medium formula-enhanced allusiveness produces depths far beyond the limpid surface of the poem. Since modern readers lack the environment in which such art first flourished, we can only hope to recover the range of a phrase's meaning by looking at all its occurrences and calculating the effect it would have on any one scene if an audience imported into its understanding of the scene at hand a recognition of all the other situations in which a particular phrase had been or might be used. The technique differs from the novel. The reader of *The Europeans* or *Ulysses* only gradually learns, page by page, just how rich are certain phrases applied by James or Joyce to their protagonists. Every novel creates its own language, whereas Greek oral epic relied on an audience's long experience of a rich dictional tradition, already loaded with meanings, to engage and move its hearers immediately.

Take, for example, the way in which the *Odyssey*'s characterization of Telemakhos happens with the help of formulaic style. The first time we see Telemakhos (1.113), Athene in the guise of Mentes has just arrived at the palace in Ithaka. Telemakhos sees her before any of the others notice:

τὴν δὲ πολὺ πρῶτος ἴδε Τηλέμαχος θεοειδής

tên de polu prôtos ide Têlemachos theoeidês

Godlike Telemakhos, surely the first one to see her

Theoeidês, "in appearance like a god," is one of four noun-epithet formulas attested for Telemakhos in the nominative or subject case. That the poet even used an epithet for Telemakhos here, when we first see him, signals that the scene immediately following is important for our understanding of character. The epithet is like a single musical note sounded at the start of a composition. Moreover, it occurs in contrast to any of the other three epithets for Telemakhos that Homer might have used, had he molded the line a bit differently (*hierê is* "sacred strength," *pepnumenos* "intelligent," and *hêrôs* "the hero"). As the poem advances, the epithet *theoeidês* comes to relate to an essential theme of the *Odyssey*, how appearance sometimes conflicts with actual identity or ability. Odysseus (in disguise) sermonizes on "appearances" after being mocked during the games of the Phaiakians (8.166–85). In the dramatic situation of this passage, having a good "appearance" (*eidos*) implies that one is neither a good speaker nor, in fact, very bright. Significantly, the young islander Eurualos, who has athletic ability but no rhetorical grace, is the object of Odysseus's admonishment, for in the course of the Phaiakian episode, we see him learn. By the end of book 8, he has the wit and poise to offer Odysseus a sword and an apology. Now, this process of education is precisely what happens to Telemakhos in the course of the *Odyssey* as a whole, as many critics have remarked. The adjective *theoeidês* marks out Homer's handling of this traditional theme, which we can call "the hero grows up." When an audience keyed into the traditional phrase system first hears Telemakhos described as "having the appearance of a god," it receives a package of thematic messages and potential narrative directions. Yet this process is not without suspense. The son of Odysseus could turn out to be like others who share this epithet: Paris in the *Iliad* (*Alexandros theoeidês*), a less than heroic figure who relies on looks to get by, or Eurualos, naively arrogant but educable. In fact, each of these two thematic alternatives comes up in the course of the *Odyssey*: the adjective *theoeidês* is used three times to describe one or other of the pair of chief suitors on Ithaka, the arrogant young men Eurumakhos and Antinoos, dangerous types who dislike Telemakhos. The good-but-not-perfect youth arises as well, in the figure of the seer Theoklumenos, to whom the epithet *theoeidês* is applied five times, and whose very name ("god-hearing") dovetails with its meaning. When this young fugitive encounters Telemakhos, we see an important stage in the growth of the latter; he without questioning befriends the outlaw, thus showing how he has assimilated the cultural code concerning guest-friends. Such is the artfulness of formulaic repetition that similar thematic threads can be traced by following the deployment of any epithet in the poem.

Another powerful device used by the *Odyssey* is characterization by speeches. It has been estimated that more than half the poem is presented in this format. As well as being a poetic style, speechmaking was most likely a key cultural phenomenon. Ancient Greeks of all periods admired rhetorical ability. The *Iliad* tells how Akhilleus was raised up to be a "speaker of speeches and doer of deeds" (*Il.* 9.443). Part of the appeal and influence of Homeric poetry on later ages comes from its excellence at *mimesis*, the representation of direct speech. (Plato, on the other hand, pinpointed the same mimetic technique as the central danger within Homeric epic when he banned it from the ideal city-state of *The Republic*.) Such speeches can be commands, threats, or promises made by one character to another; public addresses to assemblies; recollections made in the company of dinner companions; or even monologues addressed to one's own heart and mind, like the speech Odysseus makes as he finds himself in danger of drowning (5.299–312).

Instead of telling the audience what is going on in the mind of characters in the poem, the composer makes these figures talk for themselves. As a result, we get the sense of intimacy, of intense interaction between Homeric heroes and their environment, and of the distinctive ways in which they present themselves to the world. A further refinement on the technique consists of juxtaposing the speeches of different characters in order to express conflict or imply deeper unexpressed emotions. The exchange between Helen and Menelaos in book 4 (lines 235–89), as each tells a story for the benefit of their visitors, represents this contrastive art at its highest form. Without a hint from the narrator's own voice, the impression is nevertheless created that the aging hero and his wife who once caused so much destruction are still immersed in their mutual grievances and protestations. The series of encounters between Odysseus and his wife Penelopeia, extending from book 19 through book 23, allow us to intuit the shape of their relationship more than any information the narrator could have relayed. And the close parallels created by such serial use of direct speeches—for example, the five fictions told by the disguised Odysseus on Ithaka, or the encounters Telemakhos has with Nestor and Menelaos—further enrich the poem by subtle variations. Whereas with the formula the poet plays on an audience's shared knowledge of allusion and association, with speeches the poet can produce new and multiple points of view.

A third characteristic technique, the simile, might be seen as a combination of the traditionality of the formula and the innovative use of speech. The Homeric simile often includes more detail than we might think necessary to make a comparison. Consider two examples that occur at the start of book 20 as Odysseus, lying awake, grows angry at the sight of serving women who sleep with the suitors:

> . . . The heart grumbled inside him
> the way a dog will growl, standing over her tender
> pups and anxious to fight with a man she does not know.
> His heart growled that way. Their wrongdoing vexed him.
> (lines 13–16)

After describing how Odysseus subdues his anger—"But shortly he struck his breast and scolded his own heart"—the poet continues:

> His heart obeyed him well: it bore up and stayed firm.
> Yet the man went on tossing this way and that way
> much like a cook at a blazing fire, turning a stomach
> packed with blood and fat this way and that way,
> moving it as fast as he can, longing to roast it.
> So Odysseus tossed both ways and he wondered: (lines 23–28)

The seemingly extraneous details, however, evoke many things that a briefer comparison misses. If the poet had simply said "his heart growled like a dog," the image might strike us, but a chance for further emotional impact would be lost. The expanded version, in a manner both oddly out of synch and entirely appropriate, associates Odysseus with a *female* figure— the mother of the puppies—who barks to defend them against an intruding *male*. In terms of the overall plot, Odysseus (by way of the simile) has become like Penelopeia, a fiercely independent female resisting male incursions in her house. More immediately, we might be reminded of the scene not long before, when Odysseus, arriving in disguise at his own palace, is recognized by Argos, the hound he left behind twenty years previously. Now tick-ridden and uncared for, unable to move from the dung-heap where he lies, the dog wags his tail pitifully and, as his old master passes by, expires (17.290–327). The slight dissonance created by the simile reminds the audience that Odysseus, though apparently old and useless at the moment (like Argos), will soon take on the role of watch-dog and even hunter, as he punishes the suitors. Similes, therefore, artfully employ in a compressed format two other techniques frequent in Homeric poetry, the use of flashbacks and of foreshadowings.

The second simile mentioned above, in which the hero is compared with a sausage, might seem at first comically commonplace, even arbitrarily antiheroic. The only apparent point of connection comes from the similarity of movement, as both hero and meat revolve like rotisseries. Yet again, Homeric technique relies on our recognition of the gap between the immediate plot-event and the rhetorical reshaping of it. Odysseus cannot sleep because he is at a moment of crisis, anxious about his ability to plan and carry out a slaughter, while the anonymous cook in the simile only has to deal with food preparation. Nevertheless, we can imagine that the veteran fighter might well yearn to *be* the peacetime chef, so that the simile then is "focalized" by the very consciousness of the character it purports to describe. It is worth recalling, after all, that the very first time we glimpse Odysseus in the poem he is longing to see the smoke rising from his native hearth. Furthermore, the cook and the hero both crave something deeply. The cook's longing is made explicit—he wants to have roasted meat—and he, at least, has the means to carry this out. By bringing to mind such a universal want, the poet makes his audience feel, almost taste, the overwhelming immediacy of Odysseus's desire for revenge, without at this point even mentioning it. The implication is that Odysseus, too, will soon be in charge (not to say cook the suitors' goose). Finally, both similes in this cluster, the dog and the cook, make public, at least in their memorable imagery, otherwise internal, private movements of thought. By reference to recurrent everyday actions, they make natural and unproblematic what is in fact a one-time, somewhat questionable, revenge of epic proportion.

History and the *Odyssey*

The advances made by archaeology, linguistics, and the comparative study of culture over the past century have made it clear that the world depicted by the Homeric epics is a poetic creation. It has elements of eras in Greek civilization reaching from 1400 B.C. to the Peisistratid period in Athens, in the mid-sixth century. Like Greek culture, it has absorbed influences from the Near East and Egypt, perhaps even from the Black Sea and beyond. At the same time, the basic elements of the Homeric world are constants in Mediterranean history and social life: the crafts of fighting and sailing; trade; colonization; viticulture and agriculture; and settlement-building. Although techniques in all of these change over the centuries, the activities themselves show long stretches of continuity, even into the twenty-first century.

      This is not the place for even the briefest sketch of Greek history. It will be enough to note that speakers of Greek about 1900 B.C. must have moved apart from speakers of closely related languages (the dialects within the "Indo-European" group that would evolve into the Italic, Indic, Germanic, Celtic, Slavic, and other language families) and traveled from either the steppes of southern Russia, or the Caucasus region, pushing into the Balkans, then farther south. Around the shores of the Aegean, they encountered already established high civilizations, among them the Egyptians and "Minoans" (a non-Greek people centered on Krete). In time, a Greek warrior culture based on citadel sites and chieftainship borrowed from and then replaced the Minoans and other early peoples of what is now central Greece and the islands. The "Mycenaean" period (ca. 1600–1200 B.C.), named after one of the key citadel centers, ended—it is not clear why—with a series of destructions, of which the Trojan War is most likely an abstract, distilled reminiscence.

      After antiquity, the existence of Troy and the war for it were regarded as merely fables. When travel to the east revived in the eighteenth century, antiquarians began to note the close similarity between actual landscapes and Homeric descriptions of the area of Asia Minor associated with the old legends. In the nineteenth century, the Romantic quest for origins and the growing European devotion to an idealized classical past combined to spur more attention to the physical remnants of that past, culminating in the 1870s with the investigations of a wealthy amateur archaeologist, Heinrich Schliemann. At the large mound of Hissarlik, in what is now western Turkey, Schliemann dug and discovered the remains of an ancient city, layer upon layer, dating back to the twelfth century b.c. and well beyond. Long-buried "Troy" was suddenly brought to light.

Excavations at the site continue to this day. While no inscription or object pinpoints this site as the place that the Greeks besieged and de-stroyed, the spot was clearly an extensive and rich city, with great defensive walls and gates not unlike those described in the *Iliad*. There is little doubt that this was Troy. Several of its layers ("Troy VI and VIIa") dated by archae-ologists to about the time of the Trojan War (as computed by the ancients themselves) show evidence of a sack and fire. Whether Greeks from the mainland—Agamemnon of Mycenae, Menelaos of Sparte and compan-ions—led the attack sometime between 1325 and 1200 b.c., cannot be proven. Nor is it known who the Trojans were, in ethnic and linguistic terms, or where the remnants of their populace might have gone.

Migrations from the mainland to Asia Minor, especially the coastal settlements of Ionia, began after the collapse of Mycenaean palace culture on the mainland of Greece. It is perhaps during this period that the story of a great culture in those places, once overcome by Greeks, gained popularity. It is not impossible that the saga of the Trojan War goes back, even in versified form of some sort, to the actual events of the twelfth century b.c. The poems we have preserve some elements that are of Mycenaean date, both linguistically and culturally. Thus, the heroes of both epics regularly use bronze weapons and implements; iron, which became the most com-mon metal after the demise of Mycenaean culture (in the so-called Dark Ages of 1100–800 b.c.), is rarely mentioned. Chariot-fighting is known. The design of shields, helmets, and swords matches objects found from the twelfth century. Places named in the text as sending troops and ships in many cases were not inhabited after the twelfth century, and so the poems must preserve an ancient historical memory of them. And the warrior confederacy that took Troy seems to fit with the pattern of citadel settlement from the period that the epics purport to describe. Archaeology shows that Pulos and Tiruns, Mycenae and Thebes were important centers in the Bronze Age, and these cities figure prominently in the epics.

At the same time, it is clear that centuries of transmission and reshap-ing of the poems within an oral tradition have allowed historical elements from other eras to intertwine with the older threads. Although chariots are used, for example, heroes stop and step down from them to do battle (unlike their employment in cultures farther east)—it has been thought that the poet is unsure how they were employed in actual warfare. Some objects and place-names from as late as the sixth century B.C. have been detected within the epics, although the composers obviously have tried to archaize. The political structures of the polis ("city-state"), first crystalized in the eighth century B.C., and the importance of Apollo's shrine at Delphi, another eighth-century phenomenon, are other, major non-Mycenaean traits. It has been argued that the emphasis on a unified Greek expedition itself is to be linked with the evolving "Panhellenic" institutions of the eighth century, which brought together Greeks of all regions after several centuries of isolation (see Nagy, 1999). A number of signs thus point to a period four centuries after the Trojan War as the crucial incubation period for continually developing epic traditions.

If the ruined citadel, object of this legendary siege, has been revealed, what of the place Odysseus left to go to Troy, and its history? Ithaka today is a rocky island some thirty miles off the west coast of mainland Greece. Small enough to hike the length of in a day, it is neither rich in antiquities, nor famous—except as the home and kingdom of Odysseus. As with the city of Troy, there is no way of telling for certain whether the island now called Ithaka or Thiaki was the spot imagined by the poet of the *Odyssey*. Ongoing excavations by a team from Washington University, St. Louis, have so far uncovered what could be Mycenaean remains, the identity of which is still unclear. At any rate, it is worth remembering that even within the poem, life on Ithaka hardly measured up to the splendor of palaces visited by Telemakhos on the mainland. The young hero tells his host Menelaos that his home island, unlike Sparte, does not have space enough for horse-breeding. In other ways as well, we can expect that Ithaka was less powerful and important. Deprived of large forces, its chieftain Odysseus must operate by other means: his intriguing indirect and cunning character fits the reduced resources of his compact kingdom.

Yet the household of Odysseus, even in its minor way, shows the signs of a royal economic center. The king has herds and flocks on other islands and on the mainland. Servants, such as the pig-herder Eumaios, who have been acquired by sale or conquest, maintain the resources of the great house. Women are constantly at work in the palace producing textiles. And the great storeroom of Odysseus, which Penelopeia visits in book 21, is full of gold, bronze, and iron. Such imperishable goods were used throughout early Greek times to build reciprocal exchange relationships, by way of ostentatious gift-giving, with other aristocrats. The presents of Menelaos and Alkinoos fit such a system; Odysseus, as we learn in book 1 (line 177), was in the habit of visiting others, even before his wanderings. Out of action for twenty years, however, he has not only lost opportunities to participate in such all-important prestige exchanges, but has also suffered threatening losses in livestock from the depredations of the suitors. The beggar's disguise that he assumes on Ithaka lies dangerously close to the truth. The *Odyssey* seems to recognize that the dividing line between comfortable existence and penury is thin. No doubt, in the subsistence economy within which most Greeks in most eras have labored, this lesson makes sense. The poem's insistence on loss and gain reflects real anxieties that the economic misfortune of just one man could blight the lives of his descendants for a long time afterward.

Modern readers look to politics and economics for their "history," yet we should recall that one can also speak of history on the level of feelings and attitudes conditioned by a set of actual experiences. How Greeks of the past responded creatively to the strains and challenges of their own times—that, too, is history. Framed within the tale of Odysseus's return, the abiding notion that each person needs a *place* is taken as a practical fact, without apology, sentimentality, or melodrama. Only in the fictions created by Odysseus (e.g., 14.199ff.) do we hear of men roaming for the sake of adventure alone. One senses that beneath the eloquence and economy of the *Odyssey* depiction there lies the experience of generations of Greeks yearning for home—political exiles, warriors, colonizers, sailors, traveling bards. Because the disturbed centuries when the numerous Greek city-states arose—from 900 to 700 B.C.—coincided with the development of epic poetry, it is even more likely that audiences would have been found sympathetic to a homecoming story like this one. In its distillation of feeling, and its celebration of survival, rather than its representation of social facts, the epic makes good its claim to tell the truths of the past.

The Gods of Homer

Another facet of the appeal of Homeric epic is its persuasive picture of a world beyond the human. The gods and goddesses of archaic Greece are like humans in nearly every way but one—they never die. Ageless and immortal, fed on nectar and ambrosia, with clear *ikhôr* in their veins instead of blood, the gods live at ease in cloudless calm on the snowy height of Mount Olumpus in northern Greece. Theoretically they could ignore the death-bound humans. But in the Greek imagination the gods need people as much as people need them. The Homeric poems are enthralled by this symbiotic bond of gods and mortals, a relation always teetering between adoration and antagonism.

The gods are much more than a Homeric fantasy. For millennia, Greeks worshiped the divinities mentioned in the epics, and many more. We can never be sure what they actually had in mind while doing so. But if we take the *Odyssey* as a guide, it was something like this: gods are inquisitive, meddlesome, proud of their favorite humans, and dangerously quick to anger. To maintain their favor, mortals must offer sacrifice, making sure to fill heavenly nostrils with the savor of roasting meat. The ritual of pouring out wine, coupled with prayer, also works to appease gods. The hero strives to win the only immortality available to humans: epic fame (*kleos*). To do so, he must win out over opposition, with divine help, or must lose spectacularly by spiting it. Odysseus could be seen as involved in a religious quest, testing the efficacy of his attitude toward the divine, and determining for himself whether the gods will hear and aid him.

The divine is everywhere in Homer; this poetry is deeply theological. One reason that epic dwells so much on feasting and drinking, for example, is that these are crucial ritual events: in archaic Greece every meat meal was also a religious act. Every daybreak is actually the work of a goddess, Dawn. Moon and sun, rivers, caves, and trees are either gods or have divine inhabitants. At a deeper emotional level, we hear throughout the *Odyssey* of humans actually descended from Zeus or Ares or Poseidon. Odysseus the hero of this poem has an interesting ancestry—his maternal grandfather Autolukos (whose name means "the very wolf") is a trickster and a thief who, in some versions of myth, was son of the conniving god Hermes himself. The Homeric version downplays this shady past, sticking instead to the story that Hermes taught Autolukos the art of burglary (19.395–98).

This raises the issue of the morality of Homer's gods. Not long after the epics took shape, philosophers were already criticizing their divinities. Said one sixth-century moralist, Xenophanes: "Homer attributes to the gods all that is most shameful among mortals. Stealing, adultery, and deceiving one another." In the early fourth century B.C., Plato went so far as to ban Homer's poetry from the idealized morally upright city that he sketches in his work *The Republic*. The good order of a state, in his view, was threatened not only when its leaders read about and imitated characters whom Homer depicted as failing to control their emotions. It was also put in jeopardy if the inhabitants believed in less-than-perfect divinities.

But if Homer's gods make poor ethical paradigms, they nevertheless embody real truths. There *are* powers greater than us at work in the world. These powers seem capricious and sometimes cruel. Overwhelming emotions—melting desire, intoxication, the rage of war—where else could these come from if not from gods? To call such experiences, respectively, Aphrodite, Dionusos, and Ares, was to name them but at the same time to control them. For the gods, once humanized, function like an extended and somewhat dysfunctional family, one in which there is at least some order. Ruling from on high is Zeus, who backs up his commands with a white-hot thunderbolt. Hades and Poseidon, his brothers, have their places, on sea and under earth. Other gods and goddesses fall into line as sons or daughters of Zeus. There is a nice economy in such a polytheistic system—one god balances another, in a mode almost comically domestic. If mother (Here) says no, you can always ask father (Zeus). Humans get to hedge their bets by praying to as many gods as they wish.

When it comes to the *Odyssey*, Athene deserves special attention. Although we never hear the tale in Homer, the unusual birth of the virgin goddess from Mêtis ("cunning intelligence") was well known (see "Plots and Performances," above). We might question why this goddess of craft— including warcraft—becomes so attached to the modest mortal Odysseus. Primarily, it seems, because he is like her: indeed, his regular epithet is *polumêtis* (literally, "having much cunning intelligence"). Yet one senses an element of competition in their relationship. A revealing conversation between goddess and protégé occurs in book 13, when Odysseus has just returned to his island. In reply to his convenient fiction, about how he arrived home, Athene replies with friendly rebuke and a touch of pride:

> ... It seems you will never
> stop your lying, not even here in your own land.
> You love such guile and fakery, right from your feet up!
> Come on now, stop such talk. Both of us know well
> how you're shrewd, the best by far among all men
> with words and plans. And I'm well known among all Gods
> for wisdom and counsel. Yet you're failing to know me: (lines 293–99)

Plenty of mythic stories tell of humans who matched themselves with gods and lost. So part of the suspense of the *Odyssey* must arise precisely from this dangerous divine and mortal collaboration. Will Odysseus somehow cross the line? Is he good enough to win the admiration and aid of the goddess? Or will he boast too much of his own ability, risk Athene's jealousy, and court abandonment or death?

In the *Odyssey*, Zeus, his brother Poseidon, and his daughter Athene are more than arbitrary or independent powers. The poet, from the start of the epic, emphasizes the complex family relations and repercussions involved as the three divinities become wrapped up in issues of human justice. Zeus, the chief god, is responsible for maintaining justice on the cosmic level. If anyone, Greek or Trojan, is mistreated, Zeus can be summoned to witness the outrage and take corrective action. He sometimes does with blazing thunderbolt. At the same time, both Athene and Poseidon have claims against the Greeks for personal injuries (the desecration of Athene's Trojan temple and the blinding of Poseidon's son, the Kuklops Poluphemos). So Zeus, while keeping order in the world, must also work for Olumpian

harmony. In this regard, the adventures of Odysseus bring the gods them-
selves to a new realization of their limitations and interdependence. Thus,
one religiously observant human can alter the configurations of the divine.

In this sense of ethics, human and divine, the *Odyssey* especially differs
from simpler narratives of vengeance. This epic is not about brutal payback
or gratuitous violence. Throughout the poem, the justice of major actions—
human or divine—is carefully scrutinized, debated, and evaluated. Compet-
ing claims are argued and weighed by the various figures involved. Already,
we can see at work the analytical spirit that pervades Plato's examination of
justice in his *Republic* centuries later. At first sight, the world of the *Odyssey*
may seem lawless. Clearly, its inhabitants live without formal, written rules
established and enforced by legal authorities. But justice does not require
law. In fact, the Greek word *dikê*, most often translated as "justice," is closer
to the ideas of custom, habit, and propriety. The way things normally are,
when family, community, and world are in order, is the way things should
be. And this does not depend on adherence to some externalized code of
behavior.

Dikê, in this archaic Greek sense, can even describe the working of
nature. When, for instance, Odysseus meets his mother in the underworld,
and cannot embrace her, she tells him that it is the "way" (*dikê*) of mortals,
when they die, to have their soul fly off like a dream, while the body is
burned (11.218–24). Animals can have *dikê*, too. But both humans and
animals sometimes go beyond the boundaries of this natural "justice."
They do so when they disturb the order of things, either by refusing to give
others their rightful due, or by trying to take somebody else's goods or
honor. Such actions—the opposite of *dikê*—are called in Greek *hubris*.

In the *Odyssey*, the suitors of Penelopeia embody hubristic behavior. Not
only are they breaking the norms of hospitality, an important part of *dikê*;
they court the queen arrogantly, without regard to precedent, truth, or
custom. They ruin the household and dishonor its inhabitants. By contrast,
Odysseus throughout the poem employs his native wit in adapting himself
to the way of things and the will of the gods. It is this, rather than a pious
righteousness, that makes him "just" in Homeric terms. His miraculous
victory over the 108 suitors is a confirmation that Zeus and the Olumpian
gods maintain equilibrium in the world. Overstepping the limits eventually
brings reprisal. Odysseus is the agent of such divine justice.

To appreciate fully the ethical stance of the *Odyssey*, it will help to know
something more about the link between justice and hospitality. In ancient
Greek, the concepts of "host," "guest," and "stranger" are expressed by one
and the same word: *xenos*. This unified idea, so different from the way in
which we split apart the three notions, can be seen at work throughout the

Odyssey. Again and again the poem foregrounds the theme of *xenia* (the guest-host relationship). The plot unfolds in relation to this notion, and characters, from the Kuklops to the suitors, are judged by how well they adhere to the ideal of the proper treatment of strangers. *Xenia*, in sum, represents the epitome of Odyssean morality.

It is not surprising that in a preliterate, archaic culture, where there were no recognized international institutions or norms, the correct behavior toward outsiders was made into a sacred obligation. (The same phenomenon can still be observed today in isolated small-scale cultures.) This was in effect the only way in which individuals could survive beyond the bounds of their local community. Zeus had a special title, *Xenios*, to denote his role as protector of strangers. Any infraction was thus an offense against the chief god.

Xenia represents one key instance of a larger cultural requirement for reciprocity. This greater principle can be seen at work in a number of other areas alluded to by the Homeric poems. Animal sacrifice, prayer, and warfare were based on the idea that equilibrium must be maintained by giving or paying back either favors or hostility, either among humans or between humans and gods. The reciprocal expectations underlying *xenia* can explain the semantics of the term. Just as any "stranger" was a potential "guest"— and had to be so treated—any "guest" was by implication a potential "host," as he was expected to pay back whatever treatment was received.

The entire Trojan War saga can be interpreted as a mythic example of the catastrophes brought on by improper guest-host relations. Paris, the young Trojan prince, was a guest of Menelaos in Sparte when he ran off with his host's wife, Helen. The Greek chieftains who had sworn to help Menelaos were obliged to avenge this crime against *xenia*, even to the extent of besieging and razing Troy. (In this way, myth works like a legal precedent, justifying societal practices by reference to one case.) Odysseus's return from Troy is therefore the continuation of a moral lesson about the need for maintaining equilibrium on the intersecting social and cosmic levels. If Odysseus is treated well, all is well with the world.

As with most socially significant actions in the *Odyssey*, importance can be measured by how often the theme recurs. Furthermore, the repetition comes in the form of stylized, almost predictable "scripts"—what Homerists call "type-scenes." It is hard to say if the scripts are poetic devices or social rituals—one reinforces the other. Typically, the stranger is welcomed with kind words, the offer of a bath and fresh clothing, food and drink (and no questions asked until these preliminaries are over). He is encouraged to stay as long as he likes. Upon departure, he is provided with transportation and with "guest-gifts." These precious items of exchange were a combina-

tion of souvenir and statement to the world of the host's excellent be-
havior—because *xenia*, like everything else in Greek culture, could turn
competitive.

If warriors like Odysseus can become paradigms of a behavior that
divinity approves, it is not surprising that special mortals can attain a place
apart from that of other humans, closer to the gods in terms of celebrity and
power. The idea of the "hero" as someone between man and god is a specifi-
cally Greek invention. All over the Greek world, the graves of men and
women who had attained notoriety in the community were sites of worship
from at least the eighth century B.C. on, even into the Christian era. It is
worth noting that not all were by any means heroic in senses current today.
The *hêrôs* and *hêrôinê* were not primarily moral beings, but rather persons
of great strength or special connection to the divine. The power to curse, or
to do harm to others, marked the heroic status as much as did courage on
behalf of society: these were the dark side of the power to do good or to heal.
Herakles, whose exploits took him over the known world, conspicuously
combined the warrior's courage with aberrant, even berserk, behavior
(sometimes excused as "madness" sent by his nemesis Here). He died, but
paradoxically lived forever after he was taken up onto Olumpos following
his fiery death on Mount Oita. His story may be taken as a paradigm for
others—the hero fights, rules, often sins, dies, and gains postmortem fame
(a form of immortality) along with semi-divine power. Even the parricide
Oedipus was associated with heroic honors in several places; the *Oedipus at
Colonus* of the tragedian Sophocles tells of the struggle between Athens and
Thebes over claim to his prized burial site.

Among those associated with the Troy saga, such figures as Akhilleus,
Menelaos, Agamemnon, and Diomedes were worshiped with the specific
sacrificial rites of hero "cult" in shrines all around the Aegean. The dan-
gerous aspects of the hero can be glimpsed partially in stories about each of
these men, both within Homeric epic and beyond it. The godlike wrath of
Akhilleus, which brought destruction to his own companions in the war, as
much as his warcraft against the Trojans proved his heroic powers. Hun-
dreds of other heroes, many of them otherwise unknown, are named in
other literary sources or from inscriptions, since every community of any
significance might boast a local hero. The alleged burial sites of heroes and
heroines brought people eager for the blessings and protection that such
powerful ancestors might bring. Recent archaeological work has shown
that in many cases such worship started at real tombs of persons from the
Mycenaean age, perhaps places rediscovered in the eighth century and later.
At the civic level, heroic figures often stood for the pioneer founder of a city
or colony, and so epitomized a community's history and ambitions. That
the leaders of colonizing expeditions were on occasion fugitive murderers

did not detract from their heroization. The story of Odysseus unites several of these features. First, there are signs he was worshiped as a hero on Ithaka, with dedications of archaic tripods made in a cave near Polis Bay on the island (the date of dedication is disputed: eighth century or third century B.C.). Second, by the sixth century B.C. (and most likely earlier), the *Theogony* of Hesiod had assigned to Odysseus two sons by Kirke, named Latinos and Agrios, who were said to have ruled, with Telemakhos, over the Etruscans in the west. In other words, Odysseus was both local hero and father of colonizing heroes. Finally, in his justifiable anger at the suitors, Odysseus resembles his rival Akhilleus, as an exponent of divine wrath.

Character and the Domestic Triangle

The *Odyssey* contains dozens of figures. Part of the poem's enchantment lies in its ability to create a realistic fictional world, populated not just by heroes but by the slaves and servants who support them, by herders and drivers as well as bards and seers. An influential treatise on literary art, *On the Sublime* (attributed to one "Longinus" and probably written in the first century A.D.), speaks of the poem's sketches of daily life in the household of Odysseus as being "like some comedy of character" (9.15: *kômôidia tis estin êthologoumenê*).

For all its profusion of characters, nevertheless, the poem remains fixed around three mortals: Odysseus, his son, and his wife. The role of Telemakhos as a focus for the narrative and figure close to the audience has already been mentioned. What of his parents?

A folklorist would classify Odysseus, the compact, wiry protagonist who defeats huge beasts, as that universal figure, the trickster. Such characters emerge from deep within myth. Well-known tricksters from the Native Americas and Africa, characters like Spider, Crow, or Coyote, shape the way the cosmos is arranged, creating new land or inventing essential crafts or elements, such as weaving or fire. Hermes (in some versions the ancestor of Odysseus) fits this aspect—the *Hymn to Hermes* depicts his invention of sacrifice, for example—whereas Odysseus exhibits trickster qualities in a more human dimension. Like the folklore figures, he is associated with food (as the hungry beggar and master at dispensing wine to the Kuklops, as well as the only *Iliad* warrior who urges Akhilleus to eat before battle). Like the trickster, he is known for his relations with women and his slippery behavior. His adventures often involve animals. Not bestial himself, he nevertheless enjoys a "liminal" status, often on the threshold between the human and the natural worlds. One could read his character as an advance beyond the amorality of the trickster: since he knows so much about food, he can also resist temptations (cf. the cattle of the sun-god), and because he knows women so well, he can also resist Kirke and Kalupso (at least ultimately). Odysseus lives out the more rigid demands of a heroic ethos, although it may be too much to call him an ethical trickster.

But the *Odyssey* is more than a picaresque narrative about a trickster hero. The fundamental shift from folktale to epic (or, some would say, proto-novel) depends on the poet's decision to embed Odysseus in a set of relationships with other characters—a rare setting for the usually lone-wolf trickster. The *Odyssey* insists on these social connections by its very structure, interweaving the stories of Telemakhos and Penelopeia with that of Odysseus, and framing the whole within the motif of a family advancing cautiously to meet change. It is worth pointing out further that the homecoming (*nostos*) for Odysseus is both a personal and a socio-political return. This makes the *Odyssey* more complex and realistic than a simple romance about a reunited couple. Indeed, when we first hear of Odysseus in the poem, Penelopeia is not even mentioned: he sits on the shore of Kalupso's island longing to see the smoke from his hearth-fire. A larger rootedness and security is at stake in his return. Odysseus needs his place in the social pattern—as king, and warrior, aristocrat, father, husband, son—as much as he craves private intimacy with his wife. In turn, his reunion with Penelopeia renews all Ithaka; even Laertes, his father, is rejuvenated and as the poem ends, three generations stand together, in an ideal image of continuity and regeneration. This is to say, finally, that the "character" of Odysseus in the poem is a function of his openness, his ability to let himself trust a few others (like Nausikaa), to lose at least a bit of the loner's suspicion. Guile and survival instinct—the trickster's inheritance—enable him to reach home, where imagination, empathy, and a sense of wider responsibility complete his reintegration, even after twenty years away.

And what of the woman who has waited all those years? By the end of the *Odyssey*, we feel that female heroism is as important, if not more so, than the male variety. Penelopeia's heroism takes a form that William Faulkner would recognize millennia later among the survivors of his tortured South: the quiet ability to endure.

We cannot separate the characterization of Penelopeia in this epic from the poet's careful treatment of women in general. The women in the poem are all the more compelling because their portraits tend to overlap and resonate. Penelopeia and the nymph Kalupso are both weavers and devisers with a deep attachment to Odysseus; Helen resembles Kirke in her knowledge of drugs and her effect on men; Arete, queen of the Phaiakians, rules an island household, as does Penelopeia; she, like her daughter Nausikaa and the nymph Leukothee, turns out to be a helper during the heroic quest. And of course Athene—the wily and witty protector of Odysseus—takes on something of all these female roles as she stage-manages the plot and weaves the hero's homecoming. Odysseus seems as tightly bound to her as to his long-suffering wife. (Given this prominence, one theory about the poem's origin suggests that the *Odyssey* was finally set down in writing in Athens, specifically in praise of the divine patroness of that city.)

There are so many artfully drawn portraits of fascinating, strong women in the *Odyssey* that more than one critic has proposed that the poem was actually composed for a largely female audience. Going a bit further, the English novelist Samuel Butler in 1897 published *The Authoress of the Odyssey*, in which he suggested that a young woman wrote the epic (somebody like Nausikaa!). Knowing what sort of reception his rather ironic book was going to get from the "real" Homerists of his day, Butler mused: "Is it possible that eminent Homeric scholars have found so much seriousness in the more humorous parts of the *Odyssey* because they brought it there? To the serious, all things are serious."

Butler's view, unfortunately, comes with a dose of Victorian sexism—feminine composition, for him, was indicated by such *Odyssey* traits as a lighter tone, a narrative interest in money and lying, and some confusion in the description of ships' rigging. He did correctly observe that women in the *Odyssey* are never laughed at, even though people do laugh fairly often in the *Odyssey* as a whole (twenty-three times as opposed to eleven times in the *Iliad*).

What Butler and others have characterized as a difference of gender views between the two poems may have more to do with theme and content. The *Odyssey* appears to be much more humane, practical, and pragmatic; interested in the everyday rather than the exclusively heroic; more religious in the sense that it shows the immanence of the divine, and the gods' shaping of a happy ending; and more hopeful than the *Iliad* at least in suggesting that one *can* go home again. Whether these reflect a "female" viewpoint depends, of course, on how a given culture conceptualizes gender.

It is undeniable that the most exquisite touches of characterization and psychological insight in the *Odyssey* center on a woman, Penelopeia. In the course of the poem, we see her as an anxious mother, dealing with a son now reaching manhood; as a faithful wife, pining for her husband, who has been absent for twenty years; as the manager of a large, royal household; and as the object of desire for a crowd of determined young suitors. In fact, the story is as much about Penelopeia as it is about Odysseus. It is her intelligence and steadfastness that enables him to survive, once he has made it home. And it is her cunning final test of the bed that makes him acknowledge his emotional tie to her, as it emblematizes their bond.

But to list her qualities as if they are never in doubt is to lose the suspense that the poem's narrative manages to create and maintain. *Will* she stay steadfast? *What* does she really want? Recent years have seen a number of studies of Penelopeia inspired by feminist approaches (see Cohen, Felson-Rubin, Katz, and Doherty in the Bibliography). With the help of these, we can better appreciate the complexity and even ambivalence that the Homeric poet has built into the portrayal of the Ithakan queen. Penelopeia's decisions to appear before the suitors, although she professes to abhor them, and to set up the bride-contest of the bow precisely when her husband has returned, leave the audience wondering about motivation and method. Has she reluctantly given in to the suitors' demands, or instead intuited that the long-suffering Odysseus is back? Could it be that her solitary life has given her a new independence, that she (unlike her cousins Helen and Klutaimnestre) can actually make good decisions in her husband's absence? Is she really the force that holds the house together? And what might all this have meant to an archaic Greek audience? The Homeric poem's depiction—as that of the web of relations Penelopeia sustains—remains powerful and provocative as the epic lives on into the twenty-first century.

Note to the reader: Within the poem, notes are indicated by small solid diamonds directly to the left of the lines of verse.

THE ODYSSEY

The Man ♦ The man, my Muse, resourceful, driven a long way
and the Story   after he sacked the holy city of Trojans:
tell me all the men's cities he saw and the men's minds,
how often he suffered heartfelt pain on the broad sea,
striving for life and a way back home for his war-friends.
Yet he saved no friends, much as he longed to:
they lost their lives through their own reckless abandon,
fools who ate the cattle of Helios the Sun-God.
Huperion seized the day they might have arrived home.

Stranded   Tell us, Goddess, daughter of Zeus, start in your own place.   10
When all the rest at Troy had fled from that steep doom
and gone back home, away from war and the salt sea,
only this man longed for his wife and a way home.
A queenly Nymph, goddess-like, shining Kalupso,
kept the man in a hollow cave. She wanted a husband.
But now the years came round, Gods had arranged it:
the threads were spun for the man's homecoming voyage
to Ithaka. Even there he would undergo trials,
yes, among those he loved. Most of the great Gods
pitied him; only Poseidon's rage was unflagging   20
at godlike Odysseus until he came to his own land.

The Gods   Lately Poseidon had gone to remote Ethiopian
Assemble   people, far from us men, cut off from each other—
♦ some where the God Huperion sets and some where
        he rises.
Accepting rams and bulls burned by the hundred,
Poseidon sat and enjoyed the feast there. But other
Gods were joining Zeus in his hall on Olumpos.

The Father of Gods and men wanted to speak first.
His heart recalled the high-born, handsome Aigisthos:
♦ Agamemnon's well-known son Orestes had killed him.   30
He spoke to the deathless Gods, recalling that murder.
"Look at this, how these humans are blaming the high Gods,
saying evil's from heaven! No, it's a reckless

3

way of their own, beyond what's fated, that hurts them.
The way Aigisthos lately went beyond measure:
he wooed Agamemnon's wife and killed the man when he
    came home.
He knew his doom would be headlong. We told him
    beforehand,
sending Hermes, the sharp-eyed Splendor of Argos.
'Marry no wife,' he was told, 'and murder no husband:
Orestes will take revenge for Atreus's offspring   40
soon as he comes of age and longs for his own land.'
But Hermes, meaning well, failed to deter him;
now Aigisthos has paid in full for all of his evil."

Kept on an   The glow-eyed Goddess Athene answered by saying,
Island   "Father, son of Kronos, highest of rulers:
surely the man lies dead, and his death was the right one.
May all the rest of them die who act in the same way.
But now my heart is torn for artful Odysseus.
The man looks cursed: in pain and far from his people,
kept on a wave-ringed isle where the sea has its navel.   50
The place is thickly wooded, the home of a Goddess,
the daughter of Atlas, who broods on ruin and fathoms
all of the ocean's depths—he holds up the massive
columns himself which keep the earth from the heavens.
His daughter clings to that wretched, mournful Odysseus,
always cajoling, her words gently beguiling
to make him forget Ithaka. Meanwhile Odysseus,
longing to spot mere puffs of smoke from his homeland,
yearns to die. And your own heart is unfeeling,
for all that, Lord of Olumpos. Hasn't Odysseus   60
prayed by the Argive ships and offered you victims
on Troy's wide shore? Why then, Zeus, are you angry?"

A Long   Stormcloud-gathering Zeus answered by saying,
Punishment   "My child, what talk gets over the wall of your front teeth!
How could *I* forget your godlike Odysseus?
He's wise beyond all men, beyond them in holy
gifts to the deathless Gods who rule broadly in heaven.
No, it's Poseidon, the Earth-Upholder, always resentful
because Odysseus put out the eye of a Kuklops,
godlike Poluphemos, the hugest and strongest   70
of all the Kuklops. Thoosa, the Nymph, was his mother,

the daughter of Phorkus, who rules the tireless waters:
the Nymph made love in a hollow cave with Poseidon.
Since then Poseidon, the Earth-Shaker—though he's not
    murdered
Odysseus—keeps him away from the land of his fathers.

"Come on then, all of us here should ponder the question:
how will the man get home? Poseidon must let go
of anger. Since all the deathless Gods are against him,
he won't be able to fight alone with the great Gods."

A Double Plan   The glow-eyed Goddess Athene answered by saying,   80
"Father, son of Kronos and highest of rulers:
indeed if all of the well-blessed Gods are delighted
that thought-full Odysseus now should go to his own house,
let Hermes, the Guide and Splendor of Argos, be swiftly
sent to Ogugie Island and say to Kalupso,
the lovely braided Nymph, our plan is unshaken:
it's time for steadfast Odysseus now to return home.

"I'll go myself to Ithaka promptly and stir up
the son. I'll lodge bravery and strength in his spirit.
He'll tell the long-haired Akhaian men to assemble;   90
♦ he'll warn the suitors, those who are always killing
his bunched-up sheep and curl-horned, hoof-dragging
    cattle.
I'll send him to Sparte too, and deep-sanded Pulos,
for news of his father's homecoming. Maybe he'll find out
there and his own good name among men will be stronger."

Down to   She stopped and tied at her feet the beautiful sandals
Ithaka Fast   of long-lived gold that carried her over the water
and over the measureless land as fast as a wind-breath.
She took a rugged spear, sharp at the bronze point,
heavy and long, well made for downing ranks of heroic   100
men who enraged her—this child of her powerful Father!
She left by leaping down from the heights of Olumpos.

Suitors at Play   She stood on Ithakan ground near Odysseus's courtyard,
close to the outer gate. Holding the bronze spear
♦ she looked like a stranger, Mentes, lord of the Taphians.
She came on the proud suitors gambling with pebbles,

entertaining themselves in front of the doorway,
squatting on hides of bulls they'd slaughtered themselves
        there.
Heralds, a number of helpers moving around them,
mingled water and wine in bowls for the suitors.   110
Others wiped off tables with hole-dotted sponges
and set them again. They piled on plenty of meat-cuts.

Welcoming   Godlike Telemakhos, surely the first one to see her,
a Guest   had sat by a crowd of suitors, sad in his own heart.
He'd pictured a good man, his father: what if he came home
now and scattered the suitors through all of the palace,
gaining esteem again and the rule of his own house?
He mulled and sat among suitors but, spotting Athene,
he walked to the courtyard door in a hurry, embarrassed:
the stranger had stood there a while. Standing beside her,   120
clasping her right hand, he accepted the bronze-pointed
        weapon
and spoke to his guest—the words had a feathery swiftness—
"Good health to you, stranger! Here you'll surely be cared for.
Take some food then say whatever your needs are."

Pallas Athene followed him after he'd spoken.
Soon as they stood inside the high-roofed building,
he placed the spear he'd carried close to a lofty
column inside a polished spear-rack where plenty
of steadfast Odysseus's weapons also were standing.
He led her now to a chair covered with fine cloth   130
and richly carved; under the chair was a footstool.
He took a motley chair nearby, apart from the other
suitors lest the stranger, annoyed by their uproar,
dislike her meal, for these men were all overbearing.
He hoped to ask her about his long-away father.

Bread,   A maid brought them water. She poured from a pitcher
Meat, and a   of stunning gold and they washed their hands in the silver
Good Wine   basin. She set out a polished table before them.
An honored housekeeper brought them bread and
        arranged it.
She laid out plenty of food, gracious and giving.   140
A carver hoisted and set out salvers with all kinds

of meat. He set down golden goblets beside them.
A steward poured them wine, moving around them.

Dining, Poetry,   More brash suitors came in. Soon as they sat down,
and Dance   taking the plain seats or chairs that were thronelike,
                  stewards covered their hands with water for washing,
                  housemaids piled up bread in baskets before them
                  and houseboys crowned the bowls of wine for their
                      drinking.
                  Their hands went out to the good things lying before them.

                  After the craving for food and drink was behind them,   150
                  the suitors' thoughts moved on to other enjoyments,
                  dancing and song, which always go with a good feast.
                  A steward handed the beautiful lyre to the poet,
                  Phemios. Often forced to sing for the suitors,
                  he started to play some chords, his voice engaging.

Trouble at   Now Telemakhos asked the glow-eyed Athene,
Home   holding his head close to stop the others from hearing,
                  "Stranger, friend, will you be galled if I tell you
                  these men enjoy all this, the lyre and the singing,
                  for free? They devour a man's goods without paying,   160
                  a man whose white bones could be rotting now in a
                      rainstorm,
                  lying on land or rolling in waves of the salt sea.
                  Yet if they saw him return to his Ithakan homeland,
                  all of them soon would pray more for some foot-speed
                  than any stores of gold or beautiful clothing.
                  But no, some harsh doom has killed him. I'd feel no
                  warmth or hope whatever man on the whole earth
                  told us he'd come: that homecoming day is a lost one.

Tall Tales and   "But come now, tell me something, answer me truly.
the Truth   What man are you, where is your city, who are your parents?   170
                  What kind of ship did you sail? How did your crewmen
                  bring you to Ithaka? Who do they claim to be sons of?
                  I doubt myself you came to our island by walking!

                  "Tell me a few more things, help me to know this,
                  whether you're new here now or came as my Father's

guest before. Plenty of good men came to our household
because my Father was so well known among all men."

Goddess, The glow-eyed Goddess Athene answered by saying,
King, and Sea "I'll tell you everything now; I'll answer you truly.
Captain
I claim to be Mentes. I call Ankhialos Father, 180
a wise man. I rule the Taphians, lovers of rowing.
I came here now aboard my ship with her crewmen,
sailing the wine-dark sea to a strange-sounding people,
bound for Temese's copper. My brown cargo is iron.
The ship lies to by a farm, away from the city
in Rheithron harbor, below the woods of Mount Neion.
Let's call each other friends: our Fathers were friendly
right from the start. Go and check with Laertes,
  • the old war-chief. They say he comes to the city
no longer, but lives and mourns far off on his own land. 190
His maid is an old woman who sets out his dinner
and wine after weariness claims all of his body,
climbing hard knolls in his wine-bearing orchard.
I came here now because they said that your father
was home. Instead the Gods are blocking his way back.

Alive and "For godlike Odysseus is not yet dead on some hard ground.
Home Soon I'm sure he's alive, somehow, maybe on broad seas,
maybe a foam-ringed island where dangerous tribesmen
hold him against his will and keep him from sailing.
In fact I'll tell you myself, just as the deathless 200
Gods thrust in my heart the way it will all end—
though I'm no seer, I don't know much about bird-signs—
he won't be away from the well-loved land of his fathers
for long even if iron shackles constrain him.
He'll plot some way to come back. He's widely resourceful.

A Beautiful "Come on now, tell me something, answer me truly:
and Doubtful are you, tall as you are, the child of Odysseus?
Bloodline
Your beautiful eyes and head strangely resemble
the man's. We often met and spoke with each other
before he sailed to Troy, where others would sail off 210
too in their hollow ships, the best of the Argives.
Since then I've seen no Odysseus, nor has he seen me."

Telemakhos promptly gave her a sensible answer.
"So then, stranger, I'll tell you myself what the truth is.
◆ My Mother tells me it's so—how can I know it
myself?—no one is ever sure of his bloodline.
I've wished, in truth, that I were the son of a well-blessed
man overtaken by age, surrounded by good wealth.
But no, the sorriest man's doom was my Father's,
the man they say I was born to, now that you ask me."   220

Wrongs of the   The glow-eyed Goddess Athene answered by saying,
Suitors   "Surely the Gods have not decreed that your bloodline
will always be nameless—not since Penelopeia has
                borne you!
Come on though, tell me something, answer me truly:
who are these crowding diners? Why do you need them?
Is it a feast? A wedding? It's surely no picnic!
The men strike me as overproud and insulting,
eating your house up. A good man walking among them,
watching their shameless acts, would really get angry."

An Emptied,   Telemakhos promptly gave her a sensible answer.   230
Dishonored   "My guest, now that you press me, asking your questions,
House   my house was meant to be truly wealthy and handsome
once—as long as my Father stayed in his homeland.
Now the Gods will otherwise: planning our bad times,
making the man more lost than anyone ever
from common sight. I'd never mourn his passing
so much if he died on Trojan soil among war-friends;
or later, the war wound up, in the arms of his loved ones.
Then all the Akhaians would raise a tomb for the dead man.
In days to come he'd gain a name for his son too.   240
But now storm-winds have carried him off as though
                nameless.
He's gone, unseen and unheard of, leaving me mourning
and smarting.

                "I don't grieve or wail for my Father
only: Gods have caused me other worrisome hardship.
The noblest men around us, lords of the islands—
Same, Doulikhion, densely wooded Zakunthos—
and those who rule our rock-strewn Ithakan island,

all come courting my Mother, wearing our house down.
She won't say no to a wedding she hates, and she cannot
make them stop. They go on eating and wasting   250
our home. They'll waste me too, they'll wholly destroy me."

The Wrath of Pallas Athene now got angry and told him,
Odysseus "Look at this! How you need your long-gone Odysseus
truly to get his hands on the shameless wooers!
If only he came right now and stood at the outer
doorway holding a shield, two spears and a helmet—
the way he looked when I saw him myself for the first time
in our own house. He enjoyed himself and he drank well,
back from Ephure, Mermeros's son, the household of Ilos.
Odysseus went there sailing a fast-running vessel   260
to look for deadly poison, useful for coating
his bronze-tipped arrows. Ilos, though, would not give it:
he dreaded the rage of Gods living forever.
My Father, greatly loving the man, gave him the poison.
If only the same Odysseus now were facing the suitors,
they'd all be dead in a hurry—that bitter a marriage!

Calling an "Surely all this lies on the knees of the great Gods,
Assembly whether he comes back home for revenge in the great hall
or fails to return. But you? I say you should ponder
how to drive the suitors yourself from the great hall.   270
Come on then, listen closely, do as I tell you.
Call the Akhaian war-chiefs at dawn to assembly.
Speak to them all, let every God be your witness
and order the suitors to go right now to their own lands.
Your mother may, if her heart enjoins her to marry,
go back to the hall of her greatly powerful father.
They'll build her a wedding there, arranging the many
bride-gifts, all that should go with a daughter they so love.

Sailing to "I'll offer you wise counsel—if only you'll take it!
Pulos Man the best ship that you have with twenty rowers.   280
Go off and ask of your father: he's gone for a long time.
A man may tell you, or maybe a rumor you hear from
Zeus—he often brings good news to you people.
Go and talk first with godlike Nestor in Pulos.
Later ask light-haired Menelaos in Sparte:
he came home last of the bronze-clad Akhaians.

Then, worn as you are, if you hear that your father's
alive and headed for home, hold out for another
year. If you're sure, however, he's gone from the living,
come back home to the well-loved land of your fathers.   290
• Raise a mound up high: honor the dead man
duly and fully. And give your mother a good man.

Killing the   "When all that's done, your work and traveling ended,
Suitors   now in your mind and heart you really must plan it,
how to kill the suitors still in your great hall,
whether in stealth or openly. Staying with boyish
ways is not what you need: you're boyish no longer.
Or don't you know of the name that godlike Orestes
won among all men? He killed that sneaking Aigisthos
who'd killed his father—he'd killed the renowned
        Agamemnon.   300
So you, my friend. I see you're handsome, a tall man.
Be brave and every man in the future will praise you.

Leaving Soon   "But now I'll go to my race-fast ship and my crewmen.
The men are likely annoyed: I'm keeping them waiting.
Take care of yourself and ponder well what I told you."

Stay Longer   But now Telemakhos gave her a sensible answer.
"My guest, surely your words are thoughtful and kindly—
a father's way with a son. I'll never forget them.
But stay, come on now: although you're anxious to set out,
wait till you've bathed and filled your heart with enjoyment.   310
Then go to your ship in high spirits holding my present—
a rich and beautiful heirloom. Let it remind you
of me, the gift of a friendly stranger to stranger."

A Bird   The glow-eyed goddess Athene gave him an answer:
Soars Away   "Don't hold me any longer. I'm anxious to set out.
Whatever gift your heart has told you to offer,
save it for when I come back; I'll carry it home then.
Choose the loveliest—then in return you will fare well."

The glow-eyed Athene spoke that way and she left him
suddenly soaring, birdlike. There in his young heart   320
she'd placed boldness and strength: he'd remember his
        father

better now than before. He watched her in deep thought,
his heart amazed, for he knew his guest was a Goddess.

The Long Way
Home
from Troy

He walked at once like a man and God to the suitors.
They sat there still. The bard was renowned as a singer:
they heard him out as he sang of the wretched Akhaians'
long way home from Troy, made hard by Pallas Athene.
Upstairs in her room the wondrous music was too well
heard by Ikarios's daughter, mind-full Penelopeia.
Shortly the queen came down the stairs of her high house,   330
but not alone: two maids followed behind her.
Closer now to the suitors, the goddess-like woman
stood by a strong support of the well-built roofbeams,
holding a shiny veil in front of her two cheeks.
Loyal maids were close, left side and right side.
She spoke with tears in her eyes to the God-gifted singer.
◆ "Phemios, many other songs you know can be charming,
the doings of men and Gods made famous by poets.
Sing one now as you sit here—the others may relish
their wine in silence. But stop that song about wretched   340
Troy that always wears the heart in my own breast
down. Unforgettable pain has fallen on *me* most,
my longing for one dear head, remembering always
the man so widely esteemed in Hellas and Argos."

The New
Music

But now Telemakhos gave her a sensible answer.
"Mother, why deny a faithful singer his own joy,
whatever rouses his mind? Poets are never
to blame; somehow Zeus is to blame when he hands out
all he decides to each of us bread-eating people.
Don't chide this man for singing of harsh doom for
          Danaans.   350
For people will praise a song most if its music
sounds more new than the other music around them.
Let your heart and soul listen and bear up.
Not only Odysseus lost the day he would come home
from Troy: plenty of other people were lost there.
Rather go to your room and care for your own work,
loom and spindle. Tell your handmaids to manage
their own tasks. We men will care for the talk here,
all of us, mainly myself—I rule in my own house."

Amazed, the lady went upstairs to her bedroom,   360
keeping at heart her child's sensible answer.
Arrived upstairs in her room with the women, her
    handmaids,
she wept for Odysseus, the man she loved, until glow-eyed
Athene tossed some honeyed sleep on her eyelids.

Call for a   Suitors made new noise in the shadowy great hall,
Gathering   Each of them praying to lie in bed with her close by.
Then Telemakhos shrewdly started to tell them,
"My Mother's wooers, with all your pride that is lawless,
dine and enjoy for now. But none of this uproar:
plainly it's a beautiful thing to hear out a singer   370
like Phemios—how his voice resembles a great God's!
At dawn, however, let's go and sit in assembly,
all of us. There I'll openly give you my own word:
get out of my hall. Enjoy your dinnertimes elsewhere,
eat up your own wealth, one house or another.

"Yet if it strikes you somehow as better and cheaper
that one man's goods be lost with none of you paying,
go on wasting. I'll call to the Gods lasting forever:
somehow Zeus may grant the workings of vengeance.
Then you could die inside my house without paying."   380

A Leader's   He spoke that way. Suitors were biting their lips hard,
Tricky Answer   struck by Telemakhos, how he'd spoken so bravely.
At length Antinoos answered, the son of Eupeithes:
"Telemakhos, surely the Gods themselves are your teachers:
you talk so high to us all, you've spoken so bravely!
May Zeus, the son of Kronos, never create you
lord of sea-ringed Ithaka, though it's yours from your
    father."

But now Telemakhos gave him a sensible answer.
"Antinoos, don't be angry, whatever I say now.
I'd surely want to be king if Zeus would allow it.   390
You think it's the worst thing for a man to be ruling?
It's not so bad to be king. Promptly your own house
takes on wealth and you're honored most as the ruler.
In fact there are plenty of other lords of Akhaians
on sea-ringed Ithaka, men both younger and older;

one might rule since godlike Odysseus perished.
But I'll be lord of our own house and our helpers,
those whom godlike Odysseus won for me fighting."

Another
Leader's
Tricky Answer

Then Eurumakhos, son of Polubos, answered,
"Telemakhos, all this lies on the knees of the great Gods,   400
whichever Akhaian is sea-ringed Ithaka's ruler.
Hold on to your wealth still—be lord of your own house.
May no man arrive in force to take your belongings
against your will, so long as Ithaka's lived on.

But Who Was
That Stranger?

"But now, good man, I want to ask of that stranger.
Where did the fellow come from, what was the homeland
he claimed, where was his bloodline, the land of his fathers?
Maybe he brought you news? Your father is coming?
Or maybe he came here wanting help for his own work.
How quickly he rose and left, hardly remaining,   410
not to be known! Yet his looks were not low-born."

A Grown Son's •
Tricky Answer

Now Telemakhos gave him a sensible answer.
"Eurumakhos, surely it's lost, the return of my Father.
I trust the news no longer, wherever it comes from.
I don't care about omens, whoever my Mother
calls to the great hall, the prophets she questions.
That stranger now was a friend of my Father's from Taphos.
He claims to be Mentes; he calls Ankhialos father,
a wise man. He rules the Taphians, lovers of rowing."

Still Telemakhos knew in his heart Mentes was deathless.   420

A New Day
Ending

Others went back to their pleasures—spirited singing
and dancing a while—they stayed till evening's arrival
entertaining themselves. With darkness approaching
they left to take some rest, each man to his own house.

An Old and
Caring Nurse

Telemakhos's room was raised over the handsome
courtyard, built up high, a place with a broad view.
He went there now, pondering all of his troubles.
A caring Eurukleia joined him and carried
the blazing torches. The daughter of Ops, a son of Peisenor:
Laertes had bought her once with a lot of his own wealth,   430
paying twenty oxen—the woman was young then.

He honored her much as his caring wife in the great hall,
but not in his bed: he avoided vexing his lady.
She carried the blazing torches now for she loved him
more than the other maids—she'd nursed him in childhood.
After she opened the doors of his well-fashioned bedroom
he sat on the bed, took off his tunic, a soft one,
and placed it right in the knowing, elderly woman's
hands. She folded and smoothed it, hanging the tunic
high on a peg close to the hole-and-cord bedframe.   440
Then she went from the room, closing the door with its
     silver
handle, pulling the thong and driving the bolt in.

All night long he stayed there, wrapped in a woolen
blanket and pondering moves laid out by Athene.

BOOK 2 *A Gathering and a Parting*

Summoning
the Old
and Young
When newborn Dawn came on with her rose-fingered
    daylight,
the well-loved son of Odysseus rose in his bedroom
and dressed. He hung a sharp sword from a shoulder,
strapped two beautiful sandals under his oil-smooth
feet and left the room, his face like a great God's.

He promptly told heralds with strong-sounding voices
♦ to call the Akhaians, the long-haired men, to assembly.
The calls went out and a crowd hastily gathered.
After they'd all arrived and the assembly was waiting,
Telemakhos came. The man was holding a bronze spear   10
and not alone: two white dogs followed him closely.
Athene showered a wondrous grace on the young man;
all the people gazed at him now as he drew near.
Elders yielded: he sat in the chair of his father.

Why
an Assembly
Now?
Aiguptios spoke up first, a war-chief among them.
Stooped with age, in countless ways he had grown wise.
Yes, and his own son, joining with godlike Odysseus,
had gone in hollow ships to Troy, known for its horses.
A spear-man, Antiphos later was killed in the hollow
♦ cave of a wild one: the Kuklops made him his last meal.   20
Of three more sons, Eurunomos joined with the suitors
and two men steadily worked the lands of their father.
He never forgot the dead son. He missed him and
    mourned him
now as he spoke, shedding tears as he called out,
"Listen, you men of Ithaka! Hear what I'm saying.
We haven't held our assembly here since the morning
godlike Odysseus left our land with his hollow
ships. Who's gathered us now? Which is the younger
or older man who felt this need to assemble?
Maybe he's heard news of an army approaching.   30
The man who knows that first should plainly inform us.
Or maybe he'll air some other cause for our people.

That strikes me as good, as blessed: may Zeus be the
  bringer
of all good things to that man, whatever his wants are."

The Suitors   His prayer gladdened the well-loved son of Odysseus.
Must Go   Staying seated no longer, anxious to speak out,
he stood in the assembly's midst holding the scepter
thrust in his hand by Peisenor, a herald shrewd in his
  counsel.
Facing the old man first Telemakhos told him,
"My elder, you'll find out soon. The man who assembled   40
this crowd is not far off: pain has come to me most here.
I haven't heard the news of an army approaching.
Whatever I found out first I surely would tell you.
Another cause for our people? I'd show you and speak out.
No, it's my own need. Wrong fell on my household
in two ways. My brave father was lost—and your ruler
once, right here—a king who was kind as a father.

Powerless   "But now a far worse harm could utterly ruin
my house quite soon, destroying all my resources.
Suitors beset my Mother although she's unwilling.   50
Well-loved sons of the men here, the noblest among us,
shy at going away to the house of her father,
Ikarios, letting him see to his daughter's presents
and give her away to the man he wishes and favors.
Instead they jam our house: they slaughter our sheep here
every day, our fattened goats and our cattle.
They revel and gulp down glowing wine with abandon.
So much is lost already because there is no man—
the man Odysseus was—to keep this blight from my
  household.
We cannot stop it ourselves. If all of us tried to,   60
we'd do quite badly: we're not trained to be fighters.
If I had the strength myself I surely would stop them.
What they've done is unbearable: far from its beauty,
my house is plunder. So then. Take the dishonor
and shame on yourselves before men, the others around us,
all our neighbors. And dread the Gods when they're angry:
astonished at evil acts, they could turn and be vengeful.

A Prayer for   "By Zeus on Olumpos I plead, yes and by Themis,
Help   who calls assemblies of men herself and disbands them:
             stop them, my friends. Let me dwindle in painful   70
             mourning alone. Unless my Father Odysseus,
             a good man, harmed or spited you well-greaved Akhaians
             and now, to make me pay, you spite me and harm me,
             prodding the suitors on. I'd rather you ate up
             all my belongings yourselves, my livestock and gold-hoard.
             After you ate them someday there would be payment.
           ◆ I'd go around the city pressing my own case,
             recalling my goods till everything surely was paid back.
             But now you thrust pain in my heart that I can't cure."

The Shroud for ◆ He spoke in rage and wept, throwing the scepter   80
Laertes   hard on the ground. All the people felt pity.
             The rest of the crowd was quiet, no one was daring
             enough to answer Telemakhos, talk to him sternly—
             only Antinoos. Soon he answered by saying,
             "High talk, Telemakhos, forceful! But what are you saying,
             trying to shame us? You'd like to fasten the blame here?
             Still not one of the Akhaian suitors is guilty.
             No, it's the mother you love, that cleverest woman.
             For three years now—it's close to the fourth year—
             the lady goes on spiting hearts in the chests of Akhaians,   90
             making us all hope and promising each man,
             sending him notes when her thoughts are elsewhere and
                 plotting.

             "The mind of the lady planned this trick among others:
             standing a huge loom in the hall for her weaving,
             a broad and beautiful web, she spoke to us shortly:
             'Young men, my suitors, now that godlike Odysseus
             died, you're anxious to marry. But wait till I finish
             this work. Don't let my yarn be useless or wasted.
             The shroud's for a war-chief, Laertes, after a deadly
             portion cuts him down—remorseless death is the matter.   100
             May no Akhaian blame me now in this country
             because he lies unshrouded after he gained wealth.'

             "Those were her words. Our hearts were proud but we
                 nodded.
           ◆ So every day at the huge loom she was weaving—

and every night with torches nearby she unwound it.
For three long years her guile tricked us Akhaians.
Then the fourth year came with its rolling of seasons.
One of her maids who knew what was happening told us
and promptly we caught her unwinding the beautiful
    web-work.
She finished her work at last—unwilling but forced to.   110

The Lady Must Choose   "So now we suitors answer you, let it be known well
in your own heart and known by all the Akhaians:
send your mother away. Tell her to marry
the man her father chooses, whoever she likes best.
So long as she stalls and annoys the sons of Akhaians,
her own heart knowing the way Athene has blessed her
with all of the finest skills, thoughtful and able
designs—we've never heard of a woman in past times
knowing this way, no lovely braided Akhaians
like Turo, Alkmene, Mukene in beautiful headdress: 120
none of those minds were a match for Penelopeia's.
But now she failed this time to plan in the right way.
So long will men devour your goods and resources,
long as her thoughts hold back, these notions the Gods now
place in her bosom. The lady's building a big name
herself but she makes you long for all of your lost goods.
So we won't go ourselves to our farmland or elsewhere,
not till she marries the Akhaian man of her own choice."

Love and Fear of the Mother   But now Telemakhos gave him a sensible answer.
"Antinoos, how can I force her from home if she says no?   130
She bore and raised me. No, with my Father in other
land alive or dead, it's wrong sending my Mother
away on my own whim. I'd pay Ikarios plenty:
her father could make me suffer. Yes, and the other
◆ Powers—my Mother could call down fearsome Avengers
on leaving home. Men would also upbraid me.
So I will never say such words to my Mother.

A Clash of Eagles   "You others here, if you feel shame in your own hearts,
stay out of my hall. Tend to your mealtimes elsewhere,
eat up your own belongings, vary your households.   140
Yet if it strikes you now that it's cheaper and better
to eat up one man's goods, not punished or paying,

go on with your waste. I'll call on Gods lasting forever:
somehow Zeus will bring me the workings of vengeance.
Then you'll die inside my house without paying."

Telemakhos stopped and Zeus, watching from far off,
sent two eagles down from the high crest of a mountain.
both of them flew for a while on the breath of a fast wind,
spreading their wings out widely, close to each other.
Then they approached the center, the gathering's many   150
voices, and banked around them, rapidly beating
their wings and glaring at all their heads with a death-look.
They tore at each other's cheeks and necks with their talons
and flew away to the right, past homes of the city.

A Reading of   People marveled to see such birds with their own eyes.
the Two Birds   They pondered deep in their hearts: how would it all end?
                  An aging war-chief, Halitherses, would tell them.
                  The son of Mastor, surely the best in his own age
          ♦ at knowing the ways of birds and reading the dark signs,
            the man meant well when he spoke to the gathering saying,   160
            "Listen closely, Ithakans. Hear what I tell you—
            mainly you suitors—I'll make things known to you fully.
            Great harm is rolling down on you. Not for a long time
            now is Odysseus far from his loved ones: he's close by,
            rather, and planning doom, the murder of every
            suitor. He'll cause trouble for many besides you,
            too, living on clear-viewed Ithaka. Ponder a long time
            before then: how can we stop this? You suitors can stop it
            yourselves indeed. You know which course is the best one.
            I'm not a witless prophet for I have been well taught.   170
            I say for Odysseus everything now will be ended
            the way I foretold when Argives left for the coastline
            of Troy and Odysseus joined them, full of the best plans.
            He'd suffer often, I said, and lose all of his war-friends.
            Then in the twentieth year, when no one would know him,
            he'd come back home. All this now is to happen."

Birds Can   But shortly Polubos's son Eurumakhos answered,
Mean Nothing   "Go off, old man. Foretell big things to your children
                 at home and stop them from suffering harm in the future!
                 For this I'm far better at prophesying than you are: 180
                 plenty of birds fly back and forth in the Sun-God's

rays; not all are omens. Odysseus perished
a long way off. *You* should have died with the dead man
just like that, ending all this talk about seers,
not rousing the way you do Telemakhos's anger.
You wait for his gift for your house—if only he grants it!

Pain to Be   "No, I'll plainly tell you how it will end here.
Spread Around   If you as the older man with all of your wisdom,
hoodwink a younger man and stir up his anger,
first you'll make for a lot more pain for the young man: 190
he cannot change a thing because of us all here.
Then old man, we'll levy a fine which will make you
wince repaying. Your heart's pain will be bitter.

"I charge Telemakhos now myself as we all hear:
tell your mother to go back home to her father.
Let them arrange for a wedding, preparing the many
bride-gifts, those that go with a well-loved daughter.
But not before then, surely, will sons of Akhaians
end their rough courting. No one anyhow scares us,
not Telemakhos there, for all of his high talk.   200
And you, old man, we hardly listen to omens
you mouth which don't come true. They make you more
      hated.
So his goods will crassly be eaten without our
ever paying, long as the lady stalls the Akhaians
in marriage. We go on waiting all of our days here,
wrangling over her worth. We hardly go looking
for other women we all might properly marry."

Sea Travel   Telemakhos promptly gave him a sensible answer.
"Eurumakhos—yes, and you other high-born suitors—
I won't beg you. I'll say no more of the matter.   210
The Gods know well enough, and all the Akhaians.
But now give me a race-fast ship with some rowers,
twenty crewmen to help me travel that way and this way.
I'll sail to both Sparte and deep-sanded Pulos
for word of my Father's return—he's gone for a long time.
Maybe a man will tell me—maybe a rumor
from Zeus—he often brings good news to us people.
Then worn as I am, if I hear that my Father's
alive and heading home, I'll wait for another

year. But then if I hear he's dead, gone from the living,   220
I'll come back home to the well-loved land of my Fathers
and raise a mound up high. I'll honor the dead man
duly and fully. I'll give my Mother a good man."

A Challenge for   He spoke that way and sat down. The next one to stand up
the People   was Mentor, an old friend of handsome Odysseus
                 who'd charged him, boarding ship, to care for his whole
                      house
                 and keep things safe; the rest were to follow the old man.
                 Meaning well now, he faced the gathering saying,
                 "Listen closely, you Ithakans! Hear what I tell you.
                 Let no king holding a scepter be willingly gracious   230
                 or kind ever, knowing and caring for justice.
                 Let him be hard, always acting unfairly
                 now that no one recalls godlike Odysseus,
            ♦   people he ruled as king, and kind as a father.
                 But truly I don't blame the emboldened suitors,
                 their minds' evil designs and the force they are using:
                 their own heads are at risk for devouring Odysseus's
                 household brutally, saying he'll never return home.
                 No, I'm angry more at the rest of you people,
                 those who have sat here dumb, never a harsh word   240
                 to stop the suitors, although they're few and you're many."

Uneven Battle   But then Euenor's son Leiokritos answered,
                 "Mischief Mentor! Crazed in your head, what are you saying,
                 goading people to stop us? It's surely a hard thing,
                 even with more men as you have, to fight over dinner!
                 But even if Ithaka's Lord Odysseus came home,
                 heartily anxious to force us high-born suitors,
                 dining there in the man's house, from his great hall,
                 his wife would hardly rejoice, however she pined for
                 his coming: he'd go to his doom shamefully right there,   250
                 fighting outnumbered. So what you've told us is not right.

The Gathering   "Come on now, people, break up—each to your own work!
Is Ended   Mentor and Halitherses, Odysseus's household
                 friends from the start, will speed up Telemakhos's voyage.
                 And yet I'm thinking he'll stay right here for a long time,
                 waiting for news on Ithaka, never making this journey."

He said so much: his words cut short the assembly.
The crowd broke up, each man went off to his own house.
Suitors left for the home of godlike Odysseus.

<table>
</table>

A Plea to ◆ Telemakhos walked apart on the shore of the salt sea.   260
Athene   Washing his hands in the gray surf he prayed to Athene.
         "Hear me: you came to our house yesterday, Goddess,
         you told me to sail a ship on the haze-covered water,
         asking for news of my Father, gone for a long time.
         But everything's thwarted now by all the Akhaians,
         the suitors mainly. They're overprevailing and evil."

Sons and   While he prayed like that Athene had come close,
Fathers   taking a voice and shape that struck him like Mentor's.
         She spoke to him now and the words had a feathery
              swiftness:
         "You won't be a low or thoughtless man in the future,   270
         Telemakhos, not if your father's power has filled you:
         the man could bring his word and work to a good end.
         The voyage you go on won't be fruitless or endless.
         Yet if you're not the man's child and Penelopeia's,
         I cannot hope you'll end all this as you'd like to.
         A boy just like his father is truly unlikely.
         Most are worse and those who are better are so few.
         But since you won't be thoughtless or mean in the future
         because Odysseus's wiles won't utterly fail you,
         I then have hope you'll bring this work to a good end.   280

A Good Crew "So now slight the thoughts and plans of the suitors.
and Ship   They're such fools, lacking fairness and good sense.
         They know nothing of doom, that portion of darkness
         truly close to them—all of them dying in one day!
         The voyage you'd like should not be delayed any longer.
         Since I'm so close to the line and house of your father,
         I'll deck out a race-fast ship myself and I'll join you.

         "Go back home for now and mix with the suitors.
         Get ready with stores, place them all in containers,
         wine in amphoras and groats, the backbone of sailors,   290
         in skintight sacks. I'll go to the city and gather
         an eager crew in a hurry. Plenty of newer
         and older ships are in sea-ringed Ithaka's harbor.

I'll look at them all myself and pick out the best one.
We'll hurry and get her ready to launch on the broad sea."

Back to the   Athene, daughter of Zeus, had spoken. Waiting no longer
Old Times   after he heard the voice of the Goddess, the young man
                made his way back home. But sad in his own heart—
                he found disdainful suitors again in the great hall.
                They flayed his goats; they roasted pigs in the courtyard.   300
                Antinoos walked right up to Telemakhos laughing,
                taking his hand. He called his name and he told him,
                "High-talking Telemakhos, fearless and forceful!
                Don't keep harmful words or work in your own chest.
                Drink and dine with me rather, just like the old times.
                Akhaians will surely bring all this to a good end—
                a vessel with hand-picked rowers to hurry and take you
                to holy Pulos for news of your high-born father."

Death Warning   But now Telemakhos gave him a sensible answer.
                "Antinoos, how can I calmly dine with you prideful   310
                men and enjoy myself, acting without care?
                It's not enough you suitors devour my belongings,
                all that wealth from the times when I was a boy here.
                But now I'm grown. I've heard stories from others,
                I'm learning well, the spirit's rising inside me.
                I'll try to harm you somehow. I'll send you your death-day,
                whether I sail to Pulos or stay in my own land.
                I'll go and it won't be in vain, the voyage I spoke of,
                though I must sail as a passenger, owning no well-rowed
                ship. That way, I guess, was more to your liking."   320

Dangerous   He stopped and calmly removed his hand from Antinoos's
Teasing   clasp. Then suitors ready to dine in the palace
                mocked Telemakhos, laughing and taunting him loudly,
                some overbearing younger suitors complaining,
                "Of course: Telemakhos plans to slaughter us all here!"
                "Maybe he'll bring back war-guards from deep-sanded
                     Pulos."
                "Yes, or from Sparte: he's anxious now and a wild man!"
                "Or maybe he means to sail to Ephure's grain-rich
            ◆ land in order to bring back potions and poisons
                to toss in the wine-bowl." "He'll kill us all in the great hall!"   330
                Other younger suitors overbearingly answered,

"Who knows? Sailing his hollow ship he may wander
and die himself, far from friends, just like Odysseus."
"That way, though, he'd make the job of dividing
all his wealth much harder." "His house would be given
then to his mother." "Yes—to the man she would marry!"

The Choicest   So they went on. But the son walked down to his father's
Wine   broad and high-roofed storeroom. Gold in a tall pile
lay there, bronze, clothes in chests and various scented
oils. Bulky jars of wine, sweetened and aging,   340
stood there, an uncut, God-pleasing vintage inside them,
arranged close to the wall—should Odysseus ever
come back home after suffering great pain.
The double doors had barlike planks and were tightly
joined. Day and night a housekeeper stayed close,
a woman watching it all with plenty of know-how—
Eurukleia, the daughter of Ops, a son of Peisenor.
Telemakhos called to her now at the storeroom and told her,
"Good mother, draw some wine in the two-handled wine-jar,
the sweet one next to the choicest wine you have kept here   350
for luckless, Zeus-bred Odysseus. Maybe he'll come back
home from somewhere, saved from doom and his
        death-day.
Fill twelve jars and fit them all with their covers.
Pour groats into bags, well-sewn and of leather—
twenty measures in all, ground by the miller.
Only you must know. When it's all gathered and ready
I'll haul it away at dusk after my Mother
goes upstairs to her room, mulling her night's rest.
I'm going to both Sparte and deep-sanded Pulos
to ask of my loving Father's return. Maybe I'll hear news."   360

A Woman's   Soon as he'd spoken his loving nurse Eurukleia
Dread   ♦ wept and called out, her words with a feathery swiftness:
"How has this thought, my child, entered your dearest
head? Where do you long to go on the broad earth,
an only son, so loved? Zeus-bred Odysseus
died in some strange country far from his homeland;
now with you gone, these men will maneuver to harm you.
They'll lie and kill you in time, then split up your treasure.
No! Stay with your own right here. There is no great
need to suffer harm on the restless sea or to wander."   370

A Goddess's   Telemakhos promptly gave her a sensible answer.
Help   "Take heart, good mother. My plan's not lacking a God's help.
Just swear you won't be telling my dear Mother of all this,
not till eleven or twelve days are behind us
or Mother has missed me herself, hearing I've gone off.
Fewer tears must mar her face and her beauty."

He spoke that way and the old one swore to say nothing.
The great oath done, when all the swearing was over,
she quickly drew some wine into two-handled wine-jars
and poured groats into bags, well-sewn and of leather.   380
Telemakhos went to the hall, rejoining the suitors.

A Ship ♦   Then the gray-eyed Goddess Athene thought of a new plan.
into Water   She looked like Telemakhos going through all of the city,
choosing every crewman and passing the word out:
"Gather close to our race-fast ship in the evening."
She also asked for the race-fast ship of Noemon,
Phronios's son, the bright one. He offered her gladly.

The sun went down. When all the roadways had darkened
she hauled the race-fast ship into water and stockpiled
all the gear that a vessel with strong planking will carry.   390
She moored her next at the harbor's mouth. Plenty of
       good men
gathered around her, each man roused by the Goddess.

Drunk and   There the glow-eyed Goddess Athene thought of a new plan.
Weary   Making her way to the house of godlike Odysseus,
she poured a honeyed drowsiness fast on the suitors,
muddled their drinking and knocked the cups from their
       weak hands.
They all stood up to go and rest in the city.
No one could stay for long when sleepiness fell on their
       eyelids.

Down to the   Glow-eyed Athene spoke to Telemakhos also,
Seashore   hailing him out of the hall where people had lived well,   400
taking a voice and shape that struck him like Mentor's.
"Telemakhos! Crewmen in well-made greaves have already
sat by the oars. They wait for your word to begin work.
Come on, let's go! Don't stall this trip any longer."

Pallas Athene spoke that way and she led him.
Telemakhos briskly followed the Goddess's footsteps.
Soon as they came on down to the ship and the salt sea,
finding the long-haired crew right there on the seashore,
Telemakhos, filled with a holy power, addressed them:
"Come on, my friends, let's carry all of the gathered   410
stores from the great hall. Most of the maids and my Mother
do not know: one woman alone has heard our story."

Sailing   He spoke that way, he led them along and they followed.
at Night   They hauled goods on the strong-decked ship and they
                    stowed them,
just as the well-loved son of Odysseus ordered.
Telemakhos went on board, Athene before him,
taking a seat astern. Telemakhos sat down
close to the Goddess. Crewmen untied the cables,
boarded themselves and took their seats at the oar-locks.

Glow-eyed Athene sent them a favoring tailwind,   420
Westwind's gusts on the wine-dark sea as it sang by.
Telemakhos rallied his crewmen now and he told them
to break out line: they heard his call and obeyed him,
•   hoisting the fir-wood mast to be stepped in its hollowed
mast-block: they made it tall and braced it with forestays.
They pulled up white sail, the lines a twisting of leather,
and wind bellied the sail out. Darkening water
loudly swished at the prow of the underway vessel,
smartly cutting the waves and set on the right course.

Prayer   After they lashed their gear on the black-painted, race-fast   430
and Wine to   ship and set out wine-filled bowls, they poured a libation,
the Gods   drops for the deathless Gods, born to be always,
mainly for Pallas, the glow-eyed daughter of great Zeus.

All that night, through dawn, the ship stayed on the right
        course.

BOOK 3 *In the Great Hall of Nestor*

Go Boldly to
the King

Helios the Sun-God, leaving beautiful sea-swells,
rose in a sky all bronze to lighten the deathless
Gods and death-bound men on grain-giving farmland.
The travelers came to Pulos, Neleus's well-built city.
♦ Men were offering all-black bulls on the seashore
now to the dark-haired Earth-Shaker, Poseidon.
Nine assemblies with five hundred in each group
sat while nine bulls were readied before them.
They burned thighs for the Sea-God and tasted the entrails.

The travelers put in straight. They lowered sail on the
     balanced   10
ship and furled it. They moored and stepped on the
     beach-sand.
Athene before him, Telemakhos walked from the vessel.
The first to speak was the Goddess, glow-eyed Athene.
"No need for shyness, Telemakhos, not in the least here.
You came by sea for a good cause, to learn of your father,
what ground might cover him now, what doom he was
     faced with.
Come on then, straight to Nestor, that breaker of horses!
Let's see what guidance the king might store in his old
     chest.
Plead with the man yourself to tell you the whole truth.
He won't tell lies; he's very sensible really."   20

Where Will
the Words
Come From?

But now Telemakhos gave her a sensible answer.
"Mentor, how will it go, how should I greet him?
♦ I'm not yet trained in concise talking. Moreover
young men feel embarrassed questioning old men."

The glow-eyed Goddess Athene answered by saying,
"Telemakhos, some of the words you'll know in your own
     heart;
Power will help you with others. I think you were hardly
born and raised against the will of the great Gods."

28

Welcome to
a Feast
for Poseidon Pallas Athene spoke that way and she led him.
The man briskly followed the Goddess's footsteps.   30
They came to the stone seats where men of Pulos had
     gathered.
Nestor sat there with friends and family around him
ready to dine, spitting and roasting their cutlets.
• Seeing strangers they all came crowding around them,
taking their hands in welcome. They asked them to
     sit down.
First a son of Nestor, Peisistratos, came close,
taking them both by the hand. He sat them for dinner
on soft wool, spread out there on the beach-sand
close to Thrasumedes, a brother, and close to their father.
Peisistratos offered them entrails and he poured them then   40
wine in a golden goblet to welcome them, saying
to Pallas Athene, daughter of Zeus who carries the great
     shield,
"Stranger, our guest, pray to lordly Poseidon.
You happened to sail here now for a feast in his honor.
Pray and offer him wine—that is the right way.
Hand the goblet of honeyed wine to your comrade
then to pour. I'm sure he prays to the deathless
Gods for every man needs help from those Powers.
He's also a younger man, close to my own age,
and so I offer the golden goblet to you first."   50
He stopped and placed in her hand the goblet of sweet wine.

Goddess
Praying to God Athene was pleased. The man was thoughtful and proper
to place the golden goblet first in her own hand.
• Promptly she prayed in full to lordly Poseidon:
"Land-Upholder, Poseidon, listen! Don't be resentful,
scorning our prayers to bring this work to a good end.
Lavish renown on Nestor first and his children.
Then endow the others with gracious return-gifts—
all these Pulos men who've made your hecatombs famous.
For me and Telemakhos too, grant a return home   60
fast on our black ship as soon as we've ended our
     work here."
She prayed—and was bringing it all herself to a good end.
She gave Telemakhos now the stunning, two-handled
     goblet.
The well-loved son of Odysseus prayed in the same way.

Who Are These
Guests?
After the outer flesh was cooked and unspitted
they all took portions, enjoying a wonderful dinner.
When all the craving for food and drink was behind them
Nestor began to speak, the Gerenian horseman.
"Now is the better time for raising a question,
asking guests who they are, after they've dined well.   70
Who are you, strangers? From where are you sailing the
          sea-paths?
Are you on business? Or maybe you recklessly wander
over the sea like pirates, men who go roving,
risking their lives and causing hardship for others."

Ithaka and Troy
Promptly Telemakhos gave him a sensible answer,
taking heart from Athene. The Goddess had roused him,
making him ask for his long-gone father with boldness,
helping him gain a good new name among people.
"Nestor, Neleus's son, you crowning pride of Akhaians,
where are we from? you ask. Now I will tell you.   80
We came from below Mount Neion, Ithakan country.
The cause is my own: I don't speak for my townsmen.
I came for far-off news of my Father—maybe I'll
          hear some—
godlike and steadfast Odysseus. They say that he fought
          once
there by your side, storming the city of high Troy.
Of all the others who fought that war with the Trojans,
we know where each man died, how wretched his death was.
But Zeus has made my Father's ending unheard of,
no one can say for sure where he has fallen,
whether warlike men on land overwhelmed him   90
or Amphitrite's waters finally drowned him.

No Soothing,
No Pity
♦"So now I approach your knees. I hope you are willing
to speak of the man's sad death, whether you saw it
by chance with your own eyes or heard it told by another
roamer. Beyond all men his mother bore him to suffer.
But don't hold back to soothe me, held by your pity:
tell me plainly how it came to your own sight.
I'm pleading: if ever my Father, worthy Odysseus,
gave his word or promised you work that he made good
on Trojan soil, where Akhaians underwent great pain,   100
remember his word now and tell me the whole truth."

A Long War | Nestor answered him then, the Gerenian horseman.
and Its Ending | "My friend, you recall the anguish and mourning we went
    through
in Trojan country. Strong, unbeatable sons of Akhaians,
we suffered greatly aboard our ships, sailing the misty
seas roaming for booty wherever Akhilleus led us.
In years of war at the great city of lordly Priam
all our bravest and best warriors died there.
Ares-like Aias lies there. Akhilleus lies there,
Patroklos too, a match for the Gods in his counsel.   110
My own dear son is there, forceful and handsome
 • Antilokhos, best of them all in sprinting and fighting.
So much evil we bore besides! Who among death-bound
men could count those ills and tell you the whole tale?
Not if you lingered five long years or for six years,
asking of all the agony borne by godlike Akhaians:
you'd wear down first and leave for the land of your fathers.

A Son | "Using every trick, we actively planted the Trojans'
the Same as | misery nine long years. Even Zeus could not end it.
His Father | And no man there wanted to challenge your father's   120
war-plans: godlike Odysseus was always a standout
using every trick. Your father—truly if *you* are
the man's child—I'm taken by wonder to see you!
Your voices are truly alike, who would have thought it,
a younger man with the same sound as his father.

"Long as we stayed there truly godlike Odysseus
and I were never at odds in assembly or planning.
One mind, one spirit held us, showing the Argives
how our plans were the best by far in their shrewdness.

Brothers at | "But after we looted the high city of Priam   130
Odds | and left in our ships, a God spread out the Akhaians.
Right then the mind of Zeus was plotting a rueful
way home because of the Argives—not all were truthful
or just—they went to a sorry doom through the killing
 • rage of the glow-eyed Goddess, the powerful Father's
daughter. She made both sons of Atreus bitter.
The two of them called an assembly of all the Akhaians
with no clear order, rashly starting at sunset.
Bloated with wine, the sons of Akhaians assembled

and told their tales. Why did the gathering take place?   140
First Menelaos reminded all the Akhaians
to look to the broad back of the sea and our way home.
That hardly pleased Agamemnon. He wanted to hold back
people and to offer sacred hecatombs right there.
He hoped to calm the fearsome rage of Athene.
The fool, unaware the Goddess never would listen:
Gods' minds won't readily change, living forever.
So the two men stood there, trading their hard words,
yet the Akhaians in handsome leg-guards were wildly
shouting and leaping—both were plans to their liking!   150

Hard Ways   "Resting that night, we thought hard thoughts of each other.
Home   Harm and pain were all that Zeus was arranging.
             One group hauled their ships at dawn to the bright sea,
             stowing goods away and their low-belted slave girls.
             But half the army delayed, choosing to stay there
             with Agamemnon, Atreus's son, that shepherd of people.
             Our half boarded and rowed, moving the vessels
             fast for a God had leveled the great-bellied Ocean.

             "We came to Tenedos Island and offered our victims
             to Gods, pleading for home. But Zeus was not planning   160
             homecomings. Cruel again, he caused us to wrangle.
             One group sailed in their up-curved ships to return home
             with lordly Odysseus, richly crafty and mind-full,
             once more favoring Atreus's son Agamemnon.
             But I with my ships—plenty had followed behind me—
             escaped for we knew some Power was planning to harm us.
             Tudeus's Ares-like son fled with us, rousing his crewmen.
             Light-haired Menelaos traveled and caught us
             later at Lesbos, mulling the long course to be taken:
           ♦ whether to travel north of Khios, known for its rough land,   170
             keeping the isle of Psurie well to our port side;
             or sail south of Khios, chancing the storm-winds at Mimas.
             We asked our God to show us a sign and he gave it:
             he told us to cut through the central sea to Euboia
             in order to run as fast as we could from a bad end.

Finally Home   "A clear-toned wind came up and our vessels were racing
at Pulos   along on the fish-filled water, making Geraistos
             late at night. We offered thanks to Poseidon

with plenty of bulls' thighs for we'd measured a great sea.
Four days later the friends of that breaker of horses,   180
Tudeos's son Diomedes, were mooring their balanced
ships at Argos. I held on for Pulos, our sea-wind
unfailing after the God first started it blowing.

A Few Safe   "So I came home, my dear young man, without knowing
Arrivals   who were the saved Akhaians and who were the lost ones.
              Whatever I've heard, though, living at home in my
                   great hall,
              you'll hear too. It's only right. I've nothing to hide here.
              They say the spear-crazy Murmidons came home safely,
            ♦ led by a bright one, the great-hearted son of Akhilleus.
            ♦ And Poias's well-known son, Philoktetes, arrived well.   190
              All Idomeneus's men who raced from that long war
              he brought back safely to Krete. The seaways took no one.

A Father's   "But Atreus's son! I'm sure you've heard in your far land
Death   how he arrived, Aigisthos plotting a bad end.
              Ah, but the killer paid hard for his killing
              and rightly so. A son should survive when his father
              is killed like Orestes, avenging himself on the sneaking
              Aigisthos who'd killed his father, renowned Agamemnon.
              You too, my friend, I see you're a handsome and big man:
              be brave and men born in the future will praise you."   200

A Son Who   Promptly Telemakhos gave him a sensible answer.
Cannot Take   "Nestor, Neleus's son, you crowning pride of Akhaians:
Revenge   surely the man was avenged, all the Akhaians will
                   make him
              known well and men in the future will praise him.
              If only the Gods would array me now in the same strength!
              I'd take revenge for the galling crimes of the suitors,
              reckless and prideful men plotting to harm me.
              But Gods have woven no such joy in my own life,
              nor in my Father's. My only need now is to bear up."

Hope for   Nestor answered him now, the Gerenian horseman.   210
a Goddess's   "My friend, in fact you remind me now as you say this:
Help   plenty of suitors, they say, for the cause of your mother
              are making trouble against your will in the great hall.
              Tell me if you want them ruling, or maybe some people

hate you at home, obeying the voice of a great God.
Who knows? Your father could take revenge on their brutal
acts one day, alone or with scores of Akhaians.
If only the glow-eyed Athene chose to befriend you!
She cared that way in the past for high-praised Odysseus
on Trojan soil, where Akhaians underwent great pain.   220
  ♦ I never saw a Goddess as openly friendly
as Pallas Athene, standing plainly beside him.
So if she chose to befriend you, her heart full of caring,
every suitor would wholly forget about marriage."

But now Telemakhos gave him a sensible answer.
"My elder, I hardly think your words will become fact.
You speak so grandly—I'm taken by wonder—yet there is
      no hope
things will happen, even if Gods were to want it."

A Bright and a   The Goddess, glow-eyed Athene, answered him sharply:
Dark View   "Telemakhos, what words get over the wall of your front   230
                     teeth!
A God can easily save a man—from afar if he wants to.
I'd rather the pain myself, all of the struggle
to get back home and see my homecoming daylight,
than go to my hearth and die the way Agamemnon
died in that sneaking plot of his wife and Aigisthos.
Yet despite the Gods death is too common:
they cannot save a man they love when his cruel
doom takes him. Death is truly remorseless."

Shortly Telemakhos gave her a sensible answer.
"Let's say no more, Mentor. However it hurts us,   240
my Father's return is real no longer—already the deathless
Gods have arranged for his death, for his black doom.

The Fall of   "But now I'd like to ask another question.
Klutaimnestre   Nestor has learned fairness, a wisdom beyond men's.
They say he's reigned through three generations of people.
Plainly the man I gaze at now is undying!
Nestor, son of Neleus, tell me this truly:
how was Atreus's son Agamemnon, a ruler of broad lands,
cut down? Where was Menelaos? What was the death-plan

of sneaking Aigisthos? The man he killed was a great one.   250
♦ Was Menelaos away from Argos, wandering other
   men's lands, and Aigisthos felt bold for the murder?"

Nestor answered him now, the Gerenian horseman.
"Well then, my young man, I'll tell you the whole truth.
Of course you may guess the way it all would have happened
if Atreus's light-haired son Menelaos had sailed home
from Troy and found Aigisthos alive in the great hall.
Not one man would have piled up earth for the slaughtered
Aigisthos: vultures and dogs would have torn him to pieces,
sprawled in a field far from the city. None of Akhaia's   260
women would mourn, for the act he planned was revolting.
We had remained at Troy, ending so many struggles;
he was at ease in a room of horse-breeding Argos,
charming Agamemnon's wife with all of his banter.
The lady denied him at first. The act would be shameful
and godlike Klutaimnestre's mind was a good one.
♦ A poet was close by too—her husband had often
   told him, embarking for Troy, to guard Klutaimnestre.
But soon as the Gods' doom ensnared her and tamed her,
Aigisthos took the singer away to an empty   270
island and left him, a prize and prey for the vultures.
He wanted to take her, she wanted him too, in his own
       house.

"He burned plenty of thighs on holy altars of high Gods,
offering plenty of gifts, woven and gold things.
He'd brought his work to a big end—beyond what his heart
       hoped.

The Slow   "We'd sailed from Troy ourselves, embarking together,
Way Home for   Atreus's son and I, friends well known to each other.
Menelaos   But nearing holy Sounion's headlands near Athens,
Menelaos's helmsman was marked by Phoibos Apollo:
killed on the spot, he died from the gentlest of arrows,   280
both his hands holding the steering board of the race-fast
ship. Phrontis, the son of Onetor, was better than all men
guiding a ship whenever a storm-wind was blowing.
So Menelaos lingered there. Anxious to travel
still he buried his war-friend, paying funeral honors.

A Monstrous   "But now as he sailed the wine-dark sea in his hollow
Gale ◆   ship once more, swiftly approaching Maleia's
heights, Zeus was far off watching, plotting a hateful
turn. He sent a gale downward, gusting and screaming,
every wave hugely swollen, a match for a mountain.   290
The God split up the fleet, half of it driven
to Krete where Kudonians live by the Iardanos's waters.
Flat-faced rock is there, a headlong drop to the salt sea
at Gortun's far-out point on the haze-covered water.
Notos rolls big waves into rocks on the port side
toward Phaistos: little stone hinders the great seas.
His vessels put in there, war-friends barely avoiding
death when breakers heaved a number of vessels
at rocks. The rest of them, five ships with their dark prows,
were borne on water and wind to the coastline of Egypt.   300
There Menelaos's vessels wandered and often gathered
wealth and gold among men who spoke with a strange
    sound.

Death-Feast   "Aigisthos meanwhile plotted misery back home.
After he killed Atreus's son and mastered the people,
he ruled for seven years in golden Mukenai.
Then godlike Orestes came like death in the eighth year,
home from Athens. He killed that sneaking Aigisthos
who'd killed his father—he'd killed the renowned
    Agamemnon.

"After he slew him, Orestes gave the Argives a death-feast
over his hateful mother and spineless Aigisthos.   310
The very same day Menelaos, good at a war-cry,
came home hauling all the wealth his vessels could carry.

◆"So you, my friend: don't wander far for a long time
far from home, leaving wealth in your household
to men so prideful. They may devour and divide it,
the whole hoard—and the way you've sailed will be folly.

To Sparte   "But do go first to Menelaos. I say it and urge it
myself. The man's come home lately from far-off
people no one could hope in his heart to escape from.
Storm-winds drove him away from the course he had
    first set   320

over a sea so vast no seabird could cross it
twice in a year—it's all that frightful and spread out.
Go to him now yourself with your ship and crewmen,
or travel by land if you like. Chariot horses
are quite close by. My sons could join you and guide you
to bright Lakedaimon and light-haired Menelaos.
Plead with the man yourself, let him speak to you truly.
He won't tell lies: the man's quite sensible really."

Offering Wine
to the Gods

He stopped: the sun was down and darkness was coming.
The Goddess told them now, glow-eyed Athene,   330
"Old man, surely you said all that in the right way.
Come on then, mix our wine. Cut out the oxen's
tongues, pour wine for Poseidon and all the deathless
Gods and mull rest. The hour is approaching,
already the light's gone beneath darkness. It's not right
staying too long at the Gods' feast. Better to go now."

Ending the Day

The daughter of Zeus had spoken. They heard what she
        told them:
stewards poured water now for a hand-wash,
young men filled all the wine-bowls with good drink
and dealt them goblets. Everyone poured for the great Gods.   340
Standing they threw tongues of bulls in the hearth-fire.
They poured more wine and drank as their spirits
        inclined them.

A Good
Night's Sleep
for the Guest

Shortly godlike Telemakhos, joined by Athene,
was eager to go to the hollow ship by the salt sea.
But Nestor tried holding them back as he told them,
"May Zeus and the other deathless Gods prevent you
from leaving my home for your race-fast ship in this
        manner,
as though I utterly lacked good clothes like a poor man
or lacked plenty of blankets and cloaks in the household
for gentle sleep for myself and rest for a stranger.   350
I do own fine bedding and beautiful blankets.
Surely the well-loved son of the man Odysseus never
will lie on a ship's deck—not so long as I live here
myself or sons of my own are left in the great hall
to welcome strangers, whoever arrives at my household."

An Eagle An answer came from the Goddess, glow-eyed Athene:
Soaring Away "Dear old man, you said that well. Telemakhos truly
should mind you because it's far better to do so.
Yet as he follows closely behind you for good sleep
now in your hall, I'll go myself to the night-black   360
ship to hearten our crew and tell them of all this.
I claim my age—the only elder among them.
The rest of the crew are younger, all of the same age
as great-hearted Telemakhos, joining in friendship.
I'll lie down there by the hollow and night-black
ship for now. At dawn I'll sail for the great-hearted
Kaukones. They owe me something; the debt is an old one,
a large one. Send this man who came to your good house
next with your son to Sparte by chariot. Give him the fastest
horse-team you have, light on their hooves and the
    strongest."   370

Having spoken the glow-eyed Athene suddenly flew off,
strong as an eagle. Awe gripped everyone watching.
The old man marveled to see all that with his own eyes,
taking the hand of Telemakhos, giving him good words:
"My friend, I'm not afraid you're harmful or fretful.
You're young but plainly a God's joined you and led you—
of all the Gods with homes on Olumpos none other
◆ than Zeus's daughter, the glowing Tritogeneia,
who prized your worthy father most among Argives.

"Be kind, powerful Lady: grant me a good name,   380
me and my honored wife and all of our children.
I'll offer a heifer myself, a yearling with wide brows,
unbroken, not yet led to the yoke by a cowherd.
I'll kill her myself, her horns layered with fine gold."
He made that vow and Pallas Athene heard him.

Wine   So Nestor led the way, the Gerenian horseman,
and Prayer with sons and sons-in-law to the beautiful palace.
to Athene   Soon as they came to the far-famed house of that ruler,
taking the plain seats or chairs that were thronelike,
the old man mixed a honey-sweet wine in a great bowl   390
for all the arrivals. The wine had aged for eleven
years. A housemaid having loosened the lid-dress,
the old man mixed a bowl and prayed for a long time

♦ then to Athene, daughter of Zeus, who carries the Aigis.
They poured drops to the Gods and drank as their hearts
    wished.
Next the people went to rest, each to his own house.

A Good Day's
End

Right there Nestor, the old Gerenian horseman,
told Telemakhos, loved as the son of godlike Odysseus,
to lie on a corded bed in the echoing hallway.
Peisistratos, good with an ash spear, a leader of good men—   400
and still the only unmarried son in the great hall—
lay nearby. In the inmost room of the high house
Nestor's wife cared for their bed and their closeness.

Time for
a New Feast

When newborn Dawn came on with her rose-fingered
    daylight,
Nestor rose from his bed. The Gerenian horseman
went outside and sat down, presiding on polished
stones in front of the large gates of the palace.
The white stones with their oil-like shine had been sat on
long before by Neleus, a match for the Gods in counsel.
But now, struck down by his doom, he'd gone into Aides'   410
house and Gerenian Nestor, a guard of Akhaians,
sat there holding the scepter. Down from their own rooms,
sons crowded around him: Ekhephron and Stratios,
Perseus, Aretos and godlike Thrasumedes.
A sixth one came—Peisistratos, warrior leader.
Godlike Telemakhos too was led there to sit down.

Nestor began to speak, the Gerenian horseman.
"Be lively, you sons I love, do as I wish now!
I hope to appease the Gods and mainly Athene,
who openly came to our bountiful feast for Poseidon.   420
Come on then: one of you go to the fields for a heifer,
bring her fast as you can, a cowherd may drive her.
One of you go to great-hearted Telemakhos's night-black
ship and invite his men; let two of them stay there.
One of you go to ask the goldsmith Laerkes
to join us and layer his gold on the horns of the heifer.
The rest of you stay here together. Order the housemaids
inside to arrange our home for a praiseworthy banquet.
Bring chairs, logs for a circle and glittering water."

Golden Horns   They all moved as he spoke. Led from an old field   430
                the heifer arrived. Great-hearted Telemakhos's crewmen
                came from the balanced and race-fast ship. And the
                    smith came,
                hands holding the bronze tools of his artwork:
                carefully crafted tongs, hammer and anvil
                for working gold. Athene also arrived here
                to share in the rites. An old chariot driver,
                Nestor gave the gold and the smith gilded the heifer's
                horns with care so the Goddess would gaze on her gladly.

A Heifer   Guiding the heifer's horns were godlike Ekhephron
Dies for the   and Stratios. Water for hands came from a room in a
Goddess   flowered   440
               basin brought by Aretos, a basket of barley
               grains in his other hand. Thrasumedes, steady in battle,
               held a sharpened ax nearby for striking the heifer.
               Perseus held the blood-bowl. An aging chariot driver,
               Nestor began at the basin, washing, then sprinkled some
                    barley
          ♦   grains and prayed to Athene at length. He cut off the heifer's
               hairs to throw in the fire. After they prayed and scattered
               barley, the son of Nestor with high heart, Thrasumedes,
               promptly approached and struck: the ax tore through the
                    muscled
               neck and the heifer's power went slack. Ritual wailing   450
               rose from daughters and wives of sons, from the lady of
                    Nestor,
               honored Eurudike, eldest of Klumenos's daughters.

Wine on the   Men now raised it from earth—the earth with its wide
Smoking Meat   ways—
               and held it. Peisistratos slashed the throat, a leader of
                    good men.
               Black-red blood ran out; the bones were drained of their
                    spirit.
               They quartered the body fast and cut out the whole thighs,
               each in the right way, then covered the thighs with a double
               layer of fat. They laid raw flesh on the thigh-parts.
               The old man burned them on split logs, pouring a
                    bright wine

over as young men held five-pronged forks alongside.   460
After the thighs were burned they tasted the entrails
and cut the rest into pieces. They spitted and roasted
them all, holding the sharp spits in their fingers.

A Feast and a   Pretty Polukaste, the youngest daughter of Nestor,
Send-Off   Neleus's son, had bathed Telemakhos meanwhile.
After the bath she rubbed him well with a fine oil.
She tossed a beautiful mantle and tunic around him.
He came from the bath like a deathless God in his
        young form
going to sit by Nestor, a shepherd of people.

Soon as the outer flesh was cooked and unspitted   470
they sat and dined. Good men watched them and
        helped them,
pouring wine into gold, refilling the goblets.

After the craving for food and drink was behind them
Gerenia's horseman, Nestor, started to tell them,
"My sons, guide our rich-maned horses under a chariot's
yoke to move Telemakhos on with his travels."

He spoke that way, they heard him well and obeyed him.
Fast-running horses were yoked to a chariot quickly.
A housekeeper placed her bread and wine in the wagon
with meats that a Zeus-bred king would be used to at dinner.   480

Two Days to   Telemakhos promptly mounted the beautiful chariot.
Sparte   Peisistratos, Nestor's son and a leader of good men,
mounted alongside. He took the reins in his own hands,
lashed and drove the horses which willingly took off
for the open plain, leaving the high city of Pulos.
The double yoke they bore rattled the whole day.

The sun went down. When all the roadways had darkened
they came to Pherai and entered Diokles' household—
the son of Ortilokhos, born as a child to Alpheios.
They passed the night there, welcome guests in the
        household.   490

When newborn Dawn came on with her rose-fingered
    daylight,
they yoked the horse-team, mounted the colorful chariot
and drove along through the gate as the portico echoed.
They lashed and drove the horses which willingly took off,
coming in time to a wheat-filled plain. The journey was over
there and then. Both of the lively horses had held up.
The sun now set and all the roadways were darker.

<table>
<tr><td>A Wedding
Feast</td><td>They came to a land of hollows and dips, Lakedaimon.
They drove to the home of highly praised Menelaos
and found him hosting a wedding feast for his lovely
daughter and son, with family and friends in the household.</td></tr>
</table>

A Wedding
Feast

    They came to a land of hollows and dips, Lakedaimon.
    They drove to the home of highly praised Menelaos
    and found him hosting a wedding feast for his lovely
    daughter and son, with family and friends in the household.
  ♦ He'd send the bride to the son of Akhilleus, breaker of front
       ranks:
    at Troy Menelaos had promised her first when he nodded,
    saying, "Yes." Now the Gods were blessing the marriage.
    He'd send the daughter away by chariot horse-team
    then to the Murmidons' well-known city—her man was their
       ruler.
    The son was brought Alektor's daughter from Sparte.   10
  ♦ She'd marry a strong and well-loved man, Megapenthes.
    A slave girl had borne him. The Gods had no children
    for Helen after the first. She'd borne one beautiful daughter,
    Hermione, having the look of gold Aphrodite.

    So they dined in the huge house with its high roof,
    family and friends of the highly praised Menelaos,
    reveling. Striking his lyre, a God-gifted poet
    sang in their midst. A pair of tumblers had started
    leading their dances, whirling around in the center.

Welcomed
Strangers

    Nestor's renowned son and warlike Telemakhos   20
    pulled up close to the gate, stopping their horse-team.
    Lordly Eteoneus came from the palace and saw them.
    The ready squire of highly praised Menelaos,
    he carried news through the house to that shepherd of
       people,
    standing close and his words had a feathery swiftness:
    "Menelaos, nourished by Zeus, strangers are nearby,
    a pair of men who look to be sons of the Day-God.
    Tell me, should we unyoke their spirited horses,
    or send them off to another host who'll befriend them?"

    Blond-haired Menelaos got angry and told him,   30
    "Boethous's son, Eteoneus! Foolishness never

marked you before but now your blather is childish.
We often ate and welcomed men's presents as strangers
ourselves on the long way home, trusting in great Zeus
to end our sorrow one day. Unharness the strangers'
horses and bring me these men. They'll join us for dinner."

He stopped and the squire went fast through the household,
calling on other ready squires to join him and follow.
The sweated horses were eased from under their harness.
Helpers tied them at stalls where horses were well fed: 40
they tossed them a mixture of white barley and emmer.
The chariot leaned on a shining wall by the entrance.

A House of   Led in the godlike house the guests were in wonder.
Wonder   They stared at the home of a ruler nourished by great Zeus,
the sunlike glow of the place, its luster like moonlight—
the high-roofed home of the highly praised Menelaos!
After enjoying all they could see with their own eyes,
they went to a smoothly polished bathroom for washing.
Handmaids cleaned and rubbed their bodies with good oil.
They tossed woolen mantles and tunics around them.   50

Guests took chairs near Atreus's son Menelaos.
Bringing them water a maid poured from a stunning
pitcher of gold and they washed their hands in the silver
basin. She set a polished table before them.
A modest housekeeper brought them bread and arranged it.
She gave them plenty of food, gracious and giving.
A carver hoisted meat: salvers of all kinds
were set out. Golden goblets went to each setting.

Join in the   Blond-haired Menelaos welcomed them saying,
Feast   "Take some food and enjoy! Later we'll ask you,   60
after you've dined and drunk, who are your people.
Your parents' bloodline is hardly lost on you both here:
I'm sure you're sons of men nourished by great Zeus,
   ♦ sceptered kings. Your parents could hardly be low-born."

He took a chine of rich beef while speaking and laid it
before them—the chine set down to honor his own place.
Their hands went out to the good things lying before them.

After their craving for food and drink was behind them,
Telemakhos turned to the son of Nestor and told him,
his head held close to stop the others from hearing,   70
"Son of Nestor, joy of my heart, have you noted
all this gleaming bronze in the echoing household,
amber and gold, the shine of silver and ivory?
It's like the inner court of Zeus on Olumpos—
so much wealth!—I'm taken by wonder to see it."

The Riches   But blond-haired Menelaos, hearing his low voice,
of Gods   gave him an answer, the words with a feathery swiftness:
and of Men   "My youthful friends, no man's a rival of great Zeus
whose house and all his belongings truly are deathless.
A *man* might rival me though—or maybe he cannot—   80
♦ in wealth. I wandered often and suffered a great deal
hauling treasure home by ship and arriving
eight years after. I wandered past Phoinikia, Kupros
and Egypt, far Ethiopia, Sidon's tribes and the Eremboi.
Libya too: lambs grow horns early in life there,
ewes bear young three times in the long year.
Lords of that land and shepherds never are lacking
cheese or mutton. The sweetest milk is forever
plentiful—ewes are always nursing their sucklings.

No Joy   "Yet as I roamed around there, gathering plenty   90
in All That   of goods, another man was killing my brother
Wealth   without a warning. I damn the wife who misled him.
But I can take no joy as lord of the wealth here.
Maybe you heard from your fathers, whoever they
        might be,
how much I bore in losing the house of my brother,
so well lived in, storing plenty of great things.
If only I owned one-third of that wealth in my own house,
knowing those men—my friends who died on the
        spread-out
plains of Troy so far from horse-feeding Argos—
were safe! I've often sat and wept in our great hall   100
mourning all those deaths, taking a pleasure
at times even in grief. Then at the other
times I've stopped: grief is cold, we're full of it swiftly.

Grief
Especially for
Odysseus

"But I don't grieve for them all, whatever my sorrow,
so much as I mourn one man. Each time I recall him
I hate my food and sleep. More than any Akhaian
♦ Odysseus worked and won. He was meant to be troubled,
though, that was his curse. The anguish is always
frightful—how long he's gone! And no one has made out
whether he's dead or alive. I'm sure that the old one   110
mourns today, Laertes, and faithful Penelopeia—
Telemakhos too, just born, a child when he left home."

The son as he spoke yearned to mourn for his father,
dropping tears to the floor at the name of Odysseus.
Both his hands, holding the purple cloak up,
covered his eyes. Menelaos, watching him closely,
thought for a while. His heart and head were unsure now
whether to wait for the man to ask of his father
or speak out first himself and ask about each point.

Helen

Then as he gave his heart and head to this mulling,   120
Helen walked down from her high-roofed and scented
♦ room, resembling Artemis, Goddess of golden arrows.
Adreste joined her, placing a well-made chair for the lady.
Alkippe brought a coverlet fashioned from soft wool.
Phulo carried her silver basket, a gift from Alkandre
once who was Polubos' wife, living in Egypt
at Thebes—the greatest wealth lies in those houses.
He also gave Menelaos a pair of bathtubs of silver,
a pair of tripods and ten talents of pure gold.
His wife gave too, the loveliest presents for Helen: 130
a golden staff to work with, a basket of silver—
the wheels under its frame had gold-plated wheel-rims.
Her handmaid Phulo brought and placed it beside her,
now filled with her spun yarn. Lying across it,
the staff of gold was covered with violet woolens.

A Young Man
So Like
Odysseus

The lady sat in her chair, her feet on a footstool.
She spoke to her husband promptly to ask about each thing:
"Zeus-bred Menelaos, who do these two men
claim to be now that they've entered our household?
And I, shall I feign or be open? My heart has been saying   140
strongly to speak. I never saw a resemblance so striking

in man or woman, I'm taken by wonder to see him—
a man like the son of our great-hearted Odysseus!
He left a child behind, Telemakhos, born in the palace
♦ that day when all you Akhaians, because of my own shame,
went to the walls of Troy and planned boldly for battle."

Blond-haired Menelaos answered by saying,
"I see it now, my wife, the likeness you spotted.
There are the man's feet, there are his own hands,
the hair and heads are the same, and that throwing of
    glances.   150
Just now when I mentioned the name myself of Odysseus,
remembering how he worked and suffered for my sake,
the young man painfully dropped some tears from his
    eyelids
and held the purple cloak to cover his wet eyes."

The Son's   Then the son of Nestor, Peisistratos, answered,
Longing and "Atreus's son Menelaos, Zeus-bred lord of your people:
Anxiety   just as you say, my friend is truly the man's son.
His heart is cautious, though, embarrassed to say much,
arriving and talking here in your house for the first time
with *you*—your voice giving us joy like a God's voice!   160

"Nestor sent me along, the Gerenian horseman,
to guide and help him closely. He wanted to see you,
hoping you'd say some word or move him to action.
The son whose father is gone has plenty of trouble
if no one at home is a strong guard of the great hall.
Telemakhos left that way: right now there is no one
throughout the land to watch and keep him from
    great harm."

Longing for   Blond-haired Menelaos answered by saying,
Old and   "Look at this! Truly the man's child came to my own house—
Renewed
Friendship   the man and friend who suffered so many trials for my sake.   170
I knew if he came I'd welcome him better than any
Argive if Zeus on Olumpos, watching from far off,
gave us a homeward course by ship on the wide sea.
I'd give him a *city* in Argos! I'd build him a new house
after moving his people, all that wealth and his only

son from Ithaka. First I would empty a city
lying about, a place that calls me its master.
Then we could live and meet there, nothing would keep me
away or stop us from sharing friendship and pleasure
until the darkening cloud of death would enshroud us.   180
But somehow the God himself must have been jealous.
He caused one wretched man not to return home."

Grief Pausing   His words were making them all want to be mournful.
The daughter of Zeus was crying—Helen of Argos.
Telemakhos wept, and Atreus's son Menelaos.
The eyes of the son of Nestor too were not tearless.
Thoughts about handsome Antilokhos troubled his own
        heart,
◆ the way a striking son of the Dawn-Goddess had killed him.
Recalling that brother, his words with a feathery swiftness,
"Son of Atreus," he said, "old Nestor has called you   190
sensible more than anyone. We often recall you,
asking each other questions back in our great hall.
Now if you can, say yes to me: mourning at dinner
is not my pleasure and soon the early-born Goddess
Dawn will arrive. I don't see anything shameful
in tears for a man who's died, gone to his own doom.
We only honor wretched humans in that way:
we let tears fall from our cheeks and we lop off
hair. Yes, and my brother is dead—hardly the meanest
Argive—maybe you knew him? Although I have never   200
seen or met him myself, others have told me
Antilokhos beat out everyone racing or fighting."

Blond-haired Menelaos answered by saying,
"My friend, you said all that like a person with good sense.
You act and speak in fact as though you were older—
the son of your father!—Nestor also has good sense.
A bloodline's truly known in a hurry if great Zeus
weaves good luck in the parents' lives and their children's.
Thus through all his days Nestor was granted
by Zeus to shine while growing old in his great hall.   210
His sons are shrewd and the best young men at a spear-
        throw.
So we'll stop the grief we built up before this.
Look to your food again and water for washing

your hands. Our tales can surely wait until morning.
I and Telemakhos then will talk things through with each
    other."

He paused and Asphalion splashed his hands with some
    water,
a ready squire of the highly praised Menelaos.
Their hands went out to the food still lying before them.

Pain Killing   Helen, the daughter of Zeus, now thought of a new plan.
          ♦ She promptly tossed a drug in the wine they were drinking,   220
            dulling their pain and anger. They all forgot about evil.
            Whoever swallows the drug she placed in the wine-bowl
            lets no tear fall from his cheeks for a whole day,
            not if his mother and father both were to die there,
            not if the man's own son and brother were hacked down,
            slashed by a sword of bronze in front of his own eyes.
            The daughter of Zeus had drugs quite useful and helpful,
            good ones given by Thon's wife Poludamna
            in Egypt where grain-rich farmland carries the most drugs.
            Many are helpful mixes, many are harmful.   230
            Every man has a doctor's knowledge surpassing
          ♦ the rest of men's: their blood is Paieon's the Healer.

The Beggar's   After she sprinkled the drug and called for a pouring
  Disguise   of wine again, she answered her husband by saying,
            "Son of Atreus, Zeus-bred Menelaos, and two good
            mens' sons in our house: to this one and that one
            Zeus gives good and bad for it's all in his power.
            Take your chairs then, enjoy our feast in the great hall
          ♦ and relish a story. My tale will not be unlikely.

            "I don't recall, myself, the name or the number   240
            of all the battles and trials of steadfast Odysseus.
            But one task! The powerful man suffered and worked at
            a task I saw at Troy, where Akhaians underwent great pain.
            He'd struck himself beforehand, a merciless whipping.
            He'd tossed old rags on his back—those of a house-slave.
            He'd walked into Troy, the enemy city with broad ways,
            moving along by hiding himself in his beggar's
            disguise: hardly a man from ships of Akhaians!
            He went through the town that way. All the Trojans

missed him and I was the only person who knew him.   250
I questioned the man; at first he avoided me shrewdly;
but later I washed him myself, anointed his body
with oil and clothed him again. I swore him a great oath
not to mention Odysseus's name to the Trojans
before he arrived at the race-fast ships and his campsite.
Then he told me all the plans of the Akhaians.

"After his long-edged sword cut down plenty of Trojans,
he left to bring back plenty of news to the Argives.
Now when the other Trojan women were loudly mourning,
my heart felt joy: I'd changed inside and was longing   260
for home. I hated the mad love Aphrodite
gave me that took me far from the dear land of my Fathers.
I'd left my child, my own bedroom and husband,
a man not lacking either in mind or in body."

Dread inside   Blond-haired Menelaos answered by saying,
the Horse   "Truly, my wife, you said all that in the right way.
By now I've learned the planning and thinking of many
warrior lords and traveled to plenty of far lands.
My eyes have not yet seen a war-chief like this one,
a man so steady, a loving heart like Odysseus.   270
• I'll tell you a task the man powerfully worked at
inside the smooth-scraped horse. The best of us sat there,
Argives bent on doom and death for the Trojans.
You came yourself to the place. A God must have told you,
wanting somehow to seize kudos for Trojans.
Yes and godlike Deiphobos followed you closely.
Three times you circled the hollow place of our ambush.
You stroked it and called by name the leading Danaans,
sounding like all their Argive wives with your own voice.
The son of Tudeus, I and godlike Odysseus   280
sat in the center, hearing the way you were shouting.
Two of us longed for a fight, bitterly yearning
to rush outside, or answer you quickly from inside.
Odysseus checked us, though, for all of our longing.
We all kept still for a while, we sons of Akhaians.
Only Antiklos wanted to give you an answer.
However, Odysseus pressed hard with his forceful
hands on that mouth. Saving all us Akhaians,
he held him there till Pallas Athene removed you."

Longing for | But now Telemakhos gave him a sensible answer.   290
Sleep | "Atreus's son Menelaos, Zeus-bred lord of your people,
so much the worse. For none of that kept a revolting
end from my Father—an iron heart could not help him.
Come on then, send us to bed now. Help us to lie down,
taking some sweetness at last, the pleasure of sleeping."

Soon as he'd spoken Helen of Argos instructed
handmaids to set out beds close to the walkway,
spread with beautiful violet covers and blankets
and set with layers of fleecy wool on the whole pile.
Torches in hand, the maids went out of the great hall   300
to make the beds. A herald guided the men out.
They went to sleep right there in the palace's forecourt—
Nestor's well-known son and lordly Telemakhos.
Atreus's son slept in the inmost room of the high house.
Long-gowned Helen lay alongside, a goddess-like woman.

A Plea | When newborn Dawn came on with her rose-fingered
for the Truth | daylight,
Menelaos, good at a war-cry, rose in his bedroom
and dressed. He hung a sharp sword from a shoulder,
strapped on his oil-smooth feet two beautiful sandals
and left the room. He looked like a God as he walked out.   310

He sat by Telemakhos now, he called him and asked him,
"Warlike Telemakhos, tell me why you were driven
over the broad back of the sea to bright Lakedaimon.
Your people's cause? Or your own? Tell me the whole truth."

Telemakhos promptly gave him a sensible answer.
"Atreus's son Menelaos, Zeus-bred lord of your people,
I came here hoping you'd tell me news of my Father.
My home is devoured. Our rich farmlands are wasted.
Enemies crowd my house and slaughter the livestock,
our bunched-up sheep and curl-horned, hoof-dragging
    cattle.   320
Suitors beset my Mother, haughty and high men.
So I've come to your knees, hoping you'll tell me
freely: maybe you saw the wretched end of my Father
by chance with your own eyes or heard it told by another
roamer. Beyond all men his mother bore him to suffer.

But don't hold back to soothe me, held by your pity.
Tell me plainly how it came to your own sight.
I'm pleading: if ever my Father, worthy Odysseus,
gave his word or promised you work that he made good
on Trojan soil, where Akhaians underwent great pain,   330
remember his word now and tell me the whole truth."

The Lion   Blond-haired Menelaos got angry and told him,
Returns   "Look at this! Men who'd lie in the bed of a strongly
spirited man are themselves lacking in courage.
The way a doe might rest her fawns when they're
            suckling,
newly born, in the lair of a powerful lion:
she goes off looking to graze on a hillside or grassy
vale but the lion is back too soon to his own lair—
what a sorry end for both of the young deer!
Odysseus too will bring a sorry end to the suitors.   340
I pray to Zeus, our Father, Athene and Apollo
that now he's the man he was in strong-founded Lesbos
• the day he stood up and faced Philomeleides wrestling.
He threw him forcefully. Every Akhaian applauded.
If only that strong Odysseus dealt with the suitors,
they'd all be dead in a hurry—that bitter a marriage!

What   "But on to the questions you ask. I'll hardly mislead you,
Happened   wandering far from the point. Nor would I fool you:
in Egypt   I'll tell you the tale I heard from an errorless old man,
a lord of the sea. I won't keep anything hidden.   350

• "Gods kept me in Egypt for all my longing to get back
home because I failed to offer hecatombs duly.
Gods are always wanting their orders remembered.
An island well off Egypt lies in the loudly
surging water—Pharos, people have called it—
as far from land as a hollow ship can sail in a single
day with a clear-toned sea-wind blowing behind her.
The harbor is good for mooring or launching a balanced
vessel after she's drawn fresh water from dark depths.
The Gods kept me there. Twenty days with no rising   360
wind or air on the water! No gust that can hurry
a man's good ship on the broad back of the salt sea.

Help from a   "All our food and the strength of my crew would have run out
Sea-Goddess   had not one of the Goddesses pitied and saved me—
                 the daughter of Proteus, an old and powerful sea-lord.
                 I moved the heart of Eidothee the most there.
                 She met me walking alone, away from my crewmen
                 who'd gone out roaming around the island and fishing
                 with old bent hooks, their bellies shriveled by hunger.
                 The Goddess came up close and asked me her questions.   370
                 'Stranger, are you a fool? Amazingly thoughtless
                 or lazy by choice? You take pleasure in hardship?
                 You're kept so long on this island: can't you discover
                 an end to your stay? Your men's hearts are all shrunken.'

                 "She spoke that way and I promptly answered by saying,
                 'Whatever Goddess you are, I'll answer you outright.
                 It's not by choice I'm held here; I must have offended
                 undying Gods who rule broadly in heaven.
                 Tell me yourself—you Gods know everything surely—
                 which of the deathless Gods has stopped and
                       constrained me?   380
                 How can I travel the fish-filled sea and return home?'

Ensnaring a   "The glowing Goddess answered me soon as I'd spoken.
Sea-Lord   'Well then, stranger, I'll tell you. I'll speak to you plainly.
                 A sea-lord comes this way, an errorless old man,
                 Proteus of Egypt, deathless and knowing the deepest
                 ocean waters. He serves under Poseidon.
                 He gave me birth, I'm told: that lord is my father.
                 If you could hide somehow, surprise him and hold him,
                 he'd tell you your course, how hard and far is your voyage,
                 how you can travel the fish-filled sea on your way home.   390
                 He'll also tell you, Zeus-bred man, if you want it,
                 whatever right or wrong was done in your great hall.
                 You've been away, traveling hard for a long time.'

A God Can Be   "She spoke that way but I quickly answered by saying,
Hard to Catch   'Show me yourself, right now, some trap for the old God,
                 lest he spot me first and somehow avoid me.
                 It's hard for an earth-bound man to master a great God.'

                 "I stopped and the shining Goddess answered me promptly:
                 'Well then, stranger, I'll tell you. I'll speak to you plainly.

At noon when the Sun-God arches halfway through heaven,   400
my lord arrives from the sea. An errorless old man,
he'll hide in some dark rollers under the Westwind
and move forward to look for rest in a hollow cavern.
Seals around him, the graceful sea-daughter's children,
rise from the gray waters to sleep there together.
Their breath is foul from all the depths of the ocean.
I'll marshal you there myself at the showing of Dawn's light.
I'll lay you down in the right way. Choose your companions
very well—three men from your strong-timbered vessels.

Sleeping   'But first I'll tell you all the wiles of the old man.   410
among the   He'll count the seals right off, moving among them.
Seals   He tallies them all by fives, watching them closely,
then he lies in their midst—like shepherd and sheep-flock.
Soon as you know for sure he's fallen asleep there,
you must really be forceful, look to your power,
hold him tight! He'll push and struggle to break free,
testing you every way. He'll look like a creature
that crawls the earth, like water or marvelous firelight.
Hold on still more tightly—all of you grip him.

'In time he'll speak for himself, asking you questions,   420
taking again the shape you saw when he lay down.
Then you may loosen your forceful grip on the old man,
my strong war-chief. Ask him which God is against you
and how you can travel the fish-filled sea on your
        way home.'

"She spoke that way then entered the billowing water.
I walked to the ships myself where they stood on the
        beach-sand,
my heart mulling plenty of hope as I walked on.
Soon as I came back down to the ships and the salt sea
we all made dinner. Ambrosial night was arriving:
we went to sleep right there on the shore of the salt sea.   430

Hiding under   "When newborn Dawn came on with her rose-fingered
the Skin   daylight,
I walked along the shore, the sea with its wide ways,
and prayed to the Gods often. Friends were behind me:
I'd brought three men I trusted most in a challenge.

The Goddess, meanwhile, diving under the broadly
breasted sea, hauled up skins: four seals from the water,
newly flayed. She planned a ruse on her father.
Having scooped out beds of sand by the water
she sat to wait. We went quite close to her promptly.
She made us lie down and threw a hide over each man.   440

Killing the   "What a revolting trap! The stench from the sea-fed
Smell   skins of seals was all that shocking and sickly—
who'd ever lie and sleep right next to a sea-beast?
The Goddess herself saved us, finding a great help:
she brought ambrosia, placing it under our noses.
A joy to inhale, it killed the stench of the sea-beasts.
All that morning we waited with spirits that bore up.

Struggle with   "Then seals came out of the sea, crowding together.
the Sea-Lord   They soon were lying in rows at rest on the beach-sand.
At noon the old one came from the sea. Spotting his well-fed   450
seals he marshaled them all, checking their number,
counting us first with the beasts. Never suspecting
guile was there, he lay himself on the beach-sand.

"We charged and shouted, throwing our arms around him.
The old man never forgot his crafty disguises:
he took the shape of a lion first with a full mane,
then a snake, a panther next, and a large boar.
He took on the flow of water, a tree with its high leaves.
We held on tightly ourselves, our hearts unrelenting.

The Lord of   "At last the old one tired of painful disguises.   460
the Sea   Yes and he actually spoke out, asking me questions:
Will Help   'What God, son of Atreus, helped with your ambush,
holding me against my will? What is your great need?'

"He spoke that way and I promptly answered by saying,
'You know, old man. Why do you question and fool me?
I'm kept so long on this island. I cannot discover
an end to it all and the heart's wasting inside me.
Tell me yourself—you Gods know everything surely—
which of the deathless Gods has stopped and
        constrained me?
How can I travel the fish-filled sea on my way home?'   470

"I spoke that way and the old one answered me quickly,
'Zeus and the rest of the Gods: you ought to have rendered
the right victims before embarking in order
to sail home fast on the wine-dark sea to your homeland.
Your portion now is not to look on your loved ones,
not to enter that well-built house in your homeland
before you sail once more to the waters of Egypt,
that Zeus-fed river. Offer sacred hecatombs duly
to deathless Powers who rule broadly in heaven.
Then the Gods will give you the voyage you long for.'   480

What
Happened to
All the
Akhaians?
"He spoke that way and all my spirits were broken.
That lord had told me to sail again on the hazy
sea toward Egypt—a long and wearying journey.
Even so I finally gave him an answer.
'I'll do it that way, old man, just as you told me.
But tell me something else, answer me truly:
were all the Akhaian ships unharmed when they
            came home?
The war-chiefs we left, Nestor and I, sailing from Trojan
shores: did they die a hateful death in their warships?
Or after the war wound up, in the arms of their loved ones?'   490

"I spoke that way and the old one answered me quickly,
'Son of Atreus, why ask this? Surely you need not
know and be taught my mind. You won't be a tearless
man for long, I'm sure, if you hear out the whole tale.
So many were slain back there, so many abandoned.

Odysseus May
Be Alive Still
♦ 'Only two of the bronze-coated Akhaian leaders
were lost on the way home—you'd stayed at the fighting—
and one may still be alive, held back on the broad sea.

The Doom
of Aias
'But Aias went down, his long-oared vessels around him.
Poseidon had brought him close at first to the massive   500
rocks at Gurai—he'd saved him there from a wild surf.
He might have raced from his doom in spite of Athene's
wrath but he tossed off prideful words, grand in his folly,
claiming in *spite* of the Gods he'd fled from the great sea.
Poseidon heard it all, that boisterous yelling.
Swiftly his powerful hand grappled the trident,
smashing the Gurai rocks and breaking a crag off.

One part stayed but a huge part fell in the water
where Aias had just been sitting, grand in his folly.
It dragged him down under the swirling and endless   510
water. The man was lost, swallowing salt sea.

The Murder of   'Your brother? He fled in his hollow ship to avoid doom,
Agamemnon   saved from seas I suppose by the queenly Here.
But then, about to arrive at the sheer heights of Maleia,
high winds caught him and took him away to a fish-filled
sea where he groaned heavily, borne on that water,
pushed to a far land's end, the home of Thuestes
before but now of Aigisthos, son of Thuestes.

'Now the way back home appeared to be harmless.
Gods gave him a change of wind and he came home.   520
What joy to disembark in the land of his fathers!
He touched and kissed the soil, plenty of warm tears
flowed from his eyes, he welcomed and gazed at the country.

'A lookout had watched from the rocks. Sneaking Aigisthos
had brought and sat him there; he'd promised to pay him
two gold talents. The man had watched for a whole year
lest Agamemnon get by unspotted and call back
the rush of his prowess. When word came to the palace
that shepherd of people, Aigisthos, was fast with his tricky
plans: choosing twenty men, the best in the country,   530
to wait in the trap, he ordered a feast to be ready
and went to call on Agamemnon, a shepherd of people,
with horses and chariot. What he planned was revolting:
hardly thinking of death, Agamemnon was brought there
and killed at the feast like cattle killed in their own stall.
No one was left. Agamemnon's followers died there.
Aigisthos's henchmen too were all killed in the great hall.'

Death-Feast   "Those were his words. All my spirits were broken.
I sat on the sand and wept. Wanting to live on,
to see the sunlight, left my heart for a long time.   540
But after I had enough of crying and clawing,
the lord of the sea told me, that errorless old man:
'Son of Atreus, don't cry nonstop for so long now.
We find no help in wailing. Instead you should labor
fast as you can to sail to the land of your fathers.

You'll find that killer alive, or Orestes will kill him
before you're there—and you'll take part in the death-feast.'

Odysseus and
Kalupso
"Soon as he'd spoken the heart and spirits inside me
were bold and warm again. In spite of my anguish
I spoke to that lord and my words had a feathery swiftness: 550
 ♦ 'So now I know of those men. But name me the third man,
whether alive and kept out there on the broad sea
now or dead. I want to hear, in spite of my anguish.'

"I spoke that way and the old one answered me promptly,
'The son of Laertes. An Ithakan household was once home.
I saw him shedding warm tears on an island,
kept in a Nymph's hall: Kalupso has forced him
to stay and he can't get back to the land of his fathers
lacking a ship with oars, lacking the crewmen
to send him over the broad back of the salt sea.   560

The Last Days
of Menelaos
'You now, Zeus-bred Menelaos, the Gods don't
say you'll die facing your doom in horse-feeding Argos.
 ♦ No, the deathless Gods will send you down to Elusian
Fields at the earth's far end with blond Rhadamanthus.
The lives of men down there are surpassingly easy.
No snow, no powerful storms, hardly a rainfall:
only the high-toned Westwind steadily blowing,
the Ocean cooling you all by sending you good air.
Since Helen is yours, to the Gods you are God's son.'

Once More
to Egypt
"He spoke that way then plunged in the billowing water.   570
I walked to the ships with my godlike war-friends alongside,
pondering many things in my heart as I walked there.
Soon as we came back down to the ships and the salt sea
we all made dinner. Night came down like ambrosia.
We took our rest right there on the shore of the salt sea.

"When newborn Dawn came on with her rose-fingered
        daylight,
first we hauled our vessels down to the bright sea.
After we raised and set both mast and sail on the balanced
ships our crewmen boarded and sat on the benches.
All in place they rowed, splashing the gray sea.   580

"I stood my ships once more by the waters of Egypt,
the Zeus-fed river. I offered hecatombs duly.
After quelling the anger of Gods living forever,
I raised Agamemnon's death-mound, making his
    great name
endless. With all that done I sailed with a sea-wind—
the Gods gave it—sending me fast to my own land.

To Stay
or to Go "But now come on and linger a while in my great hall.
Wait for the eleventh day to arrive or the twelfth day.
I'll give you a fine send-off, my gifts are outstanding:
a well-shined chariot led by a trio of horses;   590
a lovely goblet too for pouring your wine out
to deathless Gods. All your days you'll recall me."

But now Telemakhos gave him a sensible answer.
"Son of Atreus, don't hold me here for a long time.
I'd like to stay, to sit by your side for a whole year.
Longing for home and parents would hardly enfold me,
I'd take such anxious pleasure hearing the stories
you tell in your hall. But my crewmen must be worried
    already
in holy Pulos: you've held me here for a long time.
Whatever bounty you offer, make it an heirloom.   600
♦ I can't take horses to Ithaka. Let them remain here,
your own delight on the broad plains you are lord of,
where so much trefoil grows and plenty of tall sedge,
wheat and spelt, white barley spaced in its planting.
Ithaka lacks your wide courses and meadows.
Our goats' pastures are far more charming than horses'
but none of our islands is good for chariot driving,
lacking meadows. They slope to the sea, Ithaka more so."

The Silver
Wine-Bowl Those were his words. Menelaos, good at a war-cry,
smiled and touched his hand. He answered by saying,   610
"Your bloodline is good, dear child—everything well said!
I'll change the gifts myself, that's in my power.
Of all the presents and heirlooms that lie in my household
I'll give you the best, the one most stunning and precious:
I'll give you my wine-bowl, carefully crafted in silver
except for the edges finished in gold by the deathless

God Hephaistos. The war-chief Phaidimos gave it,
Sidon's king, that time his house was my shelter
when traveling home. I want to give it to you now."

**Building a
Good Feast**

So they went on talking that way with each other   620
as dinner guests arrived at the house of the godlike
king. They prodded sheep or brought a heart-lifting wine in;
housewives in lovely veils carried the bread-loaves.
Everyone worked well at the feast in the great hall.

Bad News for •
the Suitors

Suitors meanwhile in front of Odysseus's palace
enjoyed themselves by throwing a spear or a discus
on leveled ground just as before, full of their high pride.
Godlike Eurumakhos sat with Antinoos close by,
the ranking suitors—in manly strength they were foremost.
Noemon, the son of Phronios, came to them up close,   630
wanting words with Antinoos, asking him outright,
"Antinoos, when will we know—or maybe we won't know—
Telemakhos's time of arrival from deep-sanded Pulos?
He took my ship when he left; I need her myself now
to sail across to the spread-out dancing places of Elis.
Twelve brood mares are suckling my hard-working donkeys,
all unbroken. I'd like to drive off a donkey and break him."

Their hearts were stunned by his words. They'd hardly
    imagined
Telemakhos going to Pulos, Neleus's city. He must be
out on his land somewhere with flocks or the swineherd.   640
So now Eupeithes' son Antinoos answered,
"Tell me the truth: when did he go and who followed,
which young men? Ithaka's best or some others,
workmen and slaves? I'm sure he could find them and work
    them.
Tell me a few more things, help me to know this:
your own black ship—did he use force when he took it?
Or maybe you gave it freely because he implored you."

Phronios's son Noemon answered by saying,
"I gave her myself gladly. Would anyone do less
for such a man? His heart was caring and anxious,   650
he wanted a favor, saying no would be cruel.
The men who joined him too were the best in the country

◆ after ourselves. I saw Mentor board as their leader—
or maybe a God who looked like Mentor in each way.
Yet I wonder. I saw a godlike Mentor about here
yesterday morning. Then he left on my ship for Pulos."
He spoke that way and left for the house of his father.

The Rage of
Antinoos

The brash hearts of both were astonished and angry.
They stopped the suitors' games at once and they sat them.
Eupeithes' son Antinoos spoke to them very   660
grimly as rage mounted and filled his darkened
heart, his eyes glowing as though with a hot fire:
"Look at this! Great big work, Telemakhos proudly
ending his travels! We never thought he could do it.
Despite us all the boy went off without trouble,
hauling a ship out, choosing the best in the country.
He'll start to be far more trouble. Let Zeus be the wrecker
of all that power before it reaches a measure of manhood!
Come on then, give me a race-fast ship and twenty
        companions
to look out closely and ambush the man as he enters   670
the channel of rock-strewn Samos and Ithaka Island.
Then he'll be sad he sailed because of his father."

He spoke that way, they all approved and they urged it.
They stood up fast and reentered Odysseus's palace.

Bitter News for
the Queen

Penelopeia was not unaware of this plotting
for long in the minds and unholy hearts of the suitors,
◆ for Medon the herald told her. Outside in the courtyard
he'd heard the plans they wove while gathered inside there.
He'd gone through the house with word for Penelopeia.
She spoke to the man first when he came to her threshold: 680
"Herald, why did the high-born suitors dispatch you?
Maybe to tell the maids of godlike Odysseus
to stop their work and prepare more food for
        themselves here?
If only they stopped this wooing and crowded together
elsewhere—if only they dined here now for the last time!

"You men thronging my house and wasting all our
        resources,
mind-full Telemakhos's wealth, you never listened

before to your own fathers when you were children
telling you how Odysseus fared with your parents,
never acting or saying a word in this country   690
unfairly. The way kings are, even the godlike
hate one man and make friends with another.
My husband never was rash at all with a man here.
But your own hearts and acts are plainly disgusting.
You're never grateful for work well done in a gone time."

Medon spoke to her now, knowing and wary.
"My queen, if only the wrongs you cite were the worst ones.
No, the suitors are plotting another and far more
godless act. May Zeus not end it in this way!
They're planning Telemakhos's death, using their sharp
    bronze   700
when he comes home. He'd gone for news of his father
to holy Pulos and then to bright Lakedaimon."

No Answers   Her heart and knees went slack soon as he'd spoken.
She lost all speech for a while. Both of her eyelids
welled with tears, her voice was forceful but stopped short.
When words finally came she answered by asking,
"Herald, why did my child go off? What was the great need
to board some fast-running ship that acts like a strong horse
for men at sea while crossing all of that water?
So now even his name won't last among people."   710

Medon gave her an answer, knowing and wary.
"I don't know if a God roused him. Maybe his own heart
drove him to sail to Pulos, hoping to find out
whether his father was coming, or gone to his own doom."
He spoke that way then left for Odysseus's great hall.

Double Grief   A spirit-destroying grief surrounded the woman.
She could not bear to sit though her chairs were many.
Instead she sat on the floor of her richly crafted
room and moaned wretchedly. All of her handmaids,
younger and older help in the house, were crying
    around her.   720
Penelopeia told them, heavily sobbing,
"Hear it, my friends, how Zeus on Olumpos gave me

anguish beyond all women born and raised alongside me.
I lost a good man first, his heart like a lion's,
in every manly strength the best of Danaans,
so well known through the center of Argos and Hellas.
Now some sea-wind's carried away my beloved
son from our hall, nameless. I heard no word when he
        left here.

What Help
from an
Old Man? "Not even you, heartless women, chose to arouse me,
no one, from bed. You knew enough in your own hearts   730
the hour Telemakhos left in the hollow and night-black
ship. If I'd known my son was planning this voyage,
whatever his hurry to go, the man would have stayed here
or left his mother behind him dead in the great hall.

"One of you go then, call old Dolios quickly,
the helper my Father gave me before I arrived here
to tend the crowds of trees in my garden. Ask him to hurry,
go and sit by Laertes and tell him of all this.
Somehow Laertes may weave a plan in his own heart
to go in tears among people, those who are planning   740
to kill his seed and that of godlike Odysseus."

A Nurse's
Hard Advice But then her loving nurse Eurukleia answered,
"My dear lady, whether you kill me with ruthless
bronze or let me stay in your house, I cannot conceal it:
I knew all this myself. I gave him whatever
sweet wine and bread he wanted. He took from me great
        oaths
not to tell you before the passing of twelve days
unless you missed him yourself and heard he had gone off.
He wanted no tears to mar your face and your beauty.

"Now you should bathe, dress your body in clean clothes,   750
go upstairs to your room with your women and pray hard
to Athene, daughter of Zeus, who carries the great shield.
The Goddess to save him, even from death, is that Goddess.
Don't cause pain for that pained old man. I've doubted
the line of Arkeisios's son is wholly despised by the blissful
Gods. A man of his bloodline somehow will take back
the high-roofed house and the far spreads of your rich land."

Barley Grains   Her soothing words slowed the tears of Penelopeia.
The woman bathed and dressed her body in clean clothes.
She went upstairs to her room with handmaids around her.   760
She placed barley grains in a basket and called on Athene:
♦"Hear me, unfailing daughter of Zeus who carries the great
        shield!
If often shrewd Odysseus ever burned in your honor
the fat-rich thighs of heifers or ewes in our great hall,
remember them now. Save the son I have so loved!
Guard him against the crimes of overproud suitors."
She spoke and wailed. The Goddess heard her at prayer.

The Murder   But suitors made loud noise in the shadowy great hall.
     Plan   Some overprevailing younger suitors were saying,
"Our queen has plenty of suitors!" "And ready to marry   770
surely." "Not knowing her son's death is our own plan."
They spoke that way, not knowing how it would all end.

Now Antinoos rose to tell them a few words:
"What Power has maddened you? Stop this overwrought
        chatter
of every sort. Word might spread through the household.
Come on, stand up instead, be quiet and follow
the plan we worked on closely which all of us thought
        through."

A Black Ship   Having spoken he picked out twenty of the best men.
  out to Sea   They walked to the shore, to a race-fast ship by the salt sea.
First they hauled her down into deeper water,   780
then set the mast and broke out sail on the black ship.
They moved her oars through leather straps at the
        thole-pins,
all in order. They stretched and spread out the white sail.
Highly spirited helpers carried the gear on.
They moored her out in some deep water and left her
to take some food nearby as dusk was arriving.

Closing in on   Thought-full Penelopeia lay in her upstairs
  the Lioness   room without food, no taste of wine or a good meal,
her thoughts on death—would her handsome man-child
        avoid it?

Or maybe the overbearing suitors would kill him.   790
The way a lioness fears and plots among crowding
men who tighten their crafty circle around her,
the queen thought hard till finally weariness came on
sweetly. She sank down, her whole body relaxing.

The Phantasm   Then the glow-eyed Goddess Athene thought of a new plan.
of a Sister ♦   She made a figure taking the form of a woman,
Ipthime, one of the great-hearted Ikarios's daughters.
Eumelos had married the woman; their home was in Pherai.
Athene sent her to godlike Odysseus's household
to make Penelopeia stop her lamenting,   800
to end her shedding of tears, moaning and mourning.
The figure passed through the door-bolt and entered the
        bedroom.
Standing over her head, she spoke to her softly.
"Uneasy at heart, do you sleep, Penelopeia?
The Gods in their carefree lives are unwilling to let you
cry and mourn because your son has yet to return home.
Plainly the man has not offended the great Gods."

Penelopeia thoughtfully answered by saying—
close to the gates of dream, pleasantly dozing—
"My sister, why did you come here? Seldom before this   810
have you joined us: you live so far in your own house.
You want me to stop mourning? Let go of the many
pangs that sting my mind and trouble my spirits?
I lost a good man before, his heart like a lion's,
in every manly strength the best of Danaans,
so well known through far-flung Hellas and Argos.
Now the child I love went off in a hollow
ship foolishly, unaware of strife and assemblies.
I mourn for my son. More than I mourn for his father
I dread for my child, I tremble at what he could suffer   820
maybe on land he walks on, maybe on far seas.
For lots of enemies now are plotting against him,
eager to kill him before he's back in the land of his fathers."

Help from a   Promptly the murky figure answered by saying,
Great Guide   "Take heart. Don't be afraid so much in your good soul,
for such a guide goes with him. Others have prayed for

that Goddess to stand so close. The Lady has power.
Pallas Athene pities your wailing and mourning
now and sends me to help you, to say what I've told you."

Longing for   But thought-full Penelopeia answered by asking,   830
Odysseus   "You're truly a God? I've heard the voice of a Goddess?
Come on then, tell me about my wretched husband,
whether he's still alive and gazing at sunlight
or dead by now, gone down to the household of Aides."

Promptly the murky figure answered by saying,
"Frankly I won't go on at length of your husband,
whether alive or dead. It's wrong to be windy."

Having spoken the figure passed through the door-bolt,
joining a night-wind's breath. Ikarios's daughter
rose from sleep, her heart brightened and warmer: 840
a vision in real form had rushed through the dark night.

In Wait   But suitors, having embarked, sailed on a seaway
for a Killing   with headlong doom on their minds—Telemakhos's
murder.
A stony island lay in the midst of the broad sea,
from Ithaka halfway over to rock-littered Samos.
Asteris, not so broad, had harbors for vessels
on both sides. There the Akhaians waited in ambush.

The Gods in ♦ When Dawn rose from her bed by lordly Tithonos
Council   to bring back light to the Gods and men, the deathless and
                 dying,
             the Gods assembled and sat down. Zeus was among them,
             the high thundering God, the greatest in power.

Kalupso Clings ♦ Athene recalled and counted Odysseus's many
to Odysseus   troubles. His life in the Nymph's home had her worried.
             "Fatherly Zeus and all you Gods, happy forever,
             let no king holding a scepter be willingly gracious
             or kind ever, knowing or caring for justice:
             let him be hard, always acting unfairly   10
             now that no one recalls godlike Odysseus,
             none of the people he ruled, kind as a father.
             He lies there still on that island, feeling the same pain.
             The Nymph, Kalupso, holds him back in her household
             by force. He cannot sail to the land of his fathers,
             lacking a ship with oars and a body of crewmen
             to send him over the broad back of the salt sea.

             "Now these men are plotting to murder his well-loved
             son who's bound for home. He'd gone for news of his father
             to holy Pulos and then to bright Lakedaimon."   20

Save   Stormcloud-gathering Zeus gave her an answer.
Telemakhos "My child, what talk gets over the wall of your front teeth!
             Wasn't it you who planned all this in your own mind,
             Odysseus taking revenge on men when he came home?
             So guide Telemakhos: you know how and can do it.
             Let him arrive unharmed in the land of his fathers.
             Then the suitors can sail back in their own ship."

Free Odysseus He looked to a son he loved, saying to Hermes,
             "You've always acted here as our Messenger, Hermes.
             Tell the lovely braided Nymph my plan is unshaken: 30
             steadfast Odysseus must return. So he may travel
             without a God or death-bound human to guide him.

He'll lash and board a raft, he'll suffer a great deal
for twenty days and arrive on Skherie's rich soil,
Phaiakian land. Born close to the great Gods,
they'll honor the man like a God himself in their center.
They'll send him by ship to the well-loved land of his fathers
laden with bronze, gold and plenty of clothing—
more than Odysseus ever could take from the Trojans,
arriving safely home with his rightful share of the booty.   40
For now his lot is to go and gaze on his loved ones,
to see the high-roofed house in the land of his fathers."

Flight of the • He spoke that way and the Splendor of Argos obeyed him.
Messenger   Quickly he tied to his feet the beautiful sandals
of deathless gold that took him over the water
and over the measureless land as fast as a wind-gust.
He carried a wand that lulls the vision of humans—
a God might want that; others he rouses even from
    deep sleep.
Wand in hand, the strong Splendor of Argos went flying,
passing Pierie, diving through air to the broad sea.   50
He hurried over the wave-crests resembling a seagull
catching fish on a spread of alarming and restless
Ocean, wetting its rapid wing-beats in water:
Hermes was borne past numberless waves in the same way.

Weaving and   Now approaching the island lying a ways off,
Singing   the purple sea behind him, he stepped onto dry land.
He walked to a huge cave, the home of the lovely
braided Nymph. He found her inside and approached her.
A big fire burned at the hearth, scenting the farthest
island places with tree-smoke, citron and cedar,   60
chopped and blazing. She sang inside with a mellow
voice while moving about her loom—she wove with a shuttle
of gold. Plants bloomed and surrounded the cave-mouth:
black poplar, scented cypress and alder.
Long-winged birds were there, nesting or roosting;
little owls and hawks, terns with their long tongues,
always following waves, hard-working shorebirds.
Close to the hollow cave a grapevine was trailing,
a youthful bloom, swelling with blossom-like clusters.
Four springs, their sparkling waters close to each other,   70
flowed then changed their courses that way and this way.

Wild celery and violet spread through the balmy
meadows around them. Even a God who arrived here
would gaze on it all amazed, enjoying it warmly.

Odysseus by
the Sea

The Splendor of Argos, the Messenger, stood there and
    marveled.
But after a while when his heart had wondered at all this,
he briskly walked in the spread-out cave. He was well-
    known:
Kalupso, the shining Goddess, faced him and eyed him.
The deathless Gods are not unknown to each other,
not even those who live in homes that are far off.   80
But great-hearted Odysseus was not to be found here—
he'd gone to the shore again. How often he sat there
and wept, his heart in the pangs of sorrow and mourning!
He'd stare at the restless water, letting the tears fall.

A Welcome
First

Hermes now was asked by goddess-like, shining Kalupso,
after she sat him down on a glittering chair there,
"Why are you here, Hermes, you with your gold wand,
both esteemed and a friend? You visit so seldom.
Tell me your thoughts. My heart enjoins me to help you
work if I can, if the work may be brought to a good end.   90
But follow me first and be welcome now as a guest is."

Soon as she'd spoken the Goddess arranged for a table
 • filled with ambrosia and mixed him a rose-colored nectar.
The Messenger ate and drank, the Splendor of Argos.

The
Unavoidable
Will of Zeus

After dining and filling his heart with her good fare,
words finally came and he answered by saying,
"You asked me, Goddess to God, why I have come here.
I'll tell you the faultless truth since that's what you called for.
Zeus told me to come. It's not to my liking—
who would cross a vast and untold body of water   100
gladly? With no man's town nearby, no one to offer
the Gods a hecatomb, well-picked, the holiest victims.
But none of the Gods—no one—can baffle or run from
the mind and will of Zeus who carries the great shield.

"He says you're holding a man more wretched than all those
other men who warred at the city of Priam

for nine years then looted his house in the tenth year.
They left for home but somehow offended Athene,
who sent them a ruinous gale. The seas were a great height,
all the rest of his loyal war-friends were drowned there.   110
But wind and wave drove the man to your island.
Now you're ordered to send him away in a hurry.
It's not his doom to die so far from his loved ones:
no, his portion remains to look on his loved ones,
to go to his high-roofed house in the land of his fathers."

A Killing   He spoke that way and goddess-like, shining Kalupso
Jealousy   chilled when she spoke, her words with a feathery swiftness:
             "You Gods are cruel and faster than others at envy,
             the way you begrudge a Goddess for openly sleeping
             here with a man and making a lover her husband.   120
     ♦ So when rose-fingered Dawn chose her Orion,
             all you Gods with your easy living begrudged her.
             Orion was killed by Artemis, pure on her gold throne:
             Orion died in Ortugie, pierced by her gentle
             arrows. When lovely braided Demeter surrendered
             her heart to Iasion, making love on that farmland
             plowed out three times, Zeus knew it before long
             and hurled a glaring thunderbolt, killing him outright.

Odysseus   "So Gods begrudge me if a man is beside me.
Will Be Free I saved him myself when he came here, straddling a
                   keel-board   130
             alone. Zeus with his glaring lightning and thunder
             had blasted his race-fast prow in the midst of the wine-dark
             sea where all his brave war-friends were dead men.
             Wind and wave carried the man to my island.
             I loved and fed him myself, I told him I'd make him
             deathless too: all his days he would not age.
             But now, because no God can baffle or run from
             the mind and will of Zeus who carries the great shield,
             the man may go, if that God presses and prods me,
             over the restless sea. I cannot give him a send-off.   140
             I don't have the oars, a vessel or crewmen
             to send him over the broad back of the salt sea.
             I'll gladly counsel him, though, hiding nothing
             to help him arrive unharmed in the land of his fathers."

A Last Warning   The Guide answered her now, the Splendor of Argos:
                   "Send him away then. Beware of Zeus and his anger:
                   don't make the God enraged, hard on you later."
                   The strong Splendor of Argos left when he'd spoken.

No Longer a   So the honored Nymph went out to her great-heart
Pleasure   Odysseus now that she'd heard that message from
                        strong Zeus.   150
                   She found him sitting, crying there on the seashore as ever,
                   his eyes not drying. A lifetime's sweetness had flowed off:
              ◆ he wept for the way back home. The Nymph was a pleasure
                   no longer, he slept with her nights because he was forced to
                   in hollow caves, unwilling, although the Goddess was
                        willing.
                   Every day however he sat on rocks by the seashore
                   and wept, his heart wasted by anguish and moaning.
                   He stared at the restless water, letting the tears fall.

A Hope for   She spoke when she came up close, bright as a Goddess.
Return Home   "Poor man, stop mourning here. Don't let your whole life   160
                   waste for it's time: I'll send you away with a good heart.
                   Come on then. Chop some long logs with a bronze ax
                   and make a broad-beamed raft. Put on a half-deck
                   high enough to carry you over the hazy
                   sea. I'll lay in food myself, water and red wine
                   suiting your spirits, enough to keep you from hunger.
                   I'll give you clothes and send you a following sea-wind
                   to help you arrive unharmed in the land of your fathers—
                   if Gods will it, ruling broadly in heaven—
                   they're far stronger than I am, planning or doing."   170

Can a   She spoke that way but long-suffering, godlike Odysseus
Goddess Lie?   chilled as he spoke, the words with a feathery swiftness:
                   "You're planning otherwise, Goddess—hardly a send-off.
                   You tell me to cross great gulfs of sea on a plain raft?
                   It's hard and fearsome, even for balanced and sailing
                   ships enjoying a breeze from Zeus while trying to cross it.
                   So I won't board a raft if you are against me,
                   Goddess, not unless you powerfully swear that
                   you're not planning some other hardship or sorrow."

Swearing
by the Stux
River

He spoke that way and goddess-like, shining Kalupso   180
touched his hand and smiled. She spoke to him outright:
"You rascal for sure, you're never a fool or without wits,
ready to make a speech like that to a Goddess.
So let Earth look on and the wide Heaven above us,
◆ yes and the tumbling Stux's water—the greatest
oath for the blissful Gods, the oath which they fear most:
I won't plan some other hardship or sorrow.
I'll think and explain for you as though for my own self:
I'll make your plans as though they came to my own need.
Surely my mind is not unfair—iron is hardly   190
throughout this heart in my breast! I surely can pity."

Dining in the
Nymph's Cave

The shining Goddess spoke that way and she led him
swiftly. The man walked in the Goddess's footsteps.
They went to her hollow cove, Goddess and mortal.
◆ He sat in the chair that Hermes had just now
left and the Nymph laid out plenty to eat well—
food and drink taken by men who are death-bound.
After she sat down facing the godlike Odysseus,
handmaids brought her nectar and laid out ambrosia.
Their hands went out to the good things lying before them.   200

Dying
and Undying
Women

After they'd taken pleasure in eating and drinking,
Kalupso started to ask him, goddess-like, shining:
"Zeus-bred son of Laertes, my wily Odysseus!
You want to go home to the well-loved land of your fathers
now and so quickly? Well, be happy for all that.
Yet if you knew in your heart you're doomed to be laden
with painful struggle before you reach the land of your
    fathers,
you'd stay right here at my side and care for this household.
You'd be deathless, for all your wanting to gaze at
your wife, a woman you long for all of your days here.   210
I claim to be surely nothing less than that woman,
neither in height nor shape. In fact it is not wise,
the dead striving in shape or grace with the deathless."

Longing
for the Woman
Who Will Die

Full of his own plans, Odysseus answered by saying,
"Queenly Goddess, don't be angry: all that you tell me
I know well. My thought-full Penelopeia,
beside you, is not so tall or striking to look at.

The lady will die; you are undying and ageless.
Even so I go on longing all of my days here
to sail back home, to see that homecoming daylight.   220
If Gods on the wine-dark sea again should attack me
I'll bear it: the heart in my chest has suffered and hardened.
I've gone through plenty already, plenty of struggle
at sea and in war. This pain can be added to that pain."

The Last
Lovemaking

He said so much, the sun went down, darkness was coming.
The two of them walked to the inmost nook of the hollow
cave and loved with pleasure, staying close to each other.

To the End of
the Island

When newborn Dawn arrived with her rose-fingered
          daylight,
promptly Odysseus dressed in a tunic and mantle.
The Nymph adorned herself in the whitest of long robes,   230
a graceful and fine weave. She tied a beautiful golden
sash at her waist and set a veil over her forehead.
Planning a send-off there for great-hearted Odysseus,
she gave him a large ax that fitted his hands well.
Both of its bronze edges were sharp and a splendid
olive-wood handle joined tight at the ax-head.
She gave him a polished adze and, making their way out,
led him to tall stands of trees at the end of the island—
alder and black poplar, fir making for heaven,
dry for a long time, seasoned and ready to float light.   240
After she showed him growths where trees were the tallest,
Kalupso went back home, bright as a Goddess.

Hard Working ♦
with Wood

Now he cut down trees. He worked at a fast pace,
felling twenty in all. He trimmed them with ax-blows,
scraped them with care and cut them straight to a
          string-line.
Meanwhile goddess-like, shining Kalupso brought him
          an auger.
He bored and fitted all the planks to each other,
using wooden nails and slabs for the joining.
The way a man skilled in carpentry rounds out
the broad keel of a ship designed as a freighter,   250
Odysseus worked on the wide raft in the same way.
He set down deck-planks, closely fitted with braces,
and made some long strakes. So ended the raft-work.

Sail and Line   Now he set in a mast and fitted a yardarm.
He made a steer-oar, too, in order to sail straight.
He worked in shoots of willow throughout as a caulking
to keep out water. He piled in plenty of dunnage.
Meanwhile goddess-like, shining Kalupso had brought him
cloth for a sail: he carefully worked it and trimmed it.
He fastened braces, halyards and sheets on the new raft.   260
He drew it all on rollers down to the bright sea,
having done with the whole task on the fourth day.

Good-By to the   Shining Kalupso sent him away from her island the
Goddess   fifth day.
After she bathed and dressed him in fine-scented clothing,
the Goddess laid in dark wine in a tight skin,
another larger sack of water and one more
bag with plenty of meat that suited his spirits.
She sent him off with a wind, gentle and balmy.

Sailing to   Cheered by the breeze, godlike Odysseus bellied the sail out.
Phaiakia   He sat and kept his craft on course with the steer-oar   270
smartly. He let no sleep fall on his eyelids
   ♦ that night, watching the Pleiades, late-setting Bootes,
the Great Bear—they also call it the Wagon,
circling high in its place and watching Orion—
the only sign that takes no bath in the Ocean.
Because he was told by goddess-like, shining Kalupso
to keep that sign to port while crossing the great sea,
he sailed for seven and ten more days on those waters.
Shadowy mountains began to loom on the eighteenth
day, the closest part of Phaiakian land to his own raft.   280
It looked like a bossed shield on the haze-covered water.

The Anger of   But now the Earth-Shaker, back from Ethiopian country,
the Sea   ♦ saw him a long way off from the Solumoi Mountains.
He watched him sail at sea. His heart more angry,
the God shook his head and spoke to his spirit:
"Look at this! Gods have made new plans for Odysseus
surely during my stay in Ethiopian country.
He's close to Phaiakia now. What will his lot be?
To break from his fetters, the great sorrow that bound him?
Well but I think I can make him suffer enough here."   290

The Dread and   He gathered clouds as he spoke and, taking the trident,
Rage of   roughed the seas and aroused the squalling of every
Odysseus   sort of wind. Clouds of spray were obscuring
                water and land alike: a night was roused from the heavens.
                Eastwind and Southeasterly fell on him, blustering
                    Westwind
                and Northwind, born in the high air, gathering big waves.
                Odysseus's heart and knees felt loosened and melted.
                He called in a rage to his own great-hearted spirit:
                "How wretched I am! Now what finally happens?
                I fear all of it's true, what the Goddess told me: 300
                she said before I came to the land of my Fathers
                I'd fill with pain and struggle. Everything's borne out.
                Zeus has rounded the broad heavens with storm-cloud,
                vexing the sea, and I'm rushed by a squalling of every
                sort of wind. My headlong doom is a sure thing.

Better and   ♦"Danaans were three times, four times as happy to perish
Worse Death   on Troy's wide plains, favoring Atreus's two sons.
               If only I'd died there myself, facing my own doom
               that day the Trojan hordes kept throwing their bronze-
                   tipped
               spears at me, fighting around the corpse of Akhilleus.   310
               Honored with death-rites, my name would be spread by
                   Akhaians.
               But now it's my doom to be cut off. This end will be
                   wretched."

The Storm   A giant wave struck him down from its fearsome
Mounts   crest when he'd spoken. It twirled his raft in the water
             and threw him far from the craft, making the steer-oar
             drop from his hand. The mast was cracked in the middle
             by frightfully shifting winds that came at it gale-force.
             Sail and yardarm were down and away in the water.
             The man went under a long time, unable to bob up
             swiftly from under the drive and fall of the huge wave: 320
           ♦ his clothes from the shining Goddess Kalupso were heavy.
             At last he came back up. He spat out a briny
             mouthful and plenty of water ran from his forehead.
             He'd hardly forgotten the raft. Tired as he now was,
             he made for it fast in the waves and managed to take hold.

He sat in the center hoping to slip from his own death,
titanic rollers hauling him that way and this way.
Just as the Northwind in late summer will carry
thistles afield, and they hold on tight to each other,
now the sea-winds carried the raft this way and that way.   330
Southwind sometimes tossed him to Northwind to carry,
Eastwind sometimes gave him to Westwind to drive on.

A Timeless Veil ♦ Ino, the pretty-ankled daughter of Kadmos,
had watched him. Once called Ino, her voice like a human's,
now Leukothee honored by Gods in the salt sea,
she pitied the roaming Odysseus, burdened with trouble.
She rose from the sea like a tern from a plunge in the water,
sat on the well-tied raft and started to ask him,
"Poor man: why is the Earth-Shaker Poseidon
so fiercely angry, sowing all of your troubles?   340
He won't destroy you, though, for all of his outrage.
Do as I say—you don't seem lacking in judgment—
take off those clothes and leave your raft to the driving
storm. Swim with your hands as though you would
        reach home,
Phaiakian shores. It's now your lot to escape there.
Spread this veil below your chest as a deathless
guard, then don't be afraid of wounding or dying.
Soon as your hands have taken hold of that shoreline
loosen the veil and throw it back in the wine-dark
sea far from shore. Then turn away from the water."   350

The Goddess gave him the veil after she'd spoken.
She turned and dove once more in the billowing water
just like a tern. Then she was hidden by dark sea.

Disobeying the   But long-suffering, godlike Odysseus pondered.
Goddess   Vexed and annoyed, he told his great-hearted spirit,
"Look at me now! Some deathless God may have woven
another trap. She told me, 'Abandon your raft here.'
I won't obey, not yet. I saw with my own eyes
the land she said I'd escape to now and it's far off.
I'll do this, though, because it strikes me as better: 360
long as the wood holds out where I tightly joined it,
I'll stay right here. I'll go through trouble but bear up.

Then if the sea splinters my raft and destroys it
I'll swim: I cannot foresee anything better."

The Storm
Mounts Again

But while his heart and head were pondering that way,
the Earth-Shaker Poseidon built up a great sea,
a hard and overarching terror that smashed him
the way a powerful wind rattles a litter
of dry husks and scatters them this way and that way.
Long raft-boards were scattered. However Odysseus   370
rode one plank—he might have been driving a fast horse—
he took off clothes, the presents from shining Kalupso.
He spread that veil below his chest in a hurry,
went in the sea face first, spreading his hands out,
anxious to swim. The lordly Earth-Shaker saw him.
Shaking his head the God spoke to his spirit:
"Suffer plenty of harm now! Wander the wide sea
until you join with men nourished by great Zeus.
And yet don't hope to make a joke of your hardship."
He spoke that way, lashed the horses with rich manes   380
and soon arrived at his well-known temple at Aigai.

The Great
Storm Passes

Now the daughter of Zeus, Athene, thought of a new plan.
Tying all the sea-winds down in their courses,
she told them all to stop their blowing and rest now.
She roused a lively Northwind and opened the waves out
so that Odysseus, bred by Zeus, might mix with Phaiakians,
lovers of oars. The man avoided his death-hour.

Closer to Land

Two long days and nights he was whirled through heavy
rollers. Often his heart looked forward to dying.
When Dawn in her lovely braids ended the third day,   390
all the winds diminished at last and a breathless
calm came on. Odysseus, raised on a long swell,
looked out sharply and sighted land: it was not far.
• As welcome a sight to children knowing their father
will live when he's lain sick, suffering strong pain—
some hateful Power attacked him, he wasted a long time—
now they're glad the Gods release him from ravage:
Odysseus found that forested shoreline as welcome.
He swam on, anxious to set a foot onto dry land.

The man was just far off to be heard if he shouted   400
but caught the sound of waves thudding the reef-rocks.
Gigantic tumblers roared and pounded the dry land,
a scary noise, everything covered in sea-foam.
He saw no harbor for ships, nothing of shelter,
only threatening cliff-side, rock-face and sea-ledge.
Odysseus's heart and knees felt loosened and melted.
Bitterly angry, he spoke to his great-hearted spirit:
"And I? When Zeus allows me to gaze at a landfall
unhoped for, to swim so hard crossing a great gulf,
nothing shows, no way to emerge from the gray sea: 410
jagged ledge on the outside, breakers around it,
all that surge and moan, a cliff that's flattened and
        straight up,
water so deep in close that no one could stand on
both his feet or avoid harm in the high surf.
A giant wave might break as I'm clambering out and
throw me at hard rock. My work would be pointless.

Still More   "Yet if I swim on farther, hoping to make out
    Danger   sloping shore somewhere, a sea-water harbor,
I'm worried a gale might snatch me again in the water
and carry me off to the fish-filled sea, heavily groaning.   420
Or maybe some Power would even send me a monstrous
♦ sea-beast nourished by well-known Amphitrite.
I know the renowned Earth-Quaker is outraged."

While his heart and head were pondering that way,
a mounting crest was bearing him straight at the rough
        shore.
There his skin would have torn, bones would have broken
had not the glow-eyed Goddess Athene put in his heart now
to grab at a ledge with both his hands as he rushed past
and hold on, moaning, until the roller had gone by.
So he avoided the worst. But the wave had a backwash!   430
It struck him again and threw him far out in the water.
The way an octopus, pulled from the back of its shelter,
will hold sand-grains packed in its tentacle suckers:
so were pieces of skin torn from Odysseus's daring
hands when the mounting backwash covered his body.

Prayer
to a River •

A sad Odysseus there would have died—it was more than
his portion—had not glow-eyed Athene given him foresight:
he broke from the mounting surf that roared on the beaches
and swam beyond it, watching the shoreline and hoping
to see a sloping shelf or a seawater harbor.   440

He swam and came in time to the mouth of a lovely
flowing river. It surely looked like the best place,
without rocks, sheltered, away from the sea-wind.
Watching its flow he heartily prayed to that River:
"Hear me, Lord, whoever you are, I've prayed to you often.
I came here running from seas and the spite of Poseidon.
Surely you deathless Gods will welcome and honor
a man who's wandered, arriving here as I just now
came to your flow, your knees, with all of my deep pain.
Pity me, Lord: my claim's from a man who is lowly."   450

The River
Answers a
Prayer

He stopped and the flow promptly slowed where a Power
checked it, making for calm ahead. Safe at the River's
mouth at last, both knees of Odysseus buckled.
His sturdy hands dangled, heart quelled by the salt sea,
his whole body swollen. Seawater burbled
from nostrils and mouth. He lay breathless and speechless,
utterly worn out. A drastic weariness came on.

Cold Night
Approaching

When breath came back, his mind and spirits regathered,
he promptly loosened the Goddess's veil from his middle
and let it go where the river swirled into salt sea.   460
A big swell carried it swiftly: Ino reclaimed it
with both her hands. So Odysseus moved from the river
and lay in rushes. He kissed the plant-giving soil there.
Yet he spoke in dismay to his great-hearted spirit:
"For me more pain? What will finally happen?
Now if I watch the whole uncaring night by the river
a hard frost, I'm afraid, will join with a fresh dew,
breaking my spirit. I'm faint and gasping already.
Freezing gusts can blow from a river before dawn.
Yet if I climb some hill into shadowy forest   470
and lie in the dense undergrowth—if only the night's chill
and weariness let go, if honeyed sleep would arrive there—
wild beasts, I'm afraid, will make me their booty."

Olive and ♦
Wild Thorn

So he pondered. The latter seemed to be better:
he made his way to the woods. Not far from the water,
beside a clearing, he found two bushes to crawl in:
♦ olive and wild thorn grew in the same place.
Powerful sea-damp winds could not bluster inside them,
glaring sun could hardly throw in its light there,
rain would not get through: the plants were a tangle,   480
dense and wrapped in each other. Promptly Odysseus
crawled under. He made a wide bed with his own hands.
Plenty of leaves had fallen around and were piled up,
enough to shield two men or three, in the winter
time too, whatever storm might be raging.

So long-suffering, godlike Odysseus gazed on it gladly.
He lay in the center, piling leaves on his body.
The way a man might bank a firebrand in darkling
embers far afield where neighbors are not close,
saving a fire-seed, no need to light it from elsewhere: 490
Odysseus hid in the leaves that way and Athene
poured sleep on his eyes. She freed him from hard work
fast and from weariness: the Goddess covered his eyelids.

A New City in a
Far-Off Land

So long-suffering, godlike Odysseus slept there,
worn and wholly exhausted. However Athene
went through Phaiakian country and came to their city.
The people once had lived in Hupereia's open
♦ dancing country close to the overprevailing Kuklops
who harmed them often—the Kuklops were larger and
    stronger.
But godlike Nausithoos rose in power and led them
to homes in Skherie, far from bread-eating people.
♦ He walled their city around and built them their houses,
raised shrines to the Gods and divided the farmland.   10
♦ But then his fate downed him: he went into Aides'
house and Alkinoos, counseled by Gods, now was their
    ruler.

A Dream about
Washing

The gray-eyed Goddess Athene went to the palace,
planning on great-hearted Odysseus's way home.
She entered the richly designed room where a daughter
slept like a deathless Goddess, shapely and lovely,
Nausikaa—great-hearted Alkinoos's daughter.
Two maids were sleeping nearby, flanking the doorposts,
pretty as Graces. The doors gleamed and were closed tight
but Athene, fast as a wind-breath, came to the bedside   20
and stood above the daughter's face to address her,
looking like Dumas's daughter—the man was a shipwright.
The girl was Nausikaa's age, the joy of her own heart.
Taking that form the gray-eyed Athene asked her:
♦ "Nausikaa, how could your mother make you so careless?
Your clothes have a shiny glow but they're lying uncared for.
Marrying soon, you'll need some beautiful clothing
to wear yourself and present to those who attend you.
Surely such things give rise among men to a good name.
They'll make your father and mother honored and happy.   30
Let's go then, wash in the morning, soon as the dawn
    comes!
I'll go and help you myself, the sooner to dress you
finely. You won't remain a virgin much longer.

Already the best young men in Phaiakian country
have all come courting—your bloodline too is Phaiakian.
Come on then, rouse your well-known father at daybreak
to get a mule-cart ready. Loin-cloths and dresses
and brightly colorful cloaks can be carried in that way.
It's far better to go there riding than walking:
the washing places are very far from the city."   40

A Higher,   Gray-eyed Athene spoke that way and she left her
Radiant World   fast for Olumpos. They say the Gods' thrones are forever
there, hardly shaken by storm-winds, by pelting
rain and no snow falls: there's only the cloudless
air and spread-out sky. A white radiance drifts down,
happy Gods enjoying all their days where the glow-eyed
Goddess Athene arrived after warning the young girl.

A Mule-Cart   Dawn now came on her gorgeous throne and awakened
Nausikaa, known for her fine robes. Her dream had
          alarmed her:
she made her way through the house to talk to her parents,   50
the mother and father she loved. She found them inside
          there,
the lady sat by the hearth with maids who were helping
to spin their sea-mauve wool, and then at the doorway
she came on her father going to council with well-known
lords who were called there now by high-born Phaiakians.
She stood up close to her much-loved father and asked him,
    ◆"My dear Dad, won't you harness a mule-cart,
the high one with well-rimmed wheels, to help me to carry
our splendid clothes that are soiled to wash by the river?
Surely it's right for you, going to council   60
with high-ranked men, to have clean clothes on your body.
The five sons you love, born in your great house—
two are married, three are robust and unmarried—
are always wanting to put clean clothes on their bodies
and go out dancing. My heart cares about all this."

She stopped, too bashful to speak to her own father of
          blooming
and marrying. Yet he sensed it all as he answered,
"I won't deny you the mules—or anything, daughter!

Go on then: slaves will help you harness the mule-cart,
the high one with well-rimmed wheels, topped with a
    clothes-box."   70

Off to the   He spoke that way, he gave commands and servants
Seashore   obeyed him.
Outside they prepared a wagon, the mule-cart with good
    wheels:
they led the mules up under to the wagon and yoked them.
The daughter carried shining clothes from her bedroom
and laid them down there, piled on the polished wagon.

Her mother put the food on, all kinds to be suiting
their spirits. She gave them meats and poured wine into
    goatskin
sacks. Soon as her daughter mounted the wagon,
her mother gave her softening olive oil in a golden
flask to anoint herself and the women who helped her.   80

Holding a whip and the reins—they shone in the
    bright sun—
the daughter lashed and drove the mules. Making a clatter,
anxiously straining, they hauled clothes and the daughter,
and not alone—handmaids joined her and went too.

Laundry Time   In time they came to the beautiful flow of a river.
They found the perennial wash-pools, plenty of pretty
water upwelling to clean the clothes that were badly
dirtied. They soon unyoked the mules from the wagon
and drove them along, down to the eddying water
to graze on honey-sweet grass. Taking the clothing   90
in hand from the wagon, they brought it all to the dark pools
and stamped it in wash-holes fast, racing each other.

Soon as they washed and rinsed all of the dirt out,
they spread each garment in turn right there on the
    seashore,
where waves most often had washed pebbles on dry land.
Then they washed, anointed their bodies with rich oil
and gladly took some food on the bank of the river,
waiting for laundry to dry in the glare of the sunlight.

Ball-Game   After enjoying their meal both princess and handmaids
              threw off their headbands and joined in a ball-game.   100
              White-armed Nausikaa started them all in the dance-play,
          ♦   looking like Artemis raining her arrows in mountains,
              racing through high Teugeton or Mount Erumanthos,
              taking her pleasure in deer on the run or in wild boar
              while Nymphs, the daughters of Zeus who carries the Aigis,
              play in the fields with her. Leto's heart is delighted
              seeing Artemis hold her head much higher than all there,
              she's known with ease, though all her Nymphs are so lovely.
              The unmarried virgin outshone her maids in the same way.

The   In time she was ready to go back home on the wagon,   110
Frightening   to yoke the mules and fold the beautiful clothing,
Stranger   when gray-eyed Athene, the Goddess, thought of a new plan.
              Odysseus now might wake up, see this girl with the
                   good face
              and then be led by the girl to Phaiakian men in the city.
              So now when the princess threw her ball to a handmaid,
              it missed the girl and flew in a swirl of the water—
              they called out loudly—and woke up godlike Odysseus.

              He sat up wondering, head and heart full of questions.
              "Look at me—what land and people now have I come to?
              Are men here overbearing, savage and unjust?   120
              Or maybe they mind the Gods and are kindly to strangers.
              A sound just came of women's voices around me—
              or Nymphs'—they hold the highest ranges of mountains,
              grassy plains, river sources and meadows.
              Or now I'm somehow close to the voices of people.
              Come on, then. I will look and learn for myself here."

              So godlike Odysseus came out from under the bushes,
              breaking some shoots with his rugged hand from a leafy
              bush to cover his man's genitals shyly.
          ♦   Yet he came like a mountain lion, sure of his power,   130
              however rained on or wind-blown: smoldering vision
              bright in his head, he stalks a ram or a bullock,
              maybe a forest stag, or his belly commands him
              to enter a crowded fold and charge at a lamb there.
              Odysseus made for the finely braided girls in the same way
              to mix with them, bare as he was—he felt such a great need.

Smeared with grime from the sea, he struck them as
      frightful:
they ran to the jut-out beaches that way and this way.
Only Alkinoos's daughter stayed, helped by Athene,
who made her mind bold: she took all fear from her body.   140
Nausikaa held her ground and Odysseus wondered
whether to clasp her knees, this girl with the good face,
or stand right there and pray to the girl with some soft
      words,
ask her to show him to town and offer him clothing.

Human or   So as he mulled the latter seemed to be better,
Goddess?   to ask her with gentle words while standing a ways off—
clasping her knees might rankle the mind of a young girl.
Promptly he made a speech both gentle and clever.
♦"I clasp your knees, my Lady. Are you divine or human?
If you're a Goddess holding the breadth of the heavens,   150
I'd say Artemis, yes, the daughter of great Zeus:
in looks and height and form you two are a close match.
Yet if you're human, making a home on the good earth,
your father and honored mother are blessed with you three
      times,
your brothers are blessed three times. Surely their spirits
are always warmed and happy because of your own self,
watching you join a chorus and dance like a flower.
But blessed in his heart beyond them all is that person
who leads you, weighed with bride-gifts, right to his own
      house.
I never saw such a human, not with my own eyes,   160
man or woman—I'm taken by wonder to see you!

"One time I saw, near Apollo's altar on Delos,
a young date-palm, a shooting growth of such beauty.
I'd gone that way with plenty of people behind me.
The course would harm me, though, for sorrow was
      waiting.
Yet I gazed in the same way, my heart was astonished
a long time: such a tree had never grown from the broad
      earth.
So young woman, I marvel and wonder, doubting and
      fearing
to clasp your knees. But hard pain has beset me.

Nothing Is
Better
or Stronger
"Yesterday, after twenty days, I escaped from the wine-dark   170
sea. I was often carried by waves and a high wind
far from Ogugie Island. Now some Power has thrown me
down here, maybe to face more pain. I think it will not stop,
not until the Gods have troubled me far more.
Yet my Lady, pity me. Having suffered a great deal
I come to you first now, knowing none of the other
people who hold the land or towns in this country.
Show me your city, lend me tatters to throw on,
maybe a cloth which wrapped your clothes when you
        came here.
Then may the Gods bestow whatever your heart wants—   180
◆ a man and home—and grant you the closeness of two good
minds. For surely nothing is better or stronger
than man and woman close in thought and in holding
house. It often stings their rivals but brings joy
to well-wishers. The pair have heard that most often."

Lavish Care on
the Stranger
White-armed Nausikaa faced him now as she answered.
"Stranger, you don't look like a harmful or foolish
man but Zeus himself on Olumpos apportions a good life
to evil and good men both, to each as he wants to.
He gave you your lot; you need, doubtless, to bear it.   190
But now, having arrived in our country and city,
you won't lack clothes or anything else that is proper
for those who face us humbly, whatever their trials.
I'll show you the city. I'll tell you the name of our people:
Phaiakians hold this land and rule in the city.
I'm Alkinoos's daughter—a man with a great heart—
Phaiakian strength and power are held by that ruler."

She stopped and called to her maids, beautifully braided:
"Stay there, you maids! You look at a man and you dash off?
Surely you don't suppose an enemy stands here.   200
No man's all that clever—no one will ever
try and approach Phaiakian men on our own soil
bent on slaughter: we're much too loved by the great Gods.
Our homes are across so many swells of the ocean,
so far apart that other humans hardly engage us.
Now a wandering, wretched man has arrived here.
He needs to be cared for: every stranger and beggar

comes from Zeus; our gift may be small but it's friendly.
So help him, you maids—food and drink for the stranger!
Wash the man in a wind-sheltered place at the river."   210

Bathing Alone   After she spoke they stopped and called to each other.
They took Odysseus to shelter—so they were told to
there by Nausikaa, great-hearted Alkinoos's daughter.
They set out clothes beside him, a mantle and tunic;
they gave him softening olive oil in a golden
flask and told him to wash in the flow of the river.

A Man Like a   Among the handmaids, godlike Odysseus answered,
God Again   "Stand off a ways, you women. Allow me to wash off
brine from my shoulders myself and rub them with olive
oil—my skin has not been oiled for a long time.   220
But I won't bathe with you close by. I'm embarrassed
to do so bare among maids beautifully braided."

Silver on Gold He stopped and they moved away to talk with the princess.
Godlike Odysseus washed himself in the river,
removing the brine that covered all his shoulders
and back, wiping the restless sea's foam from his forehead.
Soon as he washed it all and anointed his body
he put on clothes the unmarried virgin had offered.
The daughter of Zeus, Athene made him taller
and stronger to look at too, dressing his thick hair   230
to hang in curls from his head like hyacinth blossoms.
The way a man might skillfully overlay silver
on gold, trained by Hephaistos and Pallas Athene
in every art to turn out work outstandingly graceful,
Athene graced Odysseus's head and shoulders the
        same way.

To Be Called   He went and sat apart by the shore of the salt sea,
My Husband   handsome, graceful and glowing. Nausikaa marveled,
speaking among her maids who were beautifully braided:
"Listen, you white-armed maids, for now I will speak out.
This man will mingle with godlike Phaiakians hardly   240
against the will of all the Gods holding Olumpos.
A while ago he struck me as coarse and unsightly;
now he looks like a God who rules in the broad sky.

If only a man like that could be called my husband,
if only he'd settle here and be happy to stay here!
Come on then, you maids: food and drink for the stranger."

Off to the City   She spoke that way, they heard her well and obeyed her.
They set out food and wine close to Odysseus.
That long-suffering, godlike Odysseus heartily ate there
and drank. He'd gone without the taste of food for a
          long time.   250

Then white-armed Nausikaa thought of a new plan.
The clothes all folded and placed in the well-designed
          wagon,
the tough-hoofed mules well yoked, she mounted
          herself then,
heartened Odysseus, called and spoke to him outright:
"Get up now, stranger, we're off to the city. I'll send you
straight to my knowing Father's house where the best men
all gather, I'm sure: you'll come to know the Phaiakians.
But do it my way—you don't strike me as unwise—
so long as we go past fields and farmers at work there,
march with my handmaids briskly. Follow the wagon   260
and mules as I show you the way myself to the city.
Once we're close to the place, look at the high wall
around it first, the lovely harbor on both sides,
the tight channel for up-curved ships on their way in.
They're hauled up high and every ship has its own place.
We assemble around a beautiful shrine to Poseidon,
built with stones hauled from deep in the quarry.
We take good care of our black ships and their tackle,
hawsers and sails—some men taper the oar-blades.
Phaiakians don't care much about quivers and long bows.   270
Mainmasts, balanced ships and oars on the vessels—
those are their joys, and getting borne on the gray sea.

Gossip and ◆"Their talk is disgraceful, though. I avoid it and no one
   Ill Will   chides me later. Very overbearing men in this country,
the viler sort, might now remark if they met us,
'Who's this hulking, good-looking stranger who follows
Nausikaa? Where did she find him? For sure it's a husband!
Maybe she picked up a roamer tossed from a vessel
of men far off, since no such people are nearby.

Or else a God came down from heaven to answer   280
her many prayers—and all her days she will own him!
She's better off to travel and find a husband
elsewhere the way she scorns men in our own land—
many a good Phaiakian man's wooing that lady.'
They'll talk that way about all this work to disgrace me.
I'd blame a woman myself who acted the same way,
at odds with her living and much-loved father and mother,
mixing with men before her marriage is well known.

The Poplar   "Ah but stranger, mark my word for the fastest
Grove   way to reach my home and to gain from my Father.   290
You'll find a roadside poplar grove of Athene,
bright and flowing with spring-water: meadow surrounds it.
My Father's land is there, teeming with orchards
and far from the city as loud shouting will carry.
Sit there. Wait for a while until we have entered
the city ourselves and arrived at the house of my Father.

Go to the   "Then as soon as you hope we've gone in the palace,
Mother   enter the city yourself and ask a Phaiakian
where Alkinoos's house is, my great-hearted father.
You'll know it with ease, a foolish child could take you   300
there because no other Phaiakian houses
rise in the same way as the house of our war-king,
Alkinoos. After our home and courtyard surround you
go through the hall in a hurry until you have come to
 ♦ my Mother. She sits in the bright glow of the hearth-fire
spinning her sea-blue yarn—it's striking to look at.
She leans on a column with maids seated behind her.
The throne my Father sits on also is leaning:
he drinks his wine like a deathless God in the same place.
But go right past him. Take the knees of my Mother   310
with both your hands, the sooner to gaze on your homeward
daylight with joy, however far you have sailed from.
If Mother's thoughts are friendly, her heart in your favor,
then you may hope to sail and look on your loved ones
back in your well-built home in the land of your fathers."

On to the City   After she'd spoken she lashed the mules with her
                        bright whip.
Promptly they left the flow of the river behind them,

the animals moving along, their hooves at a quick trot.
She managed the reins to allow her maids and Odysseus
to follow on foot. She used the lash with a close care.   320

Listen,   The sun went down as they came to the holy and well-
Goddess   known
grove of Athene. Godlike Odysseus sat there.
He prayed fast to Athene, the daughter of great Zeus:
"Hear me, unfailing daughter of Zeus who carries the Aigis.
Listen this time! You failed to listen before this
when I was struck—when the well-known Earth-Shaker
    struck me.
Make me arrive among the Phaiakians pitied and well-
    liked."

He prayed that way and was heard by Pallas Athene.
But awed by her Father's brother, she held off from facing
the man—not yet. Poseidon was bitterly angry   330
at godlike Odysseus until he came to his own land.

<table>
<tr><td>An Old Woman
from Apeire</td><td>

So long-suffering, godlike Odysseus prayed there.
Meanwhile hearty mules carried the girl to the city.
Soon as she came to the well-known house of her father
she made a stop at the gates. Her brothers approached her,
like deathless Gods around her, letting the mules out
from under the yoke and carrying clothes in the palace.
She went to the bedroom herself. Starting a fire there
was Eurumedousa, her elderly maid from Apeire.
Up-curved ships had brought her once from Apeire,
a prize to honor Alkinoos, ruler of every   10
Phaiakian clan, obeyed like a God by his people.
She'd raised white-armed Nausikaa there in the great hall.
Now she built a fire and arranged for her dinner.

</td></tr>
</table>

An Old Woman
from Apeire

So long-suffering, godlike Odysseus prayed there.
Meanwhile hearty mules carried the girl to the city.
Soon as she came to the well-known house of her father
she made a stop at the gates. Her brothers approached her,
like deathless Gods around her, letting the mules out
from under the yoke and carrying clothes in the palace.
She went to the bedroom herself. Starting a fire there
was Eurumedousa, her elderly maid from Apeire.
Up-curved ships had brought her once from Apeire,
a prize to honor Alkinoos, ruler of every   10
Phaiakian clan, obeyed like a God by his people.
She'd raised white-armed Nausikaa there in the great hall.
Now she built a fire and arranged for her dinner.

Young Girl with
a Pitcher

Odysseus meanwhile rose to enter the city.
Thoughtful and caring, Athene misted him densely
to stop the ample-hearted Phaiakians from halting
or baiting Odysseus, asking his name or homeland.
Shortly about to enter the beautiful city,
he faced the Goddess herself, glow-eyed Athene.
She'd taken the form of a young girl bearing a pitcher.   20
She stopped before him. Godlike Odysseus asked her,
"My girl, could you take me now to the house of your ruler,
the man they call Alkinoos, lord of the people?
I'm hard-tested myself. I came as a stranger
from far-off land so I don't know of your people,
the men who own this land and rule in the city."

Vessels Fast as
an Insight

An answer came from the Goddess, gray-eyed Athene:
"Well then, fatherly stranger, I'll show you the building
you look for. It stands quite close to my handsome Father's.
But follow me quietly now. I'll take you myself there.   30
Don't be staring at men or asking them questions.
People don't take well to those who are odd here:
they're not fast friends with strangers coming from
        elsewhere.
They tend to rely on their swift and maneuvering vessels

for crossing the wide sea where the Earth-Shaker Poseidon
lets them go. Their ships are fast as a bird or an insight."

A Built-Up City   Pallas Athene spoke that way and she led him
and Harbor   forward briskly. He followed the Goddess's footsteps.
                     Phaiakians, known for their ships, scarcely remarked him
                     moving along through the city. Beautifully braided,   40
                     feared as a Goddess, Athene had poured that amazing
                     mist around him. At heart she cared for him closely.

                     Odysseus marveled at balanced ships in their harbors,
                     assembly places of war-chiefs, lengthy and high-raised
                     walls topped with stakes, a wonder to gaze at.

Go to the   Soon as they reached the renowned home of that ruler,
Lady First   the glow-eyed Goddess Athene started to tell him,
                     "Fatherly stranger, there's the house that you asked me
                     to point out. You'll find the lords nourished by great Zeus
                     dining inside. Go in then, don't be a fretful   50
                     heart. A daring man does better in every
                     labor however far he's traveled from elsewhere.
                     Our Lady's the first person you'll find in the great hall.
                     Arete's the name she goes by, born in the royal
                     bloodline, the same as King Alkinoos's bloodline.

The Seed of   ♦"Nausithoos first was born to the Earth-Shaker Poseidon.
a God   His mother was Periboia, the best and prettiest woman,
                     the youngest daughter of ample-hearted Eurumedon,
                     once the king of the highly spirited Giants.
                     He caused those reckless beings to die and he died too.   60
                     Poseidon loved his daughter and fathered a boy-child,
                     the great-hearted Nausithoos, lord of Phaiakians.
                     Nausithoos fathered Alkinoos next and Rhexenor.
                     The latter was sonless, killed by the silver bow of Apollo
                     when still a groom in his hall, and with only a daughter,
                     Arete. King Alkinoos made her his own wife
                     and highly esteemed her: no woman on earth is
                          esteemed so,
                     of all those managing households under their husbands.
                     The Lady's esteemed in a heartfelt way by her loving
                     children as well, of course by Alkinoos always—   70
                     and all the people, who view their queen as a Goddess.

They welcome her loudly whenever she walks through
    the city.
That Lady is never lacking in good understanding:
♦ she settles quarrels for women she likes, and for men too.
Indeed if the Lady takes you close to her own heart,
then you might hope to look on all of your loved ones
and sail to the high-roofed house in the land of your
    fathers."

A Home of
Bronze, Gold,
and Silver

Glow-eyed Athene spoke that way and she left him,
forsaking the charm of Skherie. Over the restless
♦ sea she came to Marathon, broad roadways of Athens,   80
and entered Erekhtheus's tight-built house. But Odysseus,
now at the well-known house of Alkinoos, stood there
mulling a long time before he stepped on the threshold
of bronze. A sunlike glow, the luster of moonlight
hung on the great-hearted Alkinoos's high-roofed
home where bronze walls extended this way and that way
from threshold to farthest corners, topped with a blue frieze.
Doors of gold in the tight-built house closed on the inside.
Silver doorposts stood on a threshold of polished
bronze and the lintel was silver, the handle of pure gold.   90
Silver and golden dogs were on both sides of the doorway,
made by Hephaistos, knowing the ways of the artist.
Acting as watch-dogs of great-hearted Alkinoos's palace,
deathless creatures, all their days they were ageless.
Along the wall were chairs, set out on both sides
from threshold to farthest corner. Beautiful chair-cloths
covered them, thrown there, finely worked by the women.
Phaiakian lords had used those chairs to be seated,
dining and drinking, their holdings lasting forever.
Boys of gold, standing on well-crafted bases,   100
held in their hands the brightly flickering torches
glowing each night for those who dined in the great hall.

Women Known
for Their
Loom-Craft

The king had fifty women slaves in the household.
They grind down tawny grain using their hand-mills
♦ or weave at looms, turning wheels of the wool-staffs.
They sit and their hands are like trembling leaves of
    an aspen.
Oil and moisture seep through the tight-woven fabric.
Just as Phaiakian men are outstanding at moving

a race-fast ship through the water, their women are first-rate
loom workers. Athene has given them stunning   110
workmanship, better than anyone's craft, and their good
    minds.

More Gifts Beyond the court but close to the gates is an orchard,
from the Gods four large measures of land with fencing on all sides.
The trees grow tall there, fruit-trees in full bloom:
pear-trees, pomegranates, apple-trees glowing
with fruit, the sweetest figs and olives in blossom.
Fruit is never lacking or lost in that orchard,
summer or winter, year round. Westwind is always
blowing to help some grow and others to ripen.
Pear after pear matures, apples on apples,   120
fig after fig. The grapes are cluster on cluster:
a vineyard is planted there, heavy with fruitage.
Level ground on the warm side is for drying
grapes in the sun; another place is for plucking,
others for stepping. In front, shedding their blossoms,
are unripe grapes, while others darken slowly.

The lowest ground is a garden bed in good order.
Every kind of shoot grows there the whole year
round near a pair of springs. One seeps through the garden;
the other flows right under the courtyard threshold   130
in front of the high-roofed house—townspeople draw there.
So the Gods lavished outstanding gifts on Alkinoos.

The Knees of Long-suffering, godlike Odysseus stood there gazing.
the Lady After his heart had truly wondered at each thing,
he promptly crossed the threshold, walked in the palace
and found Phaiakian lords and counselors dropping
wine from their cups for the far-sighted Splendor of Argos,
the last God to be offered wine when they thought about
    sleeping.
Long-suffering, godlike Odysseus moved through the
    great hall
held in the dense mist Athene had poured down   140
until he came to lordly Alkinoos, then to Arete.
Odysseus threw his arms around the knees of Arete
just as the wondrous mist flowed down from his body.
Everyone hushed, seeing the man in the household.

They stared in amazement. Then Odysseus spoke out:
"Queen Arete, daughter of godlike Rhexenor,
I come to your knees and your husband's after my
        great pain.
I pray the Gods will give the rest of these diners a happy
life with each man passing down to all his children
the wealth in his hall and honors bestowed by his people.   150
But send me off in a hurry—help me return home.
I've suffered harm too long, far from my loved ones."

A God Goes ♦   He spoke that way and sat by the hearth in some ashes,
with the   close to the fire. All the people were quiet.
Stranger   At length a war-chief answered, old Ekheneos.
Of all the Phaiakians there this man was the eldest,
a standout speaker, knowing the ways of the old ones.
Meaning well he spoke to the king and the people:
"It's not becoming, Alkinoos, never the right thing
for strangers to sit on the hearth's ground among ashes.   160
Others are holding back: they wait for your own word.
Come on then, raise our guest and give him a good seat,
the chair studded with silver. Order your stewards
to mix more wine and for Zeus, whose joy is in thunder,
pour from our goblets. Zeus goes with the lowly stranger.
Let the housekeeper feed our guest whatever is inside."

A Very   Soon as Alkinoos heard—his power was holy—
Honored   he took Odysseus's hand and raised the resourceful,
Welcome   shrewd man from the hearth. He set him down on a shining
chair and made friendly Laodamas stand up,   170
the son who'd sat beside him, the son whom he loved most.
A maid brought water now and poured from a pitcher
of stunning gold. Odysseus washed his hands in the silver
basin. She drew up a polished table before him.
An honored housekeeper brought in bread and arranged it.
She laid out plenty of dishes, free with her holdings.
Godlike Odysseus ate and drank. He'd suffered a long time.

Honey-Minded Strong Alkinoos turned to a herald and told him,
Wine   "Pontonoos, mix our wine in the wine-bowl and serve it
to all in the great hall. For Zeus, whose joy is in thunder,   180
we'll pour from our goblets: he goes with a lowly stranger."

Pontonoos mixed the honey-minded wine when his ruler
had spoken and then he served them all drops for libation.

Somber
Spinners

After they poured for Zeus and drank as their spirits
moved them, Alkinoos told the gathering outright,
"Listen, Phaiakian counselors, lords of the people!
Let me speak as the heart in my chest has enjoined me.
Now that you've dined, go to your houses and lie down.
At dawn we'll gather more of our elders together,
we'll entertain our guest in the hall and we'll lay down   190
handsome victims for Gods. In time we can ponder
a send-off: without pain or struggle the stranger
may leave on one of our ships for the land of his fathers
gladly and swiftly, however far he has come from.
The man won't suffer harm or pain in the meantime—
not till he walks on his own land. There he may suffer
♦ whatever doom the somber Spinners have worked out,
spinning their thread from the hour he was born to his
    mother.

What If
the Man Is
a God?

"But now if he came as a deathless God from the heavens,
that's something new the Gods are carefully planning.   200
Before this Gods have always appeared to us plainly
whenever we killed our lustrous bulls by the hundred.
They dined among us all and they sat alongside us.
If one of us faced them alone, too, as he wandered,
they never went into hiding—we are their close kin!
So are the Kuklops and wild clans of the Giants."

What Is
More Doglike?

Odysseus, full of designs, answered by saying,
"Don't think that way, Alkinoos. I am no deathless
God like those who rule broadly in heaven—
not with my size and shape. I'm human and death-bound.   210
The men you've known who carry the heaviest burden
of pain however: I'm their match with my own pain.
I could speak in fact for a longer time of my hardship,
all the sorrow, willed by the Gods, I have gone through.
But now you should let me eat, for all of my troubles.
Nothing is more hateful and doglike than hunger:
it tells then forces a man to remember its own needs,
however worn the man is, the longing he suffers,
the way my heart still mourns. 'Eat up and drink now,'

my belly always tells me, and makes me forgetful   220
of all my other anguish. It only commands me to fill up.

"You please hurry, though, when Dawn is a bright light
help me to go, a wretched man, to my own land,
despite my suffering. Let me die when I've gazed on
my ample and high-roofed house, my slaves and my treasure."

The Crowd   They all approved what he said. They asked that the stranger
Disperses   be sent off well because he'd spoken so rightly.
             They poured wine to the Gods and drank as their hearts
                wished.
             Then they went to lie down, each man to his own house.

A Telltale   Godlike Odysseus, left behind in the great hall,   230
Mantle   sat by godlike Alkinoos close to Arete.
             Housemaids took away the settings for dinner.
             Arete, the white-armed queen, started to ask him—
        ✦   she knew the handsome tunic and mantle Odysseus
             wore was made by the queen herself and her handmaids—
             she spoke out now and the words had a feathery swiftness:
             "Stranger, I'll ask you questions first for myself here:
             who are you, where are your people? Who gave you this
                clothing?
             You wandered the sea, I thought you said, when you
                came here."

Glaring   Full of designs, Odysseus answered by saying,   240
Lightning at "It's hard, my queen, to tell you all of my troubles
Sea   because the Gods in heaven gave me so many.
             I can say this much, now that you've asked me:
             an island, Ogugie, lies far off in the salt sea,
             the home of Atlas's daughter, the clever Kalupso,
             in lovely braids but a feared Goddess. No one will join her,
             none of the deathless Gods, no man who is death-bound.
             Some Power led me, a wretched man, to her fireside
             alone, for Zeus had hurtled his glaring lightning,
             blasted my race-fast ship and plunged it in wine-dark   250
             seas where all of them drowned—the men I relied on.
             I clasped the keel of my up-turned ship and was borne off
             nine whole days. In the black of the tenth night
             Gods drove me close to Ogugie, the isle of Kalupso,

in lovely braids but a feared Goddess. Taking me in there,
she fed me and loved me warmly, yes and she told me
she'd make me deathless. All my days I would not age.

Seven Years on   "The Goddess never changed the heart in my own chest.
the Island   Although I stayed there seven years I was always
    crying for home, drenching Kalupso's undying   260
    clothes she gave me. Then the eighth year came in its
      circling
    ♦ way and she asked—she urged me to go. Maybe a message
    from Zeus was the cause; maybe a change of her own mind.
    She sent me away on a well-tied raft and she gave me
    lots of bread, sweet wine and her ageless clothing.
    She brought up a following wind, gentle and balmy.

Seventeen   "For seven and ten more days I sailed on the water.
Days at Sea   The eighteenth day, with shadowy mountains looming—
    your own land was close—my heart was delighted.
    Then I was cursed, about to meet with a great deal   270
    of struggle brought on by the Earth-Shaker Poseidon.
    He set the wind against me, it stopped me from making
    headway, astounding waves he roused would not let me
    stay on the raft and go on. Though I moaned there
      without end,
    the storm soon splintered my raft. So now I went swimming
    my way on the wide sea till water and headlong
    sea-wind brought me closer at last to your own land.

A Welcoming   "But there if I'd gone ashore, the surf would have thrown me
River   straight into huge rocks. That place was no pleasure!
    I went back out, I swam and came to a river   280
    at length, plainly the best landfall I'd spotted,
    free of rock and fairly sheltered from storm-wind.
    I fell down there, worn out. When night like a Goddess
    came I moved away from the Zeus-lavished river
    and lay in some bushes. I piled leaflets around me.
    A God then poured his boundless rest on my body.

The   "I slept in those leaves, my heart restless and saddened
Welcoming   all that night, through dawn and well into midday.
Princess   The Sun-God westered; the honeyed Sleep-God unbound me.
    Now on the shore I spotted handmaids playing,   290

then your daughter herself, the likes of a Goddess.
I humbly approached her. She never failed in her good
    sense.
You'd hardly hope that a younger woman who met you
would act so—younger people are always so carefree—
she gave me bread to eat and plenty of bright wine.
She helped me wash in the river and gave me some clean
    clothes.
Despite my hardship that's the truth I have told you."

A Grandly
Welcoming
King King Alkinoos promptly answered by saying,
"Stranger, my child was not so thoughtful in one way
clearly: she failed to bring you straight to our household   300
along with her maids when you humbly approached her the
    first time."

An answer came from Odysseus, full of the best plans.
"War-lord, don't upbraid your high-born daughter on that
    count.
She asked me indeed to follow behind with her handmaids
but I was afraid, embarrassed and therefore unwilling.
Somehow I thought your heart would be angry to see me
because we races of men on earth are often distrusting."

Again Alkinoos promptly answered by saying,
"The heart in my chest is not the kind to be angry
rashly, my guest. Good rule is better in all things.   310
In fact by Zeus our Father, Athene and Apollo,
being the man you are, with a mind like my own mind,
I'd much rather you stay here and marry my daughter—
a son-in-law now! I'd offer you wealth and a fine house
if only you'd stay. But no Phaiakian holds you
against your will. May Zeus our Father dislike that.

Help on
the Long Way
Home "To know your send-off now I'll make it tomorrow
surely. After you lie down, ready to doze off,
our men will row on a calm sea to your own land.
You'll go back home, or whatever place you would like to,   320
  ♦ even to land much farther away than Euboia.
They call that island the farthest, those who have seen it
among our people: they ferried the blond Rhadamanthus
there to join with Tituos, son of the Goddess,

Gaia. They sailed and arrived and hardly were tired—
making their way back home, all in the same day!
You'll know in your heart how vastly better my ships are.
My men are the best at scattering sea-foam with oar-blades."

A Joyful Prayer   He stopped and the long-suffering, godlike Odysseus
gladly wanted to pray. He answered by saying,   330
"Fatherly Zeus! Bring everything King Alkinoos told me
now to a good end. May his name be never extinguished
where earth gives grain. May I reach the land of my
        Fathers."

Ready for Bed   All the while they spoke that way with each other,
white-armed Arete had told her handmaids to set out
a bed in the hallway promptly with beautiful covers,
to throw down violet blankets, spread out the ruglike
layers and put thick wool on top of the whole pile.
Torches in hand, the maids went out of the great hall.
After they spread out the thick-piled bed in a hurry,   340
they stood beside Odysseus, prompting and asking,
"Get up now, stranger. The bed you wanted is ready."

They said no more. For the man, how welcome to lie down!
Long-suffering, godlike Odysseus slept there.
His corded bed lay under the echoing hallway.

Alkinoos lay in the inmost room of the high house.
The Lady was there beside him, sharing the same bed.

BOOK 8   *Songs, Challenges, Dances,*
              and Gifts

The Call of a
Herald-Like
Goddess
When newborn Dawn came on with her rose-fingered
          daylight,
Alkinoos rose from his bed. His kingly power was holy.
Zeus-born Odysseus also rose, a looter of cities.
Alkinoos led the way—his kingly power was holy—
down to the ships. The Phaiakians' built-up assembly
lay nearby. They entered and sat close to each other
on shining stones. Meanwhile Pallas Athene
moved through the city resembling the herald of mindful
Alkinoos. Planning on great-hearted Odysseus's way home,
she went up close to every man and she told him,   10
"Come on, Phaiakian counselor, lord of the people!
Go to the assembly place and learn of a stranger
newly arrived in mind-full Alkinoos's great hall.
He looks like a deathless God and he's wandered the
          great sea."

Her words aroused the strength and spirit of each man.
Promptly coming together, filling assembly
chairs, the large crowd was amazed to be seeing
the mindful son of Laertes: Athene had showered
a heavenly grace on the man's forehead and shoulders,
making him taller and much more forceful to look at.   20
She made him welcome, liked by all the Phaiakians,
held in awe and respected. He'd win in a number
of games the Phaiakians used to challenge Odysseus.

The Promise
of a Fast Way
Home
Soon as the crowd had grown, pressing together,
King Alkinoos told the gathering outright,
"Listen, Phaiakian counselors, lords of the people!
Let me speak as my own spirit enjoins me.
This guest whom I don't know has arrived in my great hall.
He's wandered from people in Dawn's land or in Hesper's.
He asks to be sent on home. He wants us to stand firm;   30
so as we often have let's hurry the send-off.
No other man—whoever arrives in my own house—
waits there sadly a long time for a send-off.

Come on then: haul a black ship down to the shining
sea for her maiden voyage. Let fifty-two crewmen
be chosen from all our people—make them our best ones.
When crewmen have lashed all their oars to the oar-locks,
let them go ashore and hurry to our house
to join our feast. I'll offer plenty to each man.

"That's my charge for the young men. Now for you others,   40
scepter-carrying lords: come to my handsome
palace and help me regale our guest in the great hall.
Let no one say no! And call my God-gifted singer,
♦ Demodokos. Surely a God gave him the best voice
to entertain us whatever his heart moves him to sing of."

A Black Ship He stopped and led the way out. All of them followed,
Is Ready   sceptered lords. A steward went for the God-gifted singer.
Young men soon were chosen: fifty-two crewmen—
the king's command—left for the tireless seashore.
After they came on down to the ship and the salt sea,   50
they hauled the night-black vessel out into deeper
water and set both mast and sail on the black deck,
moved the oars through leather straps at the thole-pins,
all in order, and finally let out the white sail.
They anchored her high on the tide, left her and quickly
walked to the mind-full Alkinoos's stately household.

Blindness   Corridors, courtyards and rooms were crowded with people.
and the Gift Many were younger there and many were older.
of Song   Alkinoos killed twelve sheep for the Gods and his people,
eight white-tusked boars and a pair of hoof-dragging heifers.   60
Flayed and dressed, they'd make for wonderful dining.

Now the herald approached, guiding their faith-full poet,
loved most by the Muse. She gave him a good and a bad
      thing:
she'd taken his eyes but gave him honey-sweet music.
Pontonoos placed a chair for him, studded with silver.
It leaned on a tall column surrounded by diners.
The herald hung the clear-toned lyre on a peg there
over the singer's head and guided his hand up
to take it. Nearby he set out a basket, a beautiful table

with wine in a goblet—the man could drink when his heart
  wished.   70
So hands went out to the good things lying before them.

Music That   After the craving for food and drink was behind them,
Draws Tears   the Muse prompted her poet to sing about great men,
a story so well known that it passed broadly through heaven:
Akhilleus, Peleus's son, had clashed with Odysseus
• once at a lavish feast for the Gods. They had quarreled
fiercely with each word. The lord of men, Agamemnon,
was glad inside: the best Akhaians were wrangling
after Phoibos Apollo had said it would happen.
The king had asked for a sign, crossing the threshold   80
of stone at sacred Putho. That's when misery started
to fall on Danaans and Trojans alike, willed by the great Zeus.

The well-known poet sang that song but Odysseus,
taking a broad and violet cloak in his strong hands,
covered his face by drawing it over his forehead,
ashamed of tears from his eyes before the Phaiakians.
Every time the godlike bard paused in his music,
Odysseus wiped off tears and, taking the cloak off,
poured out wine for the Gods from a two-handled goblet.
But soon as the singer went on—the tale was encouraged   90
by all of the best Phaiakians, loving his word-song—
Odysseus covered his face again with a low moan.

Time for the   He kept his crying away from all of the others
Athletes   but not the king. Only Alkinoos marked him:
he sat alongside and heard him heavily moaning.
He said to the oar-loving Phaiakians quickly,
"Listen, Phaiakian counselors, lords of the people!
Now that our hearts are filled with dining and hearing
the lyre—how well that singing goes with a great feast!—
let's go outside for some games, a few of our many   100
contests. Later our guest can say to his loved ones
back at home that we're far better than others
in wrestling and boxing, the best in sprinting and leaping."

He spoke that way, he led them all and they followed.
The herald hung the clear-toned lyre from its own peg,

took Demodokos's hand and guided him out of the great hall.
He led him along the same path which the others,
Phaiakia's best, had walked to be dazzled by athletes.
They came to a gathering place and joined an immense
        crowd—
thousands. Plenty of good young men were standing: 110
♦ Akroneus rose, Okuolos too and Elatreus,
Nauteus, Prumneus, Ankhialos too and Eretmeus,
Ponteus also, Proreus, Thoon, Anabesineos;
Amphialos, Poluneos's son and the grandson of Tekton.
Eurualos too, a match for the man-slaughtering Ares:
Naubolos's son, he was better than all the Phaiakians
in height and form outside of handsome Laodamas.
Three young sons of handsome Alkinoos stood up:
Laodamas, Halios and Klutoneos, godlike in bearing.

The Sprinters   A number of men would be tested first in a footrace.   120
A course was drawn from its mark. All of them flew off
swiftly together, kicking up dust on the racetrack.
The fastest sprinter by far was handsome Klutoneos,
leading as long as a mule-plowed furrow in farmland
and placing first for the crowd, the others behind him.

Wrestling,   Some men tried the hard labor of wrestling.
Leaping,   In time Eurualos came out best of the whole group.
the Discus,   Then Amphialos leaped out farthest of all there.
and Boxing   The best of all by far with a discus: Elatreus.
In boxing Laodamas won, Alkinoos's good son.   130

A Greater   After they'd all enjoyed themselves in the matches,
Name   Alkinoos's son Laodamas said to the others,
"Come on, my friends. Let's ask our guest if he's knowing
and skilled in a game. In size and shape he is not bad:
those calves and thighs, two good arms and above them
a rugged neck—he's strong. Youth has not left him,
although the man looks broken by plenty of hardship.
I'd say myself nothing is worse than the salt sea
for breaking a man, whatever strength he may put on."

Now his friend Eurualos faced him and told him,   140
"Laodamas, every word you spoke was the right one.
Go and face him yourself and say what you told us."

Soon as the good young man of Alkinoos heard that,
he walked to the center, stood there and said to Odysseus,
"You too, fatherly stranger: come on and be tested
if you have skill. It's likely you know about athletes.
♦ So long as a man is alive his name will be greater
for all that his own hands and feet can accomplish.
Come on then, try us. Scatter cares from your spirit!
Your homeward way is close: already a black ship's   150
been taken down to the sea and crewmen are ready."

Mounting   An answer came from Odysseus, full of the best plans:
Anger   "Laodamas, why do you rouse and bother me this way?
What's on my mind more than your games are my troubles:
I've gone through pain before this, plenty of hardship.
Now I sit in your gathering place, asking for only
help to go home from your king and all of your people."

But now Eurualos answered tauntingly, saying,
"No, stranger, you don't strike me as skillful,
a man for the many matches engaged in by good men.   160
More like a ship-bound man with plenty of oarsmen,
a roving captain maybe whose crewmen are traders:
you mind your freight and brood over your cargo
for greed and gain. You don't look like an athlete."

Odysseus, full of designs, glowered and told him,
"Stranger, you don't speak well, like a man who is reckless.
Clearly the Gods don't lavish favors on every
man alike: good shape, clear thought or the best speech.
Maybe a man will turn out poorer in good looks
but Gods will crown his language with grace and his people   170
will gaze and enjoy his words, strong and unswerving
but lowly and mild. When people gather he stands out:
they see the man as a God when he walks through the city.
Or maybe a man's like the deathless Gods in his beauty
but lacks the crown of language, his talk is not graceful.
You're so striking to look at—a God would not make you
otherwise—yet your mind and words are quite empty.

"You've roused my spirits, though, the heart in my own
          chest,
by speaking out of order. I'm hardly unpracticed

in sports as you say. I know I stayed with the winners   180
when young as long as I trusted my youth and my own
    hands.
But now I'm owned by hardship and pain. I suffered a
    great deal
slashing through wars with men and working through
    high seas.
Yet I will try your games, for all of my bad times.
Your words cut my heart. You've riled and provoked me."

An
Outstanding
Discus Throw

He jumped up wearing his cloak and grabbing a discus,
a strong and dense one, larger and not by a trifle
than those Phaiakians threw in games with each other.
He whirled it around in his brawny hand and he let go:
the stone hummed and Phaiakians—men of the long oar,   190
known for their ships—crouched on the ground as the
    discus
sped overhead. His hand had thrown it with great speed:
it went past everyone's mark. Using a man's voice
now was Athene, placing the mark and telling them loudly,
"Even a blind man, stranger, groping around here,
would find your mark, for it's not in a crowd with the
    others—
it's first by far. You must take heart from this effort.
No Phaiakian stone will reach you or pass you."

Remembering
Battlefields
of Troy

Her words made long-suffering, godlike Odysseus
glad. He saw a likable friend on the game-field.   200
Now with a lighter heart he told the Phaiakians,
"Approach that mark, you men! I'll throw out another
right after, I think, and just as far if not farther.
You others, however your hearts and spirits have led you,
come on and try me—you've made me overly angry—
whether in boxing, wrestling or racing. Any Phaiakian
now can face me, I won't say no, except for Laodamas:
the man is my host and no man fights with his welcome.
Surely a man is a fool, worthless or mindless,
to challenge a host to a game or fight with him outright   210
on foreign soil: all of his own hopes could be cut short.

"The rest of you, though, I won't say no or denounce you.
I'll want to watch you, face to face, and to test you.

I'm not so poor in all the games that a man plays.
◆ I know a lot about polished bows and their handling.
Shooting at packs of enemies, I was the first one
to strike my man, whatever crowd of my war-friends
stood close by, aiming and shooting at targets.
Philoktetes alone was better with arrows
during the time we Akhaians aimed at the Trojans.   220
But I was better by far, I'd say, than all of the other
men now living on earth, eaters of good bread.

"I'd never have looked for a fight with men of the old days:
not with Herakles, not with Oikhalian Eurutos,
those who challenged the deathless Gods with a long bow.
So great Eurutos died soon—aging never
arrived in his hall—Apollo was angry and killed him
because the man provoked the God as a bowman.

"I also can throw a spear—and farther than anyone's arrow!
In racing alone I think a Phaiakian likely   230
would pass me. Far too many waves overwhelmed me
cruelly and help on a raft won't last forever.
So all my arms and legs are loosened and trembling."

Dining, He spoke that way and all the people were quiet.
Dancing, and Only the king, Alkinoos, gave him an answer.
Good Song "My guest, you say all this without being graceless.
You'd like to show the manliness you are endowed with.
You're angry because a man right here on the game-field
taunted you. No one would fault your manliness truly,
not if he knew in his heart the right way of speaking.   240
Well then, mark my words: tell them to other
war-chiefs after the journey back to your great hall.
Dining close to your honored wife and children,
remember our own manliness: action that great Zeus
caused to be ours in a steady line from our fathers.
Although we're not so faultless in boxing and wrestling,
we do go fast on our feet. Aboard ship we're outstanding.
Always we love our dining, dancing and lyre-work,
changes of clothes, a warm bath and a good bed!

"Come on now: all of you best Phaiakian dancers,   250
step out. In time our guest can enlighten his loved ones

after he's gone back home: we're better than others
at sailing ships, in running, singing and dancing.
One of you go and fetch the clear-toned lyre in a hurry
now for Demodokos—somewhere it lies in our household."

The Lyre   Godlike Alkinoos spoke that way and a herald
Returns   stood up to fetch the hollow lyre from the palace.
               Meanwhile nine judges chosen from all of the country
               rose—they usually managed all of the games there.
               They leveled a dancing place and widened a handsome   260
               place for games. The herald returned with the clear-toned
               lyre and Demodokos stood in the center surrounded
               by younger men in their prime, dancers with great skill
               beating the holy ground with their feet, making Odysseus
               marvel deeply. He stared at the flash of their ankles.

A Web's •   Striking the lyre, the poet sang a delightful
Design   song about Ares and stunningly crowned Aphrodite,
               how they first made love in the house of Hephaistos
               in secret. Ares gave her plenty of presents that sullied
               the bed of her lord, Hephaistos. Promptly the Sun-God   270
               came and told him—he'd watched their lovemaking
                   closely—
               and soon as Hephaistos heard the heart-racking story
               he went to the forge, his mind brooding on evil.
               He set on its block a huge anvil to hammer out bindings
               that never would loosen: he made them to stay in the same
                   place.
               After forging the hard web, still angry at Ares,
               he went to the room where the bed was lying—his
                   own bed—
               and laid out links of the web to circle the bedposts
               and hang overhead. Many came down from the rafters
               like fine spiderweb, no one ever would spot it—   280
               surely no blissful God—its crafting was that sly.
               Then with his trap in place all over the bedposts,
               he faked a move to Lemnos, the well-built city
               he loved and a place far dearer than any.

Bound   God of the golden reins, Ares was not blind.
to the Bed   Seeing Hephaistos leave—he was known for his artwork—
               Ares rushed to the house of well-known Hephaistos,

craving the love of gorgeously crowned Kuthereia.
The Lady had just arrived from her father, powerful
   Kronos's
son. She sat in the house when Ares arrived there   290
to take her hand. He called her name as he told her,
"Now my love, let's enjoy ourselves on the bed here!
Hephaistos is not in the land. Doubtless he's gone off
to Lemnos, the Sintien people, those with the rough
   speech."

He spoke that way and she thought: how welcome to
   lie down!
The two made love in the bed. They dozed. And the
   bindings
around them started to hold, designed by crafty Hephaistos.
Unable to move their arms and legs or to sit up,
they shortly knew escape no longer would happen.

The Passion   Well-known Hephaistos approached, hardy with both
of the Gods   hands.   300
Laid Bare   Before arriving in Lemnos country he'd turned back—
the Sun-God, carefully watching, had told him the
   story—
so he arrived back home, troubled and heartsick.
He stood by the gate, a wild anger inside him,
and shouted fiercely at all the Gods on Olumpos,
"Fatherly Zeus and the rest of you Gods living forever,
look at this act here now, so painful and comic:
the daughter of Zeus, Aphrodite, always mistreats me,
lame as I am, and desires a wrecker like Ares
because he's handsome and fast. I am a hobbler,   310
born that way. No one else is to blame here,
only my parents. I wish they never had made me.

"But now you'll see these two had sex in my own bed
and lay here afterward. How it galls me to see them!
And yet for all their lust I doubt they are hoping
to lie here long. They won't be anxious to sleep here
soon! For now my trap's bindings will hold them
until her Father returns all of the bride-gifts
I handed over to pay for this doglike woman.
His daughter's a beauty, yes, but her love is without faith."   320

Laughter and   He paused and the Gods assembled close to his bronze
More Lust   house.
                    Poseidon, the Earth-Upholder, came with the Runner,
                    Hermes, and Lord Apollo came, that worker from far off.
                    But every Goddess, embarrassed, stayed in her own house.
                    The Gods, bringers of bounty, stood in the doorway.
                    Laughter rose from delighted Gods, it would not stop,
                    all of them gazed at the work of crafty Hephaistos,
                    one of the Gods glancing and telling another,
                    "No good from a bad act. The slow one catches the fast one:
                    see how slow Hephaistos overtook Ares,   330
                    the fastest of all the Gods who rule on Olumpos.
                    A skillful trap—now the adulterer owes him."

                    Those were the things the Gods might say to each other.
                    Hermes was asked by the son of Zeus, lordly Apollo:
                    "Hermes, our Messenger, son of Zeus, bringer of bounty!
                    How would you like it, held by powerful fetters
                    and lying in bed beside the gold Aphrodite?"

                    That Splendor of Argos, the Runner, answered him
                         promptly,
                    "Lordly Apollo, Faraway Archer, if only it happened!
                    If triple the number of endless bindings would grip me,   340
                    if all you Gods and every Goddess were looking,
                    at least I would lie myself by the gold Aphrodite."

The God Wants   Laughter rose from the deathless Gods when he'd spoken.
His Money   But laughter was not for Poseidon. Over and over
                    he asked Hephaistos, known for his craft, to loosen the
                         bindings
                    on Ares. The words he spoke had a feathery swiftness:
                    "Let him go and I'll pledge, just as you want it
                    among the deathless Gods: he'll pay for everything rightly."

                    But well-known Hephaistos answered, hardy with both
                         hands:
                    "Poseidon, Earth-Upholder, don't ask me to do that.   350
                    It's foolish to count on pay from a God who has fooled you.
                  • Before the deathless Gods how could I bind you
                    if Ares gets out of my web and avoids what he owes me?"

Poseidon, the Earth-Upholder, gave him an answer.
"Hephaistos, however Ares avoids what he owes you
or tries to run off, I'll pay myself what I promised."

The well-known God answered, hardy with both hands:
"I won't say no. Denying that offer is not right."

Getaway   So strong Hephaistos, after he'd spoken, loosened the
                    bindings.
Soon as the powerful bindings were loosened the couple   360
jumped up and left, Ares to Thrace in a hurry
and Aphrodite, that lover of laughter, jaunted to Kupros.
♦ Her grove is there, the aroma of incense at Paphos.
The Graces helped her bathe, anointing her body
with ageless oil of the Gods living forever.
They dressed her in lovely clothes, a marvel to look at.

That was the song of the well-known bard and it gladdened
Odysseus's heart to hear it. It gladdened the others,
Phaiakians known for their long oars and their
                    ship-craft.

The Dancers   Now Alkinoos told Laodamas quickly   370
to dance with Halios—none of the dancers was better—
and promptly they picked up a ball, a beauty in purple
made for the dance by Polubos, knowing and artful.
One of them leaned backward and threw it at shadowy
clouds and the other one leaped from the gravel and
                    caught it
with ease before he landed again on his two feet.
After they tested themselves by throwing it straight up,
they danced on the ground—the earth which nourishes all
                    men—
throwing the ball to each other. The rest of the young men
stood in the game-field stamping steadily, loudly.   380

Godlike Odysseus told Alkinoos outright,
"Lordly Alkinoos, praised by all of your people,
you claimed Phaiakian dancers here are the best ones.
They've made you right. I'm held by wonder to
                    watch them."

He made Alkinoos glad—his power was holy—
and promptly he told the Phaiakians, lovers of rowing,
  "Listen, Phaiakian counselors, lords of the people!
  Our guest would seem like a man most knowing and tactful.
  Come on, let's offer him presents right for a stranger.
  Twelve outstanding rulers live in our country,   390
  powerful lords; I myself am the thirteenth.
 ♦ Let each ruler give him a clean mantle and tunic.
  A talent of purest gold should come from each ruler.
  We'll gather it all together fast for the stranger
  to hold in his hands; he'll go to dine with a glad heart.
  Eurualos, though, should calm the man with a present
  and good words. The way he spoke is hardly our custom."

He spoke that way, they all said yes and each ruler
  dispatched a herald quickly to carry the presents.
  Eurualos answered Alkinoos also by saying,   400
  "Lordly Alkinoos, praised by all of your people,
  I'll calm the stranger myself, just as you asked me.
  I'll give him my sword, all bronze, joined to a silver
  handle. Its freshly carved ivory scabbard
  has workings on both sides. It's surely a present of great
      worth."

He stopped and placed the sword studded with silver
right in Odysseus's hands. Each word had a feathery
    swiftness:
  "I hail you, fatherly guest, and if words have been spoken
  harshly may wind from a rainstorm carry them off now.
  May Gods help you to see your wife and to reach home: 410
  you've surely suffered a long time far from your loved ones."

An answer came from Odysseus, full of the best plans:
  "Friend, I hail you also: be blessed by the great Gods.
  I pray you'll never miss your sword in the future.
  What you've said and the sword you've offered have
      calmed me."
He stopped and shouldered the sword studded with silver.

The sun went down. Outstanding presents were brought in:
high-born stewards carried them now to Alkinoos.
Sons of the handsome king, taking the lavish

presents, laid them before the mother they honored.   420
Alkinoos led them along—his power was holy—
they came and sat on the high-backed chairs of the
        great hall.
Strong Alkinoos promptly spoke to Arete:
"Bring us a chest, my wife, whichever's the best one.
Inside the coffer lay out a clean mantle and tunic.
Heat a cauldron too for the stranger, warm up the water.
After he bathes he can stare at all of the laid-out
presents our handsome Phaiakians brought to the palace.
He'll relish our food, he'll hear out songs of our singer.
I'll give him my own goblet, a beauty in crafted   430
gold to help him remember me all of his long days,
pouring wine for Zeus and the other Gods in his great hall."

Fire under the   He said so much and Arete ordered the handmaids
Cauldron   to set a huge cauldron over the fire in a hurry.
                 They stood the cauldron over the fire and they poured in
                 water for bathing. They laid down firewood beneath it.
                 Flame circled the cauldron's belly, heating the water.

A Coffer Full of   Arete meanwhile brought from its room a marvelous coffer,
Treasure   a chest for the stranger. She'd laid in beautiful presents,
                   clothes and talents of gold Phaiakians gave him.   440
                   She placed a handsome tunic inside with a mantle,
                   telling her guest, her words with a feathery swiftness:
                   "Look to the lid yourself, tighten the knot in a hurry:
                   a man could rob you later perhaps when you're going
                   home or lying in honeyed sleep on your black ship."

                   Soon as the long-suffering, godlike Odysseus heard that,
                   he pressed on the lid and tightened the knot in a hurry—
            ♦   a crafty knot which queenly Kirke had taught him.

The Joys of a   Shortly a housekeeper asked him to come to the bathroom
Warm Bath   to wash himself. How truly welcome the sight was,   450
                a tub with its warm water! No one had cared much,
                not since he'd left the home of bright-haired Kalupso.
                Till then, much as a God, he'd always been cared for.
                The maids washed him now and anointed his body
                with oil. They tossed a handsome tunic and mantle
                        around him.

Remember the   He left the bathroom, rejoined some men who were
   Princess   drinking
                 wine and Nausikaa, having a God-given beauty,
                 marveled standing there by a post of the well-built
                 hall as her eyes regarded Odysseus closely.
                 She spoke to him now, the words with a feathery swiftness: 460
                 "Be well, stranger, and go to the land of your fathers
                 remembering how you owed your life to me first here."

                 Odysseus, full of designs, answered by praying:
                 "Nausikaa, great-hearted Alkinoos's daughter,
                 may loud-thundering Zeus, the husband of Here,
                 help me to see my homecoming day and my own house.
                 I'll pray each day to you there as though to a Goddess
                 because you saved my life when you were a young girl."

     Esteem   He stopped and sat on a chair with King Alkinoos close by.
  for the Singer Already the wine was mixed and portions were laid out.   470
                 A herald approached, guiding the trustworthy singer,
                 Demodokos, loved by his people. Surrounded by diners
                 the poet sat down, his chair leaned on a column.
                 Odysseus, full of design, spoke to the herald,
              ♦ carving a slab from the chine—plenty of white-tusked
                 boar was left, the fat bulging on both sides—
                 "Herald, take this pork to nourish the singer,
                 Demodokos. Let me hail him, for all of my sorrows.
                 Poets have won the praise and honor of all men
                 living on earth because a Goddess has taught them   480
                 the ways of song. She loves the clan of her singers."

                 He spoke that way and the herald handed the portion
                 to high-ranked Demodokos. Moved and delighted he
                      took it.
                 So hands went out to the good things lying before them.

  The Wooden   After the craving for food and drink was behind them
      Horse   Odysseus, full of design, said to the singer,
                 "Demodokos, truly I praise you higher than all men,
                 whether the Muse taught you, Zeus's child, or Apollo.
                 You surely sang of the Akhaians' doom in the right way—
                 how much they struggled and smarted, all that they
                      suffered—   490

as though you were there somehow or heard from a good
    source.

"But change the song, come on now, sing of the wooden
    horse made by Epeios with help from Athene.
    Godlike Odysseus led, filling the fake horse
    first with men, and Troy's acropolis came down.
    In fact if you tell this tale all in the right way,
    I'll soon proclaim your gift myself to the whole world,
    saying the Gods freely gave you a God's voice."

Troy Is   He stopped and the man, roused by his God, was a singer:
Doomed   he started with Argives boarding and sailing on well-decked   500
    ships from Troy—they'd hurled fire on their own camps.
    But those who'd joined with well-known Odysseus
        drew near
    meanwhile to Troy's assembly, sitting and hiding.
    Trojans themselves had dragged the horse to their fortress.
    It stood there, people sat and argued around it
    a long time, in doubt, but favoring three plans:
    either to stab the hollow wood with some heartless
    bronze; haul it high and throw it on boulders;
    or let it stand and please the Gods as a great gift.
    That was the way, in fact, it was going to end now.   510
    Their doom was to die that day as their city embraced it—
    a huge horse of wood with all the best of the Argives
    crouching inside, bringers of death to the Trojans.

Winning the   He sang how sons of Akhaians poured from that ambush,
War, Shedding   leaving the hollow horse to ravage the city.
the Tears   He sang how others elsewhere were pillaging high Troy
    but Odysseus—godlike Menelaos had joined him—
 ◆ went for Deiphobos's house like Ares the War-God.
    He sang how there they faced the ghastliest fighting.
    Odysseus won at last, helped by a great-hearted Athene.   520

The well-known poet sang that song but Odysseus
    often wept. The cheeks under his eyelids
    flowed like a woman's, crying and holding the husband
    she loves when he falls in front of the city and people.
    He's tried to keep a relentless day from his children
    but now his breath is failing, she knows he is dying,

she wails and throws herself on the man. Poking her
    shoulders
and back are spears, the weapons of enemy soldiers
who'll take her off into slavery, hard labor and heartbreak.
The woman's cheeks will waste with the wretchedest
    mourning.   530

Stop the Song   So sad tears of Odysseus fell from under his eyelids.
He cried and kept the tears from all the others
but not the king. Only Alkinoos marked him:
he sat alongside and heard him heavily moaning.
He said to the oar-loving Phaiakians quickly,
"Listen, Phaiakian counselors, lords of the people!
Demodokos, hold off now from the clear-toned
lyre for not everyone's charmed by your music.
After we dined and our God-blessed singer was prompted,
our guest went on for a long time with his heartfelt   540
weeping. Some heavy sorrow surely enfolds him.
Come on then, hold off. Let everyone take joy,
stranger and guest entertainer: it's far pleasanter that way.
We arranged all this for the sake of a guest whom we honor.
We'll send him off with loving gifts, with our friendship,
for lowly strangers can stand as close as our brothers.
Even those with paltry feelings have known that.

Ships Who   "So my guest, don't hide it smartly or slyly
Know Their   now when I ask you. Answering surely is better.
Own Way   Tell me the name they called you—your mother and father,   550
those in your town and those living around it.
For no one is wholly nameless living with good men,
whether he's good or bad from the time of his own birth:
parents put down names for all of their children.
Tell us what land you're from, what city and country,
that our ship can take you there with a good mind.
Phaiakian ships indeed don't carry a helmsman
or steer-oar the way a foreigner's vessel is fitted.
Our own ships know the minds and thoughts of our sailors!
They know each town and the rich farmland of every   560
people. They move on the spread-out sea in a hurry,
even in fog or haze. They're never afraid there:
our ships aren't damaged or ever destroyed on the salt sea.

One Doomed   "Yet I heard my Father Nausithoos tell me
Ship   once that Poseidon, the Sea-God, often was angry
                 because we gave out safe passage to all men.
                 He said that someday a well-worked ship with Phaiakian
                 crewmen heading home from an escort on hazy
                 seas will be wrecked by the God, and he'll circle our city
                 with high mountains. My Father prophesied that way.   570
                 The God will end it or not, whatever his own will.

Tell Us Your   "Come on then, answer me, tell me the truth now:
Story   where have you wandered? What were the places you
                     went to?
                 Which men were there, what cities or people who lived well?
                 Tell us of both—the wilder sort, the cruel and unfair,
                 and those who were mindful of Gods and kindly with
                     strangers.

War Losses   "Tell me why you weep too, heartily grieving
                 to hear of Troy, the deaths of Danaans and Argives.
                 The Gods arranged all that, Spinners of ruin
            ♦   for men so a song would arise for those in the future.   580
                 Did one good man in your bloodline die at the city
                 of Troy? A father- or son-in-law? Those are the dearest
                 persons after our own family members.
                 Maybe a war-friend? A worthy man you rejoiced in,
                 knowing him well? Surely a friend's no less than a brother,
                 especially a war-friend having knowledge of what's best."

BOOK 9   *A Battle, the Lotos,*
          and a Savage's Cave

The Most
Beautiful Thing
of All

Odysseus, full of designs, answered by saying,
"Lordly Alkinoos, praised by all of your people,
it's clearly a beautiful thing to hear out a singer,
a man like this, resembling the Gods with his own voice.
I'd say nothing is more fulfilling and welcome
than joy like that, embracing all of the people,
when diners throughout the hall listen to good song,
seated in order, and tables beside them are loaded
with bread and meat, when wine's drawn from the
          wine-bowl
and pourers make the rounds refilling the goblets.   10
All that seems the most beautiful thing in my own mind.

Odysseus, the
Son of Laertes

"But now your heart is moved to ask of my troubles
and griefs—and make for still more weeping and moaning.
What should I tell you first or last in my story?
My troubles are countless, all from Gods in their heaven.
But first I'll tell you my name so now you will know it.
In time, having escaped from pitiless doom-days,
I'll call you my guests, however far is my homeland.
I am Odysseus, Laertes' son, known for my wily
ways among men. My name has also gone to the heavens.   20
I live on clear-view Ithaka. Neriton Mountain
is plain there, its leaves rustling. Plenty of other
islands lie around us, close to each other:
Same, Doulikhion, densely wooded Zakunthos.
• My island is lower, well out to sea in the gray dusk.
The others lie apart, toward Dawn and the Sun-God.
My land is rough but it's good for raising a young man.
I cannot gaze, myself, on anything sweeter than homeland.

Away from
Your Parents

"Kalupso, a shining Goddess, kept me a long time
back in her hollow cave: she wanted *me* as her husband.   30
Kirke had held me back in her hall in the same way,
that charmer of Aiai: she longed for *me* as her husband!
Still they never won the heart in my own chest
for nothing is more delightful surely than homeland

118

and parents, <u>however rich and far is the new home</u>
<u>a man lives in. It's foreign land away from his parents.</u>

Defeated by   "So I'll tell you my long way home with all of its troubles.
the Kikones   Zeus weighed me with hardship after I left Troy.

"Winds drove me from Troy to the Kikones' coastline
♦ at Ismaros. There I killed some men and looted the city.   40
We took their wives and shared most of the city's
wealth: no man lacked the part that was due him.
Then I ordered my men to quicken their footsteps
to leave but many were passing fools and would not go.
Drunk from too much wine right there on the beach-sand,
they killed droves of sheep and curl-horned, hoof-dragging
    cattle.
Kikones meanwhile ran and called to their neighbors,
nearby Kikones, far more people and warlike.
Inland dwellers, they knew about fighting from horses;
they'd fight men too, if the need were there, on their two feet.   50
They came at dawn, dense as leaves or the thronging
blossoms of spring. Zeus was ready with cruel
deaths and we all felt doomed. We suffered a great deal
when Kikones formed by the race-fast ships and we
    fought back,
both sides hurling bronze-tipped spears at each other.
All through morning, when holy light was increasing,
we held them off, standing fast in spite of their numbers.
But after the sunlight waned—when oxen are unyoked—
Kikones forced us back and killed more Akhaians.
<u>From every vessel six of my men in their strong greaves</u>   60
<u>died.</u> We others escaped from death on that doom-day.

The God   "We sailed on farther then, our hearts in mourning,
Sends a Storm glad to be saved from death, but losing our good men.
None of my up-curved ships went far on their journey
before we called three times to all of our joyless
war-friends, dead on the land where Kikones downed them.

"Stormcloud-gathering Zeus now raised up the Northwind
against our ships, a massive storm hiding the ocean
and land alike with cloud. Night was roused from the
    heavens:

our vessels were driven headlong, sailcloth was ripping,   70
torn into rags, three or four scraps, by the fierce wind.
We struck and stowed them below, dreading our end there.
We rowed as hard and fast as we could to a landfall.

A Nameless   "We lay there two whole nights and days without moving.
Island   Pain and weariness ate up all of our spirits.
When Dawn in her beautiful braids ended the third day,
we stood our masts again, we hoisted the white sails
and sat as the wind and helmsman steered us along well.

A Land of   "Now would I come home safe to the land of my Fathers?
Blossoms and   Not when waves and current, together with Northwind,   80
Forgetfulness
◆ drove us away from Kuthereia, rounding Maleia.
From there I was borne for nine whole days by a blasting
wind on the fish-filled sea. We came on the tenth day
◆ to Lotos-eaters' land—their food is a flower.
We went ashore there promptly, gathered some water
and ate by the race-fast ships. My crewmen were hungry.

"After we ate our food and relished a good wine,
I sent off men on a search. I told them to find out
who held this land, the bread-eating people who lived here.
I chose two men and sent a third as a herald.   90

"They promptly left and mingled with Lotos-eaters.
Their people never planned on death for our war-friends:
they gave them food to try, their blossoms of lotos.
But anyone chewing the honey-sweet fruit of the lotos
no longer wanted to bring us news or to leave there.
Rather they planned on dining with Lotos-eaters,
cropping lotos themselves and forgetting the way home.

"I took them all to the ships—they cried when I forced them.
I dragged them aboard the hollow ship and I lashed them
below deck. I told the others, war-friends I trusted,   100
to clamber aboard the race-fast ships in a hurry,
lest they devour more lotos, forgetting the way home.
They boarded quickly and took their seats at the benches
right in line, their oars splashing the gray sea.

Loners   "We sailed on farther now, heavy and heart-sore.
          We came to the Kuklops' land. A lawless and prideful
          people who trust the deathless Gods for their farming,
          they plow no field and root no plants with their own hands.
          Everything grows without their plowing and sowing—
          barley and wheat and grapevines, heavily laden   110
          with clusters for wine. Zeus brings rain for their growing.
        • They don't make laws, they don't assemble or counsel.
          They live near crests of high mountains in hollow
          caves and each man lays down laws for his children
          and wives. No one Kuklops cares for another.

The Island of   "Not too close or far from the land of the Kuklops
Wild Goats   a densely wooded island spreads away from its harbor.
          Wild goats are born and grow there in countless
          numbers for no man's footfall frightens or stops them.
          Hunters never arrive there, men who would go through   120
          pain stalking through woods or the heights of mountains.
          The land's not crowded with flocks or farms that are
               plowed out:
          every day the soil's unplowed and unplanted.
          Lacking men, it feeds a bedlam of wild goats.

          "The nearby Kuklops own no warships with red cheeks.
          They have no shipwrights there, men who could build up
          strongly timbered vessels, finishing each touch
          for sailing to people's towns. But plenty of others
          cross the sea by ship to call on each other,
          men who could work this island, making it well-tilled.   130
          The land is not so poor, it would carry in season
          every fruit and its gentle and dewy meadows
          lie by the gray sea—grapevines never would fail there.
          Fields are flat for a plow, so harvests would stand tall
          every season. The topsoil's rich as the subsoil.
          The harbor's a safe one too, no need for a mooring,
          dropping anchor stones or lashing the stern-lines.
          A man could beach a ship then wait for the sailors'
          hearts to tell them to go with a following sea-wind.

Blind Landfall   "A shiny stream flows to the head of the harbor.   140
          It springs from under a cave with poplars around it.

We sailed in there, some Power guiding us darkly
in mist at night with hardly a glow to be made out,
then fog surrounding the ship. Nothing of moonlight
showed in the sky overhead: sea-clouds had blocked it.
No one spotted the island itself with his own eyes
or saw the tumbling, drawn-out waves onto dry land
before our tight-planked ships had glided ashore there.
Vessels beached, we took down all of the white sails
then disembarked ourselves on the shore of the salt sea.   150
We fell asleep, looking ahead to the bright Dawn.

Hunting and Feasting on Goats

"When newborn Dawn came on with her rose-fingered
          daylight,
we all were amazed at the place. We roamed through the
          island
and Nymphs, the daughters of Zeus who carries the great
          shield,
flushed out mountain goats, a meal for my war-friends.
Quickly we took out arching bows and our long-tipped
spears from the ships. We formed three groups and we
          let fly:
a God soon gave us our kills, raising our spirits.
Twelve black ships had followed me: each was allotted
nine goats. For mine alone there were ten goats.   160

"So now we ate and drank all day until sundown,
feasting on honey-sweet wine and plenty of goat-meat.
The good red wine was not all gone from our vessels:
enough remained since everyone topped off the wine-urns
after we first captured the Kikones' holy city.

"We also gazed at the nearby land of the Kuklops
where smoke was rising. Men, rams and goat-flocks were
          calling.
When Helios the Sun-God set and darkness was coming,
we lay and slept right there on the shore of the salt sea.

A Gigantic Cave

"Then newborn Dawn came on with her rose-fingered
          daylight.   170
I gathered all of the men myself and I told them,
'Stay here now, the rest of you men I rely on.
I'll sail across in my own ship with some crewmen

 ◆ to find and test those people, however they turn out.
   Maybe they're overbearing, savage and unjust.
   Or maybe they're mind-full of Gods and kindly with
       strangers.'

"I spoke that way and boarded, telling my war-friends
   to board themselves. After they loosened the stern-lines
   they boarded at once and took their seats at the oar-locks,
   all in order, then beat the gray sea with their rowing.   180

"We came to the place quite soon—the island was close by—
   and saw a cave by the shore not far from the salt sea,
   high and covered with laurel. Plenty of livestock,
   goats and sheep, were kept there. Around it a big yard
   spread out, built up high: stones were embedded,
   tall pine-trees and oaks, covered with high leaves.
   An outsize man slept there. He tended the livestock
   all by himself, far from the cave, mixing with no one
   else. He lived apart with the mind of an outlaw.
   He'd grown amazingly huge, hardly resembling   190
   a bread-eating man at all, more like a wooded mountain
   crag that's high and alone, away from the others.

A Very   "I told the rest of my crew, war-friends I trusted,   — repeated phrase
Strong Wine   to stay there close to the ship for now and to guard it.
   I chose a number of men, twelve of the bravest,
   and set out. I brought a goatskin full of our dark wine,
   the sweet one Maron gave me, the son of Euanthes,
   priest of Apollo, the God who watches the city
   of Ismaros. Awed by Maron, we'd guarded his woman
   and child—he made his home in Phoibos Apollo's   200
   wooded grove—and the presents he gave me were glowing.
   Seven talents of gold he gave me, all of it well-worked.
   He gave me a wine-bowl, all silver, and plenty of good wine
   in double-handled wine-urns, twelve of them filled up—
   a drink for the Gods, uncut and sweet. None of his
       housemaids
   knew of the wine, not one slave in the great hall.
   Maron knew, his wife and their own housekeeper only.
   Whenever they drank that red, honey-sweet vintage,
   he filled one goblet and poured it in twenty measures
   of water. The scent that rose from the bowl was a wonder   210

of sweetness. No one could hold back from that dear wine!
I filled a large goatskin and took it. I loaded
food in a bag as my bold spirit sensed in a short time
a man would approach us wearing massive and savage
prowess, hardly knowing of laws and fairness.

Noisy Lambs   "We promptly arrived at the cave but spotted him nowhere
and Kids   inside. He was tending fattened flocks in some meadow.
We walked in the cave and stared in wonder at each thing:
baskets loaded with cheese, pens crowded with noisy
lambs and kids, each livestock group with its own place,   220
the older lambs kept apart from the yearlings
and both from the newborn. Whey filled all the containers,
bowls and well-made pails, those that he milked in.

To Steal   "My war-friends urged me now that first we should haul off
or to Stay   cheese to the race-fast ship and then we should hurry
back to drive off the lambs and kids from their stock-pens
down to our vessel and sail off fast on the salt sea.
I paid them no mind. But how much better was *their* way!
  ♦ I wanted to see the man. Would he offer me guest-gifts?
The man was to prove, when he came, no joy to my war-
    friends.   230

"We started a fire, gave gifts to the Gods and we took down
cheese ourselves for a meal. We sat there and waited.

The Kuklops   "He came on driving flocks. He carried a hulking
Arrives   weight of dry timber for fire for his dinner
and threw it down in the cave, causing an uproar,
scaring us all. We ran to the end of the cavern.
He drove his fattened stock in the spread-out cavern—
all of these he'd milk. He'd left at the doorway
billy goats and rams: they'd stay outside in the big yard.
He raised a huge and heavy door-stone and set it   240
in place. The hard labor of twenty-two four-wheeled
wagons could not raise that stone from the cave floor.
That's how huge a boulder he'd placed at the doorway.

"He sat and milked all the ewes and the noisy
goats in order. He gave each lamb to its mother
promptly to suckle. He curdled half of the white milk,

scooping off curds to place them in wickerwork baskets.
Half of the milk he put in its pails to be ready
for drinking himself when he liked, right there at his dinner.

Are You
Pirates?

"Soon as he briskly ended his chores in the cavern   250
he started a fire, he saw us now and he asked us,
'Strangers—who are you? What watery way do you sail from?
Are you traders? Or maybe you recklessly wander
over the sea like pirates, roaming and risking
your lives while bringing harm to others in far lands.'

The God of the
Lowly Stranger

"He spoke that way and all our spirits were broken,
afraid of his heavy voice and oversize body.
Even so I found some words and I answered,
'We sailed from Troy. We're Akhaians, driven by every
sea-wind over the endless reach of the salt sea.   260
Heading for home, we came this way by another
course by chance—or Zeus wanted to plan that.
We claim to be men of Atreus's son Agamemnon:
there's the greatest name right now under the heavens,
such was the city he ravaged, the numbers of people
he killed. We ourselves approach your knees and we
        face you
humbly though, we hope you'll offer us presents
or otherwise treat us kindly: that's lawful for strangers.
Beware of the Gods, great man. We're here and we're
        lowly.
Zeus is the God of guests who cares for the downcast   270
stranger. He goes along with guests in your household.'

Scorn
for the Gods

"I spoke that way but he answered cruelly and swiftly,
'How foolish you are, strange man, or you came from a
        long way,
telling me now to be scared of a God or avoid him.
We Kuklops disdain your Zeus, sporting his big shield,
and all the blissful Gods. We're far better than they are!
I'd never be scared by an angry Zeus into sparing
your life or your friends, unless my spirit commanded.

'Tell me where you moored your well-built ship when you
        came here.
On land nearby or far off? Help me to know this.'   280

A Wily Answer   "He spoke that way to test me. But knowing a good deal
                 I was not fooled. The words I gave him were wily:
           ♦ 'The Earth-Shaker Poseidon broke up my vessel.
                 He threw her on rocks along the coast at your land's end
                 after winds and the God drove her from sea to a headland.
                 These men and I got out from under a steep doom.'

Fast   "I spoke that way, his ruthless heart had no answer,
and Revolting   he stood up fast and lunged at my men with his two hands,
Death   grappled two of them, struck them hard on the dirt floor
                 like puppies and splattered their brains, drenching the
                       cave-sand.   290
                 Then he tore them apart to make them his dinner.
                 He ate like a mountain-fed lion, leaving out nothing,
                 devouring organs and muscles, bones and their marrow.
                 We cried out loudly to Zeus, holding our hands up,
                 watching his brutal work. But our spirits were helpless.

Thinking Twice   "After the Kuklops filled his cavernous belly
                 devouring the men's flesh and drinking his pure milk,
                 he lay and slept in the cave, stretched in the sheep-pen.

                 "Now in my own great heart I planned to approach him
                 closely and draw my sharp sword from its thigh-sheath: 300
                 I'd stab his chest, my hand probing his midriff
                 to grasp the liver. But no: some other Spirit
                 stopped me. The rest of us too would go to a steep doom
                 since no one's hands could move away the gigantic
                 stone—the cave's high door—where the Kuklops had
                       placed it.
                 So now we lay and moaned there, waiting for bright Dawn.

Two More   "When newborn Dawn came on with her rose-fingered
Killings   daylight,
                 the Kuklops built a fire. Milking all of the handsome
                 sheep and goats in order, he gave each lamb to its mother
                 to suckle. But after he briskly ended his work there   310
                 again he clutched two men and made them his breakfast.
                 Done with that meal, ready to herd fat sheep from the
                       cavern,
                 he lifted the huge door-stone with ease and replaced it
                 the way a man might simply cover a quiver.

The Kuklops whistled loudly, guiding his fattened
flocks to mountain country. He left me brooding on evil,
taking revenge—if Athene would give me that honor.

A Heated and   "This was the best plan that came to my mind now.
Pointed Shaft   The Kuklops had lain a large club by the sheepfold,
a length of green olive-wood, left there to dry out   320
and take up later. We checked it ourselves and we figured
the club was large as the mast on a black vessel of twenty
oars, a wide-beam freighter crossing the vast sea.
That's how long and broad it looked in our own eyes.
I went up close to it now and cut off a six-foot
length. I gave it to war-friends and told them to scrape it
and make it smooth. I approached and sharpened the end-
      point
myself then took it at once to harden in bright fire.
At length we hid it well under a dung-heap—
the cave was grossly piled with plenty of droppings.   330

The Pick of   "I told them to cast lots: which of my war-friends
Chance   would dare to raise that shaft, standing beside me,
and stab the Kuklops' eye, slumbering sweetly?
The lots fell on those whom I myself would have chosen,
four good men. I counted myself the fifth one among them.

Two More   "He came at dusk, herding his fine-fleeced sheep-flock.
Killings   He promptly drove his fattened flocks in the wide cave—
all of them—not one sheep was left in the wide yard.
Was that his own idea? Or maybe a God's will.
Then he raised the massive door-stone and set it.   340
He sat and milked all the ewes and noisy
goats in order. He gave each lamb to its mother.

"Soon as he briskly ended his chores in the cavern
again he clutched two men to make them his dinner.

An Offer of   "I spoke to the Kuklops now, standing beside him,
Wine   my hands lifting an ivy-wood bowl of the dark wine.
'Kuklops! Drink my wine now that you've eaten
my men's flesh. See what a fine vintage was hiding
aboard our ship. I brought you this gift and was hoping
you'd pity and send us home. But you're unbearably savage.   350

Ruthless creature, why should anyone come here,
all the men not born, after your lawless actions?'

Drunk on   ◆"Soon as I'd spoken he took the wine and gulped it
Wine   down with wonder and pleasure. He asked for another.
'Give me some more and be glad to. Tell me your own name
quickly now: I'll give you a guest's gift that will please you.
The Kuklops' grain-rich soil presents us with clusters
of large wine-grapes—grown with rain from the Day-God—
but yours is truly a flow of ambrosia and nectar.'

The Name of "I gave him more of the glowing wine when he'd spoken.   360
No-One   Three times I brought it: three times he foolishly downed it.
Then as the wine went round in the brain of the Kuklops,
I gave him a kindly answer at last to his question.
'Kuklops, you asked for my well-known name and I'll
       tell you.
But give me the stranger's present, just as you promised.
    ◆ My name is No-one: No-one's the name they have
       called me—
my Mother and Father, and all the rest of my war-friends.'

Grisly Burps "I spoke that way but he answered cruelly and swiftly,
'I'll dine on No-one myself the last of his war-friends,
the rest go first—there's a gift for a stranger!'   370

"He paused and swayed, plopped and lay on his backside,
thickset neck askew. The master of all men,
Sleep took hold of him. Wine came from his gullet
and bits of men dribbling. He drooled like a wine-drunk.

The Blinding "Now I drove that shaft into plenty of ashes
until it was hot. I emboldened all of my war-friends
with strong words: they must not cower or hold back.
Soon as the olive-wood point was going to catch fire—
green as it was, the red glow was alarming—
I moved it away from the fire. War-friends were standing   380
around me, some Power breathed great daring in each one.
Grasping the olive-wood shaft, now with a sharp tip,
we lanced that eye. Pressing hard from above it,
    ◆ I turned it around myself like a man with a drill-bit

boring through deck while helpers below him are holding
the strap at both its ends, the drill steadily twisting.
We held the fire-tipped shaft in his eye in the same way,
turning it. Blood gathered and circled the hot tip.
We burned and singed all of the eyelid and eyebrow,
we boiled the pupil, swelled and crackled the eye-roots.   390
The way a worker in bronze plunges a big ax
or adze into cold water, making it loudly
hiss and harden—that's how iron gets stronger—
the eye sizzled around our olive-wood weapon.

A Maddened   "He screamed outrageously now, the cave-stone echoed
Call for Help   around us,
we scattered in dread as the Kuklops pulled at the hot shaft.
It came from his eye soaked with plenty of warm blood.
His hand flung it away from him. Smarting and maddened,
he called out wildly for Kuklops, those who were living
around him in caves on windy crags of the mountains.   400

"They heard his cry, they hurried from this way and that way.
Standing around his cave they asked him what ailed him.
'How are you hurt, Poluphemos, yelling so loudly
throughout the ambrosial night and waking us all up?'
'What man could take your livestock without your approval?'
'Who could kill you relying on cunning or great strength?'

No-One's   "From out of the cave Poluphemos answered them strongly:
Harm   'My friends, No-one kills me through cunning, hardly by
                    great strength!'

"They answered him now and the words had a feathery
                    swiftness,
'If no one really harms you, being alone there,   410
you cannot avoid sickness sent by the great Zeus.
So you should pray to your Lord and Father Poseidon.'

But How   "They spoke that way and were gone. I laughed in my own
to Get out of   heart,
the Cave?
how my name had fooled him—my plan had been faultless.
But now the Kuklops, moaning and writhing in great pain,
groped with his hands and took the stone from the entrance.

He sat there broadly himself, stretching his hands out
to seize anyone walking outside with his fat sheep.
Somehow his brain was hoping *I* was that foolish!
I thought through other plans: which was the best one?   420
If only I'd find out, freeing myself and my war-friends
from death! I wove them all, measures and good tricks.
Our lives were at stake. A monstrous evil was close by.

Help from the Sheep "At last one plan struck my mind as the best one.
Rams in the cave had heavy wool and were well fed,
large and handsome, with darkly violet fleeces.
I lashed them together quietly, using some willow
withes the huge and lawless Kuklops had slept on.
I grouped them in threes, a man to be borne by the middle,
a ram on either side guarding each war-friend: 430
three sheep for every man. I would be riding
a ram myself, by far the best of the whole flock.
Clutching his back and bunched under his wooly
belly, I'd stay there tightly clasping his wondrous
fleece and twisting my hands in. My spirits would bear up.
So we sighed and moaned there, waiting for bright Dawn.

One Dear Ram "When newborn Dawn came on with her rose-fingered
     daylight,
shortly the males of the flock were trotting to pasture.
The noisy females with swollen udders were not yet
milked in the pens—their master was tired and wounded.   440
In pain he felt along the backs of the whole flock
standing before him, foolishly failing to guess that
a man was tied beneath each ram at the breast-fleece.
My ram, the last of the flock, now moved to the outdoors
loaded with fleece, my weight, and all of my wild thoughts.
Burly Poluphemos asked him, checking his backside,
♦ 'My dear ram: why are you leaving the cavern
last? The herd has never left you behind here:
you're always the first by far to be cropping the tender
grasses and first to arrive at the stream with your long
     strides,   450
first to show your desire to return to the sheepfold
at dusk. Now you're last of all. I think you are mourning
your master's eye. An evil man with his wretched

war-friends blinded me. He'd quelled my brain with a
    strong wine.
No-one! He's not yet fled, I think, from his death here.
If only my ram could feel and speak like a Kuklops—
say where the man scurried away from my anger—
then I could spatter his brains out this way and that way,
beating the ground through the cave, bringing my own heart
rest from the hurt that no-good No-one has brought me.'   460

Safe and Free   "He said so much, then sent the ram through the entrance.
Having gone from the cave and the stockyard a short ways,
I first got loose from the ram then loosened my war-friends.
Quickly we drove off sheep, fat ones with thin legs,
often turning around, till we came to the hollow
ship. What a welcome sight to our friends—we had safely
run from death! But they cried and moaned for the others.
I stopped their crying. Nodding my brow in the right way,
I told each man to toss up a number of fine-wooled
sheep on deck, then head out to sea in a hurry.   470
They clambered swiftly aboard, they sat at the benches
in order and pulled at the oars, splashing the gray sea.

Taunting   "But far away as a man's bellow will carry,
the Giant   I shouted back at the Kuklops, taunting him loudly.
'Kuklops! The man whose crew you wanted to gulp down
brutally there in your hollow cave was no weakling.
Surely your evil acts would soon overtake you,
ruthless beast, for devouring guests in your own house.
Zeus and the rest of the Gods are making you pay now.'

A Great Splash   "I spoke that way and his heart swelled with more anger.   480
Close Astern   He broke off the top of a bulging hill and he threw it,
splashing astern as we backed out the dark-prowed
ship and almost grazing the end of our steer-oar.
That mass unleashed an undersea force when it went down,
a rising swell of water that carried us backward
fast to the shore and drove us right on the beach there!
I took our longest pole in hand and I punted
the ship away, rousing and telling my war-friends
while nodding my head, 'Get out from under disaster,
pull on those oars!' They rowed, moving us forward.   490

Worse   "But having fared out twice as far on the water,
Taunting   I called to the Kuklops again. Crewmen around me
             scolded gently, this one or that one upbraiding,
             'Ruthless man: why make a wild one so angry?'
             'Just now he hurled a crag to the sea and it drove us
             back to the beach in our ship.' 'We thought we would die
                 there!'
             'If anyone spoke or made one sound he could hear well,
             he might have thrown a jagged boulder and smashed us,
             crumbling our decks and heads.' 'His throwing is that
                 strong.'

             "Their words could scarcely check my great-hearted spirit.   500
         •   Again I answered the Kuklops, angrily shouting,
             'Kuklops! If anyone bound for the death-world should
                 come by,
             asking about the shameful loss of your eyesight,
             tell them Odysseus blinded you, looter of cities,
             the son of Laertes, his home on Ithaka Island.'

A Prophecy   "I spoke that way and the Kuklops moaned as he answered,
Fulfilled   'Look at this—how a long-past prophecy finds me.
             A soothsayer lived here once, a good and a great man,
         •   Telemos, Eurumos's son, ranked first as a prophet.
             Growing old and foreseeing things for the Kuklops,   510
             he told me all this pain would fall on me one day:
             I'd surely lose my sight at the hands of Odysseus.
             So every day I looked for a handsome and big man
             approaching our shore, plainly vested in great strength.
             Now it's a no-good runt. A man with no power
             put out my eye when he dulled my brain with a strong wine.

A Son of   'Come here, Odysseus! Let me offer you house-guest
Poseidon   presents and urge the well-known Earth-Shaker to help you
             home. For I am his son, he claims to be Father:
             he'll mend me himself if he likes. No one beside him   520
             can do it, no death-bound man or God in his high bliss.'

             "He spoke that way but now I answered by saying,
             'If only I could make you the loser of life too,
             send your soul down to the household of Aides!
             Not even the Earth-Shaker will cure you of blindness.'

The Curse   "Soon as I'd spoken he called on lordly Poseidon,
both hands reaching for heaven, far as the stars are:
'Dark-haired Earth-Upholder, hear me, Poseidon!
If I am truly your son—you claim to be Father—
make Odysseus, looter of cities, the son of Laertes   530
and ruler of Ithaka Island, fail to arrive home.
Yet if his lot is to go there, gaze on his loved ones
and walk in a well-built house in the land of his fathers,
let him be late and poor, losing all of his war-friends,
shipped by strangers and finding harm in his own house.'

A Still Greater   "He prayed that way and the dark-haired God
Splash   understood him.
Again he raised a rock-mass far outweighing the last one,
he whirled and threw it, leaning forward with great
       strength.
It crashed in the water behind our ship with its dark prow
too close—it almost grazed the end of our steer-oar.   540
That mass freed up undersea force when it went down,
waves carried us forward and drove us to dry land:
we came to the island again where all of our well-built
ships were gathered and waiting. Around them our war-
       friends
sat in mourning, waiting and steadily weeping.

The Death of   "Arriving there, beaching our ship on the dry sand,
the Best Ram   we walked from the vessel ourselves to the shore of the
       salt sea.
We took the Kuklops' livestock out of the hollow
ship and shared them: no one lacked what was due him.
War-friends, strong-greaved men, gave me the best ram   550
after we shared the flock. Right there on the beach-sand
I killed it, burning the thighs for Zeus, Ruler of all men,
the cloud-dark son of Kronos. But victims would hardly
touch that God. He'd make plots for all of my well-planked
ships to be wrecked, along with the men I relied on.

"For now we ate and drank all day until sundown,
feasting on honey-sweet wine and plenty of mutton.
Then as the sun went down and night was arriving,
we lay and slept right there on the shore of the salt sea.

A Mournful   "When newborn Dawn came on with her rose-fingered   560
Departure   daylight,
            I rallied all of the men myself and I told them
            to hurry aboard themselves and loosen the stern-lines.
            They promptly clambered aboard, sat at the benches
            in order and pulled at the oars, splashing the gray sea.

            "We sailed on farther now, our hearts in mourning,
            glad to be saved from death but losing our own men."

BOOK 10

Mad Winds, Laistrugonians,
and an Enchantress

A Floating Island   "We came to Aiolia Island next. Aiolos lived there,
Hippotes's son: the deathless Gods are his good friends.
The island's floating, walls are entirely around it,
unbreakable bronze, and the smooth-faced cliff is a
     high one.
Twelve children were born to the king of that great hall:
six are sons in their prime, six of them daughters.
   ♦ In time he gave the daughters as wives to his own sons.
They dine each day with their much-loved father and caring
mother as countless foods lie there before them.
Their home has a savor of meat and an echoing courtyard   10
all day long; at night the husbands rest by their honored
wives on corded beds covered with blankets.

A Present of Winds   "We came to that city now and their beautiful household.
Regaled for a whole month, I was asked about each thing—
Troy and the Argive ships and the long way home for
     Akhaians.
I told him all that story myself in good order.

"Then when I asked to be sent back home on the right
     course,
the man did not say no: he arranged for a send-off.
He gave me a sack, the flayed bull had been nine years
old—and he lashed moaning storm-winds inside there!   20
The son of Kronos had made him master of every
wind to rouse or calm the way that he liked it.
Lashing them tight in my hollow ship with a glowing
silver cord, he stopped the smallest breath from escaping.
Then he sent me an airy blowing of Westwind
to carry our ships and crews away. It would not take
place as he planned. Our own folly would doom us.

A View of Home   "We sailed for nine whole days, nighttime and daytime.
Our Fathers' fields came into view on the tenth day—
we came so close we could spot men at the watch-fires!   30
But now I was tired. A honeyed drowsiness came on

135

after I worked the mainsheet for hours. I'd handed it over
to none of my crewmen, the faster to sail to our homeland.

"Then my war-friends traded words with each other,
saying I hauled back home the silver and golden
presents from Aiolos, Hippotes's son with the great heart.
A man might glance at his neighbor, putting it this way:
'Look at this—how he's loved and honored by every
man whatever country or city he goes to!
He's hauling plenty of handsome treasure as booty   40
from Troy but the rest of us, ending the same course,
travel homeward carrying hands full of nothing.
Now he's awarded friendly and gracious presents
from Aiolos. No, let's quickly see what's inside here,
how much gold and silver are stored in the big sack.'

Driven Back   "They spoke that way, the wrong plans of some crewmen
to Aiolia   swayed them, they loosened the sack and all of the freed
                     winds
               rushed out. A fast-building storm seized and carried them
                     seaward
               wailing and far from home. I had been blameless
               but now, wide awake, I heartily wondered   50
         ♦   whether to leap from the ship and die in the salt sea
               or dumbly bear it all and stay with the living.
               I bore it. I stayed right there, hiding and lying
               down in the ship while sea-winds cruelly drove us,
               all of my men moaning, back to Aiolia Island.

    Hated   "There we went ashore and gathered some water.
by the Gods   My men all ate by the race-fast ships in a hurry.
               After we tasted bread and enough of our good wine,
               I took one man as a herald along with a war-friend,
               we walked to Aiolos's well-known house and I found him   60
               enjoying dinner beside his wife and children.
               Going inside, we sat down close to the doorposts,
               right at the threshold. With heartfelt wonder they asked us,
               'How did you sail here, Odysseus? What Power attacked you
               wrongly? We sent you away in friendship to help you
               arrive at your father's house, the place that you hold dear.'

"They spoke that way and my heart hurt as I told them,
'Harmful crewmen spoiled things—they and the cruel
Sleep-God. Make things better, my friends: you have the
    power.'

Cast Out   "I spoke that way, the words I'd used had been gentle,   70
by the King   but they all hushed. The father answered by saying,
    ♦ 'Leave the island and fast, you worst of the living!
    To send you again or care for you now would be lawless:
    you are a man the blessed Gods will certainly hate now.
    Leave us! You came here hated by Gods in the first place.'
    After he'd spoken he forced us out with our deep moans.

A New   "We sailed on farther from there, our hearts in sadness.
but Narrow   My crewmen's spirits tired of the heavy rowing
Harbor   because of that blunder. No more breeze or a send-off!
    We moved along for six daytimes and nighttimes.   80
    We came on the seventh day to the high fortress of Lamos,
    the Laistrugonian town of Telepulos. Men who were herding
    homeward could call to herders away and they'd call back.
    Staying awake a man might double his pay there,
    both a cowherd and shepherd with silver-like sheep-flocks:
    ♦ the paths of night and day were that close to each other.
    We came to the well-known harbor with cliff-face around it,
    a massing of high rock unbroken on both sides.
    Headlands jutted a ways out, facing each other
    but close to the harbor's mouth, making for narrow   90
    entry. All the rest of our ships with their up-curved
    bows moored in the deep harbor close to each other.
    Waves could hardly ever roll in that harbor,
    big or small: a glowing calm was around it.
    Only my own black ship was moored at the land's edge
    a good ways off, her cables tied to a rock-pile.

Another People   "I climbed a stony rise and stood there to look out:
to Learn About   no oxen appeared, no sign of men working a furrow—
    only rising smoke could be seen in the far land.
    So now I sent off scouts to go there and find out   100
    who were the men on that land eating their good bread.
    I chose two war-friends and sent a third as a herald.

A Ghastly
Queen

"Going ashore, they took a smooth cart-path where wagons
had hauled down wood from mountain heights to the city.
Close to the town they met a girl drawing some water,
Antiphates' hearty daughter—Laistrugonian people.
She'd ambled down to a spring, Artakie's graceful
flow of water from there to the city.
They walked up close to the girl and asked her questions:
who was her king, who were the people he ruled here?   110
She promptly showed them the high-roofed house of her
    father.

"But after they walked in the well-known house they
    discovered
his wife was huge as a mountain crag and revolting.

Devoured at
Once

"Swiftly she called her husband now from assembly,
the famous Antiphates, bent on a grisly end for my war-
    friends.
Swiftly he grabbed one man and made him his dinner!

Uneven Battle

"The other two jumped up fast and ran to our moorage.
The king roared through the city, strong Laistrugonians
heard him and came in throngs from this way and that way,
a countless number not like men but like Giants.   120
They hurtled man-crushing boulders down from the
    cliff-tops,
a frightful bedlam soon rose from the moorage
where men were quashed and decks of vessels were
    buckled.
They speared them like fish and carried them home to be
    foul meals.

One Ship
Runs Off

"While they were killing most of my men in that deep port,
I'd taken the sharp sword from my thigh-sheath,
hacked at the dark-prowed ship's cables and cut them,
hurriedly rousing my crew. I told them to lean on
their oars to get us out from under disaster.
They all flung up the salt sea, dreading their own doom,   130
glad to be running away in my ship from those beetling
cliffs. But all the others were lost back there in a body.

The Island of
an Enchantress

"We sailed on farther now, our hearts in mourning,
glad to be saved from death but lacking our good friends.
♦ In time we came to Aiaie, the island where Kirke,
a fair-haired but feared Goddess, lives with her human
way of talking. Her brother is troubling Aietes
and both were born to Helios the Sun-God, the giver
of men's light, by Perse, their mother, fathered by Ocean.
Our vessel quietly made for that rock-littered shoreline.   140
The harbor was good for ships: some God was our pilot.
We disembarked and lay there a day, then another
day and night, our worn-down hearts feeding on anguish.

Far-Off Smoke   "When Dawn in her beautiful braids ended the third night,
I took a spear and a sharp sword in my right hand.
I briskly climbed away from the ship to a high place,
hoping to see men working or hear them talking.
I climbed a stony rise and stood there to look off.
I scanned the ground with its broad pathways and spotted
smoke from Kirke's hall through dense forest and thicket.   150
Now in my mind and heart I pondered the matter,
whether to go and check this bright smoke I had spotted.
But while I pondered first it struck me as better
to go to the race-fast ship on the shore of the salt sea
and help my crew to a meal. Then we could find out.

A Great Stag   "Not far from the ship with its up-curved bow I was walking
along when a God took pity—I was alone there—
sending a huge, high-antlered stag in my own path.
The deer had ambled down just now from a woodland
glade to drink at a river: the sun was a heavy   160
weight as he walked. I struck him hard at the backbone's
midpoint, the brazen spear went straight through his body,
he moaned and fell in the dust. When the spirit had
     flown off
I stepped on him, pulling the bronze spear from his back-
     wound.
I laid the weapon down on the ground and I pulled up
shoots with my own hands, plenty of willow and
     brushwood.
Making a cord about six feet long with a good twist,
I lashed the hooves together—the stag had been fearsome—

and walked on back to the ship, hanging the torso
around my neck, the spear as a prop. One hand and my
    shoulder   170
could not carry the weight: the beast was too heavy.

A Good Meal "I threw it down by the ship and prodded my war-friends,
and a
Good Sleep   walking around to each and telling him softly,
'My friends, we won't go down, whatever our sad state,
not to Aides' house before our death-day's arrival.
Come on now, long as there's food and drink at the fast ship,
let's look to a meal and not be wasted by hunger.'

"I spoke that way and they took to my words in a hurry,
uncovering tear-filled eyes on the shore of that restless
sea to gaze at the stag: the beast was a great one.   180
After the joy of seeing it all with their own eyes,
they washed their hands and made us a wonderful dinner.

"We ate and drank the rest of that day until sundown,
feasting on honey-sweet wine and plenty of deer-meat.
Then as the sun went down and night was arriving,
we lay and slept right there on the shore of the salt sea.

Hard New "When newborn Dawn came on with her rose-fingered
Orders   daylight,
I gathered all of the men myself and I told them,
'My hard-suffering war-friends, hear what I say now.
How can we know, my friends, where Dusk or the Dawn is?   190
Where does Helios rise, the bringer of men's light,
where does he go under ground? Ponder it fast then:
where does a plan remain? I think there is no plan.
I climbed to the top of a rock-strewn hill for a good view
of all the island, the wreaths of endless water around it.
The land itself lies low and I saw with my own eyes
smoke in the center through dense forest and thicket.'

The Unlucky "I spoke that way but the spirits were breaking inside them
Lot   recalling Antiphates, Laistrugonian war-work,
the crimes of a monster-hearted, man-eating Kuklops.   200
They cried aloud, their eyes running with big tears.
But nothing came of all their mourning and wailing.
I counted them out myself, all of my strong-greaved

men into two groups. I joined then both to a leader:
I led one group and godlike Eurulokhos the other.
Promptly we shook our lots in a helmet of bright bronze.
The lot of great-hearted Eurulokhos fell out.
So off he went with twenty-two of my war-friends,
all in tears. They left us mourning behind them.

Lions and   "They found the home of Kirke soon in a hollow: 210
Wolves   shining stone, raised quite high, with a broad view.
     ♦ Mountain wolves and lions surrounded the building,
       all of them charmed by Kirke—she'd given them bad drugs.
       They made no charge at my men but rather they stood up
       tall and fawned around them, swishing their long tails.
       Dogs will fawn that way for a homecoming master,
       always bringing them scraps from a feast to delight them.
       The hard-clawed wolves and lions fawned in the same way
       around my men, who eyed the beasts and were frightened.

Called inside   "They stopped at the outer gate of the Goddess with fair hair,   220
by the Goddess   hearing inside the beautiful singing of Kirke.
       She moved at a grand loom that lasted forever
       doing her Goddess's work, a glowing and fine weave.
       Polites began to say, a leader of good men,
       the man I trusted and cared for most of my comrades:
     ♦ 'My friends, someone is moving inside at a great loom.
       What beautiful song—the floors are echoing music!
       A Goddess maybe? a woman? Let's call to her quickly.'
       Soon as he'd spoken the others called to her loudly.
       The Goddess came out promptly, opened her bright doors   230
       and called them inside. They all unknowingly followed.
       Only Eurulokhos held back, sensing a trap there.

Men into Pigs   "She led them inside to easeful chairs and they sat down.
       She mixed them a cheese and barley meal with her yellow
       honey and Pramneian wine. But she added a harmful
       drug to their food to make them wholly forget home.
       After she gave that drug and they downed it, the Goddess
       struck them fast with her rod. She shut them all in a pigsty
       then as they grew snouts and grunts, the bristles and bodies
       of pigs. Their minds were just as before, they had not
            changed;   240
       but penned in there they squealed when Kirke tossed them

acorns and hazelnuts, hard fruits of the cornel
to crunch—good feed for pigs that wallow in mud-beds.

A Story
of Shock and
Witchery

"Eurulokhos hurried away to our swarthy and race-fast
ship to tell us the news—the men's lot was revolting.
But nothing came out. Try as he might he could not speak,
his eyes flowing with tears, the pain overwhelming,
all his heart and mind bent on that sorrow.
Amazed at the man, we kept on asking him questions
till finally he told us how our war-friends were lost there: 250
'We went through the woods as you told us, shining
          Odysseus.
We found a beautiful, built-up home in a glade there,
shining stone, raised quite high, with a broad view.
Someone sang inside and moved at a great loom,
maybe a woman or Goddess. We called to her loudly,
the lady came out promptly, she opened her bright doors
and called them inside. They all unknowingly followed.
But I held back myself, sensing a trap there.

'They all vanished together. None of them came out
later, although I stayed and watched for a long time.'   260

Don't Take Me
Back There

"Soon as he'd spoken I threw a sword over my shoulder,
the long bronze one with silver knobs. My bow was
          about me;
I ordered him now to take me back by the same trail.
But clasping my knees with both his hands he implored me
as though in mourning, the words with a feathery swiftness,
'Zeus-fed man, don't take me unwillingly, leave me,
because I know you'll never be guiding your war-friends
back or return yourself. No, with these others
let's run fast! An evil day can still be avoided."

Help
from a God

"But after he spoke that way I answered by saying,   270
'Eurulokhos, stay in this place of course if you want to,
dining and drinking close to the hollow and black ship.
But I'll be going. What I feel is a strong need.'
Having spoken I left the ship at the salt sea.

"In time as I passed through the awe-filled Goddess's hollow
approaching Kirke, skilled with drugs in her great house,

the God of the Golden Wand suddenly faced me—
Hermes. Not far from the house, resembling a young man
with wisps of a beard, he looked quite graceful and youthful.
He took my hand, called me by name and he asked me,   280
'Where are you now, wretched man, alone on this hillside
without your knowing the place? Your war-friends in Kirke's
house were changed into pigs and locked in her pigsty.
Now have you come to free them? I say you will never
go home yourself. You'll stay right there with the others.
Come though, I'll keep you from harm myself and I'll
      save you.
Take this helpful plant when you enter Kirke's
house for its power will guard and save you from evil
days. I'll tell you all the deadly cunning of Kirke.
She'll make you a mix and toss her drugs in your dinner.   290
Yet she cannot bewitch you, not if I give you
 ◆ this helpful plant and stop her. I'll speak about each point.

Don't Say No   'When Kirke strikes you there using her long rod,
to the Goddess   take out the sharp sword by your thigh and attack her—
charge the Goddess as though in a rage to destroy her!
You'll shock and scare her; she'll ask you to lie alongside her.
You shall not say no to the bed of a Goddess.
But ask her to free your men and make you a guest there.
Command her to swear the greatest oath by the blessed
Gods that she won't keep plotting evil and anguish,   300
not to harm or unman you soon as you're naked.'

Molu   "The Splendor of Argos, having spoken, gave me a
                  plant-drug
pulled from the soil. The God showed me its good pith:
although the roots were black its blossom was milklike.
Molu the Gods call it, hard for a death-bound
man to uproot but the all-powerful Gods can.

A Tense Heart   "Hermes left me now for the heights of Olumpos,
away from the forested island. I went to Kirke's
house and my heart mulled so much as I walked there.
I soon stood at the gates of the Goddess with lovely   310
hair and called out. Kirke, hearing my loud voice,
came out promptly. The shining doorway was opened:
she called me inside. I followed, my heart in a tense state.

She led me along to a chair studded with silver,
finely crafted; under the chair was a footstool.
She made me a mix in a golden goblet to drink down,
putting a drug in, her heart set upon evil.
She gave me the cup. When I drank and it failed to
    bewitch me,
she struck me hard with her long rod and she told me,
'Go to the sty now—wallow with all of your men there!'   320

Shock and a   "She stopped and I drew the sharp sword from its thigh-
Plea for Sex   sheath.
I charged the Goddess as though I meant to destroy her!
She yelled wildly and stooped to clasp me at both knees,
wailing and begging, the words with a feathery swiftness,
'What man are you, where is your city, who are your parents?
I'm seized by amazement: you drank my drug and were not
    charmed.
No one, no other man, has taken this drug and withstood it
after he sent it past the wall of his front teeth.
Now this mind, your chest, are not to be spellbound.
Are you resourceful Odysseus? The Splendor of Argos,   330
God of the Golden Wand, often has told me
you'd come from Troy in your ship, a black one with great
    speed.
Come on then, slide your sword in its sheath. Both of us
    quickly
should go to my bed together! Loving each other
in bed will bring us closer to trusting each other.'

When the Man   "But after she spoke that way I answered by asking,
Is Naked   'Goddess Kirke, how can you ask me for kindness
after you changed my men into pigs in your great hall?
Clasping me here, plotting tricks when you ask me
to go to your room, to lie in your bed and be loving,   340
how would you harm or unman me there when I'm naked?
I'd never desire to go upstairs to your own bed,
unless you agreed, Goddess, to swear me a great oath:
no new plots, no other planning to harm me.'

"I spoke that way and she promptly foreswore as I'd asked her.
After she'd sworn, when all the oaths were behind her,
I went myself to the beautiful bedroom of Kirke.

Nymphs in the
Great Hall "Handmaids meanwhile worked hard in the great hall.
   The four female helpers who lived in the household
   ♦ were born of surrounding groves, woodlands and fountains;   350
   of holy rivers flowing down to the salt sea.
   One maid tossed her covers, gorgeously purple,
   over the chairs, then set down smooth cloths
      underneath them.
   A second helper drew up tables of silver
   close to the chairs and golden baskets were placed there.
   A third one blended sweet, mind-of-the-honey
   wine in a silver bowl, then set out goblets of pure gold.
   The fourth maid brought in water and started a big fire
   under a giant cauldron, heating the water.

Joys of the
Bath "Soon as water boiled in the cauldron of bright bronze,   360
   Kirke sat me in a tub and poured from the bulky
   cauldron over my head and shoulders, warm as I wanted,
   until she'd taken the spirit-devouring stress from my body.
   After I'd bathed she anointed me richly with fine oil,
   then tossed a beautiful mantle and tunic around me.
   She sat me down on a chair studded with silver
   and finely crafted; under the chair was a footstool.
   A maid brought in water and poured from a lovely
   pitcher of gold. I washed my hands in the silver
   basin. She set out a polished table before me.   370
   An honored housekeeper brought me bread and arranged it.
   She laid out plenty of food, gracious and giving,
   and urged me to eat. But it brought no joy to my great heart.
   My mind was elsewhere—I sat with inklings of evil.

Still Alone at
Dinner "When Kirke noticed the way I sat without putting
   a hand to her food, what strong sadness possessed me,
   she came up close and her words had a feathery swiftness:
   'Odysseus, why do you sit here resembling a dumb man,
   taking no food or drink and gnawing your spirits?
   Maybe you sense more tricks. But those you have no need   380
   to fear: I foreswore guile when I made you a strong oath.'

   "After she spoke that way I answered by asking,
   'Ah but Kirke, where is the man in his right mind
   who'd take your food or drink this wine at your table
   before he freed and gazed at his men with his own eyes?

So if you want me to eat and drink and you mean it,
release them. Let me see my trusted friends with my
    own eyes.'

Pigs into Men   "Soon as I'd spoken Kirke went out of the great hall,
rod in hand. She opened the gates of the pigsty
and drove them out. They looked like boars about nine years   390
old standing before her. Moving among them,
the lady anointed every beast with another
drug. The bristles left their bodies: Kirke had made them
grow there before, bewitching the men with a curse-like
drug but now they were human and somehow younger,
much more handsome, taller and stronger to look at.
As every man clasped my hands and recalled me,
a keen sorrow fell on them all and a frightful
wailing filled the house. Even the Goddess felt pity.

Calves and   "The bright one, Kirke, stood nearby and she told me,   400
Their Mothers   'Zeus-fed son of Laertes, my wily Odysseus!
Go to your race-fast ship on the shore of the salt sea
now and haul her out, first, onto dry land.
Store your goods and tackle, next, in the caves there.
Then come back, guiding the men you rely on.'

"Those were her words. My heart felt proud and I said yes.
I went to the race-fast ship on the shore of the salt sea
and close to the nimble vessel I found the men I relied on,
all of them wretched, moaning and shedding their big tears.
• The way young calves come frisking from stock-pens and
    circling   410
clustered cows returning to pens when they're done with
grazing—all of the jumpy calves are held in the farmyards
no longer but making a din they're crowding and circling
their mothers—my men, seeing me now with their
    own eyes,
thronged me and wept. It seemed in their hearts they had
    gone back
home in fact to the city and land of their fathers,
to rugged Ithaka's ground that bore them and nursed them.
They spoke as they wept and the words had a feathery
    swiftness,
'Nourished by Zeus!' 'We feel such joy when you come back,

as though we stepped on Ithakan lands of our Fathers.'   420
'Come on though, tell us the fate of our other war-friends.'

One Man's   "After they'd spoken I answered, telling them softly,
Fear   'The ship comes first: let's drag her onto the beach-sand.
            Let's store our tackle and all our goods in the caves here.
            Then all of you hurry and follow me closely together
            to see your friends in the sacred household of Kirke
            dining and drinking. The food will hold out forever.'

            "I spoke that way and they quickly followed my orders.
            Only Eurulokhos held back all of my war-friends,
            telling them outright, the words with a feathery swiftness,   430
            'Where are we going, you wretched men, with your longing
            for evil in Kirke's hall? If you go the lady
            will change you all into wolves, lions or wild boars
            to guard her overgrown household—yes, and you'll have to.
            That's how the Kuklops acted when some of our war-friends
            went to his sheep-yard. Brash Odysseus led them.
            They lost their lives through one man's reckless abandon.'

An Urge to Kill   "He spoke that way and I mulled it hard in my own mind
            whether to take my sharp-edged sword from its thigh-sheath
            and cut off his head, letting it plop on the ground there   440
            for all his closeness through marriage. The rest of my war-
                    friends
            held me back though, gently saying on all sides,
            'You're nourished by Zeus: leave him.' 'Maybe you'd
                    like him
            to stay right here at the shore, guarding our vessel.'
            'But take us all to the sacred household of Kirke!'

            "After their words we left the ship and the salt sea.
            Eurulokhos too would not be left by the hollow
            ship: he joined us, fearing the worst of my anger.

A Tearful and   "Kirke meanwhile had bathed the rest of my war-friends
Noisy Reunion   at home with care. She'd spread rich oil on their bodies   450
            and tossed woolen mantles and tunics around them.
            We found them all dining well in her great hall.
            But soon as they saw us, face to face with each other,
            they wailed and cried, the household wailing around them.

Spirits   "The shining Goddess came up close to me saying,
Regained   'Son of Laertes, nourished by Zeus, my wily Odysseus,
           stop this rise of sorrow now. All of the anguish
           you felt on the fish-filled sea is a thing I have known well—
           all the harm on land too from those who opposed you.
           Come on then, drink my wine and relish the food here   460
           until you've seized that spirit again in your strong chest,
           that strength when you first sailed from lands of your
                   fathers,
           rock-strewn Ithaka. Now you're wasted and listless,
           always remembering hard journeys, lacking the spirit
           of joy in your heart because you suffered so often.'

A Year with the   "She spoke that way, our hearts were proud but we said yes.
   Enchantress   We stayed there many days; we ended a whole year.
           We sat and enjoyed her wine with plenty of good meat.

Longing for   "But after a year had passed, the changing of seasons
      Home   and fading months, our long days at an end there,   470
           my trusted war-friends began to call to me saying,
     ♦ 'You strange power! Remember the land of our Fathers
           now if it's God's plan to save you and take you
           back to your high-roofed house in the land of your fathers.'

           "They spoke that way, my heart was proud but I nodded.
           We sat for a banquet all day long until sundown,
           dining on plenty of meat and drinking the sweet wine.
           Then as the sun went down and night was arriving,
           my men lay down and slept in the shadowy great hall.
           But I went up to the marvelous bedroom of Kirke   480
           and clasped her knees. The Goddess heard what I told her—
           I spoke up well and my words had a feathery swiftness—
           'Ah my Kirke, keep the promise you made me
           to send me home. My heart's anxious to go there
           now and my men's hearts wear me down by wailing
           around me whenever chance has taken you elsewhere.'

       The   "I stopped and the shining Goddess answered me promptly,
Underworld   'Son of Laertes, nourished by Zeus, my wily Odysseus,
     First   don't stay in my home any longer now if you're not free.
           But first you'll travel elsewhere: you need to be going   490

♦ to Aides' household and fearsome Persephoneia's.
You'll speak with Teiresies's ghost, the prophet of Thebes.
A blind seer, the man's mind is unshaken
and Persephoneia grants him knowledge still as a dead man.
Only that man is wise; the rest are a flitting of shadows.'
She spoke that way and the spirit was broken inside me.
I sat on the bed and cried. My heart was unwilling
to go on living, to look at light from the Sun-God.

How to
Reach the
Underworld?

"After I writhed and had my fill of that crying,
I found the words at length and answered by asking,   500
'Ah my Kirke, who's my guide on this journey?
No one's ever gone to Aides' house in a black ship.'

Many Prayers
and Offerings

"I stopped and the shining Goddess answered me promptly,
'Son of Laertes, nourished by Zeus, my wily Odysseus,
don't worry yourself about a guide for the black ship.
Only stand your mast, spread out the white sail
and sit down: the Northwind's breath will carry you forward.
After your ship has made it across Okeanos
to fruitful shore and the groves of Persephoneia—
a place of tall poplars and seed-dropping willows—   510
♦ you'll beach your ship by the eddies of deep Okeanos.
Go down yourself to the moldy household of Aides.
A branch of the Stux is there. The Kokutos empties
into the Akheron; so do the Puriphlegethon's waters.
A boulder's close to that roaring and joining of rivers.
Go up close to it, war-chief, do as I tell you:
dig a hole, a two-foot square, this way and that way;
♦ pour libations around it for all of the dead ones,
first with honey and milk, second with sweet wine
and third with water. Scatter some white barley around it.   520
Pray and vow to the frail heads of the dead there
you'll offer a barren cow, the best of your whole herd,
arriving in Ithaka's hall. You'll build a pyre of your best gifts
and slaughter a ram apart for Teiresies only—
a beast all black, the ablest ram in your whole flock.

Blood
for the Dead

'After you plead and pray to the families of well-known
dead there, offer a ram's blood and a black ewe's.
Make them turn toward Erebos; you should be turning

around to face the river's flow. Plenty of dead souls,
yes, the truly dead, will now be approaching.   530
Strongly hearten your war-friends! Tell them to hurry,
flay and burn the sheep cut down by your ruthless
bronze and sprawled out there. Pray to the Death-Gods,
powerful Aides and fearsome Persephoneia.
Drawing the sharp sword yourself from your thigh-sheath,
sit and allow none of the frail heads of the dead ones
close to the blood before you've heard from Teiresies.
The seer will come to you soon, a lord of his people,
to tell you your course, how wide and far is the right way
home on the fish-filled sea and how you should go there.'   540

Ready to Leave   "She stopped and promptly Dawn arrived on her gold throne.
at Dawn   Kirke put a mantle and tunic around me.
The Nymph herself was dressed in the whitest of long robes,
graceful and finely woven. She'd wrapped a beautiful golden
sash at her waist and tied a veil at her forehead.

"I walked through the house myself and heartened my war-
    friends,
approaching every man and telling him softly,
'No more honeyed sleeping now as you lie here.
Let's go—my honored Kirke's told me our whole plan.'
I spoke that way, their hearts felt proud and they nodded.   550

A Ghost   "Not even from there could I lead my men away safely.
into the   Elpenor, our youngest crewman, never was all that
Underworld   brave in war, not steady or strong in his mind-work.
He'd lain apart from our friends, looking for cool air
on Kirke's well-blessed house. But wine overwhelmed him:
hearing rumbles and calls of men as they moved out
he stood up fast but his muddled brain had forgotten
to go back down by the long ladder he'd climbed by.
He fell from the roof head first, breaking the neck-bone
clear of the spine. His ghost went down into Aides'.   560

Bitter News   "Then as my men were leaving I told them the story.
about   'Maybe you plan on going home to the well-loved
the Journey   land of your fathers. But Kirke's given us one more
course to Aides' house and fearsome Persephoneia's
to speak with the ghost of Teiresies, prophet of Thebes.'

"I spoke that way and the spirits were broken inside them.
They sat right there and wept, pulling their hair out.
But nothing came from all their wailing and whining.

Black Victims   "Approaching the race-fast ship on the shore of the salt sea,
by a Black Ship   we all gave way to sadness, shedding our big tears.   570
Meanwhile Kirke had also gone to the black ship,
tethering there a black ram and a black ewe.
She'd passed us with ease. Who can look with his own eyes
at Gods not wanting our looks while moving that way or
       this way?"

Leaving Kirke "Soon as we came back down to our ship and the salt sea,
first of all we dragged the ship into bright surf,
then we set both mast and sail on the black ship.
We took the sheep on board and finally boarded
ourselves, walking sadly, shedding our big tears.

Letting the "Now a good friend came, moving the dark-prowed
Wind Take Us ship from astern, a fair wind swelling the white sail
◆ and sent by Kirke, a feared Goddess who spoke like a
human
in lovely braids. Securing all our tackle aboard ship
we sat down, helmsman and wind holding our course well. 10
All day long, sail stretched out, we sped through the water.
The sun went down and the seaways were darkened.

A Deadening "We came to an end out there, to deep Okeanos's
Night ◆ flow and the country and town of Kimmerian people,
covered in haze and cloud. The brightening Sun-God
never gazes with shining rays on that people,
not when Helios climbs the star-dotted heavens
or when he turns from the sky once more to the good earth.
Deadening night spreads on those wretched people.
We sailed in there, we beached our vessel and took out 20
the sheep. We walked ourselves by the flow of that Ocean
until we came to the place that Kirke had told of.

Milk, Wine, "There Perimedes joined Eurulokhos holding
and Water for the victims. I drew my sharp sword from its thigh-sheath
the Dead and dug a hole, a two-foot square, this way and that way.
I poured libations around it for all of the dead ones,
first with honey and milk, second with sweet wine
and third with water. I scattered white barley around it.
I prayed and vowed to the frail heads of the dead there:
I'd offer a barren cow, the best of my whole herd, 30
arriving in Ithaka's halls; I'd build a pyre of my best gifts.
I'd slaughter a ram apart for Teiresies only,
a beast all black, the ablest ram in my whole flock.

The Dead Appear "After I prayed and vowed to the families of dead there,
I took the sheep and offered them, slitting their gullets
over the hole. The dark blood ran. Now they assembled,
ghosts from Erebos, those who'd died and gone under:
Nymphlike brides, bachelors, long-suffering old men,
lively girls, their hearts containing the new pain,
thousands pierced by bronze-tipped spears on the War-God's   40
plains and still wearing their blood-matted armor.
They all came thronging around that hole as a sallow
fear took hold of me—cries they made were unearthly.
Then I called to my men, I heartened and told them
to flay and burn the sheep cut down with my ruthless
bronze and sprawled out there. 'Pray to the Death-Gods,'
I told them, 'to strong Aides and fearsome Persephoneia.'
Drawing the sharp sword myself from its thigh-sheath
I sat and allowed none of the frail heads of the dead ones
close to the blood before I heard from Teiresies.   50

Bury Your Dead ◆"The ghost of my war-friend, Elpenor, came to me first off,
not yet buried under the earth with its broad ways.
We'd left his body behind, unmourned and unburied
in Kirke's hall, for another task overwhelmed us.
Now my heart felt pity, I wept when I saw him
and spoke to him shortly, the words with a feathery swiftness:
'Elpenor, how are you under this hazy darkness?
You came here faster on foot than I in my black ship.'

"I spoke that way, he moaned and gave me an answer.
'Son of Laertes, nourished by Zeus, wily Odysseus,   60
some Power harshly doomed me—and endless wine-draughts.
I slept on Kirke's house but thoughtlessly failed to
go back down by the long ladder I'd climbed up.
I fell from the roof head first, breaking my neck-bone
clear of the spine. My soul went down into Aides'.
I beg you now by our friends you left behind who are not here,
your wife, by the father who raised you from childhood,
yes and Telemakhos, left alone in your great hall.
I know when you leave this place, the household of Aides,

your well-built ship will stand on the shore of Aiaie.   70
There and then, my lord, I beg you, remember:
don't sail and leave me behind unmourned and unburied.
Lest I become a curse on you, rankling the high Gods,
burn my corpse and weapons, such as they are now.
Build me a marker, a mound on the shore of the gray sea
recalling a sorry man, so men in the future will know me.
Make that end for me. Plant my oar in the death-mound:
when I was alive I used it to row with my shipmates.'

"After he spoke that way I answered by saying,
'I'll do it, my sorry man. I'll make you a good end.'   80
We sat that way, exchanging words that we hated,
I on one side, holding my sword by the spilled blood,
my war-friend's ghost on the other, saying a good deal.

A Mother's   "Then the ghost of my laid-out Mother approached us,
Ghost   Antikleia, the great-hearted Autolukos's daughter.
I'd left her alive when I sailed to the holy city of Trojans.
I heartily pitied her now, I wept to behold her.
I stopped her, though, for all my sorrow, from stepping
close to the blood before I heard from Teiresies.

The Dead Seer   "The ghost of Teiresies came then, a prophet of Thebes,   90
holding a staff of gold. He knew me and questioned,
'Son of Laertes, nourished by Zeus, wily Odysseus,
wretched man: why did you go from the Sun-God's
brightness to look at the dead, this pleasureless country?
Move away from the hole: spare me your sharp sword
and let me drink that blood. I'll tell you the whole truth.'

No Words   "He stopped and I moved back, sliding the silver-
without   studded sword in its sheath. After the faultless
That Blood prophet drank that dark blood he started by saying,
'You ask for a honeyed return, my shining Odysseus;   100
a God will make it hard. I know that you cannot
avoid the Earth-Trembler who stores that outrage
deep in his heart: you angered him, blinding his own son.

Sacred Herds   'Yet you could make it home, for all the harm you will suffer,
♦ if only you check your spirits and those of your war-friends
after your well-built vessel approaches Thrinakie

Island. Free at last from violet sea-swells,
you'll find cattle grazing with fattening sheep-flocks—
Helios's livestock. He watches everything closely.
If only you leave them unharmed! Minding your way home   110
you might reach Ithaka still, despite the harm you will
    suffer.
Yet if you hurt them I foresee death for your war-friends,
your own ship wrecked and you, though you avoid it,
will come home poor and late with all of your men lost.
You'll find a foreign ship and your house full of trouble:
a crowd of overbearing men will devour your resources,
dote on your godlike wife and offer her bride-gifts.
Yet you'll avenge their brutal ways when you get home,
killing all the suitors there in your great hall,
whether by guile or slashing bronze in the open.   120

The Last Days   'In time you'll go on a journey. Taking a well-made
of a War-Chief   oar you'll reach a land of people who don't know
seaways. No salt savors the food that they eat there.
They know nothing at all about purple-cheeked vessels
and well-made oars that act as the wings of a fast ship.
I'll tell you a sign, quite plain: it cannot escape you.
The time another traveler meets you and tells you
you're holding a winnowing tool on your bright arm,
then you should drive the well-made oar in the ground
    there.
Offer beautiful victims to lordly Poseidon: 130
a ram, a bull and a boar that's mated with females.
Go back home then. Offer hecatombs duly
to deathless Gods who rule broadly in heaven,
each in order. Death will come from the salt sea,
arriving very gently and taking your long life,
glowing and burdened with age. The people around you
will all be blessed. Those are the truths I can tell you.'

No Words   "After he spoke that way I answered by saying,
without   'Teiresies, Gods themselves are the weavers of all that.
the Blood   Come on now, tell me something, answer me truly.   140
I've watched my dead Mother, a spirit beside me
sitting close to the blood. She's quiet and cannot
look at my face, her son's, or speak to me plainly.
Tell me, lord: how can she know I am right here?'

"I spoke that way and he promptly answered by saying,
'Let me place my easeful words in your mind then.
Of all these ghosts, people who've died and gone under,
whoever you let up close to the blood will be truthful.
Those you stop will move back from you once more.'

Alive in a
Dead World

"The ghost of lordly Teiresies left for the household   150
of Aides after he'd spoken and told me the future.
I stayed right there myself. Shortly my Mother
came and drank the dark blood. Promptly she knew me,
she wailed and spoke out, the words with a feathery
        swiftness:
'My child, how are you under this hazy darkness,
being alive? It's hard for the living to watch us,
what with great rivers—their flow is fearsome—between us.
It's mainly Okeanos: no one crosses that water
on foot but only a man with a ship that is well built.
Have you come just now from Troy with your war-friends   160
and ship a long time roaming, never a landfall
on Ithaka, not yet seeing your wife in the great hall?'

The Curse
of Troy

"After she spoke that way I answered by saying,
'Mother, I needed to come down to the household of Aides
to speak with the ghost of Teiresies, prophet of Thebes.
I haven't drawn close to Akhaia or walked on my own land
yet for I go on wandering always with sadness,
right from the start when I joined with bright Agamemnon
to fight with war-chiefs at Troy, well known for its horses.

Questions
about Home

'Come on now, tell me something, answer me truly.   170
What doom brought you down? What death
        overwhelmed you?
A long sickness? Or Artemis, Goddess and Archer,
aiming her gentle arrows in order to kill you?
Tell me about my Father and son whom I left there:
is all my esteem still theirs? Or maybe some other
man has taken hold. Do they say I'll never return home?
Tell me the thoughts and plans of the woman I married,
whether she stays by our child, keeping a safe home,
or whether she's married now to the best of Akhaians.'

"I stopped and my honored Mother answered me promptly: 180
♦ 'Your wife has waited too long. But her spirits have borne up
well in your hall, although she grieves over the always
wasting nights and days there, letting her tears fall.
No one has handsome esteem like yours. Telemakhos
      watches,
holding your land unharmed, dining at well-shared
banquets—those would be right for a judge to be sharing—
they all invite him. Ah, but your father stays in the farmland,
never going to town. No, and his bedding's
without woolen covers and glistening blankets
all through winter: he sleeps with slaves in the farmhouse,   190
close to the fire's ashes, with poor clothes on his body.
When late summer arrives and the teeming of autumn,
he makes a lowly bed where leaves have been falling
here and there on the sloping, wine-yielding vineyard.
He lies there sadly, his heart with a growing and great pain.
He longs for your homecoming. Hard old age is upon him.

'I too died and met my doom in the same way,
not from the sharp-eyed Archer there in our great hall,
aiming her gentle arrows in order to kill me.
No long sickness came on, the kind that will often   200
take the soul from the body, wasting and loathsome.
Instead I longed for you, my shining Odysseus,
your counsel and kindness. That longing stole me from
      sweet life.'

"Those were her words. I wondered, I heartily wished it,
how to embrace my Mother's ghost—she was long dead.
I reached out three times, my heart told me, 'Embrace her';
three times she flitted away from my hands like a shadow
or dream. The pain sharpened now in my own heart,
I spoke to the woman, my words with a feathery swiftness,
'Mother, why don't you stay? I'm longing to hold you.   210
Even in Aides' world, throwing our arms out
to clasp each other, can't we relish a cold grief?
Or are you a phantom sent by high-born Persephoneia
to make me moan and wail still more than before here?'

"I stopped and my honored Mother answered me promptly,
'Ah, my son, you're more luckless than all men.

Persephoneia, the daughter of Zeus, is no trickster.
It's only the way, in truth, of humankind's dying:
flesh and bone no longer held by the sinews,
it's all destroyed in the powerful blaze of the death-fire.   220
Soon as the spirit leaves its body and white bones,
the dreamlike soul is flying away and is quite gone.

'So hurry and long for Daylight! Take what you learn here,
 ♦ all of it, back to your wife and tell her in good time.'

The Long Line   "We spoke that way with each other. Women had come close
of Women   meanwhile, sent by the high-born Persephoneia:
all those ghosts had been daughters or wives of the
     best men.
They gathered around the dark blood, crowding together.
I pondered myself the ways of questioning each one
and shortly it came to my mind which plan was the best one.   230
Drawing the keen-edged sword from next to my strong
     thigh,
I stopped them from drinking the dark blood all at the
     same time.
Then each ghost came on in order revealing
her own family and birth. I questioned all of them closely.

A Woman ♦"The first one I saw was Turo. Beautifully fathered—
Seized   she claimed to be born to Salmoneus, faultless and
by Poseidon   handsome.
She told me she'd married Kretheus, Aiolos's man-child.
In time she loved a river, the God Enipeus:
of all the rivers on earth his flow was the fairest.
She often called on the beautiful flow of that river.   240
Then the Earth Upholder and Shaker took on its likeness,
he laid her down by the mouth of the eddying river,
standing a violet wave around them high as a hillside,
arching over and hiding the God and the death-bound
woman. He loosened her belt. He sprinkled a light sleep.

"After the God was done with his labor of loving,
he took her hand, called her by name and he told her,
'Be glad you loved me, woman. When seasons have come
     round

you'll bear two wonderful boys: the beds of undying
Gods are not fruitless. Care for our children and raise them.   250
For now go back to your house and don't say a word there.
I am in fact the Earth Shaker Poseidon.'

Her God's   "He spoke that way then entered the billowing water.
and Her Man's   With child, she bore in time Pelies and Neleus.
  Children   Both became powerful squires of the great God
              Zeus. Pelies' wealth was in sheep, his town Iaolkos,
              wide for dancing; Neleus lived in deep-sanded Pulos.
              She also bore Kretheus sons, this queen among women:
              Aison, Pheres and Amuthaon, chariot fighters.

Famous   ♦"I saw Antiope next, the child of Asopos.   260
Mothers and   She actually claimed she'd slept in the arms of the
Daughters   great Zeus.
              In time she bore two sons, Amphion and Zethos.
              They were the first to build up Thebes with seven
              gates, with walls and towers. They never could live well
              without such walls in Thebes, whatever their own strength.

              ♦"Then I saw Alkmene, the wife of Amphitruon.
              She bore the brave one, Herakles—heart like a lion's—
              after she made love in the arms of the great Zeus.

              ♦"Megare came, the daughter of highly spirited Kreion.
              She married Amphitruon's son whose strength was
                  untiring.   270

Mother and ♦"I saw the mother of Oidipus now. Epikaste was lovely
Son in Love   but did an outrageous thing, not knowing beforehand:
              she married her son. He'd murdered his father; he married
              his mother. The Gods made all this known among people.
              In well-loved Thebes the son would agonize greatly,
              ruling Kadmeians. The Gods' ways can be deadly,
              his mother went down to the Gate-Closer, powerful Aides,
              after hanging a noose high from her ceiling.
              Taken with grief, she left her husband with plenty
              of anguish to come—all that a mother's Avengers can
                  bring on.   280

Khloris,   "I saw Khloris in all her beauty. Finding her lovely,
Pero, and   Neleus married her, giving her numberless bride-gifts.
the Prophet
Melampous   The youngest daughter of Amphion, Iasos's good son—
             strong in Orkhomenos once, ruling Minuans—
             she reigned in Pulos and bore outstanding children,
             brash Periklumenos, Khromios, Nestor of Pulos.
        ♦ She bore Pero, a strong daughter and marvel to all men,
             courted by every neighbor. Neleus gave her
             to no one, though, unless he could drive from Phulake
             the curl-horned, broad-browed cattle of forceful Iphiklos.   290
             What hard work! Only a faultless prophet would try it—
             Melampous. But God's heavy portion constrained him:
             hard bindings of country farmhands would check him.
             Yet when days and months came to an ending,
             the year rolling around and seasons returning,
             at last the strong one, Iphiklos, loosened the bindings.
             All the omens were spelled out. Zeus's plan was
                 accomplished.

Two Sons,   ♦"I saw Lede as well, Tundareos' woman.
Alive and   She bore him two good sons with their strong hearts:
   Dead
             Kastor, a horse tamer; Poludeukes, a boxer.   300
             The grain-yielding earth holds them alive still!
             Even under the ground they're honored by great Zeus,
             one day fully alive and the other one quite dead.
             Thus they have earned esteem resembling the great Gods'.

Two Gigantic "Next I saw Aloeus's wife, Iphimedeia.
Sons Killed   She actually claimed she'd made love with Poseidon
in Their Youth
               and bore two sons. But the two were born to a brief life.
             Otos, a godlike man, and the famed Ephialtes,
             raised on the soil's rich grain: these two were the tallest
        ♦ by far and the handsomest after well-known Orion.   310
             Nine arm-lengths across already when nine years
             old, they then grew higher than nine fathoms of water!
             In time they even threatened the Gods on Olumpos,
             raising an uproar there and waging a mad war.
             To scale that heaven they planned to pile on Olumpos
             all Mount Ossa—and forested Pelion on Ossa!
             They might have prevailed if they reached a measure of
                 manhood.
             But Zeus's son Apollo, borne by the fair-haired Leto,

killed them both before the fuzz on their temples
could bloom and spread, rounding their chins with a full
    beard.   320

The Long ♦"Then I saw Phaidre, Prokris and lovely Ariadne,
Line of   daughter of Minos, that harm brooder. Theseus wanted
Dead Women to bring her from Krete by sea to a hillside of sacred
           Athens. He never enjoyed her. Artemis killed her
           first on sea-ringed Die. The God Dionusos had marked her.

      ♦"I saw Klumene too and Maira. The hated Eriphule:
       she took high-priced gold for the death of her own man.

      ♦"I cannot name them all or tell you of each one,
       every daughter and wife I saw of a great chief:
       the ambrosial night would end first. And the sleep-hour, 330
       whether I go to my race-fast ship and my war-friends
       or stay right here. You and the Gods must see to my
           send-off."

A Stranger's He spoke that way and they all were quiet a long time
Needs   as though he'd woven a spell in the shadowy great hall.
           White-armed Arete finally started to tell them,
            "How does the man strike you men of Phaiakia?
            Handsome and tall? With a mind balanced inside him?
            Though he's my guest, everyone shares in our honor.
            Don't be sending him quickly now and don't be withholding
            presents. The stranger's in need and plenty of treasures 340
            lie or stand in your halls, thanks to the great Gods."

           Old Ekheneos, a war-chief, stood up to answer.
           Among Phaiakian men this man was the eldest.
            "My friends, the words of our queen are thought-full and
                not so
            far from the mark of our own ideas. Follow them closely.
            But word and work belong to Alkinoos mainly."

The King's So now the king, Alkinoos, answered by saying,
Word   "Her words will surely stand so long as I'm living
           and ruling over the oar-loving Phaiakians.
           Our guest, for all of his hard longing to go home,   350
           should stay here now till morning. Then I will round out

the rest of our giving. All you men will share in the send-off
but I'll do the most, for I hold power in this country."

To Go Home   Odysseus, full of designs, answered by asking,
Rich or Poor   "Lordly Alkinoos, praised by all of your people,
what if you asked me now to stay here a whole year,
then sent me off and gave me outstanding presents?
I'd want that too. It's far better to sail off
with both hands full to the well-loved land of your fathers.
All my people would surely love and respect me   360
more if they saw me arrive in Ithaka that way."

The Ways   Now the king, Alkinoos, answered by saying,
of a Poet   "We'd hardly surmise, Odysseus, seeing you this way,
you'd lie and cheat like a fraud, although there are many
raised on the same dark earth, plenty of bad men
building hoaxes and lies no one can see through.
Rather your words are graceful, your heart is a good one.
You told your story with knowing ways like a singer—
all of the Argives' mourning and pain—and your own pain.

Troy and After   "Come on though, tell me something: answer me truly   370
whether you saw those godlike war-friends who followed
you closely to Troy, war-chiefs who went to their doom there.
The night is long, it's measureless—no one should doze off
yet in my hall—and tell me more of your wonderful doings!
I'd stay until Dawn's bright light so long as you bore up,
telling the tale of all your cares in our great hall."

The Harshest   Odysseus, full of designs, answered by saying,
Grief   "Lordly Alkinoos, praised by all of your people,
there's time for plenty of tales and time for a good sleep.
Yet if you long to listen I cannot refuse you.   380
I'll tell you more of our troubles, even the harshest
grief of my war-friends, those who died with me later.
Though they escaped the appalling screeches of Trojans,
they died on the way home. One woman's will was a
        bad one.

A Sorry War-   "So when holy Persephoneia had scattered
Lord's Ghost   all those women's ghosts that way and this way,
a new ghost came—of Atreus's son Agamemnon.

Though grieved like all the others gathered around him
stabbed in Aigisthos's house—they went to their doom
    there—
he knew me at once. After drinking the dark blood   390
he cried out loud, his eyes shedding their big tears.
He stretched out both his hands, longing to hold me.
The power was there no longer, all the old-time
force in that once limber body was now gone.

Which Doom   "My heart felt pity, I wept myself when I saw him
This Time?   and spoke to the man, my words with a feathery swiftness:
'Far-famed son of Atreus, the army's Lord Agamemnon,
what doom has downed you here, what death with its
    long pain?
Was it lordly Poseidon? Sinking your ships in a sea-storm,
raising the strongest winds, a merciless gusting?   400
Or men on land: did enemies gather to harm you
for rustling their flocks of sheep or beautiful cattle,
for fighting over the town's wealth and its women?'

Like a   "I spoke that way and he promptly answered by saying,
Slaughter   'Son of Laertes, nourished by Zeus, wily Odysseus,
of Beasts   Poseidon never downed my ships in a sea-storm
raising a strong wind or merciless gusting.
Men on land? No enemies gathered to harm me.
• Aigisthos caused my death. He brought on my own doom
helped by a curse, my wife. They called me to dinner,   410
they cut me down in that house like a bull in its barn-stall.
My death was the sorriest end. Other war-friends around me
were butchered like white-tusked boars, slaughtered
    without stop
like swine in the house of a wealthy, powerful master,
killed for a wedding, an eating bout or a big feast.
By now you've looked on plenty of warriors cut down,
whether they died alone or in powerful battles.
Your heart would have felt the most pity to see us
lying around that hall, over the wine-bowl
and food-piled tables, the floor a rolling of thick blood.   420
The saddest cry I heard was from Priam's daughter
Kassandre, murdered by sneaking Klutaimnestre
close to me. I raised my hands, I lay on the floor there,
struck by a sword and dying. That bitch of a woman

turned her back: although I was going to Aides
she never closed my eyes or mouth with her fingers.

Woman's
Treachery

'So nothing's more feared and doglike than woman,
the kind that thrusts in her heart the doing of such things.
My wife plotted revolting acts in the worst way,
causing her own man's death. I had been thinking,   430
traveling home, at least my children and household
would make me welcome. No, she was utterly hateful,
pouring shame on herself and on every woman
not yet born, even the woman who acts well.'

A Curse on the
Whole Family

"After he spoke that way I answered by saying,
'Look now! Zeus, watching from far off, has been cruel
ravaging Atreus's line through the plotting of women
right from the start. So many were lost due to Helen.
Now Klutaimnestre set a trap for you far off.'

"I spoke that way and he promptly answered by saying,   440
'Therefore never be kind—not to your own wife.
Don't tell her all your story, whatever you know well.
Say a few things, yes, but keep the others in hiding.

The
Trustworthy
Woman

'Yet for you, Odysseus, death won't come from your woman.
She's very understanding, wise in her counsel,
Ikarios's daughter! Mind-full Penelopeia
was barely a woman—a youthful bride when you left home
to fight that war—with a baby boy at her nipple.
Now he's a man, no doubt, and sits in the men's rows,
quite well off. His father will go there and see him,   450
the son will embrace his father: that is the right way.
My own wife, though—she never allowed me to fill my
eyes with my son. She killed me, his father, before then.

A
Homecoming
Strategy

'So I'll say this, bear it in mind and remember:
guide your ship to the well-loved land of your fathers
and hide it. Don't be open. Trust the women no longer.

A Son
Dead or Alive

'Come on now, tell me something: answer me truly
whether you've heard, somehow, my boy is alive still.
Maybe in Orkhomenos? Maybe in deep-sanded Pulos?

Or maybe with King Menelaos in wide-open Sparte.   460
♦ My godlike Orestes—he's not yet dead on the broad earth?'

"He spoke that way but I had to answer by saying,
'Son of Atreus, why do you ask what I don't know?
Maybe he's dead or alive. It's wrong to be windy.'

The Greatest   "Now as we stood there, exchanging painful and sad words,
Warrior   both of us mourning losses and shedding our big tears,
                the son of Peleus came on, the ghost of Akhilleus.
                Patroklos too and handsome Antilokhos came on,
                and Aias—in looks and shape the best of all the Danaans
                after the son of Peleus, handsome Akhilleus.   470
                The ghost of the fast-footed grandson of Aiakos knew me.
                He spoke with pity, the words with a feathery swiftness,
                'Son of Laertes, nourished by Zeus, wily Odysseus,
                tough man: what greater work than *this* will your heart plan?
                How did you dare come down to Aides where senseless
                dead men live, the souls of people who've worn down?'

Power among   "After he spoke that way I answered by saying,
the Dead   'Akhilleus, Peleus's son, the greatest by far of Akhaians:
                I came in need of Teiresies, hoping he'd spell out
                a plan to take me back to rock-strewn Ithakan country.   480
                I'm still not close to Akhaia, nor have I walked on
                my own land. I'm always harmed. But no one, Akhilleus,
                no man before or after you ever was more blessed:
                when you were alive we Argives honored you just like
                the Gods. Now you're here and powerfully ruling
                among the dead. Don't bewail your dying, Akhilleus.'

Better Alive at "I spoke that way but he promptly answered by saying,
Any Cost   'Don't talk nicely of death to me, shining Odysseus.
                I'd rather be stuck on a farm, a drudge for some other
                threadbare man with hardly a life or resources   490
                than rule all those who waste away and are dead here.

A Powerless   'But tell me news of my son, high-born and wondrous,
Father   whether he joined that war or not in the front ranks?
                Speak about faultless Peleus too—if only you heard tell—
                whether he still is esteemed by the Murmidon people.

Or maybe he's disesteemed in Hellas and Phthie
now that his hands and feet are hobbled by old age.
I cannot help him now in the rays of the Sun-God.
I'm not as I was at wide-plained Troy in the old days,
killing their army's best and defending the Argives.   500
If I could walk in my Father's house with the same strength
only briefly! They'd hate my unbeatable hands and my
      power,
the men who've treated my Father badly and taken his
      honor.'

A Powerful Son   "After he spoke that way I answered by saying,
                 'I haven't heard about faultless Peleus, your father.
                 About Neoptolemos, though, the man-child you cherish,
                 I'll tell you everything truly, just as you asked me.
                 I took him myself aboard my hollow and balanced
                 ship from Skuros to join with strong-greaved Akhaians.
                 In fact at the city of Troy when we gathered to make plans,   510
                 he always spoke up first. And he spoke without error:
                 only godlike Nestor and I could outdo him.
                 Then on the Trojan plains when we fought with our bronze
                       spears,
                 he never stayed in the crowd where warriors pressed hard.
                 He ran out strongly in front and yielded to no one.
                 He took down plenty of men in fearsome encounters,
                 I could not tell you them all, I never could name them,
                 those he killed in the ranks while guarding Akhaians.
                 But one man, Telephos's son, he killed with a bronze thrust:
                 the war-chief, Eurupulos. Plenty of men were around him,   520
                 Keteians, dying because of gifts to a woman.
                 After the godlike Memnon Eurupulos looked best.

Inside the   'Then when the bravest Argives climbed in the great horse
Horse at Troy   built by Epeios—I was in charge of the whole thing,
                 both to open that tight-built ruse and to close it—
                 all the other Danaan planners and leaders
                 wiped away tears and everyone's joints trembled
                       beneath him.
                 But not your son's, no paleness: I'd watched with my
                       own eyes
                 that beautiful face. In fact with never a single
                 tear to wipe, he asked me very often to let him   530

go out of the horse! He kept on rubbing the sword-hilt
and bronze-heavy spear. What harm he meant for the
   Trojans!

A Father's   'In time when we all had looted the high city of Priam,
   Pride   he went aboard ship with his proper share and a good prize
              unscathed—he'd never been pierced by a bronze-pointed
                 spear-throw
              or stabbed in close by a sword. Plenty of those wounds
              happen in war. Ares' rage is chaotic.'

          "I stopped and the ghost of Aiakos's fast-footed grandson
           left me with lengthening strides through the asphodel
              meadow,
           glad that I told him how his son was outstanding.   540

A Warrior's   "Other ghosts came by of those who were laid out to die once.
   Old Spite   Standing sadly each one asked about loved ones.
        • Only the ghost of Aias, Telamon's tall son,
           stood off a ways. He fumed because I had won out
           over the man in a contest close to the black ships
           for the arms of Akhilleus, spread by his honored mother.
           Sons of Troy were the judges and Pallas Athene.
           If only I'd never won a contest of that kind!
           What a head the earth now held because of those weapons!
           Aias was better in action and beauty than all the Danaans   550
           after the son of Peleus, handsome Akhilleus.

No Answer   "So I spoke to him now, asking him gently,
           'Aias, faultless Telamon's son, were you not to forget it,
           even in death, your anger because of those hateful
           weapons? Gods have made them a curse on the Argives:
           you were our tower and died for them. So as Akhaians
           mourn that head, the son of Peleus, Akhilleus,
           we always mourn yours too. No one's to blame now
           but Zeus. He hated Danaan warriors fiercely,
           all our spearmen, and caused your death on that doom-day.   560
           So then come here, lord, and hear what I'm saying.
           Tame your anger and boldness. Master your spirits.'

          "I spoke that way but the man said nothing and walked off
           to other ghosts of Erebos, men laid out to die once.

Though angry still, he might have spoken, or I might—
no, the heart in my own chest had been longing
to look to other ghosts, men laid out to die once.

A Judge and ♦"So I saw Minos, a shining son of the great Zeus,
Two Titans   holding a scepter of gold, sitting and judging
the dead. Around that lord, pleading for fairness,   570
they sat or stood by Aides' house with its wide gates.

"Next I saw the titanic shape of Orion,
herding animals down through an asphodel meadow,
beasts he'd killed himself in the lonely mountains
wielding an all-bronze club, unbroken forever.

"I saw Tituos too, a son of the well-known Gaia.
He lay spread out—nine hundred feet on the ground there!
Vultures squatted on either side raking his liver,
beaks in his guts. His hands kept failing to stop them.
He'd misused Leto, Zeus's beautiful woman   580
going to Putho once through a lovely place, Panopeus.

Teasing Thirst "Yes and I saw Tantalos suffering strong pain,
standing in water that rose to his chin but no higher.
He looked so thirsty, he longed to drink but he could not:
each time the old man stooped, wanting to drink it,
the water drained as if swallowed, making the ground look
black at his feet, some Power drying it all up.
High and leafy trees were also hanging with thick fruit:
pear-trees, pomegranates, apple-trees glowing
with fruit, the sweetest figs and olives in blossom.   590
Whenever the old man's hand went reaching to clasp one,
the wind hurled it at shadowy clouds to be hidden.

Up and Down "I saw Sisuphos too suffering deep pain.
and Up the Hill   He struggled to move a gigantic boulder with both hands.
Strained against the stone, hands and his feet set,
he pushed it high uphill. But soon as he might have
nudged it over the crest, its weight turned it around there,
the careless boulder again ran down to the flat ground.
Again he strained himself: he pushed and the sweat ran
down his body. Dust drifted over his forehead.   600

Brawling   "Now I saw a powerful Herakles figure—
and Death   ◆   a phantom; the real one gladly dines with the deathless
Designed
on a Belt   Gods married to Hebe, the beautiful-ankled
                  daughter of powerful Zeus and gold-sandaled Here.
                  The dead kept screeching around that phantom like fear-
                       struck
                  birds on every side. He looked like a dark night,
                  he held an uncased bow, its string with an arrow,
                  and glared with a steady fierceness as though he would
                       shoot now.
                  The sword-belt he wore around his chest was a scary,
                  gold-chased baldric. Alarming things were designed there: 610
                  savage bears and boars, the glaring of lions,
                  battles and deaths in brawls, the dying of strong men.
                  If only the one who designed that baldric had never
                  cause to craft it and never would fashion another!

Dragging   "The phantom knew when he saw me now with his own
Doom Out   eyes.
                  He wailed and spoke, the words with a feathery swiftness,
                  'Son of Laertes, nourished by Zeus, wily Odysseus!
                  You sorry man: are you too dragging a wretched
                  doom out as I did once in the rays of the Sun-God?
                  I was the son of Zeus, the grandson of Kronos,   620
                  yet I suffered endlessly. A man very beneath me
                  became my lord and laid his hard labors upon me.
                  He even sent me here to haul out the death-hound—
                  he planned no other test harder than that one—
                  I brought up the beast myself from the household of Aides.
                  Hermes had sent me down and glow-eyed Athene.'

Greenish Fear   "He stopped and went back off to the household of Aides.
                  I stayed there staunchly myself, hoping that other
                  war-chiefs would come, all those lost in a past time.
                  I might have spotted more, the men I had longed for   630
                  like Theseus, Peirithoos, far-famed children of great Gods.
                  But far more families of dead came crowding before that,
                  making unearthly cries. I was clutched by a green fear.
              ◆   Would high-born Persephoneia send me the Gorgo,
                  that dreaded monster's head, from the household of Aides?

Running   "I hurried back to the ship and ordered my men there
from the Land   to go aboard themselves and loosen the stern-lines.
of the Dead   They boarded at once and took their seats at the oar-locks.
          A rising wave carried us down the river-like Ocean.
          The men first rowed but later we welcomed a good wind."   640

BOOK 12   *Evil Song, a Deadly Strait,*
          and Forbidden Herds

Back to Aiaie   "Now that our ship had left behind Okeanos
                River, we came on the salt waves of the broad sea
                back to Aiaie where Dawn, the early-born Goddess,
                has places for dancing and Helios, places for rising.
                We put in promptly, we drove our ship onto beach-sand
                and disembarked ourselves on the shore of the salt sea.
                We fell asleep right there, expecting a bright Dawn.

Death-Rites   "When newborn Dawn came on with her rose-fingered
Again   daylight,
                I sent a few of my men to the household of Kirke
                to carry back a body: Elpenor had died there.   10
                We hurried and chopped up wood. Where headland
                    pushed out
                farthest to sea we mourned and buried him, shedding our
                    big tears.
                After the dead man's weapons and body were all burned,
          ♦ we raised a barrow, dragged a stele to stand there
                and placed his well-turned oar on top of the death-mound.

Dying Twice   "We went through every rite. Kirke had known well
                how we came from Aides. Quickly she dressed up
                finely and came together with handmaids who brought us
                bread and big portions of meat—and wine with its red glow.
                Bright as a Goddess, she stood in our center and told us,   20
                'Hardened men, you went alive to the household of Aides!
                Other men die just once; you will have died twice.
                Come on now, drink some wine, relish the food here
                all day long. Tomorrow, together with bright Dawn,
                you'll set sail. I'll mark each point on your way home
                in order to stop you from suffering pain from a foolish
                plan again, whether on land or the broad sea.'

                "She spoke that way, our hearts were proud but we said yes.
                All day long we ate and drank until sundown,
                feasting on honey-sweet wine and plenty of good meat.   30

171

Fatal Voices   "Soon as the sun went down and night had arrived there
               my crewmen slept by the ship, close to the stern-lines.
               Kirke took my hand and led me away from my own crew.
               I sat and she lay beside me to ask about each thing.
               I told the Goddess all my tale in good order.
               Then my queenly Kirke answered by saying,
               'So all those things have passed. Now you will listen
               to what I unfold. Later a God will remind you.

          ◆ 'First you'll approach the Seirenes, those who can spellbind
               every seaman who sails too close to their singing.   40
               Whoever goes there and mindlessly hears the Seirenes'
               voices, his wife and little children will never
               stand beside him to welcome him back home.
               All the Seirenes' clear-toned singing will charm him.
               They sit in a meadow with massive bone-heaps around them
               of rotting men, the skin shrunk on their bodies.
               Drive on past them! Soften some honey-sweet beeswax
               and stop your men's ears: none of the others
               must listen. But you, if you long to hear the Seirenes,
               men must lash you hand and foot on the fast ship.   50
               Stand by your mast-box, the lines tight to the masthead.
               Then you may hear and enjoy the songs of Seirenes.
               Yet if you plead or command your men to untie you,
               let them lash you with still more line to secure you.
               In time your crewmen will row you past the Seirenes.

A Hard Course 'I won't minutely describe what's there any further,
   to Steer   the way your course could lie. Ponder and plan it
               yourself in your heart. I'll tell you something of two ways.

               'Hanging rocks are on one side. Roaring against them
          ◆ are giant waves of blue-eyed Amphitrite.   60
               Blissful Gods have called them *Plangktai*, the "Clashers."
               Birds can't pass that way, not even the fretful
               doves who carry ambrosia to Zeus our Father:
               the smooth cliff-side always blocks them and kills one,
               though the Father sends another to make up their number.
               No ship of a man has ever escaped if it went there,
               all the planks of ships and the bodies of dead men
               jumbled by waves—fire-storms too can be deadly.
               The only seagoing ship that managed to sail through,

the *Argo*, known to the world, had sailed from Aietes.   70
Surf would have swiftly thrown her too at the great rocks
had not Here sent her through—she cherished Ieson.

The Cave   'On the other side are two crags. One of them reaches
Monster   the broad sky with its pointed crest and clouds are around it
darkly: they never break up, there's never a clear sky
around that point, not in summer or autumn.
No man could ever climb it and stand on the high peak,
not if his hands and feet were twenty in number.
The rock's too smooth, you'd think some Power had
        shined it.

'That crag has a cave in its middle, hazy and wet gray.   80
♦ It looks toward dusk and Erebos. There you can sail by
guiding your hollow ship, my glowing Odysseus.
Not even the strongest man, nocking an arrow,
could shoot from his hollow ship to that cave in the
        cliff-side.
♦ The frightful Skulla lives and yelps in the cavern.
Her voice resembles the sound of a newborn
whelp but she's huge and fierce. No one would ever
look at her gladly, not even Gods who could face her.
All of her twelve long legs and feet will be flailing.
Her six long necks reach out—a head is on each one,   90
shocking and frightful—her teeth are crowded in three tight
rows and it's black inside, full of her black death.
She stays in hiding below the waist in her hollow
cave but keeps her heads out over the frightening chasm
to fish below. She hungrily searches the cliff-base
for seals or dolphins—and larger prey she might take there,
some beast of the thousands fed by moaning Amphitrite.
No sailor yet has claimed his vessel could slip by
unscathed: every head of her snatches a crewman
and carries him high over the ship with its dark prow.   100

The Whirlpool 'You'll see the other crag is lower, Odysseus,
Monster   but close to the first: well shot, an arrow could cross them.
An outsize fig-tree is there, swelling with big leaves,
♦ and under it, God-size Kharubdis swallows the dark sea.
Three times a day she retches, she swallows it three times,
it's fearsome to watch. Don't be there when she swallows—

no one could save you from harm, not even Poseidon.
Instead stay close to Skulla's cliff-side and row by
fast in your ship. It's far better to mourn six
men gone from your ship than all the crewmen together.'   110

Can't I Fight   "But after she spoke that way I answered by asking,
    with a   'Goddess, come on now, tell me the truth about one thing:
   Monster?   can I escape somehow from deadly Kharubdis
and fight off Skulla too when she preys on my war-friends?'

"I stopped and the shining Goddess answered me swiftly,
'Reckless man, with all your care about battle
and struggle again! Won't you bow to the deathless
Gods? Skulla cannot die, her evil is deathless,
savage and hard, a terror. She's not to be fought with,
you can't be on guard, running away is your best course.   120
In fact if you stall and arm yourself by the cliff-side,
I fear she'll dash out again from her cave and attack you—
her heads will snatch off six more men from your warship.
Row on strongly past her. Call on Krataiin,
Skulla's mother—she bore that curse on you people—
she'll stop her daughter from lunging again from the cavern.

Tempting Beef   'Now you'll approach the large herds on Thrinakie Island,
of the Sun-God   where Helios's cattle graze with fattening sheep-flocks,
fifty in each of the Sun-God's herds—seven of cattle
and seven of beautiful sheep. None of them gives birth;   130
none of them ever dies. Goddesses tend them,
  ♦ lovely braided Nymphs: Lampetie helps Phaethousa,
born to the Sun-God, Huperion, by godlike Neaira.
Their queenly mother, having borne them and raised them,
sent them to live on far-off Thrinakie Island,
to guard the sheep and tight-horned bulls of their father.
If only you leave them unharmed, minding your way home,
you might reach Ithaka yet, though suffering setbacks.
But if you harm them I foresee death for your war-friends,
your ship destroyed and you, though you may not die,   140
will get home late and poor, with all of your men lost.'

Leaving the   "She stopped and right off Dawn arrived on her gold throne.
Island Again   My shining Goddess left me then for up island.
I went to the ship myself and stirred up the crew there

to get aboard in a hurry and loosen the stern-lines.
They boarded at once and took their seats at the oar-locks,
each in his place. They rowed, splashing the gray sea.
Now a good friend came, moving the dark-prowed
ship from astern, a fair wind swelling the white sail
and sent by Kirke, a feared Goddess who spoke like a
    human   150
in lovely braids. Securing all our tackle aboard ship
we sat down, helmsman and wind holding our course well.

Bad News   "But soon I spoke with a sad heart to my crewmen.
for the Men 'My friends, if only one or two of us know what
shining and godlike Kirke foretold, it is not right.
I'll tell you myself. Once you know, we may either
die or fend off death—we may run from our doom-day.

'She told me first to avoid the songs of bewitching
Seirenes, to run on past their blossoming meadows.
She told me to listen alone. You crewmen will tie me   160
hard and tight to make me stay in the same place.
I'll stand by the mast-box; your lines will knot at the
    masthead.
Then if I plead and command you all to untie me,
lash me with still more lines harder to hold me.'

Beeswax   "So I made each point quite plain to my war-friends.
Our well-built vessel meanwhile was hurriedly nearing
Seirenes' island, borne by a favoring sea-wind.
Then the wind died promptly. We moved in an airless
calm, some Power lulling all of the white-caps.
My men stood up to furl sail and they stowed it   170
below in the hollow ship. They sat at the oar-locks:
planed and pinewood oars whitened the water.
I cut a large round of wax into smaller
chunks with a sword's keen edge. It warmed with my
    kneading
and soon softened, thanks to the work of my strong hands
and rays from Helios the Sun-God, Lord Huperion.
I stopped the ears of all my war-friends in order.
Then they lashed me, hand and foot, in the fast ship.
I stood by the mast-box, their lines' knots at the masthead.
They sat and strained at the oars, splashing the gray sea.   180

Honeyed   "As far as a man's voice can be heard when he cries out
Music   we hurried along, but Seirenes certainly saw us
              approaching fast in our ship. They rose into clear song:
         ♦ 'Here, well-known Odysseus, lofty pride of Akhaians!
              Stop your ship: hear the two of us singing.
              No man's ever passed our isle in a black ship
              before he's heard the honeyed song from our two mouths.
              Instead they enjoyed it and left here knowing a great deal.
              We know everything now about Troy and its wide plains,
              Trojan and Argive suffering willed by the great Gods.   190
              We know what happens on Earth, nourishing all men.'

Running from "They raised that beautiful song and my spirit was longing
Beautiful Song to hear much more. I told my men to untie me,
              nodding my brows. But most men kept to their rowing.
              Perimedes rose with Eurulokhos quickly
              and lashed me with still more line, harder and tighter.

              "After they rowed on past, when no one could hear them
              any longer, Seirenes' voices or singing,
              my trusted war-friends briskly took out the beeswax
              I'd used to plug their ears. They loosened my bindings.   200

New Dread   "But not long after we left that island I spotted
              spray and mounting waves, then listened to loud noise.
              The oars flew down from the frightened hands of my war-
                  friends,
              they dragged and swished along in the sea till our vessel
              stopped. With no hands working the tapering oar-blades,
              I walked through the ship myself to hearten the whole crew,
              approaching every man and telling him softly,
              'My friends: hardship is not unknown to us truly.
              The harm nearby cannot be worse than the Kuklops,
              holding us deep in a hollow cave with his brute strength.   210
              And yet we escaped, thanks to my boldness and thoughtful
              planning. This too I think you'll somehow remember.
              Come on now, every man obey what I tell him.
              Stay at your benches, pull your oar-blades and row hard,
              strike at the deep salt sea! Zeus may be willing
              to grant our escape somehow and help us avoid death.
              You at the helm: thrust in your heart what I tell you
              now in the hollow ship. As you manage the tiller

steer us away from that mist, those waves and the high
    spray.
Stay quite close to this cliff. Don't be forgetful   220
and drift off course, or you'll drive us there to the
    worse fate.'

The Tightest   "I spoke that way and everyone promptly obeyed me.
Strait   ♦ I never told them of Skulla. That would be hopeless
pain and the crew should not be mastered by panic
and stop rowing, huddling below in the ship's hold.
I also overlooked a painful order from Kirke,
telling me not to arm myself for the battle.
I donned my well-known armor and, taking my two long
spears in hand, I walked on deck to the vessel's
bow. I'd wait for the first showing of Skulla,   230
a monster of rocks who'd bring great pain to my war-
    friends.
I could not spot her, though. I tired from straining
my eyes everywhere, staring at haze-covered sea-cliff.

"Moaning lowly, we moved along in that tight strait,
Skulla on one side, God-sized Kharubdis on the other,
frightfully sucking down great gulps of the salt sea.
Every time she retched, like a cauldron on high flame,
the waters roiled and swirled, sea-spray would rise up
high then fall and spatter the summits of both crags.
Every time she sucked in more of the salt sea,   240
everything whirled inside her, both of the high crags
loudly echoed and ground was bared at the bottom,
a dark blue sand. We all were seized by a pale green
fear as we watched that monster, dreading our own end.

The Other   "Just then Skulla snatched six men from the hollow
Monster   ship—the strongest hands, the best of my war-friends.
Strikes   Turning to look at the race-fast ship and those war-friends,
I saw their hands and feet rising above me
high in the air. Their voices came to me calling
my name for the last time, their hearts in anguish.   250
The way a fisherman uses a long pole on a jutting
rock to cast his bait, a morsel of food for some lesser
fish with a horn-piece too from an ox in the water,
he catches a writhing fish and throws it ashore there:

so were my writhing men raised to that cliff-side.
She ate them all right there, they screamed at the cave-
    mouth
stretching their hands to me, caught in that horrible
    struggle.
In my own eyes that was the most pitiful ending
of all, the worst I endured while searching the seaways.

A Dangerous   "After we left those cliffs of daunting Kharubdis   260
Island   and Skulla both, in time we came to the Sun-God's
peerless island, his cattle, broad-browed and handsome,
and plenty of fattened sheep of the God, Huperion.
While still at sea on my black ship I could hear them,
cows mooing along as they moved into stock-pens
and lambs bleating. Words of the prophet Teiresies,
the blind Theban, came and fell on my mind now,
Kirke too on Aiaie telling me often to stay clear,
avoid that island of Helios, a God who gladdens his people.

"So I spoke with a sad heart to my war-friends.   270
'Listen, you men. Although you've suffered a great deal
now I must tell you the words of the prophet Teiresies.
Kirke enjoined me too on Aiaie to stay clear,
avoid the island of Helios, a God who gladdens his people.
They told me our worst harm was there on that island.
Drive us instead right by the place in our black ship.'

A Dangerous   "I spoke that way but the spirits inside them were broken.
Night   Eurulokhos answered shortly with words that I hated:
'Cruel Odysseus, far too strong, never a tired-out
body! Surely you're made entirely of iron.   280
You won't allow your men, drowsy and worn down,
to walk on land right there, a sea-circled island
where we could build a meal once more to delight us.
You tell us to drift as we are through fast-falling darkness,
be driven through fog-bound seas away from the island.
But night gives birth to the harshest winds and can ruin
a ship. How could a man escape from his steep doom
if chancy gusts or a sea-storm suddenly came on,
Southwind, the wrong-minded Westwind—those that most
    often
dismember ships—whatever the will of the strong Gods.   290

Instead we should yield right now to the black night.
Let's get settled ashore by the race-fast ship for our dinner.
We'll board her again at dawn and sail on the broad sea.'

The Gravest   "Eurulokhos spoke that way and the rest were agreeing.
Oath   Then I surely knew some Power was planning to harm us.
I spoke to them all, my words with a feathery swiftness,
'Eurulokhos, clearly you've checked me: I am alone here.
Come on though, all of you now swear me a strong oath.
By chance if we find a herd of cattle or great flocks
of sheep, no one will turn recklessly evil   300
and kill those bulls or rams. I say that we rest here,
taking the food that deathless Kirke provided.'

"I spoke that way and they promptly swore as I asked them.
After the oath, with solemn swearing behind us,
we moored our well-built ship in the round of that harbor
close to a fresh-water spring. Then disembarking,
my skillful crewmen began to make us a dinner.

Bad Signs   "Soon as the craving for food and drink was behind them
on the Island   they all began to mourn, remembering dear friends
Skulla had snatched from the hollow vessel and
    gulped down.   310
They cried until the balm of sleep overcame them.

"Still in the night's last third when starlight was waning,
stormcloud-gathering Zeus raised up a high wind
against us. The storm was astounding, land and water
alike were blurred, the night roused from the heavens.

"When newborn Dawn came on with her rose-fingered
    daylight,
we hauled our ship to a hollow cave and secured her.
Nymphs had chairs and beautiful places to dance there.
I gathered the men once more and carefully told them,
'Friends, with plenty of food and drink in the fast ship,   320
let's keep away from the herds or maybe we'll suffer.
Dreaded Helios owns the cattle and strong sheep.
The Sun-God watches and hears everything clearly.'
I spoke that way, their hearts were proud but they nodded.

Running
Out of Food
"Then the Southwind blew—and it blew for a whole month.
No other wind came on but Eastwind and Southwind.
Yet as long as my men had food and our red wine
they kept away from the cattle, desiring their own lives.
But after all our food was gone in the fast ship,
they had to wander the island often to find prey,   330
fish or fowl, whatever came to their hands first.
They used bent hooks, their bellies hurting from hunger.

"I went up island myself to pray to the Powers,
hoping a God might show me a way to get on here.
After I walked through the island far from my war-friends,
I washed my hands in a cove sheltered from sea-wind
and prayed to all the Gods holding Olumpos.
♦ They only sprinkled a honeyed sleep on my eyelids.

The Worst
Death
"Eurulokhos meanwhile badly counseled my war-friends.
'Listen, you men, for all the pain you have suffered: 340
every death is hateful to men who are wretched
but starving's the sorriest way to go to your own doom.
Come on then: round up the best bulls of the Sun-God
to slaughter for deathless Powers ruling broadly in heaven.
Someday if we get to Ithakan land of our Fathers,
we'll promptly raise a wealthy shrine to the God Huperion
and set down plenty of beautiful treasure for Helios.
Yet if he's angry about his cattle with straight horns
and wants to destroy our ship and the rest of the Gods say
yes, I'd rather die just once gagging on water   330
than waste away on a lonely island slowly.'

The Wrong
Feast Begins
"Eurulokhos talked that way, my other war-friends nodded
and swiftly they rustled the finest bulls of the Sun-God
nearby, for not so far from the ships with their dark prows
the tight-horned, broad-browed, beautiful cattle were
        grazing.
So they stood around them, prayed to the high Gods
♦ and gathered tender greens from a high-leafing oak-tree—
the well-planked ship had no white barley aboard her.
Still praying, they cut those throats and they promptly
flayed them, carved out thighs, layered the red meat   360
twice with fat, then spread raw flesh on the thigh-parts.

Lacking wine to drop on the smoldering victims
they poured on water. They roasted all of the innards.
After the thighs were burned and they tasted the entrails,
they cut and pierced with spits the rest of the pieces.

Awake from a   "Just then the balmy sleep was gone from my eyelids.
Cruel Sleep   I went to the race-fast ship on the shore of the salt sea.
Soon as I came close to the ship with its up-curved
bow the cloying smell of meat-fat drifted around me.
I moaned to the deathless Gods in pain and I cried out,   370
'Fatherly Zeus and you other Gods, joyful forever,
you lulled me with cruel rest, a sleep that destroyed me.
A hateful act was planned by the men who remained here.'

Lighting Up   "A messenger swiftly rose to the God Huperion:
the Dead   long-gowned Lampetie told him we'd slaughtered his cattle.
He promptly spoke to the deathless Gods in a hot rage:
'Fatherly Zeus and the rest of you Gods, joyful forever,
avenge me now on the men of Odysseus, son of Laertes,
who brashly killed those bulls that gave me such pleasure,
both when I rose up high in the star-dotted heavens   380
and came back down from the heavens to good earth.
If they don't pay me for all those bulls in the right way,
♦ I'll go to the house of Aides and light up the dead there.'

"Stormcloud-gathering Zeus answered by saying,
'Helios! Do keep shining here for the deathless
Gods and for death-bound men on grain-giving farmland.
Shortly I'll strike that race-fast ship myself on the wine-dark
sea with glowing lightning. I'll smash it to splinters.'

"I heard all this in time from fair-haired Kalupso,
who told me she'd heard it herself from Hermes the
     Runner.   390

Plenty   "Soon as I came back down to the ship and the salt sea
of Feasting,   I railed at every man. But no one could find some
Plenty
of Omens   plan to escape: the bulls were slaughtered already.
Then the Gods were swift in revealing their omens.
bull-hides crawled, meat made noise on the sharp spits,
roasted and raw both with sounds like the lowing of cattle!

"For six whole days my war-friends, a crew I had trusted,
dined on Helios's cattle, the best they could round up.
When Zeus, the son of Kronos, brought on the seventh
day and the wind and raging thunderstorm ended,   400
promptly we all embarked and made for the broad sea,
standing our mast up tall and hoisting the white sail.

A Vengeful and   "But after we left the island, with nothing around us—
Killing Storm   no land showing, only the sky and the salt sea—
the son of Kronos raised a darkening storm-cloud
over the hollow ship and seas were graying beneath it.
We sailed but not much farther: Westwind abruptly
came on blowing, roaring soon with a gale force.
It gusted fiercely and broke off both of the mainmast
forestays, the mast fell back and all of its rigging   410
crashed in the hold. Astern, the head of our helmsman
was hit by the mast—all his skull-bones were shattered
together at once. He looked like an acrobat tumbling
down and a proud spirit was gone from the man's bones.

Deaths   "Zeus hurled bolts and thunder both at the same time.
and a Life   The whole ship trembled, struck by lightning from
                great Zeus,
she filled with sulphur-smoke, men were overboard,
                rolling—
they looked for a time like cormorants circling the
                black ship,
borne by the waves. A God had seized their return home.

"I paced through the ship myself till water was pulling   420
the keel from her side-boards. When waves carried it
                naked—
the keel had also sheared from the mast—somehow a
                backstay
was thrown down over the keel, a working of oxhide.
I used it to lash the keel and mast closely together.
I sat on them both, borne by ravaging storm-wind.

A New   "In time the Westwind and raging thunderstorm ended.
Wrong Wind   But Southwind came on fast, bringing me heart-pangs:
now I could travel the long way back to devouring
                Kharubdis!

Help from a "Swept along all night, I came with the sunrise
Fig-Tree to Skulla's cliff once more and dreaded Kharubdis,   430
    the monster who sucked down huge gulps of the salt sea.
    The tall fig-tree was there: I lunged for it, grabbed it
    and held on tight as a bat. Yet there was nowhere
    now to get good footing and nowhere to climb up
    since roots were far below and branches above me
    hung out large and long, overarching Kharubdis.
    I held on tightly until some time she might vomit
    the keel and mast I longed for. Finally they came up
   ♦ late at dusk. When a man stands up from assembly
    to dine—a judge in the many suits of the young men— 440
    that's when the wood came back from the depths of
     Kharubdis.
    My hands and feet let go. I fell from a ways up,
    a midstream thud, beyond but close to the long spars.
    I seized and sat on the wood then paddled with both hands.
    The Father of Gods and men kept Skulla from looking.
    Without his help I'd never have run from my steep doom.

Care from a "For nine whole days I was borne. Gods on the tenth night
Goddess brought me close to Ogugie. There was Kalupso
    in lovely braids, a feared Goddess who spoke like a human.
    She loved and cared for me. Why go on with that story? 450
    I told it only yesterday here in your own house,
    to you and your heart-strong wife. To me it's a bother
    to tell a story again that's plain when it's told once."

13+4, 21-23
16-19,

More Gifts for
the Stranger

He spoke that way and they all were quiet a long time,
as though he'd woven a spell in the shadowy great hall.
At length however Alkinoos spoke up and told him,
"Odysseus, now that you've come to my bronze-floored and
   high-roofed
house you won't, I think, be driven away so
far from home with all the pain you have suffered.
So I'm charging every man in the great hall,
speaking to those who've always relished the glowing
wine of our elders and listened well to our singer:
clothes for our guest are surely laid in the polished   10
chest with carefully crafted gold and all of the other
presents our own Phaiakian counselors brought here.
♦ Come on then, every man should give him a cauldron
and large tripod as well. We'll pass on costs to our people
in time since giving presents is taxing for one man."
Alkinoos spoke that way and his word was their pleasure.
Then all of them went to their own homes for a night's rest.

When newborn Dawn came on with her rose-fingered
   daylight,
they all went down to the ship with man-bracing presents
of bronze. Alkinoos went through the ship—his power
   was holy—   20
and stowed the presents himself under the benches.
They'd hardly hamper the work of men hurriedly rowing.

Slow Sunset

Then they walked to Alkinoos's home to get ready
to dine and the king slaughtered—his power was holy—
a bull for dark-cloud Zeus, the son of Kronos and ruler
of all men. They roasted thighs and splendidly dined there
gladly. The godlike singer played in their center,
honored by all—Demodokos. Ah but Odysseus
often glanced at the fiery sun, anxious to see it
set for the man was keenly longing to sail home.   30
The way a man has yearned for dinner after he's labored
all day long with wine-dark oxen plowing a new field,

then he welcomes the going down of the Sun-God
and walks at last, his thighs trembling, to dinner:
Odysseus welcomed Helios going the same way.

The Last   He told the oar-loving Phaiakians quickly—
Send-Off   mainly King Alkinoos—making his words clear:
"Lordly Alkinoos, praised by all of your people,
send me off now, pour the wine, and the rest of you farewell!
For now they're brought to an end, these wants of my own
                heart,
a send-off and loving presents. Let Gods on Olumpos   40
make them blessed. May I find when I reach home
a faultless wife and all my loved ones in good health.
You who remain here, gladden the hearts of your children
and married women. May Gods reward you with every
richness. I pray no harm will come to your people."

the only blessing on thier voyage comes from Odysseus

He spoke that way, they all were nodding and urging
the send-off now, for their guest had spoken so rightly.
Strong Alkinoos turned to his herald and told him,
"Pontonoos, mix the wine in our wine-bowl and serve it   50
to all in the great hall. Soon as we honor our Father
Zeus we'll send our guest to the land of his fathers."

Honeyed Wine   He stopped: Pontonoos mixed the wine with its honeyed
for the Gods   heart and filled each goblet. Letting the drops fall,
they honored the joyful Gods ruling broadly in heaven,
high on their thrones. Godlike Odysseus rose now.
Placing the two-handled cup in the hands of Arete,
he said good-bye and his words had a feathery swiftness,
"Farewell, my queen, and for good. Flourish till old age
comes and death: that's still the lot of us humans.   60
I go my way, and you? Feel joy in your household,
your children and people, in King Alkinoos mainly."

Help on the   Godlike Odysseus now was crossing the threshold
Voyage   after he'd spoken. Strong Alkinoos offered his herald
to guide him down to the race-fast ship at the seashore.
Arete gave him handmaids, women to join him.
One maid carried a well-washed mantle and tunic.
A second she told to help take care of the close-packed
chest and a third carried food and some red wine.

Night Travel   Soon as they came on down to the ship and the salt sea,   70
quickly some high-born escorts were stowing the presents
below in the hollow ship with all the foodstuff and red wine.
They spread a blanket and linen cloth for Odysseus
right on the deck of the hollow ship, making for sound sleep
astern as the man himself boarded and lay down
quietly. All the oarsmen sat on their benches in order.
Soon as the line at the bored moor-stone was loosened
each man leaned on his oar and flung up the salt sea.
A lovely sleep came down on Odysseus's eyelids,
a sound and sweet one—the closest thing to a death-sleep.   80

Asleep on a   The way a four-horse team when harnessed together
Fast Ship   will all take off on a plain, lashed by a quick whip,
rising swiftly and tall to race through the right course:
the vessel rose in the same way, building a shiny
and spread-out stern-wave, loud with seawater noises.
She ran on steady and sure. Not even the circling
sea-hawk, nimblest in flight, could have matched her!
Running swiftly along she cut through the sea-swells,
bearing a man resembling the Gods in their wisdom.
Before this day his heart had suffered a great deal,   90
warring with men and crossing burdensome seaways.
Now he slept quite still, unmindful of all he had suffered.

Homeland   The brightest star was rising—more than the others
it heralds the light of newborn Dawn—at that moment
the seagoing ship was drawing close to the island.

Phorkus, the Old Man of the Sea, has a harbor
in Ithakan country. A pair of headlands go jutting
and soaring out, then sloping down to the harbor as buffers
against the huge rollers raised by the storm-winds
beyond those rocks. A well-planked vessel can lie to   100
there without hawsers after reaching a moorage.
Close to an olive-tree's slender leaves at the harbor's
  ♦ head is a charming cave, misted and sea-gray,
sacred to Nymphs called *Neiades*—Nymphs of the Water.
Mixing bowls are inside, two-handled wine-jars
of stone and bees as well, storing their honey.
Long looms of stone are used by the Sea-Nymphs
to make their sea-blue clothes, a wonder to gaze at.

Spring-water flows nonstop and the cave has an entrance
facing the Northwind: men go down through that cave-
    mouth.   110
The entrance facing the Southwind though is holy and
    no one
human can go there. It's only for those who are deathless.

The crew put in, knowing the place from a past time.
They drove onto land strongly, half of the ship's length
beached, the arms of the rowers driving her that fast.
Stepping down from the well-benched ship onto land there,
first they carried Odysseus out of the hollow
ship with his bedding, the shiny blanket of linen,
and laid him, quelled by the Sleep-God, down on the
    seashore.
Then they hoisted the gifts from high-born Phaiakians   120
prompted by great-hearted Athene as Odysseus left there
for home and arranged them in piles at the base of the
    olive,
away from the path. So no one happening by there
would damage or steal them before Odysseus woke up.

A God Still • Then the Phaiakians left for home. But Poseidon
Angry   recalled the threats he'd made at godlike Odysseus
right from the start. He asked for the planning of Zeus now:
"Fatherly Zeus, I'm not esteemed any longer
by deathless Gods if humans esteem me so little,
not even Phaiakian people, those of my bloodline.   130
I said Odysseus plainly would suffer a great deal
while sailing for home, but I never entirely robbed him
of homecoming after you pledged and gave it your own nod.
Now these men have brought him, asleep in their fast ship,
to lay down there on Ithaka, lavished with endless
gold and bronze presents, clothes with a fine weave,
more than Odysseus ever could take from the Trojans
had he come home unharmed with a full share of that
    booty."

Esteem   Cloud-gathering Zeus answered by asking,
and Fear   "Earth-Trembler, you wide ruler, what have you said here?   140
of the Gods   The Gods esteem you still. It's surely a hard thing
to stop esteeming the best of our Gods and our eldest.

But now if a *man* gives in to his muscle and power
and fails to esteem you, you always can punish him later.
Do as you like, whatever pleases your own heart."

Poseidon the Earth-Shaker answered him loudly,
"Dark-cloud Zeus, how fast would I do as you say now!
But always I check myself, in awe of your spirit.
Right now I'd like to smash the Phaiakians' charming
ship as they sail back home from escort on hazy   150
seas. To make them stop this bounty of send-offs
for men I'd circle and hide their city with great peaks."

A Stone Ship   But cloud-gathering Zeus answered by saying,
"Dear friend, another way seems best in my own mind.
When all the people are watching from town as the vessel
is rowed in close to the land, change her to hard stone—
a race-fast ship like rock! They'll all be astonished
too when you circle and hide their city with great heights."

Soon as the Earth-Shaker Poseidon had heard him
he made his way to Phaiakian homes in Skherie   160
and waited. In time the seagoing vessel was closer,
driving swiftly. The Earth-Shaker approached her
and turned her to stone. He lodged her there on the bottom,
the flat of his hand pressing. Then he was far gone.

An Old   Now Phaiakian men well known for their sea-craft,
Prophecy   lovers of long oars, turned and spoke to each other,
glancing at neighbors, their words with a feathery swiftness,
"Oh no—who stopped our race-fast ship in the water?"
"Just now she was driving to port and wholly in plain view."

They spoke that way, not knowing how it had happened.   170
But then a strong Alkinoos spoke to his people.
"Look at this: surely a long-past prophecy came true.
My father often told me Poseidon was angry
because we gave our escort safely to all men.
He said the God would stun a Phaiakian well-made
ship some day returning home from escort on hazy
seas. He'd circle and hide our city with great heights.
The old one spoke that way; now everything's happened.
Come on then, let's all obey the words I am saying:

stop our send-offs for people whenever a stranger   180
arrives in our city. Let's offer twelve of our choice bulls
quickly to Lord Poseidon and ask for his mercy,
not to circle and hide our city with great heights."

Those were his words. Frightened, they gathered the choice
        bulls.
Then they offered prayers to lordly Poseidon.
Phaiakian leaders, advisors and lords of the people
stood around the altar.

Strange Home   Meanwhile godlike Odysseus,
now awake on his fathers' land, could not know it,
having been gone so long. A Goddess had poured down
mist as well—the daughter of Zeus, Pallas Athene—   190
to make him unknown. She'd tell him soon about each
        thing
but now his wife, his townsmen and friends would not
        know him,
not before the suitors paid for all of their outrage.
• So everything looked quite strange to the lord of the island:
ongoing trails, inlets good for a mooring,
rocks and soaring cliffs, trees in their full bloom.

He jumped up, stood there and studied the land of his
        fathers.
Then he moaned, using the flat of his two palms
to slap his thighs, asking himself like a mourner,
"Look at me now, what people's land have I come to?   200
Are men here overbearing, savage and unjust?
Or mindful of Gods maybe and kindly with strangers?
Where do I carry so much wealth or wander
around myself? I wish I'd stayed with Phaiakian people
far behind me, or gone to another powerful ruler
who'd make me his friend and send me right on the
        way home.
But now I'm unsure of this wealth. How can I leave it
here to become, by chance, the booty of others?
Look at me! All the Phaiakian lords and advisors
were not so thoughtful or fair—they took me to strange land. 210
First they promised a ship that would take me to clear-view
Ithaka, then they failed to end it the right way.

May Zeus, the God of lowly beggars, gazing on all men,
make them pay, avenging those who offend him.
Come on though—I surely can count my goods and
    review them.
Maybe the crew of that hollow vessel purloined some."

Visit by a
Young Man

He spoke that way and counted the beautiful tripods,
gold and cauldrons, clothing splendidly woven.
Nothing was missing. Then he longed for his homeland,
dragging himself along the shore of the loud sea,   220
steadily moaning. Now Athene approached him,
taking a young man's body, a herder of sheep-flocks,
a mild young man, the way the child of a lord is.
She wore a well-styled double cloak on her shoulders.
Her oil-smooth feet had sandals; her hand had a long spear.
Glad to see her, Odysseus walked up and faced her,
telling her briskly, the words with a feathery swiftness,
  "My friend, since you're the first one I've met in this country,
I hail you and ask: don't face me now with a wrong mind.
Save my goods instead, and myself. For I'm praying   230
as though to a God, approaching your knees like a poor
    friend.
Tell me all of the truth and help me to know well
who your people are and what is this country,
whether a clear-view island or part of the soil-rich
mainland with coastline sloping down to the salt sea?"

A Name
That's Gone
as Far as Troy

The glow-eyed Goddess Athene answered by saying,
  "You are silly, stranger, or come from a ways off
to ask about this land. It's hardly so nameless
as all that: surely many people have known it,
whether their homes are close to Dawn and the Sun-God   240
or those behind them with homes in the hazy darkness.
It's rugged land, not for the driving of horses
but not so poor. Though it's not broad in its outline,
the grain harvests are wonderful. Plenty of grapevines
yield good wine, there's plenty of rain and a dense dew.
The land's good for our goats, our cattle and sundry
trees for water is always flowing the year round.
The name of Ithaka, stranger, therefore has traveled
even to Troy—that far they say from lands of Akhaians."

Murder on
Krete Her words made long-suffering, godlike Odysseus   250
        glad. He hailed his fatherland, named by the Goddess—
        Pallas Athene, daughter of Zeus, who carries the Aigis.
        He spoke to her now and his words had a feathery
            swiftness
        but not each word was true. Holding back what he told her,
   •   always changing notions, his brain was a wizard's:
        "I knew of Ithaka too, even on ample
        Krete that's far over the sea. Now I have come here
        hauling this wealth. I left as much to my children
        when I ran off: I'd cut down Orsilokhos, well-loved
        son of Idomeneus. Fast on his feet and the winner   260
        of every race with bread-eating men on the island
        of broad Krete, he'd tried to rob me of all my booty
        from Troy. That wealth had caused me plenty of heartache,
        battling with men and crossing the heaviest salt seas.
        I'd also refused to welcome or fight for his father
        in Trojan country. I led some others, my own men.

        "I hurled that bronze-pointed spear myself as Orsilokhos
        left his farm. I'd lain in wait by the path with a war-friend.
        The sky was black that night and men could not see us:
        I wrested the man's life when no one could spot me.   270
        Soon as the pointed bronze struck him and killed him
        I hurried down to a ship where I pleaded with high-born
        Phoinikians, gave them prizes to gladden their spirits
        and asked them to set me down on Pulos or land me
        in God-bright Elis, the country ruled by Epeians.

Unlikely
Landing at
Night "But powerful gales thrust them away from that quarter—
        against their will—they never wanted to trick me.
        Wandering off from there, at nighttime we came here
        and rowed in the harbor fast, none of us mindful
        of food although we badly needed to take some.   280
        We stepped from the ship just so and all of us lay down.
        I was limp. A honeyed sleep overcame me.

        "They took my wealth from the hollow vessel in good time
        and placed it all to one side as I lay on the beach-sand.
        They boarded again and sailed for well-settled Sidon.
        I was left behind though, my heart in its deep stress."

The Goddess
and Man
Revealed

After he said all that the glow-eyed Goddess Athene
smiled and gently stroked him. She changed to a woman,
tall and beautifully shaped, skilled in the best crafts.
She answered him now and her words had a feathery
    swiftness,   290
"A man must be sneaky and smart to beat you at all your
wiles—not even a God could, chancing to meet you—
so richly thoughtful and stubborn! It seems you will never
stop your lying, not even here in your own land.
You love such guile and fakery, right from your feet up!
Come on now, stop such talk. Both of us know well
how you're shrewd, the best by far among all men
with words and plans. And I'm well known among all Gods
for wisdom and counsel. Yet you're failing to know me:
Pallas Athene, daughter of Zeus. I am always   300
there beside you, I guard you through every struggle
and made you dearly loved by all the Phaiakians.

The Final Plot

"I came here now in order to weave you a good plan.
I'll hide this wealth which the high-born Phaiakians
    gave you
leaving for home—they followed my knowing counsel.
Then I'll tell you of all the doom you will go through,
the plight in your well-built house. Your need is to bear up.
Don't tell anyone now you wandered and came home,
not one woman or man of them all. You should keep still,
undergo pain, men's force and plenty of hardship."   310

Doubting the
Goddess

Odysseus answered her then, full of his own plans.
"Goddess, it's hard for a man to know when he's met you,
however shrewd: you take on many disguises.
I do know well the way you were kind in a former
time at Troy when sons of Akhaians were battling.
But after we looted the high city of Priam
and left in our ships, when a God scattered Akhaians,
I never saw you, daughter of Zeus, nor did I catch you
boarding my ship in order to save me from torment.
I only wandered, my heart always inside me   320
piecemeal. At last the Gods freed me from trouble,
but not till I came to the fruitful land of Phaiakians.
You braced me with words, you led me yourself to the city.
Now I beg you before your Father—I don't think

♦ I've sailed to clear-view Ithaka—no, it's some other
land to be roamed and you, I think, have been teasing,
saying all this in order to muddle my own mind.
Tell me, have I arrived in my fatherland truly?"

Ithaka Surely   The glow-eyed Goddess Athene answered by saying,
"Surely those are always the thoughts in your own chest,   330
so I cannot abandon you now in your sadness,
because your wits are sharp, you're kindly and thoughtful.
Another warrior wandering home would have gladly
rushed off to see his children and wife in the great hall.
It's not your way, not yet, to learn or to know much
before you've tested your wife. Well, but the lady's
waiting still in the great hall, forever unhappy,
her days and nighttimes wasting. Often the tears fall.
I never doubted myself, though: I knew in my own heart
you'd come back home when all your crewmen had
           perished.   340
Yet I hardly wanted a war with Poseidon,
my Father's brother. He thrust rage in his own heart,
a killing spite, because you blinded his own son.

"Come on then, I'll show you Ithakan sites to persuade you.
There's the harbor of old Phorkus the sea-lord.
The olive-tree dense with leaves is close to the harbor's
head not far from the charming cave, misted and sea-gray,
sacred to Nymphs called *Neiades*—Nymphs of the Water.
You offered many flawless hecatombs often
inside that overarching cave to Nymphs of the Water.   350
And there's Neriton Mountain, wearing its green woods."

A Kiss   The Goddess cleared off haze when she spoke and the
for the Land   country
was right there. Long-suffering, godlike Odysseus gladly
hailed and kissed his land, a giver of good grain.
He called on the Nymphs at once, raising his two hands:
"You Water-Nymphs, Zeus's daughters! I thought I would
           never
see you again. But now I hail you with loving
vows and I'll bring you presents the way that I once did,
if Zeus's daughter, the war-prize bringer, will freely
allow me to live, and my own son to become tall."   360

But
How to Kill?

The glow-eyed goddess Athene answered by saying,
"Take heart: don't let your mind be troubled by those things.
Instead we should hurry and place your goods in the wondrous
cave's innermost corner. They'll keep for you safely.
Then let's ponder together which is the best way."

So with that word the Goddess entered the misty
cave and searched for a nook. Meanwhile Odysseus
brought it all inside—the gold and tireless
bronze and well-styled clothes—Phaiakian presents.
He carefully set them down and a stone was placed at the
        entrance   370
by Pallas Athene, daughter of Zeus, who carries the great
        shield.

Then the two sat down at the base of the holy
olive to plan death for the pride-smitten suitors.
The glow-eyed Goddess Athene started by saying,
"Son of Laertes, bloodline of Zeus, my wily Odysseus,
think about how you can get your hands on the shameless
men who've ruled for three long years in your great hall.
They dote on your godlike wife, they load her with her
        presents.
While her heart pines for your homecoming each day,
she pledges hope for them all—some promise for each man,   380
a message to send him—her mind is pondering elsewhere."

The Man
Cannot Do It
Alone

An answer came from Odysseus, full of the best plans:
"Look at this! Just like Atreus's son Agamemnon
I might have gone to an evil end in my own hall
unless you told me, Goddess, the truth about all this.
Come on then, weave me a plan, help me repay them.
Stand close to me too, the strength and courage inside me,
the way we loosened the fire-lit heights of the Trojans.
My glow-eyed Goddess, if only you'd eagerly stand close,
I'd battle three hundred men myself in the great hall.   390
So my queenly Goddess, I pray you will help me gladly."

The Look of a
Beggar

The glow-eyed Goddess Athene answered by saying,
"I'll surely be with you there and then: I'd hardly forget you
the hour that work's to be done. Yes, and I think some

blood and brains will spatter the floor of your large hall—
suitors' blood, the men who devour your resources.
♦ Come on then: I'll make you unknown to all of your people.
I'll parch your limber arms and beautiful skin-tone.
I'll blight your head's bright hair and dress you in poor
    clothes
making men feel disgust when they see you.   400
I'll also blur your eyes, quite handsome before this,
to make you appear shameful to all of the suitors,
then to the son and wife you left in the great hall.

Help from a   "But go up first yourself to the man who has guarded
Swineherd   and cared for your swine. Always kindly and loyal,
he loves your son and thought-full Penelopeia.
You'll find him close to the hogs. The herd has been feeding
by Korakos Rock not far from the spring, Arethousa,
taking their fill of acorns and drinking the shade-black
water that helps those hogs fatten and flourish.   410
Sit and stay there. Ask the man about each thing.
I'll go to Sparte myself, known for its beautiful women,
to call Telemakhos back, the son you cherish, Odysseus.
He went to the dancing places of wide Lakedaimon
to ask Menelaos for news, whether you still lived."

Help for the   Odysseus, full of designs, answered by asking,
Son Too   "Why not tell him then? Your heart knows everything surely.
Or maybe the son should also wander the restless
sea and suffer pain while others devour his resources."
The glow-eyed Goddess Athene answered by saying,   420
"Don't be too afraid for the man in your heart now.
I guided your son myself to win him a good name
by going there. He does no work and he sits down,
relaxed in the home of Atreus's son, its bounty before him.

Another   "Young suitors though in a black ship have been waiting,
Death Threat   anxious to kill him before he returns to the land of his
    fathers.
I think they won't. Before then Earth will have covered
a few more suitors, the men who devour your resources."

An Old Man   She spoke that way and touched him. The wand of Athene
Suddenly   parched his limber arms and beautiful skin-tone.   430

She blighted the brown hair on his head and she covered
his whole body with age, the skin of an old man.
She also blurred his eyes, quite handsome before that,
and threw some old and tattered clothing around him,
a ragged and coarse tunic, grimy from bad smoke.
She flung the hairless and bulky hide of a once-quick
stag around him. She gave him a staff and beggarly
      knapsack,
dotted with holes. Its carrying strap was a plain rope.
So they planned and parted, Athene to God-bright
Lakedaimon to bring back home the son of Odysseus.   440

BOOK 14

The House of the Swineherd

Odysseus

The man walked from the harbor now on a stony
trail uphill through woods to the heights shown by Athene,
the path to his godlike hog-man. He'd cared for Odysseus's
livestock most among slaves acquired by his master.

He found him sitting down out front where the forecourt
♦ was well built up, a handsome place with a broad view
and plenty of space around it. Built by the swineherd
himself to care for the hogs of his king who was long gone,
his work unknown to Penelopeia and aging Laertes,
he'd dragged big stones and topped them with thorn-limbs.   10
Around it he drove in stakes that way and this way,
all set close, black oakwood, its bark stripped.

Inside the forecourt twelve sties had been built up
next to each other. The sows used them for sleeping,
fifty penned in each sty to wallow or doze there—
breeding females. The males who slept on the outside
were far fewer: godlike suitors had killed them
for feasts and lowered their numbers. The swineherd would
     always
send them a fattened boar, the best of the whole herd
whose number now was three hundred and sixty.   20

Dogs were always dozing close by, savage and beastlike,
four of them raised by the swineherd, a leader of good men.
He fitted sandals now to his feet with some cuttings
of lightly colored ox-hide. Three other swineherds
had gone off this way and that way, driving their clusters
of hogs, and a fourth he'd sent himself to the city,
driving a boar. The overbearing suitors had forced him:
they'd kill it there and fill their hearts with the pig-meat.

Suddenly now the dogs spotted Odysseus,
growled fiercely and charged him. Odysseus wisely   30
sat and let the staff drop from his right hand.
There on his own land he'd have suffered outrageous

harm but the swineherd was fast in running behind them—
the ox-hide dropped from his hand as he rushed through
    the open
gate with a yell—and he scattered the dogs this way and
    that way
with volleys of stones. Shortly he said to his master,
"The dogs would surely and swiftly have torn you
apart, old man, your cries pouring shame on my own head.
Gods have given me plenty of sorrow already.
I've sat here often in pain, mourning a godlike   40
master and raising fattened boars to be eaten
by strangers while my master is wandering hungry
maybe in a far-off land, a city of strange-sounding people—
if somehow the man's alive and looks at the Sun's light.

Warmer   "But follow me now, old man, let's go to my lodging.
Welcome   After your heart has filled with food and my good wine,
    you'll tell me your birthplace and all the trouble you've gone
        through."

Speaking that way the godlike hog-tender led him
along to the house. He strewed thick brushwood to sit on
and spread out a goat-hide, a bulky and wild one,   50
shaggy and broad—his own bed. Glad to be welcomed
so and promptly, Odysseus said to the swineherd:
"My host, I pray that Zeus and the rest of the deathless
Gods lavish whatever you want. You've welcomed me fully."

The Long-Lost   Then, Eumaios the swineherd, you answered by saying,
Master   ♦"My guest, even if men poorer than you came,
    it's wrong to mistreat them. Every stranger and beggar
comes from Zeus. Our gifts are small but they're friendly
being our own. Slaves must follow that custom,
however they dread their lords powerfully ruling—   60
our new lords. For Gods blocked his return home,
a man who'd care for me staunchly, give me belongings,
a house and land—yes and a wife who had often
been wooed by men! A good-hearted master lavishes all that
on hard workers. And Gods have cherished my own work:
see how it's all flourished under my tending.
My lord would have helped me greatly if only he'd
    grown old

here at home. But he died. Let Helen's family wholly
die for she loosened the knees of thousands of soldiers.
My master went there, honoring great Agamemnon   70
battling Trojans at Ilion, known for its horses."

Not the Best   He stopped and took a belt to cinch up his tunic.
Ham Dinner   He walked to the pens and sties, full of their porkers,
chose a pair and took them both to the slaughter.
He seared them, sliced them and put each slice on its
    own spit.
Having roasted them all he set them there for Odysseus,
ham hot on the spits with a white sprinkle of barley.
Then he'd mixed the honey-sweet wine in an ivy
bowl and sat down facing his master and urged him,
"Eat now, stranger. It's all meat from the younger   80
pigs we slaves can hand you. The fat ones go to the suitors
who don't think much of the angry Gods or of pity.

The Gods'   "But blessed Gods don't like such reckless behavior.
Vengeance   They prize justice, the acts of those who are fair men.
Even a lawless enemy landing on foreign
soil after Zeus allows him some booty:
he loads a ship with plunder and sails home
but powerful dread falls on his heart of that vengeance.

"But these men know—they've heard the voice of some
    Power—
my master has died wretchedly. Now they will not court   90
right and they won't go home. They'd rather be careless,
haughtily wasting resources, sparing in no way.
Every day and evening—gifts from the great Zeus—
they kill not one or a pair of victims but far more.
They're overbearing with wine, drinking and wasting.

A Onetime   "My master's wealth was boundless. None of our war-chiefs
Vast Wealth owns as much, not on the shadowy mainland,
not on Ithaka. Twenty together could hardly
match his goods. I'll tell you myself what their count is.
♦ He owns twelve herds of cattle and sheep on the mainland,   100
twelve of swine and twelve wide-ranging goat herds,
tended by strangers there or watched by his own men.
Here on the island outskirts too, grazing and spread-out,

eleven herds of goats are watched by trustworthy goatherds.
But every day one goat is led from a herd to the suitors,
the fattest of all, the goat that looks like the best one.
I watch and guard the swine herd myself but I also
carefully choose and send the best to the suitors."

Liars and   His lord, as he spoke, ate meat with relish. He drank wine
Listeners   briskly and planned harm for the suitors in silence.   110

After dinner, his heart full of the good fare,
he filled a cup with wine, the cup he had drunk from,
and offered the full cup to his host, who happily took it.
Odysseus asked him, the words with a feathery swiftness,
"Who was the man who bought you, my friend, with his own
        wealth,
the very rich and powerful master you spoke of?
You said he died to honor the great Agamemnon.
Tell me the name of such a man—I may know him.
Zeus and the other deathless Gods will know if I happened
to spot him. I could have news. I've wandered a long way."   120

The swineherd answered him promptly, a leader of
        good men:
"Old man, no one wandering by with news of my master
would make his well-loved son or wife a believer.
Because a wanderer always needs to be cared for
he often lies. The truth is not what he wants most.
So many wanderers came to Ithakan country
and went to my lady, telling her stories they made up.
Still she welcomes them all and asks about each thing,
sadly. Tears form at her eyelids and fall down—
a woman's way when her husband dies in a far land.   130
So a man like you might spryly work up a story
if someone gave you a tunic and cloak for your trouble.

Too Late   "But dogs or fast-flying birds already have torn off
for Another   flesh from my master's bones. The spirit has left him.
Tall Tale   Or sharks devoured him at sea, the bones of my master
lie on a beach, wrapped in a layer of thick sand.
He's lost out there, all of his loved ones from now on
must mourn and I mourn most, for how will I ever
find another lord so mild wherever I travel?

Not if I sailed again to the house of my Father   140
and Mother where I was born, the home I was raised in.
And yet I mourn them less—although I am eager
to go back home and see them again with my own eyes—
the longing that holds me here is for long-gone Odysseus.
Stranger, I've scrupled to name him, though he is far off,
because of his heart's love. He cared for me deeply.
I call him a lordly friend, the man who is absent."

Your Lord Must   Long-suffering, godlike Odysseus answered,
Come Home   "My friend, you strongly deny it, saying your master
will never come home, your heart will always believe that.   150
So I won't say it myself, but rather I'll swear it:
Odysseus *must* come home! And soon as he lands here,
soon as he walks in the palace, reward me for good news:
give me a tunic and cloak, some beautiful clothing.
Whatever my needs, till then I will take nothing.
I hate the man more than the gates of Aides
who yields to his own wants and makes up a story.
Zeus be my witness, first of the Gods, and your welcoming
        table—
and faultless Odysseus's hearth, a place I will go to—
surely it all will end the way I will say it: 160
♦ this very month Odysseus truly will come home,
after the moon has waned and another is waxing.
Returning home he'll take revenge on whoever
mistreats his wife and well-known son in his own house."

The Ambush   But then Eumaios the swineherd, you answered by saying,
"Old man, I won't reward you myself for your good news.
Odysseus won't come home. Just drink and relax here.
Let's talk about other things. Don't remind me,
putting the heart in my chest in anguish. It always
returns when someone names my wonderful master.   170
We'll let it lie, your oath. And yet may Odysseus
come back home! I want it myself, and Penelopeia,
old Laertes and godlike Telemakhos want that.

"I grieve so much for the child too of Odysseus,
Telemakhos, helped by the Gods to grow like a young oak.
I thought he'd stand among men no less than the father
he always loved, a marvel in build and in beauty.

But now some deathless God has damaged his good mind
or maybe a man did: he went for news of his father
in holy Pulos. But high-born suitors are waiting   180
to snare him traveling home in order to wipe out
♦ godlike Arkeisios's bloodline on Ithaka, making
them all nameless. We'll let him be, whether he's caught
    there
or makes an escape with the hand of Zeus overarching.

Troubled   "But now say a word, old man, for your own cares.
Spirits   Tell me the truth of it all, help me to know well
the man you are. Where are your city and parents?
What sort of ship did you sail on? How did the crewmen
take you to Ithaka? Who did they claim to be sons of?
I hardly suppose you came to our island by walking."   190

An answer came from Odysseus, full of his own plans:
"Well I'll speak about that, I'll answer you truly.
Yet if we both had food and honey-sweet wine here
to eat and drink for a long time in your shelter,
dining in peace while others handle the farmwork,
my tale could easily run through the course of a whole year
and not be done with all that's troubled my spirits,
all the tasks that Gods have willed me to take on.

A Warrior ♦"The broad island of Krete, I claim, was my birthplace.
from Krete   My Father was wealthy enough, with plenty of other   200
boys in the great hall, born and raised by his own wife.
Yet the mother who gave me birth was a second
wife he'd bought. But the son of Hulakos, Kastor—
the man I claim to be born to—honored me much as the
    other
lawful sons. Esteemed as a God in Krete's country
Kastor had goods, lands and sons who were highly
praised until the Powers of death took him to Aides'
house. The sons divided my Father's belongings:
highly spirited men, casting their own lots,
they gave me very little, only a small house.   210

"In time I married a woman whose people were quite rich.
My bravery won her: I was no fool or coward
waging war. Though all that power has left me

look at the husk—I think you'll know what the grain was.
Surely a great deal of misery owns me
now but Ares gave me boldness then and Athene
drove me to smash front ranks. I picked out the ablest
men for an ambush and plotted my enemies' mayhem.
My heart was brash, I never looked for a death-blow.
I always leaped out first to kill with a spear-thrust   220
whatever enemy ran away on his fast feet.

"So I was warlike. Working a farm I did not like,
tending house or raising children to stand out.
But oared ships were always things that I relished,
battles and carefully crafted lances and arrows.
A somber life to some men? Feared and revolting?
I liked it though—it was placed by a God in my own heart.
This man enjoys one task, that man another.

Driven to Troy "Before the sons of Akhaians walked onto Troy's land
I'd led my men nine times in fast-running vessels   230
to strike at foreigners, chancing on plenty of booty.
I chose what suited me first; later a good deal
came by lot. My house was a great one in no time,
causing my name to be feared and praised among Kretans.

"Then Zeus, watching from far off, plotted a hateful
course that crumpled a great number of men's knees.
I was told, along with well-known Idomeneus,
to head our ships for Troy. No one could help me
answer no. The harsh cries of people engulfed us.

"For nine years we fought there, we sons of Akhaians.   240
We wrecked the city of Priam during the tenth year
and sailed for home in our ships. But Akhaians were
    scattered
by Gods when Zeus, that Plotter, planned more harm for a
    sad man.

Driven to Egypt "I'd stayed home for only a month, enjoying my children,
my wealth and the wife I'd married, before some spirit
told me to sail once more. I'd voyage to Egypt
with godlike crewmen in ships weighed with our good
    stores.

Nine vessels were weighed down, my men were gathering
    briskly
and then for six whole days the war-friends I trusted
dined grandly. I gave them plenty of victims   250
myself to offer to Gods and prepare for our dining.
We sailed from the broad island of Krete the seventh
day and were helped by the Northwind's beautiful blowing:
we moved as if sailing downstream. None of my vessels
came to harm. As we all were healthy and quite safe
we sat down, helmsman and wind holding our course well.

Death   "Five days later we reached the gentle waters of Egypt.
or Slavery   I stood my up-curved ships by the river of Egypt
and spoke to them all myself, the crewmen I trusted:
'Stay here close to the ships and safeguard the squadron.'   260
I urged scouts to find good spots to be lookouts.

"They yielded to brashness instead. Pushing their own
    strength,
 ♦ they promptly ravaged handsome fields of Egyptian
farmers and hauled off women and helpless children—
they'd murdered the men. But shouts went fast to the city,
the call was heard and with Dawn an army had shown up,
filling the whole plain with foot-soldiers, horsemen
and glaring bronze. Then Zeus, whose joy is in thunder,
threw a revolting scare in my men: no one was daring
to stand and face that menace closing on all sides.   270
Many of us died right there, cut down by the sharp bronze.
Others were led off alive and forced into slavery.

Pity for   "But Zeus himself now put a thought in my own mind—
the Humbled   although I wish I'd died there, gone to a black doom
Stranger   that day in Egypt, since pain would welcome me
    quite soon—
I pulled my well-worked helmet away from my head fast,
the shield from my shoulder, the spear fell from my
    right hand,
I went by myself to their king's chariot horses,
grasped his knees and kissed them. He pitied and saved me.
I wept as he sat me and drove me home in the chariot.   280
Despite the ash-wood spears of throngs who approached me,

men who were anxious to kill, glutted with fury,
the king stopped them. He dreaded the anger of great Zeus,
the God of guests who rages most against wrong acts.

Another Liar "I stayed there seven years. I gathered a good deal
of wealth from Egyptian people. They all were forthcoming.
But then as the eighth year came and moved in a circle,
• a man arrived from Phoinikia. A liar and nibbler,
he'd surely caused people plenty of trouble.
He coaxed me and changed my mind: he got me to sail off   290
to where his house and wealth were—Phoinikian country.
And there I stayed by the man's side for a whole year.

The God "When all those months and days came to an ending,
Storms Again soon as the year rolled by and the seasons had circled,
he took me aboard a seagoing vessel to Libya.
His plan was a lie, that I'd help him ferry some cargo;
he wanted to sell me, in fact—and sell for a huge price.
I went aboard sensing a plot but he forced me.

"Yet as our ship ran on with a beautiful Northwind
passing central Krete, Zeus was planning to kill *them*.   300
Soon as we sailed past Krete, with nothing around us—
no land showing, only the sky and the salt sea—
Zeus, the son of Kronos, heightened a dark cloud
over the hollow ship. Waves were graying beneath it,
the God thundered and hurled a bolt at the same time,
rattling the whole vessel. Struck by that lightning
she filled with sulphur, and all the crewmen were tumbling
• over, looking like cormorants circling the black ship,
bobbing on crests. The God stole their return home.

A Saving Mast "But Zeus himself, as agony clutched at my own heart,   310
placed in my hands the unwieldy mast of the dark-prowed
ship to help me escape once more from the worst harm.
I held on tight. Caught in that murderous windstorm,
for nine days I was carried along. Then on the tenth black
night a gigantic swell caught me and rolled me
• ashore among Thesprotians. Pheidon, their ruler and war-
chief,
cared for me, no pay asked, for his own son had found me

cold and worn down. His hand had helped me to stand up.
He took me home himself to the house of his father
and gave me clothes to wear, a mantle and tunic.   320

Come Home   "There I heard of Odysseus. Pheidon had loved him,
Openly   a guest on his way, he said, to the land of his fathers.
or Disguised He showed me all the wealth amassed by Odysseus,
             bronze and gold, iron wrought with a struggle—
             that wealth could feed his heirs to the tenth generation—
             so much treasure lay in the house of that ruler.
        •   He told me the man had gone to Dodone to hear out
             plans from Zeus, God of the oak-tree with high leaves:
             how to return to fruitful Ithakan country?
             Openly? In secret? He'd been away for a long time.   330
             The king swore in his house before me, tendering
                   wine-drops
             to thank the Gods, that a ship was launched and her
                   crewmen
             ready to take the man to the well-loved land of his fathers.

Disloyalty and   "But first he sent me away. Thesprotian sailors
Greed Again   were bound by chance for Doulikhion, known for its
                        grainfields.
             He told them to take me with care to Akastos, the ruler.
             But then a vicious scheme entered the crewmen's
             minds to make my pain and misery thorough.
             Soon as the seaworthy ship was far from the mainland
             they promptly made it the first day of my slave-life.   340
             They pulled off my clothes, that fine mantle and tunic,
             and threw old rags and a wretched mantle around me,
             the tatters I'm wearing now—you see with your own eyes.
             They came at dusk to clear-viewed Ithakan farmland.
             They lashed me tight on the well-planked ship with some
                   twisted
             line and disembarked themselves in a hurry
             to eat a meal right there on the shore of the salt sea.

             "But now the Gods themselves loosened my bindings
             with ease and I promptly covered my head with some
                   old rags.
             Sliding down the smooth loading plank till I breasted   350

the sea, I pulled with both my hands through the water.
I soon came out of the surf apart from the sailors
and climbed from there into woods and copses in full
    bloom.
I lay huddled and heard them loudly complaining,
searching around me. In time they knew there was nothing
more to be gained by looking, so they reboarded
the hollow ship. Gods themselves had concealed me
deftly. They also led me straight to the lodging
of one shrewd man. For now my lot is to live still."

Failing to Kill But then Eumaios the swineherd, you answered by saying,   360
    "Ah poor stranger, you've roused my spirits a good deal
telling me all you suffered and how you have wandered.
But not quite rightly, I think: what you said of Odysseus
cannot sway me. Why does a man of your standing
need to lie, and in vain? I know well of my master's
coming home and just how much he was hated by
    each God.
Yet they failed to kill him there among Trojans
or later, the war wound up, in the arms of his close friends.
All the Akhaians then would have built him a great tomb.
The man had also won renown for his child in the future.   370
But now the Storm Powers have carried him off without
    honor.

Lies "I live far off with my hogs. I never go to the city
from Another myself unless our thought-full Penelopeia
Wanderer asks me to come when news arrives from elsewhere.
Then people sit by the stranger and ask about each thing,
all of those who mourn their king who is long gone
and those who gladly devour his goods without paying.
But I don't like it, all that asking and prying,
   ◆ not since a man from Aitolia fooled me with stories.
He'd killed a man, he said, and wandered the whole earth.   380
He came to my house, I welcomed him here as a friend
    would,
he said he'd seen Odysseus, a guest of Idomeneus
on Krete rebuilding vessels a sea-storm had battered.
My lord would be home, he said, by summer or autumn.
He'd bring back stores of wealth and his godlike war-friends.

"Old man with your many woes, a Power has brought you.
Don't lie to make me cheerful. Don't be a charmer.
I won't respect you for that or befriend you, but rather
from awe of Zeus, the strangers' God, and from pity."

The Truth or Death

Full of designs, Odysseus answered by saying,   390
"Truly the heart in your chest is deeply distrustful.
Even with oaths I cannot move or persuade you.
Come on then, make an agreement now and for later
time for us both, and let the Gods holding Olumpos
witness my word: if your lord comes back to his own house
give me the clothes, a mantle and tunic, and send me
off to Doulikhion—that's quite dear to my own heart.
But then if your lord's not home the way I have told you,
loosen your slaves to throw me down from a great cliff.
You'll make another wretch think twice about lying."   400

The Best Boar

But now the godlike hog-tender answered by saying,
"Ah my stranger: that's my merit and good name
with people in times to come and men of our own age:
I take you inside my house and offer a guest's fare
only to take your spirit away and to kill you!
Then I could freely pray indeed to the son of Kronos.

"But now it's time for some food. My men will be back here
soon to prepare a tasty meal in our small house."
And just as the two men spoke that way with each other
swine and men were approaching, the rest of the hog-men.   410
They penned the sows in the usual place for a night's rest
while shocking squeals rose from the animals penned in.
Shortly the godlike hog-tender called to his work-friends:
"Bring me the best boar to kill for our guest here
from far away. We'll enjoy it ourselves for all of the
        hard work
and pain we've borne so long because of the white-tusked
boars while others devoured our work without paying."

Prayers, Good Cooking, and Thanks

He stopped to cut some wood and his bronze was relentless.
Others dragged in a boar, a fat one at five years,
and stood him close to the hearth. Nor did the swineherd   420
forget the deathless Gods—the man's heart was devoted—

he threw in the fire some hairs from the head of the white-
     tusked
boar as a first rite then prayed to all of the great Gods:
"Let wise Odysseus come back home to his own house."
Then he stood and struck the boar with a leftover oak-split:
the life left it. His work-friends cut its throat and adroitly
singed and quartered it. Taking pieces from every
leg to offer first, the swineherd laid them in thick fat,
strewed them with barley and threw them all in the
     hearth-fire.
They sliced the rest into cutlets. Carefully spitted   430
and promptly roasted, pulled from the fire and unspitted,
meat piled up on a board. Standing again there
to carve, the swineherd's heart knowing the right way,
he sliced up all the meat. The portions were seven:
one share went with a prayer to the Nymphs and to Hermes,
the son of Maia. The rest he allotted to each man.
He honored Odysseus most with a long chine of the white-
     tusked
boar and clearly delighted the heart of his master.
Odysseus spoke to him now, full of his own plans:
"Eumaios, I pray you're just as dear to our Father   440
Zeus as to me. I'm poor but you honored me most here."

A Slave   Then Eumaios the swineherd, you answered by saying,
of a Slave   "My Power-like guest, eat well! Whatever is lying
before you, enjoy: it's God who grants or withholds it,
the way his own heart likes. For Zeus can do all things."

He offered the first cuts to the Gods, born to be always,
and poured some glowing wine for them. Handing the
     goblet
then to Odysseus—wrecker of cities—he sat by his own
     share.
Mesaulios passed out bread. The swineherd had bought him
all on his own, seeing his master was long gone.   450
Unknown to Penelopeia and aging Laertes,
he'd bought the man from Taphians, using his own means.

Rain and Wind   So hands went out to the good things lying before them.
in the Dark   After the craving for food and drink was behind them,

Mesaulios carried the bread off. They longed for a
    night's rest,
every man quite full of the bread and the good pork.

Night came on, moonless and grim. Zeus let it rain there
all night long and the Westwind blew, always the rain-wind.
Odysseus spoke to them, mainly testing the swineherd
to see if the man would remove and give him his own
    cloak—   460
he cared a lot for him now—or encourage a friend to:
"Listen, Eumaios, and all the rest of you work-friends.
I'll brag and tell you a story. Wine is the silly
ruler that makes a man, even the wisest, a gentle
chuckler or singer. It makes him stand up and dance too.
It often provokes a word that's better unspoken.
But now that I've started to speak, let nothing be held back!

A Bitter Night   "I long to be young once more. My strength was unshaken
    at Troy ♦ the time we set up an ambush at Troy and we led it—
Odysseus and Atreus's son Menelaos were leaders   470
and I was third in command—so they had ordered.
Soon as we came to a high wall of the city
we lay around the place under some dense brush,
reeds and marsh, crouching under our weapons.
The grimmest night came on: swoops of the chilling
Northwind and layers of falling snow from above us
freezing everyone—ice formed on our shield-rims!
All the rest of our group had mantles and tunics
and slept calmly, shields guarding their shoulders.
I'd foolishly left my cloak behind when I set out   480
with war-friends because I'd hardly thought it was
    that cold—
I'd taken only my shield along and a bright belt.

The   "Then in the night's last third when starlight was changing,
Helping Lie   I spoke to the man close by, godlike Odysseus.
My elbow nudged him right: at once he could hear me.
'Son of Laertes, nourished by Zeus, wily Odysseus,
I won't be alive much longer, not with this killing
frost. I have no cloak—some Power beguiled me—
only a tunic. There's no escape any longer.'

"I spoke that way and his mind formed an idea.   490
Ah what a man and mind for planning and fighting!
He spoke to me shortly, his voice low as he answered,
'Be quiet now. The other Akhaians must not hear.'
Head propped on an elbow, he said to the others,
'A vision came from the Gods, my friends, in my sleep now.
We've gone too far from the ships. Someone should
          run back,
tell Atreus's son Agamemnon, that shepherd of people,
strongly to urge more men to come from our warships.'

Help   "Andraimon's son Thoas stood up when he'd spoken
Then and Now   and promptly took off his heavy, violet mantle   500
to run to the ships unencumbered. Taking his warm cloak,
I lay down gladly till Dawn arrived on her gold throne.

"If only I had my prime! That strength was unshaken.
A swineherd here in the house might give me a mantle
both to be kind and show regard for a good man.
Or I am scorned for the bad clothes on my body?"

Then Eumaios the swineherd, you answered by saying,
"Old man, you praise men well and your story was flawless.
So far none of your tales are improper or useless.
You won't lack clothing, therefore, or anything due to   510
a lowly and hard-tried stranger coming across us—
for now. At dawn, however, you'll scuffle with tatters
again for we don't have lots of mantles and tunics
to change or try on: there's only one for each person.
Soon as the well-loved son of Odysseus comes home,
the man will clothe you himself in a mantle and tunic.
He'll send you wherever your heart and spirit have
          called you."

Sleeping   He jumped up now and made a bed for Odysseus
Indoors and   close to the fire, throwing down fleeces and goat-hides.
Outdoors   Odysseus lay there. The swineherd threw on his body   520
a huge and dense cloak he kept on hand for a quick change,
to wear when a fiercely cold storm should arise there.
Odysseus now could rest. Sleeping around him
were all the younger men but Eumaios avoided

beds like theirs, a place too far from the best boars.
He dressed to go outside, quite pleasing Odysseus:
the man took care of the stock when his master was far off.
Tossing a sharp sword over his rugged shoulder,
the swineherd donned his thickest cloak as a wind-break
and hefted the hide of a large goat that was fed well.   530
To fight off dogs and men he carried a sharp spear.

Then he walked out. He'd go to sleep by the white-tusked
boars under a hollow rock, safe from the Northwind.

Awakened by a ◆ Pallas Athene meanwhile went to broad Lakedaimon
Goddess   to tell the renowned son that great-hearted Odysseus
                  now was home and to urge the son to return home.
                  She found Telemakhos lying close to the outstanding
                  son of Nestor in highly praised Menelaos's
                  court. The son of Nestor was mastered by gentle
                  sleep but honeyed sleep was not for Telemakhos's anxious,
                  waking heart through the endless night because of his
                        father.

                  Glow-eyed Athene stood nearby and she told him,
                  "Telemakhos, wandering far from your household no longer   10
                  becomes you. You left behind such wealth in your palace
                  and overbearing men could divide and devour it—
                  all your goods—your sailing here would be useless.
                  So hurry and urge Menelaos, good at a war-cry,
                  to send you off. You'll find your mother without fault
                  at home and already her father and brothers have urged her
                  to marry Eurumakhos. Tossing presents around her
                  more than all the suitors, he's piled up bride-gifts.
                  She mustn't remove wealth from your house without your
                        approval.
                  You know what spirit lies in the breast of a woman: 20
                  she wants the home of the man she marries to get rich;
                  she'd hardly think of a former child any longer.
                  A spouse she loved? If he dies she won't be inquiring.
                  So go there yourself and entrust all your belongings
                  to one good maid, whoever strikes you as best there,
                  until the Gods have shown you the bride you will honor.

Night Sail   "I'll tell you another thing to thrust in your own heart.
                  The boldest suitors are lying intently in ambush
                  close to rock-strewn Samos in Ithaka's channel,
                  eager to kill you before you arrive in your homeland.   30
                  I think they won't. Before then Earth will have covered
                  all the suitors, men who devour your resources.
                  Steer your well-built ship away from those islands.

213

Sail by night as well: a wind will follow behind you
from one of the deathless Gods who'll shelter and save you.

To the
Swineherd
First
"Soon as you reach the nearest Ithakan shoreline
hurry your ship and all of your men to the city.
But you go first to the swineherd, the man who is duly
tending your stock. He also thinks of you warmly.
Stay for the night. Then send him off to the city,   40
taking the news to thought-full Penelopeia
saying her son has arrived now safely from Pulos."
Those were her words. She left for the heights of Olumpos.

Night Quarrel
Telemakhos woke up Nestor's son from a pleasant
sleep with a prod of his heel. He said to him briskly,
"Son of Nestor, Peisistratos! Wake up and harness the full-
    hoofed
horses under your chariot. Let's get on with our travels."

But Nestor's son Peisistratos answered by saying,
"No way, Telemakhos! We can't drive through a murky
night however anxious to go. Dawn will arrive soon.   50
Wait for the son of Atreus, known for a spear-throw,
that war-chief, Menelaos. With gifts in our horse-car
and gentle words he'll send us off on our journey.
For all his days a guest remembers the person
who treats him well as a stranger and offers him
    friendship."

Longing for
Home
He stopped and Dawn promptly arrived on her gold throne.
Approaching them soon was Menelaos, good at a war-cry—
out of his bed alongside Helen in her beautiful tresses—
and after the well-loved son of Odysseus saw him
he hurriedly put on a shining tunic that covered   60
his frame and he tossed a bulky cloak on his thick-set
shoulders, war-chief style, to go out and meet him.
Telemakhos, loved by godlike Odysseus, told him,
"Atreus's son Menelaos, Zeus-fed lord of your people,
send me off right now to the cherished land of my Fathers.
Already my heart's longing to go to my own house."

Menelaos, good at a war-cry, answered by saying,
"I won't hold you here, Telemakhos, not long,

now that you're yearning for home. I would be angry
at other hosts who went too far to be friendly—   70
or very unfriendly. Balance is better in all things.
It's just as wrong to rush off a stranger unwilling
to go as to hold one back who's anxious to leave you.
Befriend the stranger at hand; send the stranger who
    wants that.

The Riches of ♦"But stay till I load your car with beautiful presents—
Hellas   gaze at them here with your own eyes! I'll order the women
to make you a meal from plentiful stores in our great house.
It's praise and honor for both for us, yes and a great help
to dine here well before you travel far on the endless
earth. If you choose to pass through the center of Argos   80
and Hellas, I'll join you myself: I'll harness a horse-team
and take you to men's cities. No one will send us
away as we came, they'll give us presents to haul off,
maybe a tripod of well-worked bronze or a cauldron,
maybe a pair of mules or a goblet of pure gold."

Losing the Self   But now Telemakhos gave him a sensible answer.
"Atreus's son Menelaos, Zeus-fed lord of your people,
I choose to go home right now. The day that I set out
I left no one behind to guard my belongings.
Let me not lose myself as I look for my godlike   90
Father—or lose the priceless wealth in my great hall."

Soon as he heard that, Menelaos, good at a war-cry,
promptly told his wife and all of the handmaids
to make him a meal from plentiful stores in the great house.
Boethous's son Eteoneus came to him quite close—
he'd risen from bed, he lived not far from his master—
and Menelaos, good at a war-cry, told him to kindle
a fire and roast the meat. The man heard and obeyed him.

Wealth from   His lord went down to a room beautifully scented,
the Treasure   and not alone: Megapenthes and Helen joined him.   100
Room   Soon as they came to the place where treasure was laid out,
the son of Atreus took a two-handled goblet
and told his son Megapenthes to carry the silver
bowl as Helen, meanwhile, went to the coffers
of richly embroidered robes, the work of her own hand.

A goddess-like woman, Helen took up and carried
the largest robe, the one most finely embroidered.
It shone like a star and had settled under the others.

The Best Wine-
Bowl, the
Finest Robe

They went back through the house. Approaching
        Telemakhos
now the light-haired Menelaos spoke up and asked him,   110
"Telemakhos, pray that Zeus, the husband of Here
and loud thunderer, takes you home as your heart hopes.
Now from all the treasure that lies in my household
I'll give you the best, the one most stunning and precious:
I'll give you the well-wrought wine-bowl, solidly silver
except for the edges, finished in gold by a deathless
God, Hephaistos. The war-chief and ruler of Sidon,
Phaidimos gave me the bowl when his house was my
        shelter.
Then I was traveling home; I want to bestow it on you now."

The war-chief son of Atreus, after he'd spoken,   120
placed the two-handled cup in his hands. Strong
        Megapenthes
brought the wine-bowl of dazzling silver and set it
before him. Her cheeks lovely, Helen approached him,
the splendid robe in her hands. She said to him outright,
"Dear child, I'll give you a present also to help you
recall the hands of Helen. At the hour of your longed-for
wedding your bride can wear it. Till then it should settle
close to your well-loved mother at home. May you gladly
arrive in your well-built house in the land of your fathers."

She stopped and gave him the robe. He took it with
        pleasure.   130
A war-chief himself, Peisistratos laid out the presents
with care in the chariot's gift-chest, gazing at each one.

A Last Dinner

Then light-haired Menelaos led them straight to the palace.
They sat down there on thrones and chairs in the great hall.
A maid brought them water, she poured from a pitcher
of stunning gold, and they washed their hands in her silver
basin. She set out polished tables before them.
An honored housekeeper brought them bread and
        arranged it.

She laid out plenty of foods, gracious and giving.
Boethous's son carved the meat and set out the right shares.   140
Pouring the wine was a son of highly praised Menelaos.
Their hands went out to the good things lying before them.

Last   After the craving for food and drink was behind them,
Good-Byes   Telemakhos yoked the horses promptly with Nestor's
well-known son and they mounted the colorful chariot.
They drove along to the gate, the portico echoed
and light-haired Menelaos, Atreus's son, was behind them,
his right hand holding the honey-minded wine in a golden
goblet to pour for the Gods as the chariot left there.
Standing close to their horses he hailed them and told them,   150
"Young men, be happy and take my greetings to Nestor,
a shepherd of people. The man was kind as a father
all that time we sons of Akhaians fought with the Trojans."

Telemakhos promptly gave him a sensible answer.
"Gladly, you Zeus-fed man, and just as you say it:
we'll tell all that to Nestor the hour we arrive there.
If only I'd find Odysseus too in my Ithakan household!
I'd tell him the way I found such wholeness of friendship
before I left you and brought home plenty of good gifts."

Wild Eagle and ♦ Just as he spoke a bird flew by on his right side.   160
Tame Goose   An eagle carried a large white goose in its talons,
a tame goose from the yard. Women had cried out,
all of the men gave chase, but after it came close
the eagle veered to the right, in front of the horses.
They watched it with joy, all their spirits were warming,
and Nestor's son Peisistratos started by asking,
"Now Menelaos, nourished by Zeus, lord of your people,
say if the sign from God was for you or for us two?"

Loved by Ares, Menelaos pondered the question:
how could he know and render the sign in the right way?   170
Her long robe flowing, Helen spoke out before him.
"Listen! I'll prophesy myself what the deathless
Gods thrust in my heart, the way I think it will happen.
The eagle that clutched a goose raised in our own yard
came from the mountains, its place of birth, of its nestlings.
Odysseus too will wander far and suffer a great deal

before he returns for revenge—or now he's already
home and planting harm for all of the suitors."

Then Telemakhos gave her a sensible answer.
"May loud-thundering Zeus, the husband of Here,   180
arrange that! I'd pray to Helen herself as a Goddess."

Chariot Travel He stopped and lashed the horses. Both of them swiftly
made for the plain when they'd galloped fast through
      the city.
The double yoke they bore rattled the whole day.

After sunset, when all the roadways were darker,
they came to Pherai and entered Diokles' household,
the son of Ortilokhos, born as a child to Alpheios.
They spent the night in his house, welcomed like strangers.

When newborn Dawn came on with her rose-fingered
      daylight,
they yoked the horse-team, mounted the colorful chariot,   190
drove along through the gate as the portico echoed,
and lashed the horses. They took off gladly with spirit.

The Need to   In time they were racing close to the high city of Pulos.
Get Home Fast Telemakhos spoke to the son of Nestor and asked him,
"Son of Nestor, how will you pledge what I ask you
and make it happen? We claim to be friends for a long time
because our Fathers were friends. We're also the same age
and all our travels have made us more of the same mind.
While Zeus cares for you, stop at my ship: I want to be left
      there.
The old one would keep me against my will in the palace,   200
♦ he'd longed to regale me. I must be home in a hurry."

He stopped and the son of Nestor heartily mulled it.
How could he promise and bring this off in the right way?
He pondered a while and then it seemed to him better
to turn their team to the race-fast ship at the seashore.

In time he loaded astern the beautiful presents,
garments and gold, the wealth Menelaos had given.

He heartened Telemakhos—words with a feathery
   swiftness—
"Hurry aboard now, tell your crewmen the same thing
before I arrive back home with news for my Father.   210
Both in my heart and mind I certainly know this:
my Father's spirit is overbearing, he won't let
go himself; he'll race here and call you, he won't go
back without you! For now he'll really be angry."

He spoke that way and drove the fine-coated horses
back to the city of Pulos, quickly reaching his own house.

Telemakhos heartened his crewmen now and he told them,
"Stow our gear in order, you men, in the black ship.
Let's board ourselves and get underway in a hurry."
He spoke that way, they heard him well and obeyed him.   220
All of them soon boarded and sat at the oar-locks.

The Son
of a Man
Once Rich
   While he worked, offered victims and prayed to Athene
close to the stern, a man approached from a far land,
a stranger in flight from Argos—he'd murdered a man
   there.

  ♦ A seer, the stranger came from the line of Melampous
who lived one time in Pulos, a mother of sheep-flocks.
Wealthy in Pulos, the house he'd owned was outstanding.
But later he fled to another land, far from his country
and highly spirited Neleus, the grandest person alive then,
who'd kept much of Melampous's wealth for a whole year   230
by force. Melampous was bound in Phulakos's great hall,
tightly chained, meanwhile, suffering great pain
because of Neleus's daughter. That folly and passion
were put in his brain by Erinus, the home-killing Goddess.

A Woman
Won for the
Winner's
Brother
   Yet he escaped from doom: he herded the mooing
cows from Phulake down to Pulos, making the godlike
Neleus pay for his brutal acts and taking the daughter
home—to marry his brother! Then he was gone to another
land for his lot was to live in horse-pasturing Argos.

A Seer's
Bloodline
   Melampous now would rule great numbers of Argives.   240
He took a wife there, built his house with a high roof

◆ and fathered Antiphates and Mantios, powerful children.
Antiphates fathered Oikleies, a man with a great heart.
Oikleies fathered Amphiaraos, a rouser of armed men,
heartily loved by Apollo and Zeus, who carries the great
    shield—
they loved him in every way. But the threshold of old age
never came: he fell at Thebes because of bribes to a woman.
He'd fathered a son, Antilokhos; another, Alkmaion.

Mantios also fathered sons, Polupheides and Kleitos.
Dawn on her golden throne fastened on Kleitos,   250
thanks to his beauty: she gave him life among deathless
Gods on Olumpos. Amphiaraos died and Apollo
made the highly spirited Polupheides a seer,
by far the best among men. In a feud with his father,
he settled in Huperesie for good, a seer for all men.

Homeland   His own son, named Theoklumenos, came here
Lost for a   now and stood not far from Telemakhos's fast black
Long Time   ship as he prayed and poured out wine for the great Gods.
He spoke to him promptly, the words with a feathery
    swiftness,
"My friend, as I find you here burning those victims,   260
I plead by your rites, your God—I plead by your very
life and the lives of your crewmen, those who have
    joined you—
tell me the truth I ask for, don't keep it in hiding:
who are you men? Where are your city and parents?"

Telemakhos promptly gave him a sensible answer.
"Well then, stranger, I'll tell you all you have asked for.
I'm from Ithaka, born to my Father Odysseus—
if ever he lived. He's dead and his loss has been cruel.
Just now I took some crewmen to sail on my black ship.
I came here to ask of my Father, gone for a long time."   270

A godlike man, Theoklumenos answered by saying,
"I'm out of my homeland too, after I cut down
a man of my own blood. His many family members
rule the Akhaians firmly in horse-pasturing Argos.
I ran to avoid my death, to keep from a black doom,
causing my own lot now to wander among men.

Take me aboard your ship for I came to you humbly.
Don't let them kill me: I think my enemies chased me."

Underway
North Telemakhos promptly gave him a sensible answer.
"I'd push no willing man away from our good ship.   280
Join us now and you're welcome to all that we have here."

He spoke that way to the man. Accepting his bronze spear,
he set it down on the deck of the ship with its up-curved
bow and they swiftly boarded the seagoing vessel,
Telemakhos sitting astern and, seated beside him,
Theoklumenos. Men were loosening stern-lines.
Telemakhos rallied them all, telling his crewmen
to handle and work the tackle; they promptly obeyed him.
They hoisted the fir-wood mast to be stepped in its hollow
mast-block and made it stand steady with forestays.   290
With twisted lines of ox-hide they hauled up the white sail.
Glow-eyed Athene sent them a following sea-wind,
driving swiftly across the sky to make for the fastest
run of the ship back home on the waves of the salt sea.
They passed the Krounoi and Khalkis, beautiful waters.

The sun went down and all the seaways were darkened.
They sailed near Pheai. A wind from Zeus was behind them,
they passed the brightness of Elis, ruled by Epeians.
From there they made for the islands that hurried to
     meet them,
wondering whether they'd run past death or be lost there.   300

Back on Ithaka Meanwhile Odysseus ate at the home of the godlike
swineherd with other work-friends sharing the good meal.
After the craving for food and drink was behind them,
Odysseus tested Eumaios, asking to find out
whether he'd still be kind: would he tell him to stay here
a while at his house? Or hurry him off to the city?
"Listen, Eumaios, and all the rest of you work-friends.
At dawn I'd like to wander off to the city
to beg and not be a drain on you here or your workmen.
Advise me well. Join me now with a good man   310
to guide me there. Then I'll need to wander the city
alone for gifts like a small wine-cup or wheat-bread.
I'd like to go to the house of godlike Odysseus

too with tidings for thought-full Penelopeia.
I know I'll mingle there with overbearing suitors.
Let's see if they offer me food—they have plenty of dishes.
I'd promptly work for them well, whatever they asked for,
because I can tell you—listen closely and hear me—
with help from Hermes the Guide, favoring all men's
work by making it widely honored and well known,   320
I say no one is better than I am at serving,
whether it's chopping wood or making a good fire,
roasting and slicing meat or pouring the wine right—
all those jobs a poor man does for a great man."

Don't Go   Deeply moved, Eumaios the swineherd, you answered,
to the City   "Ah, my guest, why is this thought in your mind here?
With all your heart you must be longing to die there
now if you're bent on joining that party of suitors,
men whose pride and force have reached to the iron
sky. You're hardly the kind who wait on the suitors.   330
Young men dressing well in mantles and tunics
with always a shine on their foreheads and beautiful faces—
those are their waiters. All the tables are well shined,
weighed with plenty of meat, with bread and the best wines.
Stay here. Not one man is annoyed by your presence,
not I or any work-friend, the others who've joined me.
But soon as Odysseus's well-loved son has arrived home,
he'll dress you in clothes himself, both mantle and tunic.
He'll send you wherever your heart and spirit are calling."

One of the   Long-suffering, godlike Odysseus answered,   340
Dearest Men   "I pray, Eumaios, you're just as dear to our Father
Zeus as to me: you've stopped my roaming and deep pain.
Nothing is worse for any man than to wander.
But men have wracking troubles because of their godless
bellies and oncoming pain, roving and sadness.

"Now that you've asked me to stay and wait for the
        young man,
come on and tell me: the mother of godlike Odysseus,
the father he left behind at the threshold of old age,
are they alive, by chance, under the rays of the Sun-God?
Or dead by now, gone down to the household of Aides?"   350

Lost and
Mourning
Parents A leader of men, the swineherd answered by saying,
"Well then, stranger, I'll frankly tell you the whole truth.
Laertes goes on living. Yet he is always praying
to Zeus that life will drain from his limbs in his own house
because he's mourned so hard for the son who is not there.
He mourned for a mind-full wife too: nothing
    distressed him
more than her death—too soon it made him an old man.
She'd also died mourning the highly praised Odysseus.
A heartsick death. No one should die in the same way
here at home as a friend showing he loves me.   360
Long as the lady lived, for all of her sadness,
I often took some pleasure in asking her questions.
The woman had raised me herself along with a hardy
 ♦ daughter and youngest child, Ktimene, loving her long
    robes.
She raised and esteemed me barely less than her
    own child.
When both of us came to the early prime that we longed for
she gave her in marriage on Same, garnering countless
bride-gifts. She clothed me too in a mantle and tunic,
the handsomest wear. She gave me sandals and sent me
out to the field. She more than heartily loved me.   370

A Lady
Out of Touch "Now I lack all that, however the blissful
Gods help me to thrive in the work I have charge of.
From Gods I get food and wine; I give to the poor ones.
There's no good news, however, to hear from my lady,
no word or work since harm fell on her household—
those overbearing men. Yet slaves have a great need
to talk with their lady closely and hear about each thing,
enjoying her food and wine. They love carrying something
home to the field—that always warms the heart of a helper."

Some Pleasure
in Old Pain An answer came from Odysseus, full of the best plans: 380
"Look at how you were young, my swineherd Eumaios,
wandering off so far from your homeland and parents.
Come on now, tell me: answer me truly whether
 ♦ your people's town with its wide roads was demolished,
the city your honored mother and father had lived in.
While you worked alone with cattle or fat sheep,

were you taken by cruel men to their ship? To your master's
house to be sold? I'm sure he paid them a high price."

An answer came from the swineherd, a leader of good men:
"Now that you press me, stranger, asking your questions,   390
listen in silence. Sit with your wine and enjoy it.
These nights are vast as Gods, time for our sleeping,
time for the joy of listening. No one should lie down
before his time! Too much sleep can be tiring.

"You others now, if your hearts and spirits have said so,
go outside to sleep. Soon as the day breaks
enjoy your food, then herd the swine of our master.
We two will stay in the house, drinking and dining.
We'll take some joy recalling the tales of each other's
cares and sorrows. For men take pleasure in pain too   400
after they've suffered often and wandered a great deal.

Gentle Deaths   "Now I'll tell you this tale to answer your questions.
           ♦ An island called Surie—maybe you heard tell—
           ♦ north of Ortugie, lies where Helios recircles.
           It's not too densely crowded yet it's a good land
           for oxen, herds of sheep, lots of vineyards and grainfields.
           Hunger never approaches that country, no other
           hateful sickness falls on the poorest of those men.
           Rather when people have grown too old in a city
           Apollo arrives with a silver bow, Artemis joins him   410
           and both release their gentle arrows to kill them.
           Two cities divide the whole island between them.
           My Father Ktesios ruled both parts of the island—
           a son of Ormenos, known to resemble the great Gods.

A Woman   "Phoinikians came one day. Known for their sea-craft,
Beguiled   nibbling and thousands of baubles, they landed their
                 black ship.
           Now a Phoinikian woman, tall and lovely,
           had lived in my Father's house. Her skills were outstanding.
           In time the very slyest Phoinikians beguiled her.
           First a man made love to her close to the hollow   420
           ship where she washed—a move that spellbinds the female
           mind as well—even the woman who acts right.

Then he asked her, 'Who are you? Where did you
   come from?'
She promptly showed him the high-roofed house of my
   Father
but called bronze-rich Sidon her home and her birthplace.
'I'm Arubas's daughter,' she said. 'His wealth was like rivers.
But Taphian pirates dragged me off as I came back
home from a field. They brought me here and they sold me
to that man's house. My master paid them a good price.'

"The man who'd made love to her secretly answered,   430
   'How would you like to go, sail with us back home
to see the high-roofed house of your father and mother—
see them too? They're alive, they're known to be wealthy.'

A Robbery Plan   "But now the Phoinikian woman answered by asking,
   'That might well happen if all you crewmen were willing
to swear an oath to take me back to my home safe.'

"She stopped and they all swore the way she had asked them.
After the oaths were ended, with swearing behind them,
the woman spoke up again, telling them outright,
'No more talk. None of you crewmen should hail me   440
at all, whether we meet on a roadway or somehow
close to the well, or people will go to the palace
and talk to the old one. The king might feel he should tie me
hard or chain me—and plan the deaths of you all here.
So mind my word. Go on with your trading and stowing.
After the ship's quite full of your wares and belongings,
let a messenger run to me fast at the palace.
I'll bring you whatever gold comes to my hand there.

Kidnap   'Yes and I'll gladly give you more for my passage.
I've taken care of my good master's child in the great hall,   450
a clever boy who scampers along with me outdoors.
I'd like to bring him aboard. He'll get you a great price
wherever you take him to sell to strange-sounding people.'
So with that word she went to the beautiful palace.

   •"The men remained with us there, trading a whole year,
filling their hollow ship with plenty of good stores.

Then when the hollow vessel was loaded to sail off
they sent a runner to take the news to the woman.
Their savviest man, he came to the house of my Father
bearing a golden necklace beaded with amber.   460
While all the maids and my queenly mother were gazing
closely and handling the gold, making pledges to buy it
now in the great hall, the man quietly nodded.
The woman caught his nod. Soon as he left for the hollow
ship she took my hand and led me out of the palace.
She found some tables and golden cups in the forecourt
where men had dined and worked, surrounding my
    Father—
they'd gone to their chairs for talk in the people's
    assembly—
she hurriedly took three cups to stash in her breast-fold
and haul away. I thoughtlessly followed behind her.   470

"After sunset, when all the roadways were darker,
she led me down to the well-known port in a hurry.
There was the fast-running ship and Phoinikian crewmen
boarding briskly to follow the ways of the salt sea.
After they boarded us both, Zeus gave them a fair wind.

Shark Food   "For six whole days, night and day, we were sailing.
Then Zeus, the son of Kronos, gave us the seventh
day and Artemis, Rainer of Arrows, struck the woman.
She made a thump in the bilge, resembling a gull-splash.
They threw her over the side and made her the plunder   480
of sharks or seals. I was abandoned and heartsick.

"Wind and wave drove us to Ithaka's coastline.
Laertes bought me then, using his own wealth.
So my eyes have come to gaze on this island."

Nothing   Nourished by Zeus, Odysseus answered by saying,
Is Worse Than "Eumaios, you greatly moved the heart in my own chest
to Wander by telling me all that, each heartfelt pain you have suffered.
And yet beside the bad there surely were good things
lavished by Zeus: after pain you arrived at a gentle
master's home, he offered you food and his good wine   490
gladly. Your life goes well; but I was a roamer
through many people's towns before I arrived here."

A Great
New Day
for the Father
and Son

So the two men spoke that way with each other
and soon slept. But not for long, only a short time:
Dawn came fast on her beautiful throne. At the seashore
too Telemakhos's men struck sail. Hurriedly taking
the mast down, rowing their ship to a mooring,
they tossed out anchor-stones, tightened the stern-lines
and disembarked themselves on the shore of the salt sea.
They made a meal there, glowing wine mixing with water.   500

Good Pay for
Good Work

Soon as the craving for food and drink was behind them,
Telemakhos spoke up first with sensible orders:
"You crewmen sail our black ship now to the city.
I'll go to the fields myself and look to the herders,
then go on to the city at dusk from the farmland.
At dawn I'll set out pay for the sea-work before you:
a choice dinner with honeyed wine and the best meat."

A Poor Place
for a Guest
Now

A godlike man, Theoklumenos spoke up and asked him,
"Where do I go, dear child? Whose house will I enter?
What man or ruler of rock-strewn Ithakan country?   510
Or shall I go straight to your own house and your mother?"

Telemakhos tried to give him a sensible answer.
"I'd tell you otherwise yes, go to our own house:
we don't lack welcomes for strangers. But now it's a bad
          choice—
worse for yourself, since I'll be away and my Mother
cannot see you. She seldom shows herself when the suitors
are home but stays in her upstairs room with her weaving.
I'll name you another man though, someone to go to:
Eurumakhos, mind-full Polubos's son, is outstanding.
Ithakans now regard this man as a great God.   520
He's best of the men by far, the one who is most bent
on marrying my Mother and taking Odysseus's honor.
But Zeus who lives in the sky will know on Olumpos
whether a harmful day will end before they are married."

A Sign of the ◆
Right Power

Soon as he'd spoken a bird flew by on his right side,
Apollo's nimble sea-hawk messenger, talons
clutching a pigeon. It plucked feathers that littered
the ground between the ship and Telemakhos's body.
At once Theoklumenos called him aside from his crewmen,

clasped his hand, spoke his name and addressed him: 530
"Telemakhos, surely that bird flew by on your right side
at God's command. I knew when I saw it the hawk was
     an omen.
No other family will rule Ithakan country
besides your own. Your line will always have power."

But shortly Telemakhos gave him a sensible answer.
"If only your words, my guest, could come to a real end!
You'd promptly know of my friendship, all of my own good
bounty and those who met you would say you are well
     blessed."

A Good Place   He spoke to Peiraios next, a crewman he trusted.
for a Guest   "Peiraios, Klutios's son, you minded me better   540
Now   in every way than the others who joined me for Pulos.
               Guide our stranger now to your family household.
               Esteem and welcome him gladly until I arrive there."

Peiraios, known for a spear-throw, answered by saying,
"Telemakhos, whether you go or stay here a long time,
I'll welcome and care for the man myself as a good guest."

Now to the   Those were his words. He boarded ship and commanded
Swineherd   crewmen to board themselves and loosen the stern-lines.
             They boarded quickly and took their seats at the oar-locks.

Meanwhile Telemakhos bound some beautiful sandals   550
under his feet and lifted a spear, rugged and pointed
with bronze, from the ship's deck. Stern-lines were cast off:
crewmen pushed away for the city, Telemakhos telling
them all to do so. The well-loved son of godlike Odysseus,
fast on his feet, then hiked until he came to a front yard:
there were the droves of swine and the swineherd, a
     good man
napping close by, known to be mild to his masters.

Fawning Dogs   Soon in the farmhouse the godlike hog-tender kindled
a fire and prepared a meal along with Odysseus.
At dawn the others were sent off, driving the pig-herds.

Telemakhos came. The loud-barking dogs were not barking:
they fawned around the man. Godlike Odysseus,
noting the dogs were fawning and footsteps were coming,
promptly spoke to Eumaios, the words with a feathery
  swiftness,
"Eumaios, the man approaching us there is your work-
  friend,
surely someone you know. The dogs are not barking,
they're fawning around him. I hear the tramp of his
  footsteps."   10

A Father-Like   The words were not all spoken when there at the doorway
Welcome   stood his own dear son. Amazed, the hog-tender
  jumped up,
dropping the bowls from his hands—those he had
  worked with
mixing the glowing wine—he rushed to his young lord,
kissing Telemakhos's head, both of his handsome
eyes and hands. The tears fell from his own eyes.
  ◆ A loving father welcomes his dear son in the same way,
arriving home in the tenth year from a far land,
his only son, full-grown, for whom he's agonized often.
So the godlike hog-tender hugged and kissed him all over   20
as though his lordly Telemakhos now had escaped death.
He wept as he spoke and the words had a feathery swiftness,
"Sweet light, you came Telemakhos! Truly I thought I'd
never see you again when you shipped out to Pulos.
So now enter, my dear child, for my heart takes
pleasure seeing you newly arrived in my own house
from elsewhere. You don't come often to farmlands or
  herdsmen
because remaining in town is right in your own mind
to watch those damaging men, that mob of suitors."

A Bed   Telemakhos promptly gave him a sensible answer.   30
Full of Spiders   "So it will be, uncle. But *you* are the reason
       I came here now, to see you again with my own eyes,
       to hear you say if my Mother stayed in the great hall
       or married another man—if the bed of Odysseus
       lies there in loathsome spiderwebs, lacking its sleepers."

       An answer came from the swineherd, a leader of good men:
       "The lady stays on surely. Her spirits have borne up
       there in your hall although she saddens over the always
       wasting nights and days, letting the tears fall."

The Father   He spoke that way while taking Telemakhos's bronze spear.   40
Yields   The young man passed over the stone threshold and
to the Son   walked in.
       His father, Odysseus, rose from his chair as he came on.
       Telemakhos checked him though from where he was
          standing:
      "Stay there, stranger. We'll find a seat in our farmhouse
       elsewhere surely. The man beside me will make one."

       After he'd spoken Odysseus went to the same seat.
       The swineherd piled up green shoots with a full fleece
       on top and the well-loved son of Odysseus sat there.
       Eumaios laid before them trenchers of roasted
       pork from the night before, left over from dinner.   50
       He hurriedly set out piles of bread in their baskets.
       After he mixed a honey-sweet wine in the ivy
       bowl he sat down facing godlike Odysseus.
       Their hands went out to the good things lying before them.

Who Is the   After the craving for food and drink was behind them,
Stranger?   Telemakhos turned to the God-blessed hog-man and
          asked him,
      "Uncle, where did the stranger come from? How did a
          ship's crew
       sail him to Ithaka? Who do they claim to be sons of?
       I hardly suppose he came to our island by walking."

In Need and   Then Eumaios the swineherd, you answered by saying,   60
Lowly   "Well now, my dear child, I'll tell you the whole truth.

♦ He claims the broad island of Krete as his birthplace.
He says he wandered, moving through plenty of cities
among men: that's the lot some Power has spun him.
Just now he sneaked away from a ship of Thesprotian
seamen and came to my house. I'll place him in your hands:
do as you like. He claims to be needy and lowly."

At Least
Some Help for
a Stranger

But now Telemakhos gave him a sensible answer.
"Eumaios, my heart is truly galled by your words here.
How can I welcome a stranger now in my own house?   70
I'm still young, I don't have trust in my hands yet
to fight off someone, an older man who is bridled.
My Mother's heart and mind have pondered it both ways,
whether to stay with me there and look to the household,
esteeming her husband's bed and the voice of our people,
or go off now with some man, the best of Akhaian
wooers who offers the most gifts in the great hall.

"As for your guest, because he came to your own house
I'll dress him in beautiful clothes, a mantle and tunic.
I'll give him a two-edged sword and sandals for footwear.   80
I'll send him wherever his heart and spirits are calling.
Or if you like, keep and care for him right here.
I'll send you all the food myself and the clothing.
The man should not be a drain on you or your workmen.

"But I won't let the stranger walk off and mingle
with suitors. Those men are far too prideful and reckless.
Maybe they'd taunt him, making my agony frightful.
It's hard for a man to accomplish much against many,
even a strong man: the crowd by far will be stronger."

Better
to Die Fighting
the Outrage

Long-suffering, godlike Odysseus answered,   90
"My friend, surely now it's right if I speak out,
for all your words have really torn at my own heart.
You say those men, the suitors, are reckless and planning
against your will? With a man like you in the great hall?
Maybe you want them to rule? Or maybe the country's
people hate you, heeding the voice of a great God.
Or maybe you blame your brothers, people a man trusts
as fighters and more when great conflict is building.

"If only I were young as the spirit inside me!
A son of blameless Odysseus—even Odysseus,   100
home from his wanderings—surely your lot would be
     hopeful.
Indeed let foreigners cut off my head in a hurry
if I weren't evil itself for all of those wooers
the hour I arrived in the hall of Odysseus, son of Laertes.
Yet if their numbers downed me, being alone there,
I'd rather go down hacked to death in my own hall
than watch disgusting acts go on without let-up,
pushing and striking of guests, women and handmaids
dragged around in shame through a beautiful household,
wine drawn off and wasted, men who are brashly   110
devouring food, no end to it, always the same way."

An Only Son ♦ Now Telemakhos gave him a sensible answer.
"Well now stranger, I'll tell you. I'll answer you truly.
All the people are not so angry or hate-filled.
I don't have brothers to blame, those who are trusted
as fighters and more when great conflict is building.
No, the son of Kronos made our family one line:
the only son Arkeisios had was Laertes;
he only fathered Odysseus; I was Odysseus's
only son. He left me in the hall, he never enjoyed me,   120
now there are droves of enemies right in our own house.
All of the noblest men around us, rulers of islands
like Same, Doulikhion, densely wooded Zakunthos,
and all those ruling rock-strewn Ithakan country
have tried courting my Mother, wearing the house down.
She won't say no to a wedding she hates and she cannot
make them stop. They go on eating and wasting
my home and too soon me—they'll utterly wreck me.

"But all these troubles lie on the knees of the great Gods.
Be quick now, uncle, go to our thought-full Penelopeia,   130
tell her I came back home from Pulos safely.
For now I'll stay here myself. Come back to your own
     house
after you tell my Mother only: no other Akhaian
should know since many suitors are planning to harm me."

The Old One

Then Eumaios the swineherd, you answered by saying,
"I know you and mind you: the man you ask
        understands you.
Come on though, tell me the truth: answer me whether
I go on the same road with news for Laertes,
that doomed man? Though he greatly mourned for
        Odysseus,
he went on tending the farm. He ate in the house there,   140
drinking with slaves when the heart in his chest
        inclined him.
Ah but after you sailed your vessel to Pulos,
they say he simply stopped, no eating or drinking.
He looks to no fields, he sits there, moaning and sighing,
mourning your loss, bones and muscle wasting."

More Pain,
Little Help

Telemakhos tried to give him a sensible answer.
"More pain. We'll let him alone, for all of our sorrow.
If people could have by chance all of their wishes,
I'd first have the day of my Father's return home.
Go with my news and come back. Don't wander the
        farmland   150
later to look for the old one. Just say to my Mother,
'Send your maid, the housekeeper, fast and in secret.'
That woman can take the news to aging Laertes."
Roused that way the swineherd put on some sandals,
tied them under his feet and was gone to the city.

A Tall and
Skillful Woman

Athene was not unaware Eumaios the hog-man
had gone from the house. She promptly approached like a
        woman,
tall and lovely, in crafts outstandingly skillful.
She stood at the farmhouse door, quite clear to Odysseus.
Telemakhos failed to see her before him or notice—   160
the Gods do not appear so plainly to all men.
• The dogs and Odysseus saw her. The animals whimpered,
not a bark, and ran to the other side of the farmhouse.
She moved her eyebrows, godlike Odysseus nodded
and left the house. He walked by the high wall in the
        front yard,
stood there and faced her. Athene spoke to him swiftly.
"Son of Laertes, bloodline of Zeus, my wily Odysseus!

Don't hide it now: tell the news to your own son.
After you plan that doom, the deaths of the suitors,
go to your far-famed city. I'm eager to fight there.   170
I won't be far away myself when you battle."

Returning ◆ Then he was touched by the golden wand of Athene.
Youth   First she made a well-cleaned cloak and a beautiful mantle
cover his chest. She raised his height and his youthful
looks next: he was dark, his cheeks were again full,
the beard on his chin once more growing and dark brown.

With all that done she left him again. Odysseus walked back
toward the farmhouse. His well-loved son was astonished,
he kept on looking aside, afraid of this new God.
He spoke at last and the words had a feathery swiftness,   180
"Stranger, you look so utterly changed from a while back—
you wear fine clothes, your color's no longer an old man's—
you're surely a God ruling broadly in heaven!
Be gracious and help us gladly offer you victims
and well-worked presents of gold. Be kindly and spare us."

Not a God   Long-suffering, godlike Odysseus told him,
"I'm not a God. Why make me out to be deathless?
I am your father. Because of me you have often
smarted and moaned. You've borne with men who are
           brutal."

Painful Doubt He stopped and kissed his son, letting some tears fall   190
down to the ground. He'd always firmly checked them
           before this.
Telemakhos, not yet sure the man was his father,
pressed him with words again. He answered by saying,
"You're not Odysseus, not my Father: some Power
has fooled me to make me moan still more and bewail him.
No death-bound man could ever cause this to happen,
not by his own wits, unless a God were to come down
himself and make him old or young without effort.
Just now you were old in fact, wearing your poor clothes;
now you look like a god ruling broadly in heaven."   200

An answer came from Odysseus, full of the best plans:
"Telemakhos, don't be amazed so much if the father

you love is present. Too much awe is unseemly.
In fact no other Odysseus will ever arrive here!—
such as I am. I often suffered and wandered a great deal.
I'm here in the twentieth year in the land of my Fathers.
The work was all Athene's. The bringer of war-wealth
makes me the way she wants—a Goddess can do that.
First I resembled a poor man, then I regained youth,   210
all my body adorned with beautiful clothing.
It's easy for Gods ruling broadly in heaven
both to raise a death-bound man and deface him."

Hugs and   He spoke that way, sat down and Telemakhos
Tears   hugged him.
At last he wailed and wept for his wonderful father.
Both men felt it rise, that longing to vent grief,
they cried aloud, even shriller than sea-birds,
an osprey or sharply taloned vulture whose nestlings
a fieldhand's wrested away before they are fledglings.
They let the tears as pitifully fall from their eyelids.

But Helios's light would now have set on their crying   220
had not Telemakhos asked his father abruptly,
"So now what kind of a ship, dear Father, has brought you
with sailors to Ithaka? Who did they claim to be sons of?
I hardly think you came to the island by walking."

How to Attack   Long-suffering, godlike Odysseus told him,
"Well my son, I'll surely tell you the whole truth.
Phaiakians brought me, sailors known for their sea-craft.
They send off others as well, whoever arrives there.
They led me over the sea as I slept in their fast ship.
They set me down on Ithaka, gave me outstanding   230
presents of gold, bronze and clothes with a fine weave.
That treasure lies in a cave, thanks to the great Gods.

"I came here now with Athene's planning and guidance
in order to plot the deaths of our enemy suitors.
Come on then, count up all those wooers and help me
know what kind of men they are and how many.
My own heart is flawless now, I can ponder
and plan things, whether we two can stand up against them
with no one else or whether we look for some helpers."

Overwhelming But now Telemakhos gave him a sensible answer.   240
Numbers   "Oh my Father, I often heard of your great name,
            your spear-man's hand, the shrewdness of all your counsel.
            But now you speak too grandly. I'm taken by wonder:
            how can two men fight such powerful numbers?
            The suitors are not ten men, frankly, or twice ten—
         • they're far, far more. You'll know of their count in a hurry.
            Two and fifty men from Doulikhion came here,
            young, well-chosen; six helpers had joined them.
            A crowd arrived from Same: twenty and four more.
            Twenty sons of Akhaians came from Zakunthos.   250
            Twelve are from Ithaka too, all of the bravest.
            Medon joined them, a herald; a bard with a God's voice;
            and two more helpers, skillful carvers of roast meat.
            If all of them face and fight us, crowding inside there,
            I fear the revenge you take will be bitter and deadly.
            So if you can, ponder gaining some helpers,
            those who could guard us both, willing and heart-strong."

Help   Long-suffering, godlike Odysseus answered,
from the Gods "I'll tell you myself then. Thrust in your heart what you
                  hear now.
            Ponder Athene helping us both with her Father   260
            Zeus. *Then* should I plan on others to guard us?"

            But now Telemakhos gave him a sensible answer.
            "Those you mention of course are able defenders.
            Their thrones are high in the clouds. They're also the rulers
            of other men and all the Gods who are deathless."

            Long-suffering, godlike Odysseus answered,
            "They won't hold back from the hard fighting a long time,
            those two Gods, when all the suitors and we two
            measure the strength of Ares there in my great hall.

The Beatings "But now as for you: at the first showing of Dawn's light   270
to Come   go back home and mix with the swaggering suitors.
            The swineherd will bring me down to the city in good time.
            I'll look quite old again, the wretchedest pauper.
            If I'm mistreated at home, the heart in your own chest
            must bear each hurt, however badly I suffer,
            even dragged by the feet through the house to the outdoors

or battered by things they throw at me. Watch it and bear up.
Tell them surely to stop such brainless behavior
but speak to them gently. The suitors will hardly obey you.
Yet the day of their downfall truly is close by.   280

Sooty Weapons   "I'll say this also—thrust in your heart what I tell you.
Soon as Athene, full of her plans, puts it inside me,
I'll nod my head your way. After you spot me,
take all of Ares' tools that lie in the great hall
and put each one away in the innermost upstairs
room to hide. Then smoothly lie to the suitors
after they miss the weapons. Say if they ask you,
'I took them away from the smoke. The weapons no longer
look like those Odysseus left when he ventured
to far-off Troy. The breath of the hearth-fire has grimed
     them.
The son of Kronos, besides, placed in my heart a greater   290
fear that drunk from the wine and starting a fight here
you just might wound each other, disgracing your dinner
and courtship. For iron can draw a man to its own self.'

"For us two only leave a couple of bronze spears,
two swords and a pair of ox-hide shields for our handling.
Then we can charge the suitors at last. And we'll take them
as Pallas Athene and Zeus the Counselor hex them!

Who Can Be   "Another thing to thrust in your heart when I tell you:
   Trusted?   if you're my son, you truly belong in our bloodline,   300
let no one hear Odysseus came to his own house.
Don't let Laertes know, or Eumaios the swineherd,
no household help or the lady herself, Penelopeia.
Only you and I will learn the aims of the women.
As for the male helpers, I say we should test them,
find out whether their hearts will honor and fear us,
or who's careless, belittling the man that you are now."

His glowing son was prompt to answer by saying,
"Oh my Father, I think you'll know of my spirit
very soon: nothing thoughtless will guide me.   310
But I don't think that plan of yours will advance us
both right now. Instead I ask you to ponder:
testing every worker will take you a long time

out on the farms while carefree men in the great hall
devour your goods wantonly, sparing you nothing.
As for the women, yes, I'd say you should test them,
those who treat you with scorn and those who are blameless.
Still I'd like us not to size up men in the farmsteads,
maybe rather to save that job until later—
unless you've heard from Zeus who carries the great shield."   320

Back into   All the while they spoke that way with each other,
Home Port   a well-worked ship was heading for Ithaka's harbor
carrying all of Telemakhos's crewmen from Pulos.
After they came into port—the harbor had good depth—
they hauled the night-black ship from the sea onto dry land.
Highly spirited helpers carried the gear off
briskly and took the beautiful gifts to the Klutios household.

A Mother's   A herald was promptly sent to Odysseus's palace
Great Relief   bearing a message to thought-full Penelopeia:
Telemakhos, now on a farm, had ordered his vessel   330
to sail to the city; the queen, strong in her spirits,
should not be afraid or worry, shedding her soft tears.
By chance the godlike swineherd encountered the herald
taking the same news on the way to that woman.
Soon as they entered the high-roofed house of the godlike
king the herald spoke up, surrounded by handmaids:
"Just now, my queen, your well-loved son has
        returned home."

The swineherd though came close to Penelopeia
to tell her all that her well-loved son had enjoined him.
Then after he gave her all the news he was told to,   340
he left the hall and courtyard. He hiked back to the pig-farm.

No Murder   Ah but the suitors' hearts were dismayed and discouraged.
after All   They left the hall, moved by a high wall of the courtyard
not so far from the palace entrance and sat down.
Eurumakhos, Polubos's son, began to address them.
"My friends, a huge and overbearing labor is ended:
we thought Telemakhos never would leave on this voyage.
Come on then, let's haul our best black ship to the water,
gather a crew of rowers and send off a message
fast to our men on the island—tell them to sail home."   350

He'd hardly said all that when Amphinomos, shifting
his place, spotted a ship in the fathomless harbor.
Crewmen were taking in sail and holding the oars up.
He broke out laughing, blithely telling his cronies,
"Let's not rush them a message—they're home here already!
Maybe a God told them or maybe they spotted
Telemakhos's passing ship but could not overtake her."

New
Murder Plans
He stopped and they all stood up to go to the seashore.
The black vessel was briskly hauled onto dry land
and highly spirited helpers carried the gear off.   360
The suitors went in a crowd to the place of assembly,
no others allowed to be seated, younger or older.

♦ Antinoos, son of Eupeithes, spoke to them outright.
"Look at this! Gods have saved this man from a bad end.
Our watchmen sat for days on crags where the wind blew,
often taking turns. At the setting of Helios we never
passed the night on land: we sailed on the open
sea in our race-fast ship, hoping with God-bright
Dawn to ambush Telemakhos—take him and kill him.
Some other Power, meanwhile, was guiding him
        back home.   370

Any Field or
Road
"For us here now let's plan Telemakhos's sorry
death again. He mustn't escape: so long as he goes on
living I don't think all our efforts will flourish.
The man himself is clever, a knower and planner,
our island people no longer favor us wholly.
Come on then, before he gathers all the Akhaians
again to assembly—I think he won't be relaxing
but rather vent his rage by telling the whole crowd
the way we plotted a headlong murder and lost him.
They'll hardly praise us hearing we acted wrongly.   380
They also must not wrong *us*, drive us away from
our land or force us to go to a foreigners' country.

"Take him first! Kill the man in a field, or a cart-path
far from the city. We'll hold his wealth and belongings
ourselves and split them fairly. We'll offer the palace
of course to his mother to own—and the man she will
        marry!

Or Should the   "Yet if my words don't please you, maybe you'd rather
Suit Be Ended?   the man live on with all the goods of his fathers.
                  Let's stop gathering then to devour his pleasant
                  store of wealth. Let each man bring from his own hall   390
                  presents to woo and win her. The lady can marry
                  the man who offers most. Her lot is his coming."

First the Will of   After he'd spoken they all were utterly silent.
the Gods   Then Amphinomos rose in the assembly to speak out.
                  A shining son of Nisos, the son of lordly Aretios,
                  he'd led the suitors who came from Doulikhion's grain-rich,
                  grassy island. In time he'd pleased Penelopeia
                  most with his talk. The man's heart was a good one.
                  He meant well now as he faced the gathering saying,
                  "My friends: I'd never want Telemakhos murdered.   400
                  Killing the son of a king is a frightful action.
                  I say first let's ask the Gods for their own plan.
                  If Zeus with all his laws and greatness will say yes,
                  I'll kill him myself and tell the rest of you, 'Kill him.'
                  But not if the Gods recoil. Then I would say, 'Stop.' "

                  Amphinomos spoke that way and his words were
                      appealing.
                  They promptly rose and walked to Odysseus's palace,
                  entered and found polished chairs where they sat down.

A Plea from   A new idea now came to thought-full Penelopeia:
the Queen   she'd show herself to the lawless and prideful suitors.   410
                  She knew of the end they'd planned for her son in the
                      great hall—
                  Medon the herald had told her—he'd heard them plotting.
                  So she came with her handmaids down to the great hall,
                  closer now to the suitors. This brightest of women
                  stood by a post supporting the well-built roof-beams,
                  holding a lustrous veil that covered her cheekbones.
              ♦   She turned on Antinoos, called him by name and
                      reviled him:
                  "Antinoos, clutching your pride, you worker of evil!
                  They say on Ithakan land among men of your own age
                  you're the first in counsel and speech. Yet you are not so: 420
                  you're mad. Why do you plot such doom, Telemakhos's
                      murder?

Don't you care for humble pleading? But Lord Zeus
cares and watches. It's wrong to plot harm for another.

A Father in
Flight

"Don't you recall your father came here and pleaded,
humble and fearing the people? They'd raged at him fiercely
because your father had joined with Taphian pirates
to raid Thesprotian cities—they were our friends then.
His people wanted to kill him, tear out the man's heart
and eat his piles of wealth that suited their spirits.
Odysseus checked and stopped them, their zeal
        notwithstanding.   430
Now you'd freely devour his home and marry his woman,
cut off his child from life and sicken me greatly.
I tell you to stop. I tell the others to stop too."

Denials

Eurumakhos, Polubos's son, gave her an answer.
"Ikarios's daughter! My thought-full Penelopeia,
take heart. Don't let your breast be alarmed about all this.
For now the man's not living, no, and he won't live,
who'll lay a hand on your son Telemakhos wrongly,
not while I live myself and look on the good earth.
So I will tell you, be sure it will come to a fast end: 440
the dark blood of that man at once would be flowing
around my spear. For Odysseus, looter of cities,
often sat me too on his knees and settled his roast meat
right in these hands. He often gave me his red wine.
So now I hold Telemakhos dearer than every
man by far. I say he should not fear death from the suitors.
Not from us men—from Gods it can't be avoided."
His talk was heartening, yet he'd joined in the death-plot.

The lady walked upstairs to her glistening bedroom.
She cried for her dear husband Odysseus till glow-eyed   450
Athene sprinkled honeyed sleep on her eyelids.

Back at the
Farmhouse

The godlike swineherd approached the son and Odysseus
briskly at dusk. They'd stood there, ready for dinner:
a year-old boar had been slaughtered. However Athene,
standing close to Odysseus, the son of Laertes,
touched him again with her wand. She made him an
        old man:
She dressed him in ugly clothes to hinder the swineherd

from knowing the man on sight or going to thought-full
Penelopeia with news, not guarding the secret.

First Telemakhos spoke up, telling the swineherd,   460
"You're back, godlike Eumaios: what news from the city?
Are manly suitors home from their ambush already?
Or waiting to catch me still as I sail to my own house?"

Then Eumaios the swineherd, you answered by saying,
"It never came to mind as I moved through the city
to ask those questions. My heart told me to swiftly
get back home as soon as I stated your message.
One of your own men joined me, a quick-footed herald,
telling your mother first—he gave her our message.

"I do know something else I saw with my own eyes.   470
Hiking above the city and Mound of Hermes,
by chance I spotted a nimble vessel approaching
Ithaka's harbor. Plenty of men were aboard her,
loaded with sharp, two-edged lances and round shields.
I thought they might be suitors. Still I am not sure."

He stopped and Telemakhos smiled—his power was holy—
catching his father's eye but avoiding the swineherd's.

A Hearty Meal   So now as the work was done and dinner was ready,
and a   they sat and ate. No heart lacked a share of the good meal.
Good Sleep

After the craving for food and drink was behind them   480
they thought about rest, the gift of sleep, and they took it.

Off to the City   When newborn Dawn came on with her rose-fingered
                daylight,
Telemakhos, well-loved son of godlike Odysseus,
tied beneath his feet two beautiful sandals
and took a rugged spear fitting his hand well.
Anxious to go to the city, he said to the swineherd,
"Uncle, I'm off to the city so that my Mother
can see me there. I doubt she'll stop crying before then—
all those tears, that joyless mourning and wailing—
not till she looks at her son. I charge you with one thing:
guide our sorry guest to the town. There he can cower   10
for food and those inclined may give him a cupful
of water and bread. There's no way now I can burden
myself with all such beggars: my own heart is too troubled.
So if the stranger's very annoyed it will only
make things worse. I like telling the truth here."

An answer came from Odysseus, full of his own plans:
"My friend, I'm hardly longing myself to be left here.
Better to plead in town than beg in the farmland
for food for in town any man who wants to can help me.
I'm not at the age to stay on a farm any longer   20
the way I am, obeying all the rules of a head man.
So you go on. This man you ordered will take me
soon as I'm warmed by the fire and sunlight is warmer.
My clothes are wretchedly poor, I fear the morning
frost could break me down—you say the city's a long way."
After he spoke Telemakhos walked from the farmhouse,
moving fast and brooding on harm for the suitors.

Very Loving   In time he came to the house where people had lived well.
Women   He stood the spear in its place: it leaned on a high post.
Then passing over the stone threshold he walked in.   30
The first to see him by far was the nurse Eurukleia,
spreading fleeces on chairs whose wood had been well-
                carved.
She cried out, came to him straight, and plenty of other

243

maids of steadfast Odysseus gathered around him,
kissing his head and shoulders. They welcomed him
   warmly.

Thought-full Penelopeia came from her own room,
♦ looking like Artemis, bright as the gold Aphrodite.
She threw her arms around the son she had so loved,
crying and kissing his head and both of his handsome
eyes. She wept and her words had a feathery swiftness,   40
"You came, Telemakhos! Oh, I thought I would never
see you again, sweet light, when you sailed to Pulos
against my will in secret for news of your well-loved
father who's gone. Tell me how you met him or saw him."

Time for the Vengeance of Zeus

But now Telemakhos gave her a sensible answer.
"Please don't rouse the heart in my chest as you make me
mourn, Mother. I've run just now from a steep doom.
You should bathe and put fresh clothes on your body.
Go upstairs to your room with your women and handmaids.
Vow to all of the Gods you'll render them flawless   50
hecatombs, praying Zeus will act in revenge now.

"I'll go to the assembly place to welcome a stranger
myself who joined us—we came together from Pulos.
I sent the man ahead with my godlike crewmen,
telling Peiraios to take the man to his own house,
welcome and honor him gladly until I arrive there."

He spoke that way and because her answer was wingless
she left him to bathe. She put clean clothes on her body
and vowed to all the Gods she'd render them flawless
hecatombs, praying Zeus might take his revenge now.   60

An Outward Show of Regard

Telemakhos made his way through the hall to the outdoors,
taking a spear. Two white dogs followed him closely.
Athene showered grace and awe on the young man:
everyone gazed and admired him now as he drew near.
Brash and disdainful suitors gathered around him
sounding fine, but at heart they were planning to hurt him.
Shortly he moved away from the large crowding of suitors.
where Antiphos, Mentor and Halitherses were sitting—

close friends of his father right from the outset—
Telemakhos took a chair. They asked about each thing.   70

Presents from
Menelaos
Peiraios came on now, known for a spear-throw.
He'd led the stranger through town to this place of
        assembly.
Soon Telemakhos turned to him, walked to the stranger,
but first Peiraios wanted to speak and he asked him,
"Telemakhos, hurry and send your maids to my household.
I want to send you back the gifts Menelaos gave you."

Still Telemakhos gave him a sensible answer.
"Peiraios, we don't know how these doings will turn out.
Maybe the manly suitors will cut me down in the great hall
in secret and split up all the wealth of my Fathers.   80
I want you to have them with joy—not one of the suitors.
If I can seed their doom though, make for their own deaths,
you'll carry the gifts to my house in joy and in my joy."

A Welcome for
the Stranger
He stopped and led his hard-tried guest to his own house.
After they entered the building where people had lived well,
the two men laid their cloaks on a chair and a high-backed
throne and then walked to the polished chamber to take
        baths.
Handmaids washed them, rubbed their bodies with rich oil,
then tossed a beautiful mantle and tunic around each.
They left the bathroom then and sat on the good chairs.   90
A handmaid brought them water: she poured from a pitcher
of stunning gold and they washed their hands in her silver
basin. She set out a polished table before them.
An honored housekeeper brought them bread and
        arranged it.
She laid out plenty of meat, graceful and giving.

A Woman's
Longing
Telemakhos's mother faced them too in the great hall.
She leaned in her chair by a post, spinning her fine wool.
Their hands went out to the good things lying before them.

After the craving for wine and food was behind them,
thought-full Penelopeia started by saying,   100
"Telemakhos, soon I'll surely go to my upstairs

room and lie on a bed that's turned into mourning,
always wet with tears from the time that Odysseus
left me for Troy with Atreus's sons. Still you have not yet
dared to tell me, before the brash suitors came in the
    palace,
about your father's homecoming. Maybe you heard tell."

News   Telemakhos promptly gave her a sensible answer.
from Pulos "Well then, Mother, I'll tell you myself what the truth is.
and Sparte We went to Pulos first, to Nestor, a shepherd of people.
There in his high-built house he gave me a welcome,   110
glad as fathers for sons newly arriving from far off
after a long time gone. He cared in that joyful
way with his own dear sons, young men who are well-
    praised.
Yet he told me he'd heard nothing of steadfast Odysseus,
whether alive or dead. No one on earth had informed him.

"He sent me on by horse-team though, a tight-fitted chariot,
to Atreus's son Menelaos, known for his spear-throw.
I saw Helen of Argos there, the cause of so many
Argive and Trojan struggles willed by the great Gods.
Menelaos, good at a war-cry, was quick with his questions: 120
why did I need to travel to bright Lakedaimon?

Deer in the "After I told him the whole truth of the matter,
Lion's Den   that ruler found his words and answered me this way:
'Look at this! Men who'd lie in the bed of a strongly
spirited man are themselves lacking in courage.
The way a doe might rest her fawns when they're suckling,
newly born, in the lair of a powerful lion:
she goes off looking to graze on a hillside or grassy
vale but the lion's back too soon to his own lair—
what a sorry end for both of the young deer!   130
Odysseus too will bring a sorry end to the suitors.
I pray to Zeus, our Father, Athene and Apollo:
make him the man he was in strong-founded Lesbos,
the day he stood up and faced Philomeleides wrestling.
He threw him with force and every Akhaian applauded.
If only that strong Odysseus dealt with the suitors,
they'd all be dead in a hurry—that bitter a marriage!

What
Happened
in Egypt 'But on to the questions you ask. I'll hardly mislead you,
wandering far from the point. Nor would I fool you:
I'll tell you the tale I heard from an errorless old man   140
and lord of the sea. I won't keep anything hidden.
He told me he saw your father in strong pain on an island,
kept in a Nymph's hall: Kalupso had forced him
to stay. He can't get back to the land of his fathers,
lacking a ship with oars and lacking crewmen
to send him over the broad back of the salt sea.'

"Those were the words of Atreus's son Menelaos,
known for a spear-throw. With all that ended I sailed off.
Gods gave me a sea-wind sending me fast to my homeland."

The Prophet's
Word He spoke that way, stirring the heart in her bosom.   150
♦ Godlike Theoklumenos spoke to her also.
"Honored wife of Odysseus, son of Laertes,
he can't know all the truth. Hear out my own words,
I'll prophesy fully what's coming. It's not to be hidden,
Zeus be my witness, first among Gods, this table
for guests and blameless Odysseus's hearth I have come to:
truly the man's right now in the land of his fathers!
He sits or creeps, he learns what harm has been done here.
He's planting seeds of doom for all of the suitors.
That was the omen I saw: I sat on the well-benched   160
ship and spelled out a bird for Telemakhos quickly."

But mind-full Penelopeia answered by saying,
"Stranger, if only these words of yours could become real!
You'd quickly know of my friendship, all of my presents
would make a man who met you say you are well-blessed."
They all went on speaking that way with each other.

More Games
and Feasts Suitors enjoyed themselves in front of Odysseus's
palace meanwhile, hurling a spear or a discus
on leveled ground, maintaining their swagger as always.
The hour for dining was close: sheep-flocks from all sides   170
came from the fields with guides who'd led them
        before this.
♦ So Medon spoke to the suitors—of all the heralds
they liked him most—he was always there when they feasted:

"Young men with all your hearts enjoying the games here,
come to the palace now and get ready for dinner.
It's never wrong to take good food at the right time."

He stopped and they all stood up to follow the man's words.
Soon as they entered the house where people had lived well,
they set their mantles down on chairs or on high thrones.
Helpers slaughtered goats and sheep, fatted and full-grown.   180
They cut down huge hogs and a bull from the herder,
preparing the banquet.

Leaving the   Meanwhile Odysseus hurried
Pig-Farm   to go with the godlike swineherd from country to city.
              A leader of men, the swineherd started to tell him,
              "My guest, you're plainly anxious to walk to the city
              today as my master told us. Yet I would rather
              leave you here on the farm right now as my watchman.
              I might be ashamed and afraid though: the master could
                   scold me
              later and strong reproofs from a master are jarring.
              Come on now, let's be gone. Much of the daylight's   190
              passed and shortly at dusk I'm sure you'll be colder."

The Looks of a   Full of designs, Odysseus answered by saying,
Beggar   "I know you and mind you: the man you charge
                   understands you.
              Let's get going. You be our leader the whole way.
              But loan me a walking stick if you happened to trim one—
              I'd like it to lean on. You talked about slippery footpaths."

              He stopped and tossed his wretched knapsack over a
                   shoulder.
              His bag was dotted with holes; its strap was a plain rope.
              Eumaios gave him a good stick, suiting his spirits.
              The two set out, the dogs and herders remaining   200
              behind to guard the pens. So a king, led to his city,
              looked like an old man, the sorriest pauper
              propped on a stick, his body covered with bad clothes.

The Fountain   After walking the rocky trails and approaching
          ♦ the city slowly, they came to the pretty flow of a well-built
              fountain where people came to draw their water.

Made by Ithakos, Neritos once and Poluktor,
it stood by a grove of poplars that thrived on its water.
The trees were all around it; cool streams were a cascade
down from the rocks. An altar had risen above them   210
to Nymphs and every wayfarer gave them a present.

Melantheus, son of Dolios, met them while driving
his goats along, the best in all of his own herds—
food for the suitors. A pair of herders had joined him.
He saw the others and called out, starting to taunt them,
the meanest words rousing the heart of Odysseus:
"It's all so true now—the ugly leading the ugly!
God brings like to like—always the same thing.
Niggardly pig-man, where are you taking your fat pig,
that bothersome pauper, the kind that licks off a meal-plate?   220
He'll stand and scratch a shoulder on plenty of doorposts
whining for scraps—never for cauldrons or weapons!
Loan me the man: I'll make him watch at my stock-pens,
scour them out and haul green shoots to the kids there.
He'll drink up whey and build his legs into big thighs.
Or maybe he's learned cheap tricks and he won't be willing
to do real work. He'd rather hide in the country,
moping and begging for feed for his ravening belly.
I'll tell you this much though, be sure it will happen:
if ever the man's in godlike Odysseus's household,   230
lots of stools will be thrown at his head by the suitors.
They'll smack his ribs and wear him down in the palace."

He spoke that way and crazily kicked at the beggar's
hip as he passed by. He failed to knock him aside there:
Odysseus kept on steadily, pondering whether
to leap on the man and take his life with a staff-blow
or hoist him high and smash his head on the hard ground.
Instead he bore up, keeping the kick in mind. But the
        swineherd
glared and scolded the man, raising his hands into prayer.
"Fountain Nymphs, you daughters of Zeus, if Odysseus ever   240
burned his goats and lambs for you, wrapping the
        thigh-parts
richly in fat: help my prayer to become real,
let the man come home, led by some Power!
Then he would scatter, Melantheus, all of your smugly

put-on glory now. You're always insulting and roaming
the city while bad herdsmen ruin your livestock."

More Insults   Melantheus answered him promptly, a driver of goat-flocks:
"Look at this, dogs that talk! His mind is too noisome.
I'll take him aboard some ship, a black one that's well-
   benched.
Far from Ithaka later he'll bring me a full price.   250
If only Telemakhos died right now in the great hall,
struck by Apollo's silver bow or killed by the suitors
the way Odysseus's day of return is dead in some far land!"
He stopped and left them there as they walked on slowly.

On to the   He went off briskly himself to the house of his ruler.
Palace   He strolled inside and sat at once among suitors
across from Eurumakhos, liking him most of the men there.
Servers placed a portion of goat-meat before him.
An honored housekeeper brought him bread and arranged it
for eating.

        Odysseus, led by the godlike swineherd,   260
approached and stopped. Around them chords from a
   hollow
lyre came closer: the poet Phemios struck them
and sang inside. Odysseus took the swineherd's hand and
   told him,
"Eumaios, truly the beautiful house of Odysseus!
Readily known from all those houses around it,
this part flowing from that part, the courtyard a build-up
of wall and coping, the gates well-paired at the entrance
and carefully worked: no man alive could dispraise it.

How   "Plenty of men, I know, are settled for dinner
and When   inside where meat-smells rise and the sounds of a calling   270
to Go In?   lyre which Gods have made the friend of a good feast."

Then Eumaios the swineherd, you answered by saying,
"You easily know all that—you're never unknowing!
Come on though, let's consider how we can work this.
Will you go first in that house where people have lived well
and mingle with suitors while I remain on the outside?
Or stay out here if you like and I will enter.

You should not linger though—someone may spot you,
punch you or throw things. Mull all that, I would tell you."

Long-suffering, godlike Odysseus answered,   280
"I know you and mind you: the man you charge
    understands you.
Go in before me. I'll stay back here on the outside.
Thrashings are not unknown to me, nor is a pelting:
my heart holds up. I've gone through plenty of hardship
at sea and in war. This pain can be added to those pains.
Besides, no one can hide the squeeze of his belly,
a curse that hands out plenty of evil to mankind.
Because of hunger our strong-planked vessels are well-
    rigged
for tireless seas and bringing their enemies great harm."

A Very Old Dog   Now as the two men spoke that way with each other,   290
             ◆ a dog lying nearby raised his head and his two ears.
               Steadfast Odysseus once had raised him, this Argos,
               but never much enjoyed him, sailing before then
               for holy Troy. Young men in the past had taken
               the dog hunting for deer, rabbits and wild goats.
               But then he lay there scorned when his master had
                   left home,
               close to some piles of dung not far from the doorway—
               oxen and mule droppings that slaves of Odysseus
               would haul off soon to manure stretches of farmland.
               So Argos lay there, ticks all over his body,   300
               until he suddenly sensed Odysseus close by,
               started wagging his tail and dropping his two ears.
               Ah but he could not move close to his master.
               Odysseus looked aside, wiping a tear off,
               hiding it deftly and briefly asking Eumaios,
               "Very strange, Eumaios—a dog lying by dung-heaps?
               His frame looks good but I'm not sure of his racing,
               whether his quickness afoot matches his good looks.
               Or maybe he's only a dog like those at a table,
               cared for mainly as handsome show for their masters."   310

Bygone Speed   Then Eumaios the swineherd, you answered by saying,
  and Power   "This dog in fact belonged to a man who is now dead
               far away. If his flair and frame were now as they once were

the day Odysseus went to Troy, leaving the dog here,
you'd soon be amazed at the sight of his quickness and
    power.
No game he flushed in the thickest depths of the forest
ever escaped him. How skilled he was as a tracker!
But now he's wretched. His master is far from his fathers'
land and dead. The women around here are careless
the way that slaves, soon as their master no longer   320
rules them, no longer want to work in the right way.
So Zeus watching from far off takes half of a good man's
worth as soon as the day of slavery grasps him."

He stopped and entered the house where people had
    lived well,
going straight to the hall and the high-born suitors.

But Argos blackened in death, seized by a grim lot
now in the twentieth year when he spotted Odysseus.

Poor Men in   By far the first to notice the swineherd had entered
the Great Hall   the house was godlike Telemakhos, hastily nodding
to call him closer. Eumaios, looking around him,   330
took a nearby stool the carver had sat on while slicing
lots of meat for suitors who ate in the household.
He carried the stool to a place by Telemakhos's table
and sat across from him there. A herald who'd taken
a share of meat laid it before him with bread from a basket.

Not long after, Odysseus walked in his own house.
He looked like an old man, the wretchedest pauper
propped on a stick with shabby clothes on his body.
He sat inside the door on its threshold of ash-wood
and leaned on the cypress doorpost, formerly worked on   340
well by a carpenter, smoothed and straight to a string-line.
Telemakhos called the swineherd closer and told him,
after taking a large loaf from the beautiful basket
and all the meat that both his hands could encompass:
"Take this food to give to the stranger and tell him
to walk around and beg from all of the suitors.
It's no good thing for a man in need to be bashful."

A Beggar
Making
His Rounds He spoke that way, the swineherd listened and walked up
close to the man, his words with a feathery swiftness,
"Stranger, Telemakhos offers you food and he tells you   350
to walk around and beg from all of the suitors.
It's no good thing for a man in need to be bashful."

Odysseus, full of designs, answered by praying:
"Lord Zeus, make Telemakhos happy among men!
Whatever his heart hopes for, let all of it happen."
He took the food in both his hands and he set it
down in front of his feet on the moldering knapsack.
He ate as long as the poet sang in the great hall.

After he dined and the godlike singer was resting,
suitors made loud noise in the hall. However Athene,   360
moving close to Odysseus, son of Laertes,
stirred him to gather bits of bread from the suitors.
He'd find out who'd act right and who'd be lawless.

Even so the Goddess would save no suitor from death here.

He walked along from left to right, begging from
        each man,
stretching his hand around as though he'd begged for a
        long time.
They pitied and gave him food, surprised at the stranger,
asking each other his name and where he had come from.

Bothersome Then Melantheus told them, that herder of goat-flocks,
Paupers "Listen, you men who court a queen who is famous!   370
About this stranger, I certainly saw him before this.
The swineherd led him in fact right to the palace.
But I'm not sure what the man claims for a birthplace."

Soon as he'd spoken Antinoos chided the hog-man.
"Far-famed pig-herd! Why do you bring such a person
into our city? Aren't there enough roamers and other
annoying paupers, the kind that lick up the meal-plates?
Don't you dislike their gathering here and devouring
your master's goods? Now you've called in a new one."

Who   Then Eumaios the swineherd, you answered by saying,   380
Would Ask for   "You don't speak fairly, Antinoos, though you're a noble.
a Pauper?   Who'd go abroad himself and ask that a stranger
           be brought here unless the man could work for our people?
      ♦ A prophet, a healer of ills, a master of woodwork,
           yes and a singer whose godlike song is our pleasure:
           we call such men from everywhere over the boundless
           earth but no one calls for a ravenous beggar.

           "Of all the suitors, though, you're always the hardest
           on slaves of Odysseus—mainly on me. But I never
           care so long as our thought-full Penelopeia   390
           lives in the hall with godlike Telemakhos close by."

The Threat of a   But now Telemakhos gave him a sensible order:
Footstool   "Stop your talking. Few words when you're answering
                 that man.
           It's always Antinoos's way, using the harshest
           terms to arouse anger—and urge the rest of them likewise."

           He spoke to Antinoos too, the words with a feathery
                 swiftness,
           "Father for son, Antinoos, how you care for me truly!
           You'd order a guest to be scared from my hall with your
                 pushy
           talk. May God never allow it to happen. But reach out,
           offer him something. I don't mind, I ask you myself to.   400
           Don't be afraid of my Mother now or the other
           maids who work in the house of godlike Odysseus!
           Well but no such thoughts are there in your own chest.
           You'd rather devour a lot yourself than give to another."
           Soon as he'd spoken Antinoos answered by saying,
           "High talk, Telemakhos, brave and strong with your big words!
           But now if all the suitors gave him what I'd give,
           your house would keep this beggar away—and for three
                 months."
           While speaking he gripped and flashed from under the table
           a stool he'd rested his oil-sleek feet on while dining.   410

The Beggar   But all the rest of them gave, filling the knapsack
Was Rich Once ♦ with bread and meat. Having tested Akhaians
           freely Odysseus could move back to his threshold.

First he stopped by Antinoos, asking him simply,
"A gift, my friend. You're not the worst of Akhaians:
you look like the best, I'd say, with the air of a ruler.
So you should offer me more bread than the others.
Then over the endless earth I surely would praise you.

"I formerly lived myself in a wealthy and happy
    home among men. I often gave to a pauper,   420
    whoever he was, whatever need he arrived with.
    I owned slaves by the thousand and plenty of other
    goods that men live well by—those we know as the
        rich men.

On to Egypt   "Then Zeus, the son of Kronos—somehow he willed it—
    wrecked me by packing me off with pirates who wandered
    away to Egypt. A long journey—he meant to destroy me.
    I stood my up-curved ships by the river of Egypt.
    I spoke to them all myself, the crewmen I trusted:
    'Stay here close to the ships and safeguard the squadron.'
    I urged scouts to find good spots to be lookouts.   430
    They yielded to brashness instead. Pushing their own
        strength,
    they promptly ravaged handsome fields of Egyptian
    farmers and hauled off women and helpless children.
    They murdered the men. But shouts went fast to the city,
    the call was heard and with Dawn an army had shown up,
    filling the whole plain with foot-soldiers, horsemen
    and glaring bronze. Then Zeus, whose joy is in thunder,
    threw a revolting scare in my men. No one was daring
    to stand and face that menace, closing on all sides.
    Many of us died right there, cut down by the sharp bronze.   440
    Others were led off alive and forced into slavery.

"They gave me in time to a friend who'd joined them while
        sailing
◆ to Kupros, powerfully ruled by Dmetor, son of Iasos.
    From there I came here now. I've suffered a great deal."

A Much More   Now an answer came from Antinoos sharply.
Painful Egypt "What Power brought this woe, spoiling a good meal?
    Stay off there in the center, away from my table,
    or soon you'll go to an Egypt and Kupros that sting you

for being a brash old man, a beggar without shame.
You stood by us all in turn, everyone gave things   450
rashly and why? No one's restrained or regretting:
we lavish the goods of others! There's plenty for
    each man."

Reproaches
and Pain Odysseus, full of his own plans, spoke as he moved back.
"Look at this! You don't seem both handsome and
    thoughtful.
You'd barely hand out salt in your own house to a beggar
if you can't bear to pull off and hand out bread when you
    sit in
a stranger's house. And yes, there's plenty at hand here."

He spoke that way and Antinoos, ever more angry,
eyed him darkly, his words with a feathery swiftness,
"Now I am thinking you won't be gracefully leaving   460
the room any longer after mouthing reproaches."

He stopped and hoisted the stool, hurled it and battered
his right shoulder behind on the back. Odysseus stood
    there
lodged like stone. Antinoos's throw did not faze him.
Quietly shaking his head, brooding on evil,
he moved back to his threshold, sat there and laid out
the well-filled knapsack. Then he called to the suitors:
"Listen, you men who court that queen who is well known!
Let me say what the heart in my chest has enjoined me.
We don't mourn so much, nor is there great pain   470
when farmers are battered fighting to guard their
    belongings,
whether their herds are of white sheep or of cattle.
But now Antinoos struck me because of my sorry
belly, a curse that hands out plenty of evil to mankind.
Yet if Gods and Avengers are somehow for poor men,
may death overtake Antinoos long before marriage."

Again the son of Eupeithes, Antinoos, answered,
"No more talk, stranger. Sit and eat or be elsewhere.
Younger men might drag you now through the household,
hand and foot, for your talk, then flay you entirely."   480

A God Playing
the Stranger

He spoke that way but others were highly offended.
Overbearing younger suitors were saying,
"Antinoos, striking a wandering wretch was not pretty.
You're doomed if the man is a God somehow from heaven."
"That's right. The Gods may look like strangers from far off.
They take on every shape and move through our cities."
"They watch men closely, both the proud and the lawful."
Antinoos shrugged off all such claims of the suitors.

Telemakhos felt great pain in his heart when the footstool
struck but he dropped no tears to the floor from his eyelids.   490
Quietly shaking his head, he brooded on evil.

A Woman's
Dismay
and Anger

When thought-full Penelopeia heard that a beggar
had just been struck in the hall, she said to her handmaids,
♦"So may Apollo, known for his bow, strike at that striker."

Then Eurunome answered, the housekeeper, saying,
"If only all of our prayers would come to a good end!
Not one of these men would last till Dawn on her gold
    throne."

Mind-full Penelopeia answered by saying,
"Good mother, they're all hateful, plotting such outrage.
Antinoos plainly is worst: the man's like a black doom.   500
A wretched stranger wanders around in my household
begging for men's scraps, enjoined by his own need.
All the others offer him food, filling his knapsack.
One man hurls a stool and strikes him low on the shoulder."

A Wife
Upstairs,
Her Husband
Below

So she talked with her maids and sat in her own room
upstairs while godlike Odysseus ate in the same house.
She called for the godlike swineherd now and she told him,
"My shining Eumaios: go and order the stranger
to come here. I want to welcome this beggar and ask him
whether he's heard by chance or seen with his own eyes   510
my steadfast Odysseus. He seems to have traveled a
    long way."

Odysseus the
Poet

Then Eumaios the swineherd, you answered by saying,
"My queen, if only the Akhaians below would be quiet!
This man could tell you a story to spellbind your own heart.

I kept him for three nights—I held the man at my
    farmhouse
three full days when he came to me, fleeing his black ship
by stealth—and he'd still not ended his story of hardship.
  ♦ The way a man will stare at a poet taught by the deathless
Gods to sing his tale of longing for people
anxious to hear his music whenever he sings it: 520
I was enthralled when he sat in my house in the same way.
He claims to be friends through his father's line with
    Odysseus.
His home is on Krete, the land of Minos's bloodline.
From there he came this way, suffering deep pain
and wandering often. He claims to have heard of Odysseus
nearby with people in rich Thesprotian country.
Alive he'll haul back plenty of wealth to his own house."

If Only   Mind-full Penelopeia answered by saying,
the Man "Go and call him. He'll face me and say it himself here.
Were Home Suitors will play their games outside by the doorway   530
or maybe inside the house. Their spirits are giddy
because their riches lie untouched in their own homes—
bread, sweet wine, their slaves taking a little.
Instead they jam our house and slaughter the best sheep
day after day, our fattened goats and our cattle.
They revel and gulp down glowing wine with abandon.
So much is lost already because there is no man
such as Odysseus was to fend off blight from the
    household.
But then if Odysseus came—if he walked on his own land!—
my lord and my son would avenge their crimes in a hurry."   540

A Telling ♦ She stopped and Telemakhos sneezed loudly, the whole
Sneeze   house
echoed around him and laughing Penelopeia
said to Eumaios, her words with a feathery swiftness,
"Go for me, tell the stranger to stand here before me.
Don't you see? My son sneezed at my whole speech!
So death will surely become the end of the suitors,
all of them: no one can run from death or his own doom.
I'll tell you something else to thrust in your own heart:
if all the truth is told by our guest as I know it,

I'll dress him in beautiful clothes, a mantle and tunic."   550
She spoke that way, the hog-tender minded and walked out.

Close to the beggar shortly his words had a feathery
     swiftness:
"Fatherly guest, our mind-full Penelopeia,
Telemakhos's mother, calls you. Her heart has been telling
her now to ask of her husband, for all of her deep cares.
So if you tell her the whole truth as she knows it,
she'll dress you in mantle and tunic, clothes that you surely
need the most. Then you can beg for food in our country,
filling your stomach. Whoever wants to will help you."

A Meeting   Long-suffering, godlike Odysseus told him,   560
after Dark   "Eumaios, I'll gladly reveal all of my story
soon to Ikarios's daughter, mind-full Penelopeia.
I know Odysseus well: we suffered in common.
But now I'm anxious. This hardened body of suitors
can reach to the iron sky with their bluster and outrage.
Not long ago as I walked around through the great hall
doing no harm, a man struck and gave me a sharp pain.
Telemakhos hardly could stop him; nobody else could.
So ask Penelopeia now, although she is anxious,
 ♦ to wait until sunset, stay behind in the great hall   570
and ask me then for the day of her husband's return home.
I'll sit close to the fire because the clothes I am wearing
are wretched. You know it yourself—I begged from you
     first here."

He spoke that way, the hog-man listened and left him.
Penelopeia asked when he came to her threshold,
"Haven't you brought him, Eumaios? What's the wanderer
     thinking?
Maybe he's worried unduly or otherwise bashful
now in my home. But a bashful tramp is a poor one."

Then Eumaios the swineherd, you answered by saying,
"He spoke quite rightly—I'm sure others would think so—   580
he wants to avoid the overbearing pride of the suitors.
He asks that you stay here, wait till the Sun-God has
     gone down.

Surely for you as well, my lady, it's far more
graceful to talk and hear out strangers in private."

Mind-full Penelopeia answered by saying,
"The man's not thoughtless. He sees the way it could
        happen:
no group of death-bound men, doubtless, have ever
been like the suitors—insulting, reckless and scheming."

Dangerous   The godlike swineherd left her after she'd spoken.
      Men   He'd told her all; he mingled now with the suitors   590
             and spoke to Telemakhos—words with a feathery
                     swiftness—
             moving his head in close to stop the others from hearing,
             "Dear man, I'm going to guard the swine and the holdings,
             your livestock there and mine. Take charge of it all here.
             First keep safe yourself. Plan in your heart well
             not to be harmed. Many Akhaians are dwelling
             on evil. May Zeus destroy them before they can harm us."

             Now Telemakhos gave him a sensible answer.
             "So will it be, uncle. Go when you've eaten.
             Come back in the morning and bring us beautiful victims.   600
             I and the deathless Gods will manage it all here."

More Dance   After he'd spoken the swineherd sat on a well-shined
  and Song   chair and his heart swelled with food and the good wine.
             Then he walked to his hogs, leaving the court and the
                     great hall
             thronged with diners. Dance and song were their pleasure
             now as the latter part of the day was arriving.

A Threatening Pauper

A common beggar came in, a man who had often
whined in the town of Ithaka. Known for his belly's
craving he drank and ate nonstop. Lacking robustness
and real strength, he only struck the eye as a big man.
His name was Arnaios. His honored mother had
   named him

♦ at birth but all the young men labeled him Iros,
because he'd go with a "message" anyone gave him.

Now on a whim he'd drive Odysseus out of his own house!
He railed at the man, his words with a feathery swiftness,
"Make way at the door, old man, or be dragged by your
   feet out   10
fast! Can't you plainly see that everyone's winking?
They want me to drag you, though it shames me to do it.
Get up or our quarrel could change that fast to a fistfight."

Threats from the New Beggar

Odysseus, full of designs, glared darkly and answered,
"Strange man, I've said and done nothing to harm you.
If diners take up plenty to give you I won't whine.
One threshold can suit us both: there is no need
to grudge the shares of others. You look like a hobo;
I'm one too. We should look to the Gods for a good life.
Don't be rash with your fists, don't get me angry,   20
or old as I am I'll soak your mouth and your big chest
with blood. Then I'll enjoy some quiet, and more so
tomorrow for then I take it you won't be returning
again to the hall of Odysseus, son of Laertes."

Eager to Brawl

Then the rambler, Iros, angrily told him,
"Look at this! How the glutton can maunder as glibly
as old baker women! I'm planning some bad things:
both my hands will clobber him, breaking his teeth out—
they'll litter the ground like a pig's, rooting in cornfields.
Tighten your belt now. All these men will be watching   30
a good fight. But how will an old man fight with a
   young one?"

261

A Goat's   So there on the gleaming threshold in front of the high-
Stomach   raised
              doors the two men wholeheartedly angered each other.
              As though his power were holy, Antinoos heard them
              both and chuckled, enjoyably telling the suitors,
              "My friends, nothing before has happened to match this.
              Some God has brought a rare delight to the household.
              The stranger and Iros now are at odds with each other,
              mad for a fistfight. Let's goad them on in a hurry!"

              Soon as he'd spoken they all jumped up with a good laugh   40
              and promptly crowded around the tramps in their tatters.
              Antinoos, son of Eupeithes, spoke to the whole crowd.
              "Listen, you bold suitors! Here's what I tell you:
              some goats' stomachs lie on the fire where we put them,
              bloated with fat and blood, a course in our dinner.
              Whoever wins this fight—the man who is stronger—
              may stand and take for himself the stomach he chooses.
              He'll always dine with us too: no other roamer
              will then be allowed to mix with us, begging for food here."

No Others in Antinoos spoke that way and his word was their pleasure.   50
the Fight   But wily and crafty-minded Odysseus answered,
              "You friends, an old man weighed with sorrow can never
              hope to fight with a young man. A worker of harm though,
              my own belly, goads me to take on his punches.
              Come on now, all of you here, swear me a strong oath:
              no one favoring Iros will deal me a reckless,
              heavy blow and force me down for my rival."

              He spoke that way and they all swore as he'd asked them.
              After the oaths, with all the swearing behind them,
              Telemakhos spoke up next—his power was holy—   60
              "My guest, if your heart and bold spirit are prodding
              you now to fight this man, don't be afraid of the others.
              Whichever Akhaian strikes you battles with me too:
              I am the host and all these masters have said so—
              Antinoos, yes and Eurumakhos, both of them shrewd men."

Great Strength He stopped and they all avowed his words. So Odysseus
Suddenly   tightened rags at his groin, suddenly baring
                huge and graceful thighs. He showed them his muscled

arms, broad chest and shoulders. Athene had come close,
making the frame seem large for her shepherd of soldiers.   70
All the suitors were highly amazed when they saw him.
One man looked at his neighbor, putting it this way:
"Iros will soon be un-Iros! He'll find the trouble he
      looked for—
what thighs the old man showed from under his tatters!"

A Scrotum for
the Dogs

He spoke that way, the spirits of Iros were badly
shaken and still the slaves were cinching his belt up,
pushing him forward, the flesh on his body atremble.
Antinoos called him names, he chided and told him,
"It's better you died now, bull-head! Better you weren't born
if all you can do is tremble and shamefully dread him—   80
an old man weighed with pain and sorrow he came with.
Yes and I'll tell you plainly how it will end here:
if the old man wins this fight, the stronger of you two,
I'll throw you aboard a black ship bound for the mainland
♦ where King Ekhetos rules, a mangler of all men.
He'll cut off your ears and nose with merciless bronze there.
He'll rip off your scrotum and toss it to mongrels to
      eat raw."

How Hard to
Strike

Soon as he'd spoken Iros's legs were seized by an even
greater trembling. Dead center, both with their hands up,
long-suffering, godlike Odysseus wondered   90
just how hard to strike: should the man fall and be killed
      here?
Or punched less hard and left sprawled on the dirt floor?
He thought it through and shortly it seemed to him better
to punch less hard and keep the Akhaians from wonder.

Sudden Agony

Their weight drawn up, Iros punched at the right side,
grazing a shoulder. Odysseus bashed his neck at the earlobe,
splintering bone. The red blood flowed in a hurry
from Iros's mouth, he fell in the dust with a loud moan,
gnashing his teeth and kicking the ground. High-born
      suitors
raised their hands and could die laughing. Odysseus   100
dragged him out by a foot and came to the courtyard,
the portico gates. He sat him down by a wall there,
propped up well. He pushed a staff in his right hand

and spoke to the man, his words with a feathery swiftness,
"Now you can ward off pigs and dogs as you sit here!
Wretched yourself, don't go mastering every
beggar and stranger. You might be garnering worse harm."

A Toast to the   He stopped and shouldered again his raggedy knapsack
Stranger   dotted with holes—its carrying strap was a plain rope—
and walked back to his threshold. He sat as the suitors   110
came inside. They laughed and welcomed him saying,
"May Zeus be kindly, stranger, may all of the deathless
Gods grant you the most, whatever your heart wants,
now that you stopped that craving beggar from roaming
the land." "We'll shortly pack him off to the mainland
to King Ekhetos, that mangler and killer of all men."
Godlike Odysseus smiled at this omen-like prayer.

Then Antinoos laid out the oversize belly,
swollen with fat and blood. Amphinomos carried
a pair of loaves from a basket and placed them before him.   120
He toasted him, raising a golden goblet and saying,
"Fatherly stranger, be well. May all of your future
luck be good, though now you have plenty of hardship."

Long-suffering, godlike Odysseus answered,
"Amphinomos, truly you strike me as knowing and tactful.
So was your father—I heard tell of his good name—
Nisos, a man from Doulikhion, wealthy and fearless.
You're his son, I'm told, and resemble the man in your
        good tact.

Nothing Frailer ♦"So now I'll talk to you plainly. Listen and take heed.
Than   Of all the breathing and crawling things on the broad earth,   130
Human Joy   nothing fed by the land is feebler than mankind.
People suppose they'll suffer no harm in the future
while Gods make them excel and their knee-joints are lively.
But then when the blissful Gods bring them a bad end,
they suffer against their will, trying to bear up.
So men's minds on the earth are such as the Father
of men and Gods brings them clearly on that day.
I too might well have been blessed among people at
        one time.

But often I acted recklessly. Yielding to power
and force I relied for help on my Father and brothers.   140

A Warning to
Leave
"So I say now let no man ever be lawless.
 Quietly take from the Gods whatever they might give.
 I've watched the suitors here, reckless and scheming,
 wasting resources and badly treating a man's wife.
 That man will not be away from his country and good
        friends
 much longer—I tell you he's close. May a Power
 take you home before then. I hope you won't face him
 the hour he arrives back home in the land of his fathers.
 It won't be bloodless, I think, when he parts with suitors,
 once that man is walking under his own roof."   150

He stopped and poured for the Gods. He drank of the
        honeyed
wine himself then placed the cup in the hands of the
        people's
marshal while Amphinomos moved through the great hall,
his head sadly drooping, heart filled with foreboding.
He'd hardly escape his doom: Athene had bound him
too to be downed by a spear from Telemakhos's
        strong hand.
For now he sat again on the chair he got up from.

Another
Showing of the
Queen
Then the glow-eyed Goddess Athene was moving
the heart of Ikarios's daughter, mind-full Penelopeia:
she'd show herself to the suitors in order to open   160
  ♦ their hearts. She'd make herself esteemed by Odysseus
    more than before—by both her son and her husband.
    She called with a silly laugh to the housekeeper saying,
    "Eurunome, how my heart is longing—never before this!—
    to show myself to the suitors, though they are hateful.
    I'll talk to Telemakhos too: my son would do better
    than joining all the swaggering suitors so often.
    They talk to him nicely but plan to murder him later."

All of Her
Beauty Lost
The housekeeper answered her now, Eurunome told her,
"Truly my child, you said all that in the right way.   170
 Go and talk to your child, keep nothing in hiding.

First you should bathe and rub your face with a rich oil.
Don't go down as you are. Your cheeks have been sullied
with tears and it's no good thing to be sorrowful always.
Now your child's reaching the age you have prayed for
most to the Gods—you see him growing a good beard."

But thought-full Penelopeia answered by saying,
"Don't press all this, Eurunome, for all of your caring.
Bathe my body and rub my face with a rich oil?
Not since the Gods holding Olumpos ravaged my beauty   180
the day my godlike Odysseus left in his hollow
ship. But tell Autonoe now and Hippodameia
to join me and stand beside me there in the great hall.
I won't go alone to those men. That could be shameful."

She spoke that way and the old one went through the
     great hall
to tell the women there to go to their lady.

Beauty upon   First the glow-eyed Goddess Athene had new plans.
Beauty   She poured a honeyed sleep on Ikarios's daughter.
                The lady leaned backward, all of her body relaxing
                soon on her couch. Meanwhile shining Athene   190
                gave her ambrosial charms to awe the Akhaians:
                she brightened her beautiful face first with a deathless
                oil used by stunningly crowned Aphrodite,
                anointing and anxious to go and dance with the Graces.
                She made her taller too, a fullness to gaze at.
                She caused her body to shine like ivory new-sawn.
                Done with that work, the glowing Goddess departed.

A Longing for   White-armed handmaids came to her now from the
Gentle Death   great hall.
                With voices nearby the lady was freed from her honeyed
                sleep and rubbed her cheeks. She said to the handmaids,   200
                "A balmlike sleep enclosed me, for all of my sorrow.
                If only sacred Artemis now would hurriedly bring me
                such balmlike death! With no more grief in my spirit
                I'd stop wasting my life in longing for one dear
                husband with all his prowess, the best of Akhaians."

Upbraiding
the Son

She spoke that way then walked downstairs from her
    glowing
room and not alone: two handmaids had joined her.
Closer now to the suitors, the goddess-like woman
stood by a strong support of the well-built roof-beams,
holding a shiny veil in front of her two cheeks.   210
Loyal maids were close to her left side and right side.
The suitors' knees wilted. Hearts lustful and spellbound,
they all prayed to lie in bed with her close by.

But first she spoke to Telemakhos—there was her dear son.
"Telemakhos: now your head and heart are steady no longer.
Even before as a child you acted more shrewdly.
Now you're tall, you've reached a measure of manhood—
indeed someone might say you were born to a rich man,
watching you grow so handsome, a stranger would
    say so—
yet your heart and head aren't right any longer.   220
Look at the act that took place now in our great hall,
how you allowed a guest to be badly mistreated.
What if a stranger who sat down here in our own house
were gravely harmed this day, roughed up and dragged out?
Outrage and shame among men would fall on your
    own self."

No One to
Help

Telemakhos promptly gave her a sensible answer.
"Mother, I won't be vexed because of your anger.
I see it all in my heart, I know about each thing,
the best and the meanest. I was boyish before this.
But truly I cannot fathom everything wisely.   230
Men have addled me, sitting on that side and this side,
their minds on evil. I have no one to help me.
At least this brawl between the stranger and Iros
ended wrong for some suitors: our guest was the stronger.

Longing for
the Gods

"I pray to Zeus, our Father, Athene and Apollo
the suitors be overpowered now in the same way,
lolling heads in our hall—men in the courtyard,
men in the house—the joints of everyone loosened
just like Iros, plopped outside at the courtyard
gate with his head lolling. He looks like a drunkard: 240

he cannot stand up straight on his feet and he cannot
go home, wherever he lives, his joints are so loosened."

Grand Flattery   After the two of them spoke that way with each other,
Eurumakhos had some words for Penelopeia.
"Ikarios's daughter, mind-full Penelopeia,
if every Akhaian in Ieson's *Argo* could see you,
far more suitors would crowd your household tomorrow,
dining and wooing. You're the best of our women
in fullness of beauty, and poised ideas are inside you."

Longing for   But thought-full Penelopeia answered by saying,   250
Her Husband   "The deathless Gods, Eurumakhos, ravaged my goodness,
beauty and body that day the Argives boarded
for Troy, my husband Odysseus going among them.
If only he came back home and cared for my life here!
My name would be greater then, my face would be fairer.
But now I'm laden with all the harm some Power has let
    loose.

Counsel   "The day Odysseus left the land of his fathers,
Years Ago   he held my right wrist in his hand and he told me,
            ◆ 'Ah my woman: I doubt the well-greaved Akhaians
will all come back from Troy without being wounded.   260
Trojans they say are men ready for battling,
hurling spears, drawing bows for their arrows,
leaping on fast-footed horses—those that can shortly
make for a winner in great fights that are close-matched.
So I don't know if a God will return me; I could be taken
there at Troy. But care for everything right here.
Remember my Father and Mother too in the great hall.
You do so now but do so more when I'm far off.
In time when you see our child growing a good beard,
marry the man you choose and abandon your household.'   270

"The man spoke to me so. Now everything's happened.
The night will come when a hateful marriage will face me,
doomed as I am. When Zeus took all of my gladness
dreadful pain came into my heart and spirit.
Your way was never the way of suitors before this.
Wanting to court for themselves a woman of good name,
a rich man's daughter, they truly strived with each other,

gathered and brought their fatted sheep and their oxen.
They dined the friends of the bride, offered outstanding
presents and never devoured her goods without paying."   280

Her words made long-suffering, godlike Odysseus
glad: she'd wheedle gifts while charming their spirits
with gentle words, her mind elsewhere and plotting.

Presents for   The son of Eupeithes, Antinoos, answered her once more:
a Queen   "Ikarios's daughter, mind-full Penelopeia!
             If any Akhaian wants to offer you presents,
             take them: it's not good grace to deny what you're given.
             We won't leave though, not for our land or another,
             before you marry a man here, the best of Akhaians."

Antinoos spoke that way and the suitors were well-pleased.   290
Every man dispatched a herald to bring gifts.
Antinoos's helper brought a large, finely embroidered
robe with a dozen linking brooches of pure gold,
each one fitted with catches gracefully rounded.
A richly crafted necklace came from Eurumakhos quickly,
gold and beaded with amber, bright as the sunlight.
The squires of Eurudamas brought in earrings with
        pendants
with trios of mulberry clusters, graceful and shining.
Then for his lord Peisandros, son of Poluktor,
a helper came with a stunningly beautiful necklace.   300
Akhaians brought her one fine present after another.
The lady, the brightest of women, went to her upstairs
room with her handmaids carrying beautiful bride-gifts.

Night   The suitors turned to dancing now and delightful
Approaching song in the hall, waiting for dusk to arrive there,
             enjoying themselves. The dusk was dark that
                 approached them.
             Shortly they set up light-stands, three in the great hall,
             to make things brighter. They laid firewood around them,
             dried for a long time, newly chopped with a bronze ax.
             They set up torches between them—steadfast Odysseus's   310
             handmaids lit them in turn. But Zeus-bred Odysseus,
             full of his own designs, spoke to them briskly:
             "Maids of Odysseus, your lord's been gone for a long time:

you all should go to the room of the lady you honor,
help her to smile as you sit upstairs in her long room,
your hands combing her wool and working your spindles.
I'll tend to the lights myself for all of the men here.
Even if diners remain till Dawn on her gold throne
suitors won't outstay me. I'm very enduring."

More Harsh   He spoke that way but they laughed and glanced at each
Words   other.   320
           ♦ Melantho, with pretty cheeks, would scold him without
                shame.
             Her father was Dolios but Penelopeia had cherished
             the girl as her own child, giving her toys that her heart loved.
             The maid did not feel sorry for Penelopeia.
             She loved Eurumakhos now and slept with him often.
             Now she turned on Odysseus, scolding him loudly,
              "Madcap stranger! Someone's clobbered your brains out.
             Don't you want to sleep? Go to the blacksmith's
             forge or a lowbrow inn? No, you would brashly
             rant at all these men, looking so fearless   330
             now and heart-strong. Does wine have your head? Or you
                always
             think this way, tossing out words like an old fool.
             You beat down Iros, a tramp. Did *that* make you giddy?
             Watch out: a man much better than Iros may stand up
             soon with close-packed fists and batter your old head,
             sending you out of the house all bloody and filthy."

Sudden Fright Odysseus, full of designs, glared darkly and told her,
              "I'm going fast to Telemakhos, bitch, and tell him
               your answer. Right here he'll slash those limbs from
                  your body."

             He spoke that way and his words scattered the women,   340
             they all went off through the house, the knees of the
                handmaids
             loosened by fear. They thought he'd told them the plain
                truth.

Still More   Odysseus stood close to light up the blazing
Taunts   fire-stands and marked each man. He thought out
             every move, for his plans would not be undone now.

Still Athene would hardly stop the disdainful suitors
from stinging his heart with insult: heavier sorrow
must sink in the heart of Odysseus, son of Laertes.
So Eurumakhos, Polubos's son, started to speak up,
mocking Odysseus, making all of his friends laugh: 350
"Listen, you men courting a queen who is famous!
Let me say what the heart in my chest has commanded.
This man has arrived at Odysseus's house with a God's help:
look at the way he's glowing there like the torchlight,
all from his hairless head—a totally bald one!"
Then he spoke to Odysseus, looter of cities.
"My guest, would you like to work? If I were to hire you
on far-off land, your pay would surely be steady.
You'd plant some tall trees and gather the wall-stones.
I'd keep you in food myself—it never would run out.   360
I'd help you to clothes; under your feet would be sandals.
Or maybe you've learned cheap tricks and won't be so
        willing
to do hard work. You'd rather hide in the country,
moping and begging for feed for your ravening belly."

A Counter   An answer came from Odysseus, full of his own plans.
Challenge   "Eurumakhos, how I long for a battle between us!
Working in springtime when long days are arriving,
I'd take a well-arched scythe out to the field-grass;
you'd take the same. We'd test ourselves in that hard work,
no food until late at dusk, surrounded by tall grass.   370
Or maybe we'd try two oxen, the best we can drive out:
hulking and dark, both of them fattened with good hay,
matched in their age and girth, their muscles untiring.
On four measures of land, good sod for our plowing,
you'd see what a straight line I'd make of my furrow.

"Or if the son of Kronos would bring on a battle
today from somewhere, if spears, a shield and an all-bronze
helmet were mine, snugly clamped at the temples,
then you'd see me scrambling with men in the front ranks.
You'd stop this talk, insulting a man for his belly.   380

"But you're too proud and scornful. Your thinking is cruel.
Doubtless you see yourself a forceful and big man
because you've joined with others—a few who are not good.

If only Odysseus came to the land of his fathers!
How fast would that door, a wide way to go out through,
be all too tight for your dash to the gates of the courtyard!"

Another Footstool
He spoke that way and Eurumakhos, heartily angered,
glared at him darkly, the words with a feathery swiftness,
"You dirt, I'll cause you trouble soon for your talking
to plenty of men so brashly and looking so fearless   390
now and heart-strong. Does wine have your head? Or you
        always
think this way, tossing out words like an old fool.
You beat down Iros, a tramp: did *that* make you giddy?"

He spoke that way and took up a stool but Odysseus
crouched at Amphinomos's knees—the Doulikhion suitor—
and looked afraid. Eurumakhos battered a pourer's
hand whose wine-jug fell to the floor with a loud clang,
the pourer screeched, staggered and fell in some ashes.

Good Dining Spoiled
Suitors roared again in the shadowy great hall.
One man looked at his neighbor and spoke to him this way: 400
"If only he'd died elsewhere, this wandering stranger,
before he came here! He'd never have caused such an
        uproar.
Now we fight about tramps. Our dining may look fine;
it won't be a joy. The worst among us will win out."

Time to Leave
Then with a holy power Telemakhos told them,
"A Daimon has crazed you now, you hide it no longer:
you're gorged and drunk. Now that the God has
        aroused you,
now that you're done feasting, go to your houses and
        lie down
soon as the spirit moves you. I'm pushing no one
        away here."

◆ He spoke that way and they all were biting their lips hard,   410
amazed at Telemakhos now for talking so boldly.
Rising to speak out next, Amphinomos told them—
the shining son of Nisos, the son of lordly Aretios—
"My friends: to answer a man who speaks to us rightly
no one should smart or sound like an enemy ranting.

Stop mistreating the stranger, or any of the other
slaves who work in the house of godlike Odysseus.
Come on, let wine be dropped from the cupbearer's goblet
to thank the Gods. Then go to your houses and lie down.
Let's leave the stranger here in Odysseus's great hall,   420
Telemakhos's ward. This is the house that he came to."

Wine for the   He spoke that way and they all liked what he told them.
Gods and Men   Amphinomos's helper, a squire and Doulikhion war-chief
named Moulios, mixed a drink for them all in the wine-bowl
and went around to serve them. They offered the blissful
Gods their drops, then drank the honey-sweet vintage.
After they poured for the Gods and drank as their hearts
        wished
they went their ways, each man to rest in his own house.

BOOK 19

Memory and Dream
in the Palace

Hiding the
Weapons

Now godlike Odysseus, left behind in the great hall,
planned with Athene's help to murder the suitors.
He spoke to Telemakhos—words with a feathery swiftness—
"Telemakhos, all of the War-God's tools must be taken
well inside. Then calmly lie to the suitors
after they miss the weapons: say when they ask you,
'I took them away from the smoke. The weapons no longer
look like those Odysseus left when he sailed off
to Troy. Wherever fumes have reached them they're sooty.
Some Power has also thrown in my heart a much greater   10
fear that drunk from your wine and standing to fight here
you just might wound each other, shaming your dinner
and courtship. For iron draws a man to its own self.'

The Maids Are
Kept Away

He spoke that way. Telemakhos heeded the father
he loved and called for the nurse. He told Eurukleia,
"Come on, good aunt: keep our maids in their own rooms
now as I take my Father's arms to the storeroom.
They're handsome but grimed by smoke in the house and
      untended.
My Father left them behind when I was a small boy;
now I want them stored. The fire's breath should not
      touch them."   20

A well-loved nurse, Eurukleia answered by saying,
"Dear child, if only you'd take on thoughtfulness always
about your house and all the wealth you should safeguard!
Come on then, who will join you, holding the torchlight?
Aren't you letting a maid light you and lead you?"

Telemakhos promptly gave her a sensible answer.
"The stranger will. I won't allow a man who has taken
my food to be lazy, however far he has traveled."

Golden Light
from a
Goddess

He spoke that way and, all her words being wingless,
she barred the doors of the hall where people had lived well.   30
So both men now, the shining son and Odysseus,

jumped up to carry helmets, sharp-pointed lances
♦ and high-bossed shields out. Their guide was Pallas Athene:
she carried a golden lamp, beautifully glowing,
and shortly Telemakhos called out loud to Odysseus,
"Father, what great wonder my eyes are beholding,
how the walls of the house with their beautiful panels,
pinewood beams and columns reaching the high roof,
glow in my eyes as though they're light from a great fire.
Surely a God's in the house, some ruler of broad sky."   40

An answer came from Odysseus, full of the best plans:
"Be still now. Check your thoughts, don't ask me such
        questions.
That's the way of the Gods who rule on Olumpos.
But you should get some sleep. I'll linger behind here
to trouble the maids again and bother your mother.
The lady no doubt will languish asking of each thing."

Soon as he'd spoken Telemakhos went from the great hall,
shining torchlight before him, to rest in his own room.
He'd often slept there—when sleep came on with its
        sweetness.
Now he lay there again, waiting for bright Dawn.   50

Husband   And so Odysseus, left behind in the great hall,
and Wife   schemed with Athene's help to murder the suitors.
Not Speaking

In time thought-full Penelopeia came from her own room.
She looked like Artemis truly, or gold Aphrodite.
Her chair was placed by the fire, a spot she was used to.
The chair had whorls of ivory and silver worked by an
        old-time
craftsman, Ikmalios. Joining the chair and below it
he'd crafted a footstool; a large fleece had been thrown on.
So she sat there, mind-full Penelopeia,
as white-armed handmaids came from their own hall   60
to carry away mounds of bread, tables and goblets
used by the overbearing suitors for drinking. The
        handmaids
dumped on the floor the fire-stands' ashes and piled up
plenty of fresh logs at the stands for lighting and warming.

Another Bitter   The maid Melantho scolded Odysseus again now.
Scolding   "Are you still here, stranger, to pester us all night,
wander around the house and peer at the women?
Get outdoors, you dirt! Be glad you were fed here
or soon you'll be going outside battered by torches."

Odysseus, full of designs, glared darkly and answered,   70
"Some Power has crazed you. Why is your heart so
    against me?
Because I'm grimy and throw bad clothes on my body?
I beg in your land this way because of my own need.
My ways are those of a poor, wandering scraper,
though I once lived myself in a wealthy and happy
house among men. I often gave to a pauper,
whoever he was, whatever need he arrived with.
I owned slaves by the thousand and plenty of other
goods that men live well by—we call them the rich men.
But Zeus, the son of Kronos, willing it somehow,   80
wrecked my life. Beware woman: you too could be losing
all that glow that makes you shine among maids now.
What if your lady also hardens her anger?
Odysseus too may arrive—there's something of hope there.
Yet if the man is lost and will never return home,
already the son, Telemakhos, helped by Apollo,
is like the father. No reckless maid in the great hall
escapes his notice. The man is a baby no longer."

Those were his words. Mind-full Penelopeia
listened and called the maid herself to upbraid her.   90
"You bold and shameless bitch, your acts are an outrage
I know well: you'll pay for it all with your own head.
You knew this too, you heard it all from my own mouth,
how I would ask the stranger soon in our great hall
about my husband because I've ached for him so much."

Husband and • She spoke to Eurunome quickly, the housekeeper close by:
Wife Speaking   "Eurunome, bring us a chair and fleece in a hurry
to seat our guest. He'll tell his tale from the outset.
He'll hear me too, I want to ask him my questions."

Those were her words. Eurunome hurried and
        brought them   100

a polished chair. She placed it and threw on a sheepskin.
Long-suffering, godlike Odysseus sat down
and mind-full Penelopeia started by saying,
  "Stranger, the first question I'll ask you is this one:
who are you, where do you hail from, what city and
      parents?"

High Praise for   An answer came from Odysseus, full of his own plans.
a Woman   "No one alive on the endless earth could dispraise you,
                lady: truly your name has arrived in the broad sky
            •   like that of a faultless king's, a man who has dreaded
                the Gods and mastered many powerful humans   110
                while holding justice high. Black soil on his farmland
                yields barley and wheat, his groves are heavy with ripe
                      fruit,
                livestock breeding always, the waters are fish-filled
                thanks to his rule, and under him people are thriving.
                But ask me now about anything else in your great hall,
                not my birth or bloodline, the land of my Fathers.
                Don't be filling my heart with more and more sadness
                recalling all that. I've grieved so much and it's not right
                to moan and cry as I sit in the home of another.
                Surely it's bad to bemoan things over and over.   120
                Let me not irk your maids, trouble your own self
                or say that I swam in tears with wine-heavy feelings."

Memories and   Thought-filled now, Penelopeia answered by saying,
Longing   "Stranger, the deathless Gods ravaged my body's
               goodness and beauty the day those Argives boarded
               for Troy, my husband Odysseus boarding among them.
               If only he came back home and cared for my life here!
               My name would be greater then, my face would be fairer.
               But now I mourn beneath the harm some Power has let
                     loose.
               All the nobles around us, ruling the islands   130
               of Same, Doulikhion, densely wooded Zakunthos
               and men with homes in clear-view Ithakan country
               all are unwanted suitors wearing my house down.
               So I don't fret about strangers, men who approach me
               humbly or heralds doing the work of the people.
               I still long for Odysseus, wearing my heart down.

The Loom   "Suitors press me to marry; I'm winding my own guile.
      ♦ The shroud came first, breathed in my heart by some Power.
        I stood a huge loom in the palace for weaving,
        a broad and fine-threaded web. I spoke to them shortly: 140
        'Young men, my suitors, now that godlike Odysseus
        died you're anxious to marry. Wait till I've ended
        my shroud-work: don't let yarn be useless and wasted.
        The shroud's for a war-chief, Laertes, after a deadly
        portion cuts him down—remorseless death is the matter.
        May no Akhaian blame me now in this country
        because he lies unshrouded, a winner of great wealth.'

        "Those were my words. Their hearts were proud but they
            nodded.
        So every day at the huge loom I was weaving.
        And every night with a torch nearby I unwove it!   150
        Three years I had them fooled: the Akhaians did not know.
        But then the fourth year came with its rolling of seasons,
        waning months and all of the daylight ending.
        The suitors got my maids, heartless bitches, to help them.
        They all came, they caught me and scolded me harshly.

        "So I ended my work, not willing but forced to.
        I cannot avoid a marriage now and I cannot
        plan otherwise. My parents have urged me to marry.
        My son smarts when all our goods are devoured here.
        He knows things now as a man, he cares for his own house   160
        greatly for ours was a household honored by great Zeus.

Not from Oak   "But tell me your own bloodline: where did you come from?
  or Stone ♦ You're not from storied oak, I'm sure, or an old stone."

        Odysseus, full of designs, answered by saying,
        "Honored wife of Odysseus, son of Laertes,
        you'll never stop that, will you, asking my birthplace?
        I'll tell you now, though you turn me over to still more
        pain than I'm gripped by. That's the way when a man goes
        far from his father's home as long as I'm gone for,
        rambling through plenty of men's cities in deep pain.   170
        Even so I'll answer all of your questions.

♦"Krete's a lovely land in the midst of the wine-dark
sea with its soil circled by water. No one can count them,
the people who live there—ninety cities in all now!
Tongues mingle with tongues, here are Akhaians,
there Kudones; great-souled Kretans from old times;
three clear strains of Dorians; godlike Pelasgians.
Knosos is there, the greatest city where Minos
ruled from the age of nine. He spoke with Zeus and he
    fathered
my own Father, the great-hearted Deukalion.   180
Deukalion also fathered lordly Idomeneus,
who sailed for Troy with Atreus's sons in their horn-prow
♦ ships. My name is Aithon. Then it was well known
though I was younger. My brother was older and stronger.

    "I saw Odysseus there and I gave him the welcome
due to strangers. Strong winds had brought him to Krete.
He'd headed for Troy and was far off course from Maleia.
♦ He stopped at Amnisos. The cave of Eileithuie is right there
but no good harbor—he barely escaped from the high wind.
He came to the city fast and he sought out Idomeneus.   190
He claimed as a stranger-guest to be honored and loved
    there.
But that was the tenth or eleventh dawn since my brother
had left in his horn-prow ship for Ilion's country.
I brought Odysseus home myself, entertained him
gladly and warmly—my house had plenty inside it.
For those who'd joined him, all the rest of his war-friends,
I gathered from people and gave out barley, some glowing
wine and bulls to slaughter for Gods—and replenish their
    own hearts.
For twelve long days the godlike Akhaians remained there,
checked by the powerful Northwind. No one could
    keep both   200
feet on the ground! Some menacing Power disturbed it.
But winds fell on the thirteenth day and they sailed off."

He told her all those lies, making them seem true.
She listened and tears flowed, her face as if thawing
far-off snow-melt high on the ridge of a mountain—
the Westwind piles up snow and Southeasterly melts it,

making for streams and widening rivers that rush down.
Her lovely cheeks were a melt of tears in the same way.
She cried for her man—and he sat nearby. But Odysseus,
with heartfelt pity for all the sobs of this woman,   210
kept his eyes unmoving, as though they were iron
or polished horn. He checked his tears and beguiled her.

A Test   After she'd taken her fill of wailing and sobbing
of Memory   the lady spoke once more. She answered by asking,
        ♦"Stranger, now I'm thinking of testing you closely.
        If all that's true, your entertaining my husband
        and godlike friends in your hall just as you said now,
        tell me the sort of clothes he wore on his body,
        the kind of man he was, and the men who had joined him."

An answer came from Odysseus, full of the best plans: 220
"It's hard to say, woman, being away so
long a time. The twentieth year has already
arrived since he sailed and left the land of my Fathers.
Yet I'll tell you how he looks in my mind now.
Godlike Odysseus wore a mantle of thick wool,
purple and doubled around. Its gold brooch had a double
working of clasps and the face design was a beauty:
a dog was holding a spotted fawn in its front paws,
it glared at its trembling prey and everyone marveled
how the dog, though of gold, kept glaring and throttling   230
the fawn which flailed its hooves, anxious to race off.
Yes and I closely noted the tunic circling his body,
its shine resembling the dried-out skin of an onion—
that fine and soft—at times it glowed like the sunlight.
Plenty of women gazed at the tunic in wonder.

Clothes for a   "I'll say this too, thrust in your heart what I tell you:
Great Guest   I'm not sure if Odysseus's clothes came from his own house
        or whether a war-friend gave them, boarding their fast ship,
        or maybe a host elsewhere. Odysseus often
        befriended people—few Akhaians could match him.   240
        I gave him a bronze sword myself, a beautiful purple
        mantle that doubled around and a tunic with fringes.
        I sent him off on his firm-decked vessel with honor.

The Closest   "His men? A slightly older herald had joined him.
War-Friend   I'll tell you now what sort of man was the herald.
                 Round-shouldered, with dark complexion and thick hair,
                 his name was Eurubates. Odysseus prized him
                 more than all his war-friends. Both had the same thoughts."

Evil, Unspeak-   He spoke that way and aroused her longing to cry more.
able Troy   She knew the signs were true the beggar had told her.   250
                 After she took her fill of moaning and sobbing,
                 she spoke to the man once more. She answered by pledging,
                 "Now my guest, although you were pitied before this,
                 I'll make you honored, a well-loved friend in my great hall.
                 I gave him the clothes myself, those you remembered.
                 I folded and took them out of their room, and I added
                 the shining brooch to make him glad. But now I will never
                 welcome him home to the well-loved land of his fathers.
                 Odysseus went with an evil doom in that hollow
                 ship to Troy—it's Evil itself—no one should name it."   260

The Husband   Full of designs Odysseus answered by saying,
Is Very Near   "Honored wife of Odysseus, son of Laertes,
                 don't keep spoiling your beautiful face any longer,
                 wasting your heart and mourning your husband. Though
                     no one
                 blames a woman for mourning her husband who's
                     perished—
                 the pair have made love, she's borne him their children—
                 and more for Odysseus who looked, they say, like a
                     great God—
                 still you should stop this grieving. Hear out my story:
                 everything's true that I tell you, nothing's in hiding.

                 "I heard myself of Odysseus's homecoming lately.   270
             ◆ The man's close by in rich Thesprotian country.
                 Alive he'll bring home lots of beautiful treasures
                 he sought throughout that land. But war-friends he trusted
                 all were lost. His hollow ship went down in the wine-dark
                 sea when he left Thrinakie Island. Zeus and the Sun-God
                 were angry because his men had slaughtered the God's
                     bulls.
                 All his crewmen died in the roar of the high sea.

"But rollers tossed Odysseus, riding the ship's keel,
ashore on Phaiakian land. Their line is the Gods' own:
they took him to heart fully as though he were great Zeus.   280
They gave him plenty of presents, glad they could send him
home unharmed. Odysseus might have arrived here
a while ago but he felt in his heart it was better
to come back wealthy, to travel over the wide earth.
Odysseus knows plenty of schemes better than any
death-bound man—no other person could match him—
so I was told by Pheidon, Thesprotia's ruler.
He swore to me, pouring wine for the Gods in his own
        house,
a crew was ready, a ship's been hauled to the water
and men would send him now to the well-loved land of his
        fathers.   290

Great Wealth   "But first he sent me off. Thesprotian shipmen
Coming   were bound by chance for Doulikhion, known for its good
                        grains.
He showed me all the wealth amassed by Odysseus,
enough to feed his heirs to the tenth generation—
that much treasure lay in the house of the ruler.
He told me Odysseus went to Dodone to hear out
plans of Zeus from the God's oak with its high leaves:
how to return to the well-loved land of his fathers?
Openly? In secret? The man had been gone for a long time.

Arrival   "So he is quite safe now. Already approaching,   300
at Long Last   very close, he won't be away from his loved ones
and fathers' land for long. I'll swear to it fully,
Zeus be my witness first, the highest and best God.
I swear by faultless Odysseus's hearth I arrived at:
truly it all will end the way I have told you.
This very month Odysseus finally sails home
when the old moon's waned and the new one is waxing."

No, the Man   But mind-full Penelopeia answered by saying,
Is Lost   "Ah my guest, if only your words could become real!
You'd quickly know of my friendship, all the gifts I'd lavish   310
making those who met you say you are well blessed.
But now my heart foresees the way it will happen:
Odysseus won't come home, nor will your send-off

take place for our household masters are hardly
the way Odysseus was, a *man* among men—if he ever
lived. He honored strangers and sent them away well.

A Bath and Oil   "Now you handmaids, wash the stranger and set out
for the   a bed with covers and blankets glistening brightly
Stranger   to warm him well till Dawn arrives on her gold throne.
Then you'll bathe and anoint him early tomorrow.   320
He'll sit right there at Telemakhos's side in the great hall
while planning to dine. And any man who annoys him
or maims his heart will fare far worse, never availing
a thing in my house, despite the extreme of his anger.

"For how will you know, my guest, whether I stand out,
the best of women in thoughtful counsel and insight,
the way you've sat in my hall to dine unanointed
and wearing rags? Men exist for a short time.
The man who never cares or knows about caring
is cursed and all men pray he'll suffer in good time   330
while living and after his death everyone mocks him.
Ah but the man who's blameless and knows what is
        blameless:
strangers carry his name and honor a long way
to throngs of people. Many call him the best man."

Only an Older   Yet Odysseus answered, full of his own plans,
Woman   "Honored wife of Odysseus, son of Laertes:
glowing blankets and covers on beds are distasteful
right from the first day I left behind me the snowy
mountains of Krete, boarding a ship with its long oars.
Tonight I'll rest as I've always rested on other   340
sleepless nights, lying down on unlikely
cots and waiting for Dawn, bright on her gold throne.
Foot-baths too no longer agree with my spirits:
none of your women now will handle these old feet.
Of all those helpers working hard in your household
♦ maybe an older handmaid, knowing and careful,
whose heart has borne as many troubles as I have—
if such a woman should touch my feet I would let her."

Mind-full Penelopeia answered by saying,
"Dear guest, no man so tactful ever arrived here,   350

not one friendly, far-off stranger joining my household—
so wise and well thought out are all of your sayings.
One old woman is heartily thoughtful and caring,
having nursed and raised my sorry husband:
her hands held him after his mother had borne him.
She'll wash your feet despite her weakness and old age.

"Come on then, thoughtful Eurukleia, stand up and
        wash him.
The man is old as your master. Doubtless Odysseus's
feet are now like this and his hands could be just so—
people in pain and misery age in a hurry."   360

No Thanks Soon as she'd spoken the woman covered her old face,
from Zeus   shedding some warm tears and answering sadly,
"I'm helpless, child. Odysseus! Zeus must have loathed you
beyond all men in spite of your God-fearing spirit.
No one burned for that God, who revels in thunder,
so many fat-rich thighs and hecatombs ever.
You offered so much while praying you'd come to your
        old age
healthy and shining, and raise your son to be well known.
But Zeus has removed your way back home—and
        yours only.

So Like   "Women undoubtedly mocked my lord in a far-off   370
Odysseus   land of strangers after he came to some well-known
house like you, stranger, mocked by all of these bitches.
So now to avoid their many disgraceful insults
you won't allow them to wash you. I'm hardly unwilling,
told by Ikarios's daughter, mind-full Penelopeia.
I will wash your feet both for Penelopeia's
sake and your own. The heart inside me is caring
if troubled. Come on though, hear some words I will
        tell you:
plenty of harshly tested strangers have come here,
yet I can say I've never seen such a likeness—   380
your shape, your voice and feet are so like Odysseus's."

The Scar   Full of designs Odysseus answered by saying,
"So everyone tells me, woman, those who have seen us

both with their own eyes. We closely resemble each other.
Now you've seen it yourself and told me the same thing."

He spoke that way as the woman, holding a shining
basin for washing his feet, poured out the water—
plenty of cold then splashes of hot. As Odysseus
sat by the fire though, he turned his face to the dark side
♦ suddenly thinking *the scar*: what if she grasped him   390
there and saw it? His work would be out in the open!
She came close, she started to wash her master and
    promptly
saw the scar—from a boar's white tusk in the old days.

The Name of ♦ He'd gone to Parnesos. Autolukos lived with his sons there,
  Odysseus   his mother's kindly father—and better than all men
at swearing and stealing! A God himself had endowed him:
he'd pleased the God Hermes by burning the best thighs
of goats and sheep. Hermes favored him gladly.
Autolukos once had gone to farm-rich Ithakan country,
arriving there for the newborn son of his daughter.   400
Eurukleia placed the boy on his friendly
knees after he dined. She spoke up and asked him,
"Autolukos, find us a name to give to your grandson.
This child of your own child often was prayed for."

Autolukos promptly answered the woman by saying,
"My daughter and son-in-law, give him the name I will
    tell you.
Because I came here 'at odds' myself with so many
on richly nourishing ground, with women and men both,
let the boy's name be 'Odysseus.' Soon as the child grows,
a man who arrives at the great house of his mother's   410
line at Parnesos, the place of my wealth and resources,
I'll give him treasure there and send him off happy."

A Bull   In time Odysseus went for that ruler's outstanding
and a Feast   gifts and Autolukos welcomed the man with a handshake
and gentle words. The sons of Autolukos joined him.
Amphithea, his mother's mother, embraced him,
kissing her son-in-law's head and both of his fine eyes.
Lordly Autolukos promptly called to his highly

praised sons to get ready to dine. They followed his
        prompting
and shortly led in a bull, a five-year-old beauty.   420
They killed and flayed it, cut off the limbs and adroitly
sliced off smaller pieces. They carefully spit them,
roasted them all and gave out everyone's portion.
All day long they ate and drank until sundown;
no one's hunger or heart went lacking a good share.
Soon as the Sun-God sank and darkness arrived there
they lay right down and took the gift of a night's sleep.

The Hunt   When newborn Dawn came on with her rose-fingered
                daylight,
        they all went out for a chase: Autolukos's own sons,
        the dogs as well and godlike Odysseus joined them.   430
        They climbed the steep mountain, wooded Parnesos
        clothed in green and soon arrived in some windy
        hollows. The Sun-God was newly lighting the farmland—
        Helios rose from the gentle flow of deep Okeanos—
        when hunters arrived at a glen. Racing before them
        the dogs had followed a scent: closing behind them
        were sons of Autolukos, joined by godlike Odysseus
        pressing the dogs closely, shaking a spear with its lengthy
        shadow. Nearby was a huge boar, lying in dense brush.
        Strong and sea-damp winds could not bluster inside there,   440
        glaring Helios could hardly throw in his own light
        and rain could not fall through: the brush was that thickly
        tangled and mounds of leaves had fallen as well there.

A Torn Leg   But then with hounds and horsemen stamping around him
        and driving closer, the boar rushed out of his thicket,
        nape-hair bristling and fire glinting in both eyes.
        He stood at bay, quite close, and Odysseus charged him,
        briskly hoisting the lengthy spear in his thick-set
        hand and hot for a thrust. But the boar was ahead of him,
                slashing
        above the knee, his tusk with a long rip at the flesh there,   450
        a sidelong tear, though it fell short of the man's bone.
     ◆ Odysseus caught him too, driving the glowing
        spearhead straight at the right shoulder and through it.
        The boar squealed and fell in the dust and its spirit
        flew off. Autolukos's well-loved sons were around him,

anxious to bind the wound of handsome, godlike Odysseus.
They carefully staunched the blackish blood as they sang out
prayers then shortly left for the house of their father.

Healing and   In time Autolukos healed him, helped by his children.
Homecoming   They made him well and gave him outstanding presents.   460
                They sent him gladly and swiftly back to his fathers'
                land on Ithaka. There his honored mother and father
                rejoiced at his homecoming day and asked about each thing,
                how he'd suffered the wound. He told them the story
                well of the boar's white tusk that slashed him while hunting
                with sons of Autolukos after he'd gone up Parnesos.

The Truth Is   The old woman remembered the scar when she felt it
Out   now with the flat of her hand. The leg she had lifted
                fell from her grasp to the bronze basin that clattered,
                tipped over and puddled the floor with its water.   470
                Joy and sorrow seized her heart at the same time,
                her eyes welled with tears and her voice was caught in
                her throat as she touched the chin of Odysseus saying,
                "Dear child, you're truly Odysseus! Yet I was not sure
                before I handled more of my master's body."

A Killing Threat She spoke that way, her eyes going to Penelopeia—
                she wanted to show her well-loved husband was right here!
                The lady though could not face her or know him:
            ◆   Athene had shifted her thoughts. Meanwhile Odysseus
                felt for the old one's throat, he clasped it with one hand,   480
                pulled her close with the other and threatened her saying,
                "Good aunt, why would you kill me? You nursed me
                        yourself once
                there at your breast. Now with all of my great pain
                I'm back in the twentieth year to the land of my Fathers.
                What you know was thrust in your heart by some Power.
                Still don't talk. No one else must know in the great hall.
                I'll say this too, I'll tell you how it will end here:
                if Gods bring down the high-born suitors beneath me,
                I won't spare you, my own nurse, when I slaughter
                the other women, the rest of the maids in my great hall."   490

Hard as Iron   But thoughtful Eurukleia answered by saying,
                "My child, what talk gets over the wall of your front teeth!

You know how steady I am, how strong and unbending.
I'll surely hold out hard as granite or iron.
And I'll say this—thrust in your mind what I tell you—
if Gods bring down the high-born suitors beneath you,
I'll tell you about these women, your maids in the great hall,
those who dishonor you here and those who are blameless."

And answer came from Odysseus, full of his own plans.
"Good aunt, why name them? No, there is no need.   500
I'll watch them closely myself—I'll know about each one.
Just keep my story quiet and trust in the high Gods."

He spoke that way and the old one went through the
        great hall
to get more foot-wash—all the other had spilled out.
After she washed him well and rubbed him with rich oil,
Odysseus pulled his chair again to the hearth-fire,
closer and warmer. He hid the scar with his tatters.

The   Now mind-full Penelopeia started to tell him,
Nightingale   "My guest, I'll ask you a small thing of my own here.
The hour for welcome rest will soon be upon us—   510
for those whom honeyed sleep may hold in spite of their
        troubles.
But I? Some Power gave me trouble without end:
every day my only joy is in mourning and wailing.
I look to my work and my maids' work in the household.
When night's arrived and sleep has taken them all in
I lie in bed, sharp cares come crowding around me,
stabbing my racing heart. Saddened and troubled,
  ♦ I'm like Pandareos's daughter, the nightingale singing
sharply in green forest when spring's newly arriving,
perched among dense leaves on the bough of a high tree.   520
She pours out echoing song and varies it often
bewailing her dear child Itulos, son of that ruler,
Zethos: she killed the child with a sword without knowing.
So my heart is in halves, waking this way and that way:
whether to stay with my child, keep everything safe here,
my wealth and handmaids, the huge house with its
        high roof,
revering my husband's bed and the voice of our people;
or go off now with the man who's best of the Akhaians

courting me, bringing countless gifts to the great hall.
My son was a child before, a careless youngster   530
who stopped me from going, leaving the house of my
          husband
to marry. But now that he's grown to a measure of manhood
in fact he prays I'll go away from the great hall
again. He frets for his goods, devoured by Akhaians.

Twenty Geese •"Come on though, hear out a dream of mine and explain it.
and an Eagle   Twenty geese in my house have come from the water
to eat my grain. I'm warm and glad to be watching.
But then a large, hook-beaked eagle flies from the
          mountains
and breaks each one of their necks. They lie where he
          killed them,
piled in the great hall. The eagle soars to the bright sky.   540
I scream myself. I cry although I am dreaming,
women in lovely Akhaian braids are around me
mourning sadly—my geese were killed by an eagle.

"The bird flew back then. He perched high on a jutting
roof-beam and spoke with a man's voice to console me:
'Take heart, widely renowned Ikarios's daughter.
No idle dream, your splendid vision will end well.
The geese were your suitors. I was an eagle
before but now I'm back in this form as your husband
who'll bring a revolting doom on all of the suitors.'   550

"He spoke that way, sweet sleep let go of me promptly,
I looked around and saw the geese in my great hall,
eating grain by a trough. They'd eaten before there."

The Suitors   Full of designs Odysseus answered by saying,
Will All Die   "Lady, this is no dream to explain by a bending
this way or that way. Surely Odysseus showed you
himself the way it will end: the suitors will all die.
Not one man will avoid his doom on that death-day."

Two Kinds of   But mind-full Penelopeia answered by saying,
Dreams   "Dreams can be useless, my guest, and endlessly baffling.   560
Surely they don't all end for people as clear fact.
Our dreams move like shadows through either of two gates,

one of them made of horn, the other of ivory.
Those that pass through the well-sawn ivory gateway
tend to be guileful—the words they carry are empty.
Those however that pass through the gateway of polished
horn can bring you truth—when a human can see that.
My frightening dream, I think, was not from the polished
horn. How welcome to me and my child if it *had* been!

Axes in a Line   "But I'll say this—thrust in your heart what I tell you—   570
the dawn that's coming is cursed, taking me far from
Odysseus's home because I'll set up a contest
with axes he used to arrange just so in the great hall,
twelve in a line in all, straight as the ribs of a vessel.
Standing back, he'd shoot through them all with an arrow.
I'll set up the same contest now for the suitors.
The man who can deftly string the bow with his own hands
and shoot an arrow through all twelve of the axes
wins my hand. I'll leave the house of my marriage,
a place of so much beauty, wealth and resources.   580
I think I'll recall it someday, even while dreaming."

Odysseus, full of designs, answered by saying,
"Honored wife of Odysseus, son of Laertes,
don't delay this contest now in your own house.
Odysseus, full of his plans, will arrive here before then,
well before a suitor handles the polished
bow or strings it and sends a shaft through the iron."

Tearful Rest   Mind-full Penelopeia answered by saying,
Again   "If only you chose, my guest, to remain in the hall here
delighting me! Sleep would never be strewn on my eyelids.   590
But doubtless there's no way for men to be sleepless
always: the deathless Gods have arranged for a portion
of each thing for death-bound people on grain-giving
        farmlands.
So now I'll go upstairs myself to an upper
room and lie on the bed. It's turned into sorrow,
always wet with tears from the day that Odysseus
left for Troy—Evil itself!—no one should name it.
I'll lie up there while you lie down in the house here,
a bed on the floor. Or maids will set up a plain bed."

Having spoken she walked upstairs to her glowing   600
room and not alone: handmaids had joined her.
After she entered the upstairs room with her women,
she cried for Odysseus, the husband she loved, till the
    glow-eyed
Athene tossed some honeyed sleep on her eyelids.

To Kill the
Women

So godlike Odysseus, ready to sleep in the forehall,
spread an untanned bull's-hide and plenty of fleeces,
the wool from sheep the Akhaian suitors had slaughtered.
Eurunome tossed a cloak on the man when he lay down.
Odysseus planned on danger there for the suitors,
lying awake. When women came from the great hall,
those who were used to going to bed with the suitors,
laughing among themselves and chatting together,
the noise they made aroused the heart in his own chest.
He thought things out in his head and heart for a while
        there: 10
whether to rush them and cause the killing of each one,
or let them have their sex with the pride-smitten suitors
one last time. The heart grumbled inside him
♦ the way a dog will growl, standing over her tender
pups and anxious to fight with a man she does not know.
His heart growled that way. Their wrongdoing vexed him.

But shortly he struck his breast and scolded his own heart.
"Bear up, my heart. You bore an action more shameless
the day that Kuklops overpowered and gulped down
hearty war-friends. You held up then till the right plan   20
brought you out of the cave—you thought you would die
        there."

Help from the
Goddess

He spoke that way, scolding the heart in his own chest.
His heart obeyed him well: it bore up and stayed firm.
Yet the man went on tossing this way and that way
much like a cook at a blazing fire, turning a stomach
packed with blood and fat this way and that way,
moving it fast as he can, longing to roast it.
So Odysseus tossed both ways and he wondered:
how could he get his hands on the pride-swollen suitors,
♦ one against many? Athene came to him close by.   30
Down from the heavens, she'd taken the form of a woman
standing over his head and asking him shortly,
"Why are you still awake? Most hapless of all men!

Your house is in fact right here, your wife's in your
    own house
and anyone surely would want your child for his own son."

Full of designs Odysseus answered by saying,
"Goddess, it's true. You've said everything rightly.
Yet in my heart and mind I'm pondering one thing:
how can I lay my hands on pride-swollen suitors
being alone? They're always crowding inside here.   40
My head keeps pondering more boldly what's later:
even if you and Zeus would help me to kill them,
where could I run from their families? Mull what I ask you."

Rustle
Their Bulls

The glow-eyed Goddess Athene answered by saying,
"Still stubborn? Others rely on some frailer,
    death-bound friend who lacks my knowledge of good plans,
but I myself am your Goddess! Through all of your
    struggles
I guard and watch you. Yes and I'll openly tell you,
even if fifty death-bound men were in ambush,
eager to kill us both on a field of the War-God,   50
still we could rustle all their cattle and fat sheep!
So now let sleep take hold. It's hard to be watchful,
awake all night. You're emerging from trials already."

Sleep for the
Man, Not for
the Woman

She spoke that way and poured out sleep on his eyelids.
Bright as a Goddess herself, she left for Olumpos.
Sleep overtook him, freeing his heart from its worries,
relaxing his man's frame. But his knowing and caring
wife woke up and cried. She sat on the soft bed.
In time when her heart had taken its fill of crying,
this brightest of women prayed to Artemis foremost: 60
"Queenly Goddess, Zeus's daughter, if only
your arrow would lodge in my breast, taking my life right
here and now! Or let me be seized by a whirlwind,
hurried away and down some shadowy byway
or thrown in the mouth of that backward flow, Okeanos,
• the way a whirlwind carried Pandareos's daughters.
Gods had killed their dear parents and left them
orphans at home, cared for by bright Aphrodite,
helped by her cheese, good wine and the sweetness
    of honey.

Here gave them more wisdom and beauty than any   70
woman's and hallowed Artemis gave them their full height.
Athene taught them her skills, their wonderful handcraft.
But after bright Aphrodite went to the heights of Olumpos
to ask for a flowery wedding at last for the daughters—
Zeus revels in thunder there and knows about all things,
both the luck and the lack of luck for men who are death-
    bound—
Windstorm-Powers meanwhile were snaring the daughters.
They gave them shortly to hateful Avengers to deal with.

Longing for the   "If Gods with Olumpos homes erased me the same way,
   Underworld   if Artemis, beautifully braided, struck me and helped me   80
                    go under the hateful earth with the face of Odysseus,
                    then I might never delight the mind of a lesser
                    man. But so much harm is bearable, even
                    crying each day, my heart crowded by troubles,
                    if only sleep takes you at night and makes you forget things,
                    all your rights and wrongs, when it covers your eyelids.

Truth-Filled   "But now some Power sends me painfully bad dreams.
   Dreams   Again tonight my man's likeness lay alongside me—
                  his looks when he left with the army. My heart was
                      delighted,
                  I thought it was not some dream but truly a vision."   90

She stopped: Dawn was arriving fast on her gold throne.
Godlike Odysseus heard the sound of her crying
and wondered a while. In his heart she seemed to be
    standing
close to his own face and to know him already.

New Signs   He gathered the wooly bedclothes, all he had slept on,
from Zeus   and placed them on chairs in the hall. He carried the
                   bull's-hide
               outdoors and set it down. He prayed to Zeus with his hands
                   raised:
               "Fatherly Zeus, if you Gods have wanted to bring me
               home by land and sea after you mangled me so much,
               let someone awake inside the house, tell me an omen.   100
               Outside too, let Zeus show me his own sign."

He prayed and was heard by Zeus, God of the great plans.
Promptly he thundered broadly from glowing Olumpos,
high in the clouds. Godlike Odysseus felt glad.

A Frail A woman also spoke from the house like an omen.
Woman's She'd milled nearby where a shepherd of people had set up
Prayer mills where twelve women in all had been grinding
barley and wheat into flour—the marrow of good men.
Having milled their grains the others were sleeping.
The frailest however had not yet finished her labor.   110
She stopped her mill and spoke, a sign for her master:
"Fatherly Zeus, Lord of Gods and us humans,
what loud thunder you send from the star-studded heavens
and nowhere a cloud! It's a sign you're showing to someone.
Poor as I am, make real this word that I say now:
today let suitors all sit down and relish
their last meal, glad in Odysseus's hall for the last time.
Those men have loosened my knees with heart-hurting
    labor,
this milling of grain. Let them dine for the last time."

She spoke that way as an omen that cheered godlike
    Odysseus   120
like Zeus's thunder. He planned to punish the offenders.

How Is the Other maids in Odysseus's beautiful household
Stranger started to gather and build a tireless hearth-fire.
Treated? Telemakhos rose from his bed, a man like a God-man:
he dressed and dangled a sharp sword from a shoulder,
strapped on his oil-smooth feet two beautiful sandals
and took up a strong spear pointed with sharp bronze.
Then he walked to the threshold and asked Eurukleia,
"Dear aunt, have you honored the guest in our household
with food and a bed? He's not still lying uncared for?   130
My Mother works that way, for all of her foresight:
she prizes a lesser, earth-born stranger at random
but sends the greater man away without honor."

A thoughtful Eurukleia gave him an answer:
"My child, don't blame a woman now who is blameless.
The stranger sat here drinking wine as long as he wanted.

He said he no longer craved food when she asked him.
Then when your guest was thinking of rest and a night's
    sleep,
the lady told her handmaids to spread out some bedding.
Yet like a man entirely wretched and luckless,   140
he wanted no fine blankets or bedding to lie on,
only the untanned hide of a bull and some sheepskins.
He slept in the forecourt. We put a cloak on his body."

Telemakhos, after she'd spoken, went through the great hall
holding the spear. Two white dogs followed him closely.
He walked to the assembly place among well-greaved
    Akhaians.

Building the   Now a goddess-like woman called to the handmaids,
Feast   Eurukleia, the daughter of Ops, the son of Peisenor:
"Hurry and move, you maids, sweep up the whole house!
Dampen the floor, throw some purple cloths on the
    well-made   150
chairs and the rest of you wipe off all of the tables
with sponges. Wash the mixing bowls, the double-
handled and well-worked goblets. Go for some water,
be off to the spring and quickly carry it back now!
The suitors won't be away from the hall much longer,
they'll come back soon: it's feasting time for us all here."

She spoke that way, they heard her well and obeyed her.
Twenty handmaids went to the spring with its dark depths.
The others labored deftly and fast in the great hall.

Anger and   The Akhaians' helpers came in next and they promptly   160
Outrage Still   and skillfully chopped up wood. Shortly the women
came from the spring, the swineherd coming behind them,
driving three of his boars, the best of the whole herd.
He let them feed right there in the beautiful courtyard
but spoke to Odysseus himself, asking him gently,
"Stranger, are all the Akhaians treating you better?
Or lacking esteem for you now as before in the great hall?"

An answer came from Odysseus, full of his good plans:
"Eumaios, if only the Gods would punish their outrage!

They form such reckless and high-handed plots in another   170
man's house. They have no shame, not even a portion."

More Taunts   Then as the two men spoke that way with each other
Melantheus walked up closely, the herder of goat-flocks,
driving nannies to town, the best in the whole herd—
food for the suitors. A pair of goatherds had joined him.
Soon as he tethered goats in the echoing courtyard
he spoke again to Odysseus, taunting him boldly,
"Still around, stranger, to pester the whole house
and wheedle from men? Not outdoors and a ways off?
I'm thinking, all in all, the two of us won't be   180
parting without a taste of our fists for your messy
wheedling. Then too there are other Akhaian dinners."

Odysseus, full of his own plans, gave him no answer.
He shook his head quietly, brooding on evil.

A Wish for   A third man came, Philoitios, a master of good men.
Better Luck   He drove a barren cow and fatted goats for the suitors,
brought from the mainland by boatmen ferrying others—
men they'd boarded—whoever arrived there and asked
        them.
He tied the animals well in the echoing courtyard,
came up close himself to the swineherd and asked him,   190
"Who's the stranger, swineherd, newly arrived here
in our own house? What clan does he say he belongs to?
Where are his bloodlines, the farming land of his fathers?
He looks doomed—though a lord or king with a good build.
The Gods, whenever they weave their anguish, can lower
a man who's often wandered—yes and a king too."

He stopped and approached the beggar, gave him his
        right hand
and spoke to him now, the words with a feathery swiftness,
"Fatherly stranger, be well. May all of your future
luck be good, though now you have plenty of hardship.   200

"You Zeus, our Father, no other God is more deadly.
You pity no man, not even a man you have fathered.
You mix us all in pain, trouble and sorrow.

"I started sweating, stranger, my eyes teared when I saw you
there recalling Odysseus. He too could be wearing
rags like those, I think, roaming among men—
indeed if he's still alive and gazing at sunlight.

"But now if he's dead and gone to the household of Aides,
I am lost. Blameless Odysseus! You made me your cowherd
when I was a child in Kephallenian country.   210
Now your herds are countless. No one was better
at breeding wide-browed cattle—you raised them like
    cornstalks!

To Run Off   "But suitors tell me to drive them here to be eaten.
or Stay   They don't care for the man's son in his great hall.
They don't tremble at Gods' vengeance, no, they are only
eager to split up the wealth of a ruler who's long gone.
So this heart in my own chest has been turning
matters often. It's very wrong, with Odysseus's
son in the house, to take my herd to some outland,
a foreigner's country. Yet it's worse to remain here,   220
bearing the pain and caring for bulls for these strangers.
Long ago, it's true, I'd like to have run off
and joined some powerful lord—I could stand it no longer.
But then I think of that wretch and how, if he came home
now from somewhere, he'd scatter suitors through all of the
    palace."

Another   An answer came from Odysseus, full of the best plans:
Prophecy of   "Herder, you don't look like a harmful or foolish
Doom   man and I know myself your heart is empathic.
So now I'll tell you the truth, I'll swear you a strong oath.
Zeus be my witness, first of the Gods, this table for
    strangers   230
and faultless Odysseus's hearth, the fire I have come to:
while you remain in the house Odysseus comes home!
You'll see with your own eyes if that's what you've wanted—
all the suitors will die who've acted like masters."

Pledges of   The man who herded his cattle gave him an answer:
Strength   "Stranger, if only the son of Kronos would make good
all your words! You'd know my strength, how ready my
    hands are."

Eumaios also prayed to all of the great Gods
that mind-full Odysseus now would return to his
        own house.

A Wrong Sign   All the while they spoke that way to each other   240
               suitors were plotting doom—Telemakhos's murder.
               But now an eagle clasping a terrified pigeon
               came from the heights and approached them all on the
                       wrong side,
               their left. Amphinomos promptly stood up to tell them,
               "My friends, clearly our plans for Telemakhos's killing
               will not go well. For now let's think about dining."

The Feast   Amphinomos spoke that way and his word was their
Begins   pleasure.
               Walking back to the house of godlike Odysseus,
               they laid their mantles on seats and chairs that were
                       thronelike.
               Slaves were slaughtering sheep and goats, fatted and full-
                       grown.   250
               They cut down huge hogs and a bull from the best herd.
               They roasted organs and shared them. Using the large
                       bowls
               they mixed wine and the hog-tender handed out goblets.
               Philoitios brought them bread—a lord of his own men—
               in pretty baskets. The goatherd Melantheus poured wine.
               Their hands went out to the good things lying before them.

A Warning   Telemakhos told Odysseus, showing his cunning,
about Strife   to sit in the strongly founded hall close to the threshold
               of stone by a lowly stool. A small table was put there.
               He poured him wine in a golden goblet and set out   260
               portions of innards. Then he spoke to the beggar:
               "Sit down, drink your wine with all of the men here.
               I'll fend off taunts myself from all of the suitors—
               fists if I must—because my house is no lowbrow
               place but the hall of Odysseus, gained for my own gain.

               "All you suitors! Hold back striking and taunting
               now from your hearts. No quarrel or strife should be
                       rising."

He stopped and every suitor was biting his lips hard,
struck by Telemakhos, how he'd spoken so bravely.
The son of Eupeithes, Antinoos, called to the others: 270
"It's hard, Akhaians, but bear with Telemakhos's big talk,
however the man scolds us or threatens us harshly.
Zeus, the son of Kronos, stopped us, or now in the great hall
we'd surely have stopped him, for all of his clear-toned
    haranguing."
He spoke that way but Telemakhos shrugged off his
    comments.

Grand Dining   Now the heralds were guiding a hecatomb sacred
Again   to Gods through the city. Long-haired Akhaians gathered
under a shady grove of far-shooting Apollo.
Soon as the outer flesh was cooked and unspitted
they all shared portions, enjoying a wonderful banquet.   280
Servers placed a portion too by Odysseus
matching their own portions. Telemakhos told them
to do so, the well-loved son of godlike Odysseus.

Another Throw   Still Athene would hardly stop the disdainful suitors
at the Stranger from stinging his heart with insult: heavier sorrow
must sink in the heart of Odysseus, son of Laertes.
One of the suitors, a man known as a scofflaw,
was named Ktesippos. He ruled his household on Same
and came trusting his wealth—said to be wondrous—
to court Odysseus's wife, whose husband was long gone.   290
He turned to the overbearing suitors and told them,
"Listen, you lordly suitors! I'll tell you my thoughts here.
The stranger's held his portion now for a long time,
rightly matched with the rest. It's wrong and ungraceful
to steal from Telemakhos's guests who came to his own
    house,
so now I'll give like a host. Maybe he'll offer
this prize himself to a bath-girl, or maybe another
slave who works in the house of godlike Odysseus."

He stopped and picked up an ox-hoof that lay in a basket
and let it fly with a powerful hand. Odysseus dodged it,   300
moving his head aside and heartily smiling
a bitter smile. The ox-hoof slammed at the hard wall.

A Death Threat ♦ Promptly upbraiding Ktesippos, Telemakhos told him,
        "Good for your heart, Ktesippos, the way it has turned out.
        You failed to hit our guest when he dodged what you
            threw him
        or *I* would have struck you for sure with a spear in
            your belly.
        Your father, instead of a marriage feast, would have
            managed
        your death-rites.

Command,   "So now let no one appear so disgraceful
Reproach,   here in this house! I'm watching, following each thing,
Plead,
and Reproach the best and the worst. Before this I was a youngster.   310
        Ah, but I watch it all and continue to bear it—
        our sheep slaughtered, wine tossed off and our bread-loaves
        bolted. It's hard for a man to hold back a whole crowd.
        Come on then: don't be enemies doing me harm here.
        Still if you're bent on killing me now with your sharp
            bronze,
        I'd want to be killed myself: far better to die here
        than go on watching disgraceful acts without let-up,
        mocking and smacking strangers, dragging the women
        around in shame throughout my beautiful household."

Help the Lady They all were dumb when he stopped. No one could answer.   320
to Choose   At length Agelaos spoke up, the son of Damastor.
        "My friends, to answer a man who speaks to us rightly
        no one should fume or rant like an enemy harshly.
        Stop mistreating the stranger now and the other
        slaves who work in the house of godlike Odysseus.

        "I have a word for Telemakhos too and his mother,
        gently hoping to please both of their good hearts.
        So long as you deeply hoped in your breasts for that hour
        mind-full Odysseus finally would enter his own house,
        no one blamed you for waiting or holding the suitors   330
        off in this hall. That course plainly was better
        if only Odysseus came back home to his own land.
        But truly now the man will never return home.
        Come on then, take a seat by your mother and tell her
        to marry the man who's best, who offers the most gifts.

You'll gladly take on all the wealth of your fathers,
dining and drinking; she'll care for the house of another."

Forcing One's   But now Telemakhos gave him a sensible answer.
Mother   "I swear by Zeus, Agelaos, and all the pain of my Father,
dying far from Ithaka somewhere or roaming: 340
I don't delay my Mother's wedding. I've told her
to choose and marry, I offer uncountable presents.
It shames me though to force her out of the great hall
against her will. May Gods not end it in that way."

Strange   Telemakhos stopped: Pallas Athene had goaded
and Sudden ♦ the suitors to laugh wildly, perplexing their whole minds—
Omens   they laughed as though their mouths belonged to some
others.
Then their meat was a bloody mess and their eyesight
blurred with tears. In their hearts they seemed to be
mourning.

Blood and   Promptly the godlike man Theoklumenos asked them,   350
Death Foretold   "You wretched men, what ravage now do you suffer?
Night's shrouding your heads and faces, yes and your
low knees.
Your wails are a kindled fire, your cheeks are all teary.
These beautiful walls and panels are spattered with
bloodstains,
ghosts crowd the doorway and crowd the courtyard,
rushing to Erebos under the gloom. The sunlight's
dead in the sky and a baleful darkness has closed in."

He spoke that way but they all laughed at him lightly.
Eurumakhos, Polubos's son, started to tell them,
"The stranger's crazy, newly arriving from far off.   360
Take him outdoors, young men, hurry and go to
the assembly place, since night is all he can find here!"

But then the godlike man Theoklumenos answered,
"Eurumakhos, I don't ask you to send me or guide me.
I have eyes and ears and both of my own feet.
The ideas in my breast have not been crafted so poorly.
I'll go outside because I know that some evil
draws close to you now. No suitor can run to avoid it,

none of you men in the house of godlike Odysseus,
insulting people and making plans that are reckless."   370

He stopped and left the house where people had lived well.
He went to Peiraios, the man who'd welcomed him gladly.

Harsh Teasing   All the suitors, exchanging looks with each other,
harassed Telemakhos now by mocking his guests there.
One overbearing younger suitor was saying,
"Telemakhos, nobody takes in sorrier strangers
than you do, holding on to a slovenly beggar
craving food and wine but lacking the know-how
for farmwork or fighting—a dead weight in your own fields.
The other one stood up now and made like a prophet!   380
My way is better by far if you follow it closely:
throw these 'guests' on a ship with plenty of oar-locks
and send them to Sicily. There they'll get you a good price."

Suitors talked that way; he shrugged off their chatter.
Telemakhos watched his father and quietly waited.
In time he'd get his hands on the insolent suitors.

The Last   Ikarios's daughter, mind-full Penelopeia,
Joyless Dinner   had placed her beautiful chair facing the doorway.
She'd heard the speeches of all these men in the great hall,
people laughing aloud while making a sweet meal   390
that suited their spirits, their helpers killing so many
choice beasts. No other dining though would be joyless
more than this one: a powerful man and a Goddess
would set that meal, for the first disgrace was the suitors'.

<table>
<tr><td>An Old
Treasure Room</td><td>

Now the glow-eyed Goddess Athene prompted
Ikarios's daughter, mind-full Penelopeia,
to place the bow and dark iron in front of the suitors—
a test in Odysseus's hall, and the start of their own deaths.
Shortly the lady walked upstairs to her high room
and took in her strong hand the beautifully rounded
key of stunning bronze attached to its ivory handle.
With several women, her maids, she went to the inmost
room where much of her lord's treasure was lying:
bronze and gold and iron wrought with a struggle.   10
The arching bow was lying there with its quiver
and weapons—plenty of groan-carrying arrows.

</td></tr>
</table>

The Story of
the Bow
♦ A Lakedaimon friend had given Odysseus presents.
His name was Iphitos, Eurutos's son. He resembled the deathless
Gods. The two had met each other first in Messene,
in wise Ortilokhos's house, a place where Odysseus
had gone to claim a debt from Messenian people.
They'd once taken three hundred sheep and their shepherds
from Ithaka, loading them all in ships with plenty of oar-
locks.
Odysseus traveled a long way to retrieve them,   20
though still young, for his father and elders had sent him.

A Guest
Murdered
Iphitos went there too. He'd lost twelve of his brood mares
and hardy nursing mules, and now he came looking.
The man was doomed. His death would come from those horses:
in time he'd face a strong-hearted son of the great Zeus,
the man Herakles. Having learned about bold acts,
he'd murder Iphitos cruelly, a guest in the man's house,
disregarding the vengeful Gods and the table
he'd set for the man. Shortly after the murder
he'd take the hard-hoofed horses away to his own house.   30

While Iphitos looked for the horses, he came on Odysseus.
He gave him the bow, once carried by Eurutos grandly
and left to Iphitos after he died in his high house.
Odysseus gave him a rugged spear and a sharp sword,
starting their close friendship. Still they would never
know each other's tables: before then Herakles murdered
Iphitos, Eurutos's son. He'd looked like a deathless
God presenting the bow but godlike Odysseus,
off to war on his night-black ship, left it behind him.
The bow would lie back there in his palace recalling   40
a well-loved friend. It was only borne in his own land.

Beautiful Old ♦ Now she came to the storeroom, that brightest of women,
Doors   and stepped on the oaken threshold, formerly worked on
well by the carpenter, leveled straight to a string-line.
He'd fitted the doorposts too when hanging the bright
        doors.
Promptly she loosened the leather thong from its
        thong-hook,
pushed in the key then pulled back on the door-bolt.
She'd aimed the key in straight and the doors were a lovely
moan like a bull's moan when grazing a meadow.
Worked by her key, they opened wide in a moment.   50

Bow and   The lady went to a high level where coffers
Axes in the were standing, filled with clothes beautifully scented.
Great Hall   Her hand reached up, she took the bow from its high peg
and took the case too that kept it brightly surrounded.
Then she sat and rested the case on her own knees.
She wept aloud, withdrawing the bow of her husband.

After she'd taken her fill of mourning and wailing,
she walked to the hall again and the high-born suitors,
holding the well-arched bow in her hands with its quiver
and weapons—plenty of groan-carrying arrows.   60
Maids were carrying chests in: plenty of iron
and bronze lay inside them for games of their master.

A Wedding   Not far from the suitors now, this brightest of women
Challenge at stood by a post sustaining the well-made roof-beams.
Long Last   She kept her glowing veil high on her cheekbones.
Her best handmaids stood on her left side and right side.

Soon she raised her voice and said to the suitors,
"Listen, my brash wooers! You men have been using
my house over and over, dining and wining
what with my man gone so long. And you never   70
were able to conjure some other plan for your long stay—
only your zeal to marry and make me your woman.
Come on then, suitors! The prize is plainly before you.
I'll start with the great bow of godlike Odysseus:
the man who can deftly string the bow with his own hands
and shoot an arrow through all twelve of the axes
will join with me now. I'll go from the house of my
        husband—
a place of so much beauty, crowded with rich life—
even in dreams I think I'll always recall it."

Tears   She stopped and told the godlike hog-man Eumaios   80
and a Scornful   to set out the gray iron and bow for the suitors.
Rebuke   Eumaios carried the bow and wept as he placed it.
                        The cowherd also wept when he saw the bow of his master.

Antinoos chided them both, telling them roughly,
"Helpless farmhands! Today is all you can think of.
Why are you bawling now, you wretches, arousing
the heart in this woman's breast? Her spirits are lying
in pain already—she's lost the husband she once loved.
Be quiet, sit there and bolt food. Or carry your sobbing
outdoors and leave the bow right there for the suitors.   90

The First to Die   "A hard enough test: I doubt it's easy to string it.
                   The man's bow was planed so smoothly and polished,
                   and no one, of all those here, is a man like Odysseus—
                   such as he was. I saw him myself as a youngster
                   and still I remember, though I was boyish and helpless."

He spoke that way but the heart in his chest was hoping
to string the bow and send a shaft through the iron.
And yet this man would taste an arrow from faultless
Odysseus's hand first: he'd badly dishonored the ruler
who sat in that hall, and he'd roused all of the suitors.   100

The Axes Are   But then with a holy power Telemakhos told them,
Arranged   "Look at this—Zeus, the son of Kronos, makes me a halfwit!

My own Mother tells me, for all of her good sense,
she'll follow another man and abandon her own house.
Yet I enjoy it—I laugh with the heart of a halfwit!
Come on then, suitors, the prize is plainly before you:
a woman who's unmatched now in the lands of Akhaians.
No one's better in holy Pulos, Mukene or Argos,
not on the dark mainland or Ithaka's own soil.
You know it yourselves. Do I need to flatter my Mother?   110
Come on then, don't be dawdling, making excuses,
avoiding the bow too long. Let all of us watch you.
I'd like to test the bow myself in my own way.
In fact if I string it and send a shaft through the iron,
I won't be galled seeing my honored Mother abandon
the house for another man. I would be left here,
the one then raising the beautiful arms of my Father."

He stopped and jumped up straight, dropping the purple
cloak from his shoulders and quickly taking the sword off.
He started to place the ax-heads after he dug out   120
a long trench for them all, straight to a string-line.
He tamped the earth around them. The rest were
          astonished,
 • watching him place them right. He'd never seen them
          before then.

The Bow   Then he tried the bow as he stood by the threshold.
Almost Strung   Three times he made it tremble, anxious to draw it,
then stopped straining each time. Yet in his own heart
he hoped to string it and send a shaft through the iron.
Now on his fourth strong try he'd surely have strung it—
Odysseus nodded *No*. For all of his longing,
again with a holy power Telemakhos told them,   130
"Look at this—either I'm wrong in the end or a weakling.
Maybe I'm so young my arms cannot be trusted:
I lack the strength to fight with an older man who is angry.
Come on then, those who are better and stronger than I am,
try the bow. Let's get on with the contest."

A Prophet's   He spoke that way and set the bow on the floor there.
Failure   He propped it against a door-leaf, shining and close-fit;
he leaned a nimble arrow too on the beautiful door-hook.
Then he sat back down on the chair he got up from.

Antinoos, son of Eupeithes, spoke to the suitors.   140
"Stand and take your turns, all of you good friends,
  from left to right. Start from the place where the wine's
      poured."

Antinoos spoke that way and his word was their pleasure.
Leiodes, Oinops's son, was the first one to stand up.
The suitors' prophet, he often sat by the lovely
wine-bowl farthest away. This man was the only
suitor who hated brashness: he'd chided all of the
      men there.
Now as the first to take up the bow and a fast-flying arrow,
he tested the weapon, standing close to the threshold,
but failed to string it. Too soon his tender and unworked   150
hands grew tired of pulling. He said to the suitors,
"My friends, I cannot string it. Another may take it.
I think this bow will steal the lives and the spirits
of many lords. Still, it's far better to die here
than go on living without the lady we've always
gathered around for. How many days have we waited?
Yet each heart is hoping, everyone's eager
to marry Penelopeia, the wife of Odysseus.
But after you try this bow and see what will happen,
you'll court some other Akhaian woman in fine clothes   160
and offer presents to win her. The lady will marry
the man who gives her the most, who arrives as her
      own fate."

He spoke that way and set the bow on the floor there.
He propped it against a door-leaf, shining and close-fit;
he leaned a nimble arrow too on the beautiful door-hook.
Then he sat back down on the chair he got up from.

Lard,   Antinoos chided him now, telling him roughly,
More Strength,   "Leiodes, what talk gets over the wall of your front teeth,
and Heat   filled with a shocking fear! I'm angry to hear it.
How can a bow steal the lives and the spirits   170
of high-born men because you're unable to string it?
You're not the man, though borne by a mother you honor,
for drawing a bow like this and shooting its arrows.
But other high-born suitors will string it in good time."

He stopped and called to Melanthios, herder of goat-flocks:
"Come on, Melanthios, light a fire in the great hall.
Put a good-size chair beside it covered with lamb's wool.
Then bring us a heavy round of lard from inside there.
We younger suitors will warm the bow and we'll grease it,
then we'll try it. Let's get on with the contest."   180

More Failures   He stopped and Melanthios briskly started a restless
fire. He brought and placed a chair with a fleece on;
he brought a large round of lard from the storeroom.
Younger suitors warmed and tested the great bow.
Yet they all failed to string it, lacking the power.

  ◆ Godlike Eurumakhos though and Antinoos held off,
the suitors' leaders. In manly strength they were standouts.

A Matter of   Two men had left the house, walking together—
Trust   the cattle herder and godlike Odysseus's swineherd.
Now Odysseus himself went out of the great hall.   190
Soon as they stood outside the gates and the courtyard,
Odysseus spoke to them both, asking them softly,
"Cow-man and you, my hog-man: how will I say this
or hide it inside me? My heart tells me to speak out.
Would both of you guard Odysseus well if he came home
very suddenly, brought by a God from somewhere?
Maybe you'd join the suitors, maybe Odysseus.
Tell me how your hearts and spirits would guide you."

The man who herded cattle answered by praying:
"Zeus, our Father, make that yearning become real!   200
I pray the man will arrive, led by some Power:
then you would know my strength, how ready my hands
    are."

Eumaios prayed to all the Gods in the same way:
"Let mind-full Odysseus now come back to his own house."

The Master   Soon as he knew for sure the thoughts of the two men
Revealed   Odysseus spoke once more, telling them plainly,
"I'm home, the man himself, with all of my deep pain,
back in the twentieth year to the land of my Fathers.
I know that only you, of all my helpers,

longed for my coming: no one else I have heard of   210
prayed that I would walk again in my own house.
So I'll tell the truth to you both, the way it will happen:
if Gods bring down these high-born suitors beneath me,
I'll find good wives for you both and offer you great wealth.
I'll build your houses next to me. You will be friends there,
both quite close to my son—Telemakhos's brothers!
I tell you it's true. Besides, I'll show you a clear sign
to make you trust me well and know in your own hearts:
the scar caused by a boar's white tusk in the old days.
I'd gone with Autolukos's sons to the slopes of Parnesos."   220

He spoke that way and pulled the rags from the big scar.
Soon as they saw it, both of them marking it closely,
they cried and threw their arms around mind-full Odysseus,
kissing his head and shoulders to welcome him warmly.
Odysseus kissed their heads and hands in the same way.

A Weapon   But now the Sun-God's light would have set on their
in the Master's   weeping
Hand   had not Odysseus himself calmed them and told them,
            "Stop the tears and moans or someone may spot us
leaving the hall then tell the men in the building.
Take turns going inside, not all at the same time: 230
I'll go first, then you. Let's work with my signals:
when all the rest of the high-born suitors inside there
hardly allow me to take the bow and the quiver,
godlike Eumaios, carry the bow through the great hall
and put it right in my hands. Order the women
to leave and bar the tight-fitting doors of the great hall.
Tell them if anyone hears an uproar and shouting,
the noise of men through the walls, no one should dash out.
Let them stay right there, quietly working.
Then you, godlike Philoitios: I charge you to fasten   240
the courtyard gates in a hurry, bar them and lash them."

He stopped and went in the house where people had
        lived well,
walking back to sit in the chair that he rose from.
Shortly both of the slaves of godlike Odysseus came in.

Another Failure   Eurumakhos now had the bow. He handled and warmed it
                   close to the fire's glow, this way and that way—but even
                   so he failed to string it. Highly praised for his great heart
                   the man he moaned and fumed, telling the others,
                   "Look at this! Pain for myself and pain for you all here.
                   I don't wail for this marriage, though it's a hard loss.   250
                   Other Akhaian women are plentiful, some on the island
                   of sea-ringed Ithaka, others in cities elsewhere.
                   But oh if we so lack such strength, we're truly so meager,
                   not even stringing the bow of godlike Odysseus!
                   Such a disgrace will be known by men in the future."

Trouble from   But now the son of Eupeithes, Antinoos, answered,
the Archer God   "It won't be so, Eurumakhos. You know it yourself too:
                   throughout the land this day is a holy feast of the Archer
                ◆ God Apollo. Who'd bend a bow? You should relax now;
                   let it lie. And the axes? What if we let them   260
                   all stand there? I don't think people will enter
                   the hall of Odysseus, son of Laertes, and steal them.
                   Come on then: let the wine-bearer pour in our goblets,
                   we'll offer the Gods our wine and, setting the well-arched
                   bow aside, we'll tell Melanthios, driver of goat-flocks,
                   to bring us the best of his whole flock in the morning.
                   We'll lay out thighs for Apollo, known for his great bow.
                   Then we can try this bow and get on with the contest."

                   Antinoos spoke that way and his word was their pleasure.
                   Stewards poured out water and, after a hand-wash,   270
                   young men filled the bowls with a wine-mix for drinking.
                   They served them all, filling the goblets. Suitors
                   offered wine to the Gods then drank as their hearts wished.

A Rankling   Crafty-minded Odysseus called out, full of his own plans:
Challenge   "Listen you men, courting a queen who is famous!
                   Let me say what the heart in my chest has commanded.
                   I plead with Eurumakhos most and godlike Antinoos,
                   surely the man who said it right when he told you
                   to stop trying the bow for now and trust in the great Gods.
                   At dawn Apollo can crown the man whom he chooses.   280
                   Come on though: give me the well-shined bow and allow me
                   to try my hand among you. Maybe I still have

strength for my body was lithe and strong as a young man.
Lack of care and wandering now may have wrecked it."

Another
Death Threat Those were his words. They all were exceedingly angry.
They worried too: the polished bow strung by a beggar?
Antinoos called him names, telling him roughly,
"Stranger, you wretch without brains, not even a smidgen!
Why aren't you glad to be dining at ease among high men,
never lacking food and well within earshot   290
of our own talk? No other stranger may hear it,
this talk of ours, no other beggar's allowed here.
Did honey-sweet wine derange you? Wine has deluded
plenty of others who gulped it fast in the wrong way.
♦ Wine once crazed the well-known Kentaur Eurution,
staying in strong-hearted Pirithoos's great hall,
visiting Lapiths. With wine crazing his spirits
he raved and caused great harm in Pirithoos's household.
Grieved and outraged war-chiefs leaped up and dragged him
outdoors through the porch: they slashed his ears and his
      nose off   300
with pitiless bronze. Mind still maddened, the Kentaur
moved away, a thoughtless heart laden with folly.
So strife arose between those Kentaurs and humans.
The first to find himself so wrong was a wine-heavy Kentaur.

"So now you: I'll show you intense pain if you grapple
that bow and string it. You'll never be faced with kindness
again in our land. We'll hurry you off on a night-black
ship to King Ekhetos, known as a maimer of every
stranger. From there you cannot be saved. So relax here,
drink your wine. Don't strive with men who are younger."   310

Marrying a
Beggar But mind-full Penelopeia answered him shortly:
"It's not graceful or fair, Antinoos, thwarting
guests of Telemakhos, those who arrive in our household.
Do you suppose, if he strings Odysseus's great bow—
a stranger trusting his hands, the strength of a beggar—
he'll take me off to his house and make me his own wife?
The man can hardly hope in his breast for that outcome.
Not one man of you, therefore, should dine with a sad heart
because of the stranger's hopes. They're very unlikely."

Eurumakhos, Polubos's son, answered her right back.   320
"Ikarios's daughter, mind-full Penelopeia,
   we don't guess he'll take you. That's surely unlikely.
   But men and women talking—that could offend us.
   In time some low-born Akhaian or other might mutter,
   'Far worse men are courting the wife of a faultless
   king and they cannot string the polished bow of Odysseus.
   Then some other wandering beggar arrives here,
   strings the bow with ease and shoots through the iron.'
   So people babble. All of that would disgrace us."

A Chance for   Mind-full Penelopeia answered him right back: 330
the Stranger   "Eurumakhos, no one's highly renowned in a country
   for lacking esteem and devouring the home of a high lord.
   Why make a beggar like this the cause of your own shame?
   Our guest, to be sure, is very rugged and quite tall.
   He claims good birth—the son of a worthy father.
   Come on then, give him the well-shined bow and we'll
        all see.
   Because I'll say this too and be sure it will happen:
   if lordly Apollo grants him fame and he strings it,
   I'll dress him in beautiful clothes, a mantle and full cloak.
   I'll give him a sharp spear to guard against people   340
   and fight off dogs, a two-edged sword, and sandals for
        footwear.
   I'll send him wherever his heart and spirit should call him."

Now Telemakhos gave her a sensible answer.
"No Akhaian, Mother, has more power than I have
   over this bow, to allow or deny as I want to—
   no man ruling on rock-strewn Ithaka, no one
   on any island down toward horse-nourishing Elis.
   None of them stops or forces my will if I'm minded
   to offer our guest this bow to carry off outright.

♦"But go to your room yourself. Look to your own work,   350
   loom and spindle now. Order your handmaids
   to do their jobs. All us men have the great bow
   to care for, and mainly myself: I rule in the household."

The lady marveled and soon went back to her own room,
   taking to heart her son's sensible answer.

She entered her room again, joined by her handmaids,
and cried for Odysseus, the man she loved, till the
    glow-eyed
Athene tossed some honeyed sleep on her eyelids.

Devoured by
His Own Dogs

Now the godlike hog-tender took up the well-arched
bow and sported it! All the suitors were yelling   360
throughout the hall, an overproud younger one shouting,
"Where are you taking the well-arched bow, you disgusting
swineherd? The dogs you raised will shortly devour you
alone and far from us men, if Apollo will do us
the favor with help from the other Gods who are deathless."

A Counter
Threat

He stopped and the swineherd placed the bow on the floor
    there,
scared by all of the roaring men in the great hall.
Then from the other side Telemakhos threatened:
"Carry the bow forward, uncle! Don't be obeying
them all or soon, young as I am, I will chase you   370
afield and pelt you with stones—I'm stronger than you are.
If only my hands were stronger than all of the suitors'
hands in our house! With so much strength I would soon be
packing a few of them off. They'd travel a sorry
road from our house for all the harm they have
    planned here."

Barred Doors

He stopped as all of the suitors were laughing with pleasure.
Their hard anger aimed at Telemakhos let go,
quickly the swineherd carried the bow through the great hall
and handed it now up close to a knowing Odysseus.
He called for the nurse Eurukleia and spoke to her briefly: 380
"Thoughtful Eurukleia, Telemakhos wants you
to go and bar the tight-fitting doors of the great hall.
Say if anyone hears an uproar and shouting—
noise from men through the walls—no one should dash out.
Let them stay right there, quietly working."

He spoke that way and, all her words being wingless,
she barred the doors of the hall where people had lived well.

Philoitios briskly walked outdoors without speaking
and soon had barred the well-worked gates of the courtyard.

A braided line from an up-curved ship was lying   390
under the porch. He lashed the gates with it tightly.
Then he returned inside to the chair that he rose from.

Like a   He watched Odysseus, already handling the great bow,
Lyre String   turning it every way and trying it out there.
Had worms gnawed the horn while its master was far off?
So a suitor might glance at his neighbor and tell him,
"Look at the bow fancier. This beggar is crafty;
no doubt a bow like that one lies in his own house.
Or now he'd like to make one, the way that he turns it
that way and this way. The wanderer knows about hurting."   400

Another younger suitor overbearingly answered,
"If only the beggar could gain wealth in the same way
now as he finds strength for stringing the great bow!"

Suitors blabbed as Odysseus, full of his own plans,
deftly raised the outsize bow and looked at it closely.
♦ At last as a man skilled with a lyre and with singing
easily stretches the newest string to its own peg
and ties the twisted sheep-gut tightly at both ends,
Odysseus strung the outsize bow with no struggle.
His right hand briskly pulled and tested the bowstring: 410
it sang to his touch like the beautiful trill of a swallow.

Passing the   What great pain for the suitors! All of their faces
Test of the Axes   were pale and Zeus made a sign, thundering loudly.
Long-suffering, godlike Odysseus felt glad:
crooked-counseling Kronos's son sent him an omen.
Taking a bare and fast-flying arrow that lay on
the table—the rest were still in the hollow quiver,
all the weapons Akhaians soon would be tasting—
he nocked the shaft on the bridge, drew back on the
        bowstring
and took dead aim, all from the chair that he sat in,   420
and shot it straight. He missed each one of the axes,
all those helves: he'd guided the bronze-weighted arrow
beyond them and out. He turned to Telemakhos saying,
"The stranger who sits in your hall, Telemakhos, brings no
shame to the test. I missed no mark, my labor was not long

stringing the bow and my strength has hardly been shaken,
not as the scoffing suitors claimed when they scorned me.

"But now it's time for a dinner indeed for the Akhaians
while there's light. Other enjoyments can follow—
the lyre and dancing—they always go with a good feast."   430

Father and Son   He nodded a sign with his brows. Telemakhos belted
Well Armed   a sharp sword on. The dear son of godlike Odysseus,
                  having a spear in hand, went close to his father's
                  chair and stood there, bronze weaponry shining.

Antinoos First Now shedding his rags Odysseus, full of his own plans,
jumped on the wide threshold clutching the bow and its
    quiver
packed with arrows. He emptied the fast-flying weapons
there at his feet and called aloud to the suitors.
"So indeed our harmful contest is ending:
but now for another target no one has struck yet—
if only I hit it! Apollo, give me a great name."

♦ He aimed at Antinoos first, a pitiless arrow.
The man was about to raise a beautiful goblet
of gold with a pair of grips, he held it with both hands   10
to drink his wine and death was far from his thoughts there:
who would guess, among his friends at a good meal,
one man in the crowd, however forceful he might be,
would cause him harm or death, the workings of
    black doom?
Odysseus aimed and struck his throat with an arrow,
the point went straight through the soft neck and the
    young man
slumped to one side. The goblet fell from his stricken
hand and mortal blood came fast from his nostrils
in thick dark spurts. He kicked at the table and moved it
away from him swiftly, dumping food on the floor there,   20
griming cutlets and bread.

The Stranger   Shouts from the suitors
Will Surely Die rose throughout the hall. Spotting Antinoos fallen
they jumped from their chairs, dashed through the room in
    a frenzy
and searched the well-built walls this way and that way.
No shield was about, no rugged spear to be hefted.
They blasted Odysseus, one man telling him fiercely,
"Stranger, shooting at men is cursed and you'll never
take part in a contest. Your headlong doom is a sure thing.
You've killed the best young man by far on the island
of Ithaka now and vultures will feed on you right here."   30

All the Suitors
Will Die First

Everyone spoke that way supposing Odysseus
killed the man unwillingly. Blind, they could not know
the lines of death for every man had been tightened.
Odysseus, full of his plans, glared darkly and told them,
"You dogs, you never thought I'd return to my own house
from Trojan country. So you wasted my household,
forced my female workers to lie alongside you
and lawlessly craved my wife while I was alive still,
dreading no God who rules broadly in heaven
and thinking no man in times to come would be outraged.   40
Now for you all the lines of death have been tightened."

A Plea
for Making
Amends

Soon as he'd spoken they all were taken by greenish
fear and each one looked to escape from a steep
doom. Only Eurumakhos answered swiftly by saying,
"If you're the Ithakan truly, Odysseus back home,
you said that right. All the Akhaians have acted
recklessly often, both in the field and the great hall.
But now the man to blame for everything lies here.
All this harm was plainly Antinoos's doing.
Not so much that he wanted or needed to marry: 50
he planned otherwise—the son of Kronos would not end
things that way—to be lord of Ithaka's well-tilled
land himself. He'd even ambush and murder your own son.
So now his death is right. But pity your own good
people in time making amends in the country
ourselves for all the food and wine in your great hall.
Every suitor will bring you the value of twenty
oxen tallied in bronze and gold. In time we will soften
your heart. Before then, no one blames you for anger."

Odysseus, full of designs, glared darkly and told him,   60
"Eurumakhos, not if you gave me all of your father's
wealth—what's yours right now then added from
        elsewhere—
I'd still not keep these hands from killing you suitors,
not till everyone paid for all of his crimes here.
Now your choice is whether to face me and fight me
or try to avoid death, to run from your own doom.
But no one escapes, I think. Your deaths will be headlong."

Fight, Then   He stopped as the knees and hearts loosened in each man.
              Still Eurumakhos called out again to the suitors:
              "Friends! Because this man won't stop his relentless   70
              hands from gripping that shining bow and its quiver—
              he'll shoot from the planed threshold till all of us die here—
              let's remind ourselves of our war-lust and quickly.
              Unsheath your swords, hold up tables before you
              to guard against fast-killing arrows, all of us charge him
              together and drive him back from the door and the
                   threshold!
              Then hurry and go through the city, raising an outcry.
              Shortly this man will have shot with a bow for the last time."

              He spoke that way, drew out a brazen and two-edged
              sword sharpened on both sides and, frightfully shrieking,   80
              bounded straight at the man. But godlike Odysseus
              shot at the same time, hitting his chest at the nipple:
              the fast point lodged in his liver. Eurumakhos's weapon
              dropped from his hand to the floor, he doubled and
                   fell down
              over a table, dumping a two-handled goblet
              and sprawling food. He beat on the ground with his
                   forehead,
              heart in agony, both feet kicking and jarring
          •   a chair. Death-mist promptly flowed on his eyeballs.

Telemakhos's Amphinomos too had made for far-famed Odysseus.
 First Killing Drawing a sharp sword he had lunged at him head-on   90
              to drive him away from the door. But Telemakhos
                   struck him
              first with a bronze-tipped spear from behind that
                   impaled him
              between the shoulders, driving straight through the
                   breastbone.
              He fell with a thud, rapping the floor with his head hard.
              Telemakhos then leaped back, letting the long spear
              stay in Amphinomos, worried some other Akhaian
              would rush him there as he pulled out the long-shafted
                   weapon
              or stab with a sword as he leaned over the body.
              He ran and came to the father he loved in a hurry.

Weapons and   He stood up close and his words had a feathery swiftness,   100
Armor Needed   "Father, I'll get you a pair of spears and a shield now,
                an all-bronze helmet—a tight fit on your temples.
                I'll arm myself as I go and I'll offer the swineherd
                and cowherd weapons. For now it's best to be armored."

                Odysseus, full of designs, answered by saying,
                "Hurry and get them. I still have arrows to guard me
                but I could be forced from the door, being alone here."

                After he'd spoken Telemakhos, minding his father,
                went to the storeroom. Finding the well-known war-tools
                he took four shields, eight spears and the brazen   110
                helmets, four in all, crested with horsehair.
                He carried them back as fast as he could to his father.
                First he armored himself: bronze circled his body.
                Both slaves donned the beautiful arms in the same way.
                They stood close to their knowing and crafty Odysseus.

The Battle   Long as the arrows held out to guard him their master
Builds   aimed at suitors again and again in the great hall.
                He struck each time and they fell, close to each other.
                After no more arrows remained for the master,
                he stood the bow against a post of the well-built   120
                hall—it leaned on a shining wall by the doorway—
                and took a four-plied shield to cover his shoulders.
                He clapped a well-made helmet next on his strong head,
                a frightening horsehair crest nodding above it,
                and grasped two hard spears pointed with sharp bronze.

Another   Another door in the well-built wall of the great room
Way Out   was raised in back by its threshold. It led to a passage
                out of the well-based hall and its doors were a tight fit.
                Odysseus told the godlike swineherd to stand there
                and watch for only a man at a time could approach it.   130

                But now Agelaos called to the rest of the suitors,
                "My friends, won't someone go right now through the back
                    door
                and tell the people to raise an alarm in a hurry?
                Then this man will have used that bow for the last time."

But now Melanthios told him, the driver of goat-flocks,
"By no means, Agelaos, nourished by Zeus. That beautiful
    courtyard
door is fearfully close and it's hard, the mouth of that
    passage.
One man could hold off plenty—if the man were a brave one.
Come on then, I could bring you arms from the storeroom
to guard yourselves. I think the arms are inside there,   140
nowhere else, laid down by his bright son and Odysseus."

Weapons for   Having spoken the goatherd Melanthios climbed up
the Suitors   through venting holes in the wall to Odysseus's arms-room.
                  From there he took out twelve big shields and as many
                  spears and helmets of bronze, crested with horsehair.
                  He left and hurriedly carried some back to the suitors.

                  Odysseus's heart and knees felt loosened and weakened
                  watching them belt on armor and brandish the lengthy
                  spears in their hands. His job now struck him as massive.
                  He spoke to Telemakhos—words with a feathery swiftness—   150
                  "Telemakhos, plainly one of the maids in the great hall
                  stirs up harmful fighting—or maybe Melanthios."

                  Promptly Telemakhos gave him a sensible answer.
                ♦"Father, I made the mistake myself—none of the others
                  made it. I left the handsome, tight-fit door of the arms-room
                  ajar. The suitors' watch was better than mine was.

                  "But go there, godlike Eumaios, close the door of the
                      arms-room
                  and find out whether one of the women has done this.
                  I'd guess Melanthios rather, the son of Dolios."

Catching the   Even now as they spoke that way with each other   160
Goatherd   Melanthios went to the room again: that driver of goat-flocks
                  hauled out gleaming armor. But godlike Eumaios
                  saw him and promptly came back to Odysseus saying,
                  "Son of Laertes, bloodline of Zeus, wily Odysseus,
                  that plague-like man has gone again to the arms-room,
                  the one we supposed ourselves. Answer me plainly:
                  should I kill him or not if I am his better?

Or haul him to you and make him pay for his many
crimes, for all the schemes he mulled in your own house?"

An answer came from Odysseus, full of his own plans: 170
"I and Telemakhos doubtless will hold off the high-born
suitors inside the hall, however they press us.
You two wrench his hands and feet up behind him,
throw him back in the room and tie a plank at his backbone
with twisted rope. Lash his body and raise him
high on one of the posts there, close to the roof-beams.
He'll stay alive but smart and suffer a long time."

The Goatherd   Those were his words. They listened well and obeyed him,
Strung Up   going off to the room. The man inside did not see them:
he rummaged for arms in the inmost part of the storeroom.   180
Both men waited, standing on either side of the doorway.
Soon as the goatherd Melanthios came to the threshold,
one hand holding a very beautiful helmet,
the other a broad old shield dotted with rust-marks—
Laertes, a war-chief when younger, had carried it often,
but now it lay there, stitching and hand-straps loosened—
the two men jumped him, grabbing his hair, and they
      dragged him
back inside. His heart slumped as they threw him and
      lashed him
hand and foot on the floor with spirit-destroying
rope. They pulled it behind him, the way they were told to   190
by long-suffering, godlike Odysseus, son of Laertes.
Knotting a twisted cord close to his torso,
they raised him high on a column, close to the roofbeams.

Then Eumaios the swineherd, you mocked him by saying,
"Surely, Melanthios, all night long you can watch here,
lying down on a soft bed just as it suits you!
You won't be missing newborn Dawn as she rises
from Ocean's flow on her chair of gold when you often
herded goats to suitors and helped them dine in the
      household."

They left him there in his tight, punishing bindings.   200
The two men donned their armor. Closing the bright door,
they hurried back to their mind-full, crafty Odysseus.

The Odds
Against

He stood there breathing rage. Those on the threshold
were four but the rest in the hall were plenty of brave men.
The daughter of Zeus, Athene came to them quite close,
in voice and form taking the likeness of Mentor.
Odysseus felt new joy when he saw her and told her,
"Mentor, keep us from death! Remember a dear friend
who treated you well. And you and I are the same age."
He stopped and supposed it might be Athene, rouser of
    armed men.   210

Threatening
the Goddess

But suitors warned her, raising a cry in the great hall,
Agelaos telling her first, the son of Damastor,
"Mentor, don't be tricked by any words of Odysseus
telling you to fight with us suitors or rush to his own aid.
I'm thinking our plans will all be realized this way:
after we kill those two, father and son both,
you'll be killed with them next for the work you were eager
to do in this hall. The price you'll pay is your own head.
Then after we've wrested all your strength with our sharp
    bronze
all your wealth will be ours, the indoor and outdoor   220
wealth to mix with Odysseus's. Nor will your own sons
then be allowed to live in your house, and your daughters
and splendid wife won't walk through an Ithakan city."

Rousing the
Leader

Athene became more angry now that he'd spoken.
She turned and hotly scolded Odysseus saying,
"Your strength and courage, Odysseus, are steadfast no
    longer,
not as they were when you endlessly warred with the
    Trojans,
fighting for nine years for white-armed, well-fathered
    Helen.
You took down plenty of men in frightful encounters,
then with your plan the wide-way city of Priam was taken.   230
How is it now, when you've come back home to your own
    wealth,
you wail at the thought of bravely facing the suitors?
Come here, old friend. Stand close, witness my war-work
and learn what sort of a man I am with your rivals.
I'm Mentor, Alkinoos's son, repaying your good work."

She stopped but gave him no great triumph beyond
    doubt—
  ♦ not yet. She wanted to test the vigor and prowess
of both these men, the well-known son and Odysseus.
Suddenly taking the form of a swallow, she fluttered
high in the smoky hall to a rafter and perched there.   240

Many Spears Now Damastor's son Agelaos heartened the suitors,
at Once Eurunomos urged them, Amphimedon too and Peisandros,
Poluktor's son; Demoptolemos also, and mind-full
Polubos: those were the best by far and the bravest
suitors alive. They'd fight to stay with the living,
the bow and showering arrows having already
sprawled the rest. Agelaos made things plain for them all
    there:
"My friends, this man's relentless hand may be checked now.
Clearly Mentor, that idle braggart, has gone off.
They're left alone right there in front of the doorway.   250
Let's not hurtle all our long spears at the same time:
you throw first, you six. If only the great Zeus
helps you to strike Odysseus, gaining your fame here!
We don't care about others if *he* can be brought down."

Help from the He spoke that way and they all threw as he told them,
Goddess eagerly. Yet Athene caused them all to be wasted.
One spear drove in a well-raised post of the great hall.
Another one struck the door fitted with close jambs.
Another of ash and heavy bronze damaged a bright wall.

Better Aim Having avoided all the spears of the suitors,   260
long-suffering, godlike Odysseus called out,
"Now my friends! I say we too should be throwing
spears at that crowd of suitors, men who are eager
to maim and strip us, to add to their earlier evils."

Soon as he'd spoken they all hurtled their sharp spears,
aiming well. Telemakhos killed Euruades.
Odysseus, Demoptolemos. Eumaios cut down Elatos.
The cattle tender, Philoitios, brought down Peisandros.
All the dying gnashed on the broad ground at the
    same time.

Suitors were moving back to the inmost part of the
    great hall.   270
Men bounded forward to pull out spears from the corpses.

Another Volley   Again the suitors were hurling sharp spears with an eager
aim but Athene caused a lot to be wasted.
One spear drove at a well-raised post in the great hall.
Another one hit the door fitted with close jambs.
A third of ash and heavy bronze damaged a bright wall.
However Amphimedon struck Telemakhos lightly,
grazing his wrist, the bronze tearing some skin off.
Ktesippos's lengthy spear passed over Eumaios's
shield and cut his shoulder and bounced on the dirt floor.   280

Again those circling a knowing and crafty Odysseus
threw their sharp spears at the crowded suitors.
Odysseus, looter of cities, lanced Eurudamas right there.
Telemakhos pierced Amphimedon. Polubus promptly
was hit by the swineherd. The cattle-man, striking Ktesippos
hard in the chest, gloated over him saying,
"Ah Polutherses' son, you lover of insults!
No more foolish or big talk: leave to the great Gods
all such speeches—they're far more powerful truly.
My spear is your guest-gift, matching the ox-hoof you
    offered   290
godlike Odysseus before, when he begged in the
    household."

Panic in the   The herder of tight-horned cattle ended his boasting.
Great Hall   Odysseus' long spear transfixed the son of Damastor
now in close. Telemakhos stabbed Leokritos, son of Euenor,
pushing the spear in, driving it straight through his belly.
He crumpled forward, striking the earth flat on his
    forehead.
Athene raised her shield, breaking their spirits
from high on a roof-beam: the brains of suitors were
    jangled,
they ran like droves of cattle around in the great hall
as though attacked and chased by a fast-flying gadfly   300
for hours in spring when the longer days are arriving.

Prey
and Predator

The way that hook-beaked birds of prey with their crooked
talons arrive from the mountains and harry the small birds
flying under a mist or scared on a flat field—
the hawks grapple and kill them, the prey are without some
way to escape or fight and men welcome those hunters—
the four were chasing the suitors through all of the
    great hall,
striking on every side. Anguished groans were rising
as skulls were cracked and blood heaved on the whole floor.

A Beggarly Plea

Leiodes ran to and grasped the knees of Odysseus   310
making a plea, his words with a feathery swiftness,
"I'm holding your knees, Odysseus, spare me, revere me!
I tell you I never spoke or acted without care
regarding your household women. In fact I kept trying
to stop the rest of the suitors from acting in that way.
They failed to obey me, to keep their hands from such evil.
Instead they've rushed to a scandalous doom for their
    brashness.
♦ I was their soothsayer also, doing you no harm.
Shall I lie here thankless later for good work?"

Odysseus, full of designs, glared darkly and told him,   320
"Yet if you claim you were their soothsayer truly,
I'm sure you offered a lot of prayers in the great hall
to keep my goal, my honeyed homecoming, far off,
to make my wife join you bearing your children.
Therefore you won't avoid this punishing death-blow."

While he spoke his thick-set hand had been grabbing
a sword that lay on the floor—Agelaos had dropped it
while dying. He stabbed Leiodes' neck in the middle.
That head, pleading its last, mixed with the dust there.

What about
the Poet?

Terpis's poet son had skulked and avoided   330
a black doom. Often forced to sing for the suitors,
Phemios held his clear-toned lyre with both hands
close to the far-side door, pondering two paths:
whether to sneak from the hall and sit at the well-built
altar of great Zeus of the Household—plenty of cattle
thighs had been burned by Laertes there and Odysseus;
or run up close and beg at the knees of Odysseus.

Sorting everything out, it seemed to him better
to clasp the knees of Odysseus, son of Laertes.
He set the hollow lyre down on the earthen   340
floor between a bowl and chair studded with silver,
then he bounded forward and clasped the knees of
    Odysseus,
making his plea—the words had a feathery swiftness—
♦"I'm clasping your knees, Odysseus, respect me, have pity.
You'll surely suffer yourself in time if you murder
a bard who only sings for the Gods and his people.
I taught myself though a God sowed in my spirit
every kind of song. It's right that I sing to you also,
as though to a God; so don't be anxious to cut my
throat. Let your own dear son Telemakhos tell you: 350
I never wanted to sing in your hall for the suitors.
I joined these men against my will as they dined here—
a crowd far stronger than I am led me and forced me."

The Bard   He stopped as Telemakhos—now his power was holy—
and the Herald   heard him and spoke up quickly, close to his father,
Saved   "Hold off. Don't pierce this blameless man with a weapon.
Let's save the herald too: Medon has always
cared for me here in our home since I was a small boy—
unless Philoitios killed him now or the swineherd—
or maybe he crossed your path as you raged in the
    great hall."   360

He stopped and Medon had heard him. Clever and cautious,
he'd cowered under a chair, hiding his own skin
with newly stripped-off ox-hide, avoiding a dark end.
Quickly he rose from the chair, doffing the ox-hide,
coming and clasping Telemakhos's knees in a hurry
to make his plea and his words had a feathery swiftness,
"Friend, I am here, hold off and appeal to your father
not to kill me with sharp bronze in the rush of his power,
maddened by all these men. The suitors were wasting
your great hall's riches. The fools never esteemed you."   370

Full of designs, Odysseus smiled and told him,
"Take heart. My son has clearly guarded and saved you.
Now you know in your heart, tell it to others:
working for good is far better than working for evil.

Go out of the hall, sit outside in the courtyard
away from death—you and our story-full singer—
until I've done whatever I must in the household."

Fish Dying on   After he'd spoken the two men walked from the great hall.
a Beach   They both sat down close to the altar of high Zeus,
peering about. They still felt close to a death-blow.   380

Odysseus looked through his house to see if a suitor
was still alive and skulking, hiding from black doom.
No, he found them all in squalor and blood there,
sprawled like so many fish pulled from the hoary
sea to a curving shore by men who've been working
nets with their close meshes. Dozens of fish there
long for swells of the sea, they're piled on the beach-sand,
the glaring Sun-God draining life from their bodies.
The suitors looked that way, piled on each other.

The Lion's   Then Odysseus, full of designs, turned to his own son.   390
Slaver   "Telemakhos, go and call our nurse Eurukleia.
I'd like to say a word to her, close to my own heart."

Soon as he'd spoken Telemakhos, heeding the father
he loved, pushed at the door and told the nurse Eurukleia,
"Rise and come now, old woman. You tended
all our maids, those who've worked in the great hall.
My Father's called, come on, he has something to tell you."

He spoke that way and because her answer was wingless
she opened the doors of the hall where people had
    lived well.
They walked inside, Telemakhos going before her.   400
She found Odysseus then, circled by dead men.
Spattered with blood and grime, he looked like a lion
who's just fed on a bull in a stock-pen for cattle,
all his chest and cheeks a smearing on either
side with blood, the beast revolting to look at:
so were the feet and hands of Odysseus filthy.

No Great Joy   After she saw that mass of bloodshed and dead men,
over the Dead   she started to wail for joy at the sight of the huge task.
Odysseus stopped her though for all of her longing.

He told her plainly, the words with a feathery swiftness,   410
"Be glad in your heart, old woman, not with a loud wail.
♦ Rejoicing over men who are killed is unholy.
The Gods' own doom leveled this mob for their cruel
acts and honoring no one man on the broad earth,
good or bad, whoever came to them humbly.
They went to a shameful end because of their brashness.

What about the   "But tell me about the women now in the great hall,
Women?   those with no esteem and those who are blameless."

The well-loved nurse Eurukleia answered by saying,
"Well then, child, I'll tell you myself what the truth is.   420
Fifty women in all have worked in the great hall,
maids we have always taught to stay with their own work,
to card the wool and bear up well in their slaves' lives.
Of those twelve in all went on to be shameless,
lacking regard for me and Penelopeia.
Telemakhos, newly grown, was stopped by his mother
from taking charge of the female slaves in the household.

"Ah but allow me to go upstairs to her shining
bedroom and tell your wife! Some God put her to sleep
      there."

An answer came from Odysseus, full of the best plans: 430
"No, don't wake her yet. You just order the women
to come here—those whose plots or acts were disgraceful."

He spoke that way and the old one went from the great hall,
taking his word to the women. She told them to join him.

Death   Odysseus turned to Telemakhos now and the pigherd
Sentence   and cowherd saying—his words had a feathery swiftness—
"Start with the job of hauling the dead out, and order
women to help you. Then wash the chairs and beautiful
      tables
using plenty of water and hole-dotted sponges.
After you've put the whole household in order,   440
take those women away from my hall with its hard base.
Between the roundhouse and handsome wall of the
      courtyard

hack them with sharp swords until you have wrested
all their souls. Make them forget Aphrodite—
their lust while privily lying under the suitors."

He stopped as the women came, all in a huddle
and shedding the biggest tears, frightfully wailing.
They carried the men out first, those who were cut down,
laying them under the porch of the well-worked courtyard,
propped on each other. Odysseus hurried them all on   450
himself with commands. They worked because they were
    forced to.
Then they washed the chairs and beautiful tables,
using plenty of water and hole-dotted sponges.
Meanwhile Telemakhos joined the cowherd and swineherd,
cleaning the floor of the strong-made house with their
    scrapers.
The women took the scrapings and settled them outdoors.

A Crueler
Death for the
Women

So after they put the whole household in order,
they took the women away from the well-founded palace.
Between the roundhouse and handsome wall of the
    courtyard
they jammed them all in a space lacking a way out.   460
Then shrewd Telemakhos spoke to the others:
"I want no simple death taking these women's
lives. They poured disgrace on the head of my Mother,
on my own head, and they often slept with the suitors."

He spoke that way and knotted a line from a dark-prowed
ship to a high column, circling the roundhouse
and stretched up high: no woman's foot would be touching
♦ ground. Then like broad-winged thrushes or pigeons
flying in nets well laid out in the bushes,
looking to roost but hating the bed that ensnares them,   470
the women's heads were lined up, necks were encircled
each with its noose that made for the wretchedest dying:
the women's feet might jerk a little but not long.

Maiming and
Murder

They brought Melanthios now through the door and the
    courtyard.
They cut off his nose and ears: their bronze had no mercy.

They tore out his scrotum, threw it to dogs to be gulped raw,
then hacked off his feet and hands in a frenzy of anger.

Soon they washed their hands and feet to reenter
the house of Odysseus. All the war-work was over.

Harder   Odysseus told the well-loved nurse Eurukleia,   480
Cleaning   "My old one, get some sulphur, a cure for this trouble.
              Bring me some fire to purge the hall. And Penelopeia?
              Ask the lady to come here soon with her handmaids.
              Encourage the rest of our women to enter the great hall."

The well-loved nurse Eurukleia answered by saying,
"Surely, my child, you're saying everything right now.
But let me bring you a mantle and tunic to put on:
don't stand this way with your broad shoulders in tatters,
not in your own house. Some would blame and resent you."

Full of his own plans, Odysseus answered by saying,   490
"Let there be fire first, right now in the great hall."

The well-loved nurse Eurukleia did not disobey him.
She brought him sulphur and fire, helping Odysseus
thoroughly purge the hall, the household and forecourt.

A Joyful   The nurse went back through the handsome house of
Reunion   Odysseus
              with news for the loyal women: she told them to join her.
              Torches in hand, the maids came out of their own room
              and gathered around Odysseus. All of them welcomed
              the man and hugged him, kissing his forehead and
                  shoulders,
              clasping his hands. The sweetest longing reclaimed him,   500
              he wanted to moan and cry, knowing them all well.

Unbelievable   The older woman went upstairs with a chortle
News   to tell the lady her own dear husband was downstairs.
The woman's knees would hurry; her feet kept stumbling.
Standing now by her head she spoke to her softly.
"Wake up, Penelopeia: see with your own eyes,
dear child, what you've pined for all of your days here.
Odysseus came, he's home, for all of his lateness!
He's killed the prideful suitors, men who were swaying
your son and devouring his wealth, troubling the whole
house."

Mind-full Penelopeia answered by saying,   10
"Dear aunt, the Gods have made you mad! They can do that,
making a man look foolish—even a wise man.
They also can make a thoughtless man understanding.
They've dazed you now; before, your mind was a sound one.
♦ Why do you fool me? My heart has plenty of sorrow
already. Why this talk? You woke me from sweet sleep
which held me fast and closed my eyes for a good while.
I haven't slept that way since the hour Odysseus
left for Troy—that Evil no one should mention.
Come on now, go back down, be off to the great hall.   20
Because if another woman, one of my own maids,
approached me with news like yours and broke up a good
sleep,
I'd pack her off myself in a nasty and hurried
way back to the hall. Your age has helped you in one way."

It's All True   Her well-loved nurse Eurukleia answered by saying,
"Dear child, I'm not fooling, everything's quite true.
Odysseus came, he's home, just as I told you—
the stranger they all mistreated down in the great hall.
Telemakhos knew him a long time as Odysseus
but charily kept the plans of his father in hiding   30
until he could take revenge on the brutish, overproud
suitors."

More Hard
Questions

She stopped and her lady gladly jumped out of bed there
to hug her old nurse. Tears fell from her eyelids.
She spoke to her then, the words with a feathery swiftness,
"Ah but if only, dear aunt! Tell me the whole truth:
indeed if the man came home the way you have told me,
how could he lay hands on those brazen suitors
being alone? They've always crowded inside here."

The well-loved nurse Eurukleia answered by saying,
"I asked and saw nothing. Groans of the dying   40
were all I heard. We sat in the inmost well-built
room in dread, the doors tightly fitted and holding
until your son Telemakhos came from the great hall
and called me—his father had sent him forward to call me.
Then I found Odysseus, circled by dead men.
They sprawled on the hard floor, he stood there
        among them,
piled on each other. The sight of the man would have
        warmed you:
smeared with blood and grime, he looked like a lion.
The corpses are all together now by the courtyard
gate and Odysseus purges the beautiful palace   50
  ♦ with sulfur. He built a great fire and sent me to call you.
Follow me! Both of your loving hearts should be marching
now into joy, for all the harm you have suffered.
Today your endless longing is ended at long last:
the man is alive at your hearth, finding you both well,
his wife and son in the hall. The suitors who caused him
trouble are all avenged right here in your household."

Some God
Must Have
Done This

Penelopeia was thoughtful still and she answered,
"Dear aunt, no boasting yet: no chortling too soon.
You know how welcome his sight would be in the great hall   60
to everyone—mainly to me and the son born to us both here.
Yet your story is not true, not as you tell it:
rather some deathless God enraged by their brashness
killed the high-born suitors for all of their wrongful,
heart-stinging acts. They honored nobody walking
the wide earth, good or bad, whoever approached them.
They suffered harm for their recklessness. Still my
        Odysseus
lost his homecoming—lost himself—far from Akhaia."

The Scar   The well-loved nurse Eurukleia answered by saying,
            "My child, what talk gets over the wall of your front teeth!   70
            Your husband's inside at the hearth and you say he
                will never
            arrive back home! You heart was always without faith.
            Come on then, I'll tell you another sign that is quite clear:
            the scar that a boar's white tusk caused in the old days.
            I saw it washing his feet. I wanted to speak out
            and tell you; he clapped his hand on my mouth and
                stopped me
            from saying a word. Your man's mind is the shrewdest.

            "So follow me now. I'll make a bet with my own life:
            kill me if I've been fooling—and make it the wretchedest
                killing."

            Penelopeia thoughtfully gave her an answer.   80
            "Dear aunt, it's hard to grasp the planning and power,
            for all your shrewdness, of Gods born to be always.
            But let's go down to my son in order to witness
            all those wooers dead, and the man who killed them."

Tense Choices ♦ She stopped and walked from her room, mulling a
                great deal
            at heart, whether to question the man she loved from a
                ways off
            or go to his side, kiss his head and cling to his two hands.
            Soon as the lady crossed the stone threshold and came in
            she sat right down, bright in the hearth-light facing
                Odysseus
            but close to the farther wall. Her husband, next to a tall post,   90
            sat there gazing down, waiting to see if his able
            wife would speak now that she saw with her own eyes.
            She sat quite still for a long time. Wonder had entered
            her heart for at times her eyes would go to his whole face,
            then she found him unknown with foul rags on his body.

A Rebuke   Telemakhos wanted to scold her, telling her outright,
            "Mother, hardly a mother, your heart so unfeeling!
            Why so far from my Father? Why don't you sit down
            close to the man and talk to him, ask him your questions?
            No other woman's like you, your heart so steadfast,   100

holding back from the man with all of his great pain—
home in the twentieth year in the land of his Fathers.
But then your heart has always been harder than granite."

Husband and   Penelopeia thoughtfully gave him an answer.
Wife Secrets   "My son, this heart in my own breast is astonished.
I hardly can say a word to ask him a question
or look him straight in the face. Yet if he's truly
Odysseus home at last, then certainly we two
will know each other better, having our own signs,
known by us both and kept in hiding from others."   110

Those were her words. Long-suffering, godlike Odysseus
smiled and promptly told Telemakhos—words with a
          feathery swiftness—
"Telemakhos, let your mother question and try me
now in the great hall. Soon she'll know it all better.
But now I'm grimy, the clothes are foul on my body,
so she scorns me. She won't yet call me her own man.

The Larger   "But you and I should ponder: what is our best course?
Danger   When someone murders a single man in a country,
Now Ithaka   a man without great numbers behind him to help out,
still the murderer leaves his brothers and homeland.   120
We have killed mainstays, the best by far in the city,
the young on Ithaka. That's what I tell you to ponder."

Telemakhos promptly gave him a sensible answer.
"See for yourself, dear Father: yours are the best plans
among all men's, they say. No one could ever
rival your counsel, no other man who is death-bound.
We'll follow you gladly ourselves. No one is lacking
strength or prowess, I'd say, so long as we're able."

Full of designs, Odysseus answered by saying,
"So I'll tell you myself what looks like the best way.   130
First you should all take baths and put on your tunics.
Tell the maids of the hall to pick out the right clothes.
Then our God-gifted bard holding his clear-toned
lyre in hand should lead us in dancing we all love.
Those who can hear outside, whether they're walking
 ◆ the road or living around us, will say it's a wedding.

That way rumors of dead suitors will not spread
broadly through town before we go to our densely
wooded and planted farms. There and then we will ponder
whatever counsel Zeus of Olumpos will hand us."   140

Sounds of a   He spoke that way, they heard him well and obeyed him.
Wedding   First they all took baths and put on their tunics.
                 Handmaids adorned themselves. The God-gifted poet
                 took up his hollow lyre and awakened their longing
                 for honeyed song, for handsome and faultless dancing.
                 The whole great house now echoed around with a playful
                 stamping of men and maids in beautiful dance-clothes.

                 People who listened outside the house could be saying,
                 "Surely a man's married the queen." "She often was
                      courted."
                 "An unkind lady. She's not holding out for the husband   150
                 she married." "Or keeping his great house till he
                      came home."
                 They'd talk that way but no one knew what had happened.

Like Gold on   Great-hearted Odysseus, now in his own house,
Silver   was washed by Eurunome. Then the housekeeper
                      rubbed him
                 with oil and tossed a beautiful mantle and tunic
                      around him.
                 Athene lavished grace on his head and she made him
                 look more muscled and taller. She managed his thick hair:
                 it curled and fell from his head like hyacinth blossoms.
                 The way a craftsman skillfully overlays silver
                 with gold when he's trained by Hephaistos and Pallas
                      Athene   160
                 in all the arts, and the work he masters is graceful—
                 she poured grace on his head and shoulders the same way.
                 He looked like a deathless God as he came from the
                      bathroom.
                 Then he sat once more on the chair that he rose from.

A Husband   Facing his wife, at last he spoke to her outright:
in Pain   "You strange power! Gods with homes on Olumpos
                 made your heart less yielding than all other women's.

No other woman's like you, your heart so steadfast,
holding back from your man with all of his great pain,
home in the twentieth year in the land of his Fathers.   170

"Come on, good aunt. Make me a bed and I'll lie here
myself tonight. This lady's heart is of iron."

The Key Test   Mind-full Penelopeia answered by saying,
"You strange power, I'm not so proud or uncaring;
I'm not so amazed. I do know well what you looked like
leaving Ithaka, sailing your ship with its long oars.

"Come on then, Eurukleia, make up the thick bed
outside my well-built room, the bed Odysseus crafted.
Set out the bed thickly: throw on some covers
of lambs' wool with cloaks and glistening blankets."   180

The Olive-Tree ♦   She spoke that way to test her man. But Odysseus
Bedpost   bridled and told his wife, who was knowing and
                  careful,
              "Woman, your words are really galling my own heart.
              Who settled my old bed elsewhere? Even a greatly
              skilled worker would find that hard. Maybe a God could,
              arriving there and wanting blithely to settle it elsewhere.
              But men? Not even the strongest man in his best prime
              could simply move it. That bed was built as a great sign
              worked out all by myself: nobody helped me.

              "An olive with long leaves had grown in the courtyard,   190
              mature and hardy. Its trunk resembled a column's.
              I built my bedroom around it until I was all done:
              my stones fit snugly, overhead it was well-roofed,
              then I added joints and doors that would close tight.
              I cut off shoots, the long-leafed hair of the olive,
              and trimmed its trunk from the ground up, smoothing
                  around it,
              skillful with bronze. I scraped it true to a string-line,
              that fine-honed bedpost, and drilled it all with an auger.
              After that start I planed the bed until I was quite done,
              inlaying it all with gold, ivory and silver.   200
              Then I stretched the ox-hide bed-straps, glowingly purple.

"So now I've explained that sign. But whether my bedstead's
firmly standing I don't know, woman, or now some
man's placed it elsewhere, cutting the olive-tree
            trunk down."

Embracing   Her knees and heart loosened now when he'd spoken.
at Last   Knowing the signs Odysseus spoke of had not moved,
              she ran up straight to him, crying, throwing her hands out,
              circling his neck and kissing his head as she told him,
              "Don't be angry, Odysseus! You have the most sense
              of all good men. The Gods joined us to sorrow,   210
              chafing because we two might stay with each other,
              enjoy our youth and arrive at the threshold of old age.
              But don't be irked with me now, bitter or vengeful
              because at first, when I saw you, I failed to be loving.
              This heart in my caring breast was always afraid some
              man might arrive and unfold lies to cajole me
              since plenty of men wrongfully plot for their own gain.
          ◆ Not even the daughter of Zeus, Helen of Argos,
              would ever have made love in a foreigner's bedroom
              had she known the Ares-like sons of Akhaians   220
              would take her back to the well-loved home of her fathers.
              But surely a God aroused her to act in that shameful
              way for she'd never kept in her heart before such a hapless
              urge. All our sorrow came first from that sorrow.

              "But now you have plainly spelled the signs of our bed out.
              No one else has ever seen our bed in the same way,
              only you and I and one of my handmaids:
              Aktor's daughter, my Father's gift when I came here,
              guarded the tightly fitted doors of the bedroom.
              You've truly prevailed on my heart, unkind as it might be."   230

The Sight   Her words provoked still more his yearning to cry out.
of Land   He wept and embraced his wife, a knowing and caring
for a Swimmer
at Sea ◆ woman, his heart's joy. So land is a welcome
              sight to a swimmer whose well-built ship has been ravaged
              at sea by Poseidon, chased by heavy waves and a high wind.
              The few who escape from the hoary rollers by swimming
              ashore with plenty of salt encrusting their bodies
              walk on the land with joy—they've run from that havoc.

The woman gazed at her welcome husband the same way,
not letting her white arms ease at all from his neck yet.   240

Now the rose-fingered Dawn would have shone on their
    crying
had not Athene, the glow-eyed Goddess, thought of a
    new plan.
She kept the long night in the west and she held back
golden Dawn by the Ocean's flow; she would not let
her quick-hoofed team be yoked—Phaethon, Lampon,
the colts of Dawn that carry her splendor to people.

To Bed   Full of designs, Odysseus spoke to his dear wife.
"My woman, we haven't arrived at the end of our trials,
not all, not yet. The work ahead is unmeasured,
hard and plentiful. I must wind up the whole thing   250
because the soul of Teiresies prophesied just that.
I traveled down one day to the household of Aides
to ask for the right way home for myself and my war-friends.

"But come to bed, my woman. It's time that we lie down,
finally taking the sweetness and pleasure of sleeping."

Mind-full Penelopeia answered by saying,
"Surely the bed is yours whenever your heart likes
because the Gods have doubtless made you arrive back
home in your well-built house and the land of your fathers.
But now that you know—some God has thrust it
    inside you—   260
tell me about those trials. I guess I will know them
myself in time. To know them sooner is not worse."

The Prophecy   Full of his own plans Odysseus answered by saying,
of the Oar   "Strange power! What's the hurry, why do you ask me
to say all that? Though I won't hide it—I'll tell you—
it won't bring joy to your heart. Nor is my own heart
glad since the prophet told me to travel to plenty
of people's towns. My hands will be holding a well-made
oar and I'll call on men not knowing the salt sea.
They take no food, he told me, seasoned with salt there.   270
They have no knowledge at all of purple-cheeked vessels

and well-turned oars that act as the wings of a fast ship.
He gave me a plain sign; I won't hide it from you now.
The day another traveler meets me and tells me
I carry a winnowing tool on my glistening shoulder,
the prophet told me to drive my oar in the ground there
and offer beautiful victims to lordly Poseidon—
a ram, a bull and a boar that's mated with females.
Then I should go back home and render hecatombs holy
to deathless Gods who rule broadly in heaven,   280
to each in order. Then death will be far from the salt sea,
arriving very gently, taking my wealthy
life, overcome with age. People will prosper
around me. That's all Teiresies told me would happen."

In Their   Mind-full Penelopeia answered by saying,
Old Bed   "Truly if Gods will bring you a happier old age,
there's hope at last you'll make an escape from your
    troubles."

So as the couple spoke that way with each other
the nurse and Eurunome, meanwhile, were making their
    bed up
with soft coverlets under the glow of their torches.   290
After they both had hurried and laid out the thick bed,
the older nurse went back to rest in her own room.
The bedroom nurse, Eurunome, guided the couple
along to bed, holding the torch with her two hands.
She led to their room and went out. The man and the
    woman
now approached the place and welcomed their old bed.

Meanwhile Telemakhos, joined by the cowherd and
    swineherd,
slowed their dancers' feet and stopped the handmaids.
They went to sleep themselves in the shadowy great hall.

Past Troubles   After the pair had taken pleasure in loving   300
they spoke to each other, taking pleasure in stories.
This brightest of women had held back in the great hall,
eyeing those men, that crowd of disgraceful suitors.
They'd slaughtered so much livestock, bullocks and fat
    sheep

because of a woman—so much wine drawn from the
    wine-jars.
Zeus-bred Odysseus told her all of the hardship
he'd brought on men and all the anguish he'd suffered.
He told it all, she gladly listened and no sleep
fell on her eyelids before he told her the whole tale.

Kikones, ◆ He told her how he'd mastered the Kikones people   310
Lotos-Eaters,   and sailed to the green fields of the Lotos-eaters.
Kuklops, Aiolos,
Laistrugonians, All of the Kuklops's acts: Odysseus made him
Kirke   pay for the stalwart war-friends he'd ruthlessly eaten.
He went to Aiolos next, who welcomed him freely
and sent him off. His fate was not to arrive in his well-loved
fatherland yet for a storm-wind seized him and sent him
away on the fish-filled sea, heavily groaning.
He sailed to Telepulos after, Laistrugonian people
who speared his well-greaved men and bombed his vessels,
all of them—only Odysseus ran in his black ship.   320
He spoke about Kirke too, her many ways of misleading.

Aides,   He told her he'd gone by ship with its many oar-locks
Seirenes,   to ask for Teiresies' help, the prophet from Thebes
Kharubdis and
Skulla,   in moldering Aides' house. He'd spotted his war-friends
the Sun-God's   there and his mother, who'd borne and fed him in
Cattle   childhood.
Yes and he heard the endless song of Seirenes.
He'd gone to the Wandering Rocks, fearsome Kharubdis
and Skulla: no man before had fled them without harm.
But then his crewmen butchered Helios's cattle
and Zeus, the high Thunderer, blasted his race-fast   330
ship with sulphurous lightning. The last of his good men
drowned together. Only Odysseus ran from that
    wrong doom.

Kalupso,   He went to Kalupso then, a Nymph on Ogugie Island.
Phaiakia   She kept him there, she longed for the man as her husband.
In hollow caves the Goddess fed him and told him
she'd make him deathless, all his days he would not age.
Yet she never prevailed on the heart in his firm chest.
Then he came to Phaiakian land with all of his deep pain:
people took him to heart like a God and esteemed him,
they sent him by ship to the well-loved land of his fathers   340

and gave him presents—bronze, gold and plenty of clothing.
He'd said the last word. Now sleep, relaxing his body,
gave him sweetness, undoing his heart from its troubles.

Off to the Farm   Athene, the glow-eyed Goddess, thought of a new plan.
Now that she knew the heart of Odysseus fully
enjoyed the bed of his wife and rested in good sleep,
she promptly roused the newborn Dawn on her golden
throne to bring men light from the Ocean. Odysseus
rose from the soft bed, he spoke to his wife and
    enjoined her,

"My woman, by now we've tired of our many   350
trials, you and I. You cried for my woeful return here
while Zeus and the rest of the Gods, for all of my longing,
snarled me in pain far from the land of my Fathers.
Now that we've both come back to the bed that we so love,
do care for all of my wealth that's here in the great hall.
The overbearing suitors devoured my sheep-flocks;
  ♦ I'll get some back by looting. Akhaians will give me
the rest of the stock till the last sheepfold is refilled.
Now I'm going out to that farm with its dense trees
to see my worthy Father. He's grieved for me often.   360
So I enjoin you, woman, with all of your good sense:
fast as the rising sun the news will be spreading
about these wooers—men I killed in the great hall.
Go to your upstairs room with the women, your handmaids,
and stay there. Don't look out or ask any questions."

Ready for   He stopped and clapped his shoulders in beautiful armor.
Battle Again   He woke Telemakhos, then the cowherd and swineherd.
He told them to take the War-God's tools in their
    own hands.
No one disobeyed him. Armored in bright bronze
they opened the doors and left with Odysseus leading.   370
By now there was light on the land but, using her own night,
Athene hid them and led them fast from the city.

Squeaking Bats ◆ Meanwhile from Mount Kullene Hermes was calling
in a Cave   the suitors' ghosts. In his hand was the beautiful golden
      wand he'd often used to weary the vision
      of men he chose or wake up men from a sound sleep.
      His wand moved and led them. They squeaked as they
          followed,
      sounding like bats that flutter and squeak through the
          inmost
      depths of a wondrous cave when a bat falls from its
          rock-face,
      the cluster where all the rest take hold of each other.

The Land of   The ghosts went squeaking that way as Hermes the Healer
the Dead   led them a long way down the moldering pathways.   10
      ◆ They moved past Leukas Rock and that flow, Okeanos,
      past the land of dreams and gates of the Sun-God.
      Soon their souls were approaching an asphodel meadow
      where ghosts have homes, the shadows of people who've
          worn down.
      They found Peleus's son there, the ghost of Akhilleus;
      ◆ Patroklos too and handsome Antilokhos close by;
      in face and frame no one was better than Aias
      among the Danaans except for peerless Akhilleus.

A Wretched   They all kept crowding Akhilleus. Moving closer
End for a   there was the ghost of Atreus's son Agamemnon,   20
Great King   mourning steadily. Others gathered around him,
      those who'd met their doom, killed in Aigisthos's
      house. The ghost of Peleus's son started by saying,
      "Son of Atreus, we thought Zeus, whose joy is in lightning,
      would love you all your days the most among war-chiefs
      because you ruled so many powerful cordons
      on Trojan land, where Akhaians underwent great pain.
      But all too soon a killing doom was to reach you
      too since no man born escapes from his own death.
      Better to die on Trojan land, facing your end there   30
      enjoying all the esteem and gain you had mastered:

343

then all the Akhaians could raise a mound in your honor.
In time you'd have won a great name for your son too.
Now your doom was to die most wretchedly back home."

Death-Rites   The ghost of Atreus's son answered by saying,
at Troy   "Well-blessed Peleus's son, you godlike Akhilleus!
  ♦ You died at Troy, far from Argos, and others around you
died there too, outstanding sons of Akhaians and Trojans
fighting over your body. You lay in the swirling
dust so greatly, a great man!—all your knowledge   40
of horses forgotten. We fought all day and we'd never
have stopped that struggling, but Zeus stopped us with
      high winds.
After we took you away to the ships from that battle,
we set you down on a bed and wiped your handsome
body with lukewarm water and oil. Many Danaans
around you shed warm tears, cutting their long hair.

Thetis,   "Your mother heard the news and came with her deathless
Her Nymphs,   Nymphs from the sea. A wondrous thing on the water,
and the Old   their rising cries! The Akhaians were taken by shudders
Man of the Sea   and now they all would have leaped up and left in the hollow   50
ships if an older and far wiser man had not stopped them:
Nestor had shown before that his plans were the best way.
Meaning well he stood in the assembly and called out,
'Stop, don't run, young men of Akhaia and Argos!
That's his mother: she came from the sea with her deathless
Nymphs to face and mourn her child who is dead now.'

      "He stopped and the great-hearted Akhaians did not flee.
The Old Man of the Sea's daughters were standing
      around you,
deeply mourning. They dressed you in clothes lasting
      forever
and all nine Muses bewailed you with beautiful voices   60
that answered each other. A tearless Argive was not seen,
the Muses' clear-toned singing moved them so deeply.

The Last Fire   "For seven and ten more days, nighttime and daytime,
we death-bound men and the deathless Gods were in
      mourning.

We gave you to fire on the eighteenth day and we
    slaughtered
plenty of fattened rams and bulls with their curved horns.
You burned in the Gods' clothes, in plenty of ointment
and good sweet honey. Many Akhaian war-chiefs
moved slowly in armor circling the death-fire
on foot or horseback. The uproar there was enormous.   70

"After Hephaistos's flames were done with you clearly,
we gathered your white bones in the morning, Akhilleus,
and set them in unmixed wine and oil as your mother
brought us a gold, two-handled urn. She said Dionusos
gave her that amphora, worked by well-known Hephaistos.
Your own white bones are inside there, shining Akhilleus,
blended with Patroklos's bones, the dead son of Menoitios.
Antilokhos's bones are a ways off, the man you
    esteemed most
among all your friends after Patroklos perished.

A Death-   "Over you all we piled a gigantic and flawless   80
Mound,   death-mound. Our holy army, the spearmen of Argos,
Games, and   worked on a jutting point by the Hellespont's broad sea,
Prizes   so to be viewed by men from far over the water—
those who are born that time and those of the next age.

"Your mother had asked the Gods for the handsomest prizes.
She set them down in our midst for the heads of the
    Argives.
By now you'd taken part in the death-rites of many
war-chiefs. Whenever a king died and went under
young men strapped on belts and got ready for prizes.
Gazing on those awards would have lifted your heart most   90
for silver-footed Thetis, a Goddess, had laid out
stunning awards for her son, so loved by the great Gods.

"And so your name's not lost in spite of your dying,
you'll always be widely known among people, Akhilleus.
Yet what joy is mine since we wound up the fighting?
Zeus plotted a wretched death when I came home
under Aigisthos's hand and a wife's that I still curse."

How Did
These Men
All Die?
All the while they spoke that way with each other
the Messenger came closer, the Splendor of Argos,
guiding down the ghosts of suitors killed by Odysseus.   100
Both were amazed, soon as they saw them, and came close:
Atreus's son, Agamemnon's ghost, recognized well-known
Amphimedon, son of Melaneus, loved by his father—
once his host when he stayed in that Ithakan household.
The ghost of the son of Atreus started by asking,
"What happened, Amphimedon? Why are you under the
        dark earth
now with all these choice young men of the same age?
Who would not choose these men as the best in a city?
Maybe Poseidon downed you all in your black ships,
raising riotous gales and mountainous rollers.   110
Or men on land? By chance did enemies harm you
for rustling beautiful flocks of sheep and their oxen?
Or fight you off around their wives and their city?
I say you should tell me, my claim is close as a house-guest.
Don't you remember the day I walked in your household
with godlike Menelaos? We encouraged Odysseus
to join us and sail for Troy on our strong-decked vessels.
Crossing the wide sea had taken a whole month.
♦ We barely prevailed on Odysseus, wrecker of cities."

Then Amphimedon's ghost answered by saying,   120
"Best-known son of Atreus, lord of men, Agamemnon,
nourished by Zeus! I remember it all, just as you told it.
♦ Now I'll tell you myself the whole of our story.
Our deaths were a ghastly end. How did they happen?

The Guileful
Web
"We courted Odysseus's wife. Her man had been long gone.
She never refused her hated marriage, nor did she end
        things.
In fact the lady planned on death, on our black doom.
Meanwhile her mind invented another deception.
She stood a huge loom in the palace for weaving,
a broad and fine-threaded web. She spoke to us briskly: 130
'Young men, my suitors, now that godlike Odysseus
is dead you're anxious to marry. Wait till I finish
the shroud—don't let yarn be useless or wasted.
The shroud's for Laertes, the time when that war-chief
is taken down by his doom's blight, a remorseless

death. No Akhaian woman must scowl in my country
because he gained such wealth but lies unshrouded.'

"Those were her words. Our hearts were proud but we
       nodded.
So every day at the huge loom she was weaving—
and every night with torches nearby she unwove it.   140
Her guile convinced and escaped us Akhaians for three
       years.
Then when the fourth year came with its rolling of seasons,
fading months and plenty of days that were ending,
one of her maids who knew of her cunning informed us.
We caught the lady at night unwinding her bright web.
She stopped working against her will—she was forced to.
In time she displayed the shroud, worked on its huge web,
washed and glowing like Helios's light or the moonlight.

The Beggar Is   "Then from somewhere the wrong Power was guiding
Maltreated   Odysseus back to an outlying farm, the home of a
                        swineherd.   150
The well-loved son of godlike Odysseus arrived there
too in his black ship from deep-sanded Pulos.
After the two of them planned a sorry end for the suitors,
they came to the well-known city—Odysseus later,
Telemakhos leading the way, going before him.

"The swineherd led Odysseus, wearing some bad clothes.
He looked like an old man, the wretchedest pauper
propped on a staff. The clothes on his body were old rags.
No one could know this man was truly Odysseus,
he came so suddenly—even the elders did not know.   160
We taunted the man harshly and hit him with footstools.
He let himself be struck for a while in his own hall.
Scolded and beaten, he showed a spirit that bore up.

Final   "But moved by the mind of Zeus who carries the great
Vengeance   shield,
at last he helped Telemakhos carry his stunning
weapons away to their room and fasten the door-bolts.
He also told his wife—the man was a wizard—
to set his bow and some gray iron in front of the suitors,
testing us doomed men, the start of our own deaths.

Not one man could stretch that powerful weapon   170
and string it right. How very much we were lacking!

"Soon as the large bow was nearing the hands of Odysseus
all of us cried out loudly, saying the weapon
should not be allowed that man, however he babbled.
Only Telemakhos heartened and told him to take it.
Now the hands of long-suffering, godlike Odysseus
deftly strung the bow. He shot through the iron
and went to stand on the threshold. He poured out the
     nimble
arrows and glared frightfully, piercing a king first,
young Antinoos. Aiming groan-carrying shafts at the others,   180
he shot so well that our men toppled in dense heaps.

"By now we knew one of the Gods was their helper.
They suddenly dashed through the hall madly and
     caught us,
striking on every side. Wretched groans were rising,
skulls were battered, blood was awash on the whole floor.

A Song   "So we died, Agamemnon. Our bodies are lying
of Praise for   still untended there in Odysseus's great hall.
Penelopeia   As yet our friends don't know in the household of each
                     man—
those who'd wash the black-red blood from our deep
     wounds,
lay us out and mourn us—all that's due to a dead man."   190

Then the ghost of Atreus's son answered by saying,
♦"Happy son of Laertes, widely resourceful Odysseus,
blessed with the marvelous, upright woman you married,
what goodness of mind in faultless Penelopeia!
Ikarios's daughter truly remembered Odysseus,
the man she'd married: so now her name and her goodness
will never die. The deathless Gods will fashion a joyful
song for men on the earth about thoughtful Penelopeia.
But not Tundareos's daughter: evilly plotting,
killing the man she married, her song will be hateful   200
to everyone. Klutaimnestre brought on a bad name
to every woman, even the woman who acts well."

So the two men spoke that way with each other,
standing under the earth in the household of Aides.

Beautiful Farmland
Meanwhile Odysseus's men went down from the city
and shortly came to the beautiful, laid-out farm of Laertes,
won by that king before with plenty of struggle.
There was the house; around it were running on every
side the sheds for bonded helpers who sat there,
ate there, worked for Laertes gladly and slept there.   210
An old Sicilian woman who lived in the farmhouse
gently cared for the aging man far from the city.

The Orchard
Shortly Odysseus told his son and the two slaves,
"You men go on to the well-built house and get ready
for dinner soon. Kill the best of the swine there.
I'm going myself to put a test to my Father,
to find out whether he'll know me now with his own eyes.
Or maybe he'll fail to. I've been gone for a long time."

He stopped and gave his War-God's tools to the two slaves
who walked in the house at once. However Odysseus   220
♦ walked in the fruit-filled orchard to test his father.
Moving down through the spreading orchard he came on
no one: Dolios's sons and all of his own slaves
had gone by chance to gather stones for the vineyard
wall and Dolios, an elderly man, was their leader.

A Ragged Old Man
Then he found his father. Alone in a well-tilled
orchard and breaking ground for a shrub, he was wearing
a patched, dirty and ragged tunic with bull's-hide
greaves bound to his legs to guard against scratches.
His hands had gloves, what with the thorns, and a goatskin   230
capped his head. The man's pain was increasing.
When long-suffering, godlike Odysseus saw him,
worn with age and his heart bearing a vast grief,
he stood beneath a tall pear-tree and shed tears.
He pondered a while. In heart and mind he was doubtful
whether to hug and kiss the man, telling him each thing—
how he was home at last in the land of his fathers—
or question the old one first and test him on each point.
So as he mulled it soon struck him as better
first to question the old man, even to bait him.   240

He walked up straight to him. Thoughtful and godlike
    Odysseus
watched him rooting the shrub, holding his head down.
The shining son came close to his father and told him,
"Old man, no lack of knowledge in caring for gardens
restrains you. You care so well that nothing at all here—
none of the fig-trees, grapevines, hardly an olive,
pear-tree or bed of leek—lacks care in the garden.
But I'll say too, and don't put pique in your heart now,
you lack good care for yourself. Together with sorry
old age you are badly grimed and your clothing is wretched.   250
It's not because you're lazy your master has not cared
surely and not because your looks are lowly and slavelike
in size or shape. In fact you look like a ruler,
the kind of man who, after he's washed and had dinner,
sleeps on a soft bed. That's right for an old man.

Who's Lord   "Come on now, tell me something, answer me truly.
of Ithaka?   What man do you serve? Whose orchard here do you
        care for?
Tell me another truth, help me to know well:
have I arrived in Ithaka? So I was told by
a man just now who met me traveling this way.   260
The man was not so clever or bold when he answered
on each point. He failed to hear me out when I asked him
about my friend who somehow might be alive still,
or maybe he's dead by now in the household of Aides.
So I'll tell you—take it inside you and listen—
I welcomed that man in the well-loved land of my Fathers
once when he came to our house. No other person,
no far-off guest who came to our home was so welcome.
He claimed he was born on Ithaka, saying his father
there was the son of Arkeisios, known as Laertes.   270
I led the man in my house myself as a good host,
enthused and friendly. Inside the house there was plenty;
I gave him a stranger's presents, all that was due him.
I gave him seven talents of gold that were well-formed.
I gave him a wine-bowl of silver with blossoming artwork,
twelve single-folding cloaks, twelve of our blankets,
twelve gorgeous mantles, the same number of tunics,
and four shapely women besides with their knowing
and flawless hand-work. He alone wanted to choose them."

Not Even
Death-Rites His father answered him then, shedding a few tears.   280
"Stranger, it's true: you came to the land that you asked of.
But prideful and reckless men have taken it over.
Those countless presents you gladly gave him are pointless.
If only you'd found him alive in Ithakan country!
He'd surely have sent you off as richly, present for present,
with grand entertainment due to the man who began things.

"Come on though, tell me something, answer me truly:
how many years have passed since you welcomed that
    stranger,
your sorry guest, my son? If the man was alive once—
doomed so far from his friends and the land of his fathers—   290
no doubt sharks ate him at sea or vultures and wild beasts
made him their prey on land. The mother and father
who gave him birth never shrouded and mourned him.
His wife with all her bride-gifts, mind-full Penelopeia,
never wailed on her husband's bier in the right way
or closed his eyes. Those are the rights of a dead man.

"Tell me another truth: help me to know well
what man you are. Where are your parents and city?
Where did you stand the race-fast vessel that brought you
here with your godlike friends? Or maybe you came here
    riding   300
a ship of others—they left you and sailed off?"

The Son Must
Reveal Himself
at Last Full of designs Odysseus answered by saying,
"I'll answer you now myself—I'll tell you the whole truth.
 ♦ I'm from Alubas. The house I live in is well known.
Lord Polupemon's son is my Father, Alpheidas.
My own name is Eperitos. Somehow a Power
drove me against my will from Sikanie right here.
My ship lies to by a farm, away from the city.

"But now five years have passed since Odysseus left us,
sailing away that day from the land of my Fathers.   310
Doomed? But the signs were good when he set out,
seabirds to starboard, making me glad when I sent him
and making him glad he left. Our hearts had been hoping
we'd meet as friends and exchange wonderful presents."

He spoke that way but a dark sadness was clouding
the old one. Gathering sooty dust in his two hands,
he dumped it onto his gray head and moaned without
      stopping.
Odysseus's heart was moved at last and a sharp sting
rose through his nostrils, watching the father he so loved.
He ran up, kissed and embraced the man as he told him,   320
"I am that man, Father, the one you have asked of.
I'm back in the twentieth year in the land of my Fathers.
Hold off grief now, all this moaning and weeping.
I'll tell you why—we need to be gone from here quite soon—
I've killed the last of the suitors now in our own house,
taking revenge for all their evil, heart-stinging actions."

A Call for Proof   Then Laertes promptly answered by asking,
"If my own child Odysseus truly has come here,
show me the plainest sign to make me believe it."

Odysseus, full of designs, answered him promptly,   330
"First look at the wound. See with your own eyes
the scar that a boar's white tusk caused on Parnesos.
You and my honored Mother had sent me to Mother's
well-loved father, Autolukos, helping me take on
presents he'd promised the time he came here and said so.
Yes and I'll also name those trees in your well-tilled
orchard you gave me once when I asked about each one,
trailing along as a boy. We walked through this very
grove and you named them all, you spoke about each one.
You gave me thirteen pear-trees and forty fig-trees,   340
ten of apple and then you named rows in the vineyard:
you gave me fifty rows that trailed each other in bearing
fruit—so many kinds of clusters that ripened
whenever Zeus weighed them down in their season."

Sure Signs,   He stopped as the knees and heart went slack in the old man.
Great Joy   Knowing the signs were sure that Odysseus gave him,
he threw both arms around the son he had so loved
then fainted. Long-suffering, godlike Odysseus held him.

Then when he breathed and spirits regathered inside him,
words came back to the man and he answered by praying: 350
"Fatherly Zeus, you Gods are still on the heights of Olumpos

if suitors have paid for their pride and recklessness truly.
But now great fear's in my breast: their Ithakan people
may come in a mass here soon and they also could send off
messengers fast to every Kephallenian city."

The Goddess
Helps an
Old Warrior
Full of designs, Odysseus answered by saying,
"Take heart: don't let your thoughts be anxious about that.
Let's go to the house that lies close to the orchard.
I sent Telemakhos there, the swineherd and cattle
herder to make a meal for us all in a hurry."   360

They spoke that way and walked to the handsome
        farmhouse.
After they entered the home where people had lived well
they found Telemakhos helping the swineherd and cowherd
slicing meat into piles and mixing the bright wine.

Great-hearted Laertes meanwhile washed in the farmhouse,
helped by the Sicily woman who rubbed him with good oil
and threw a graceful mantle around him. Moreover Athene
came up close and enlarged that shepherd of people:
she made him taller now than before and stronger to look at.
He left the bathroom, amazing the son he had so loved: 370
his father looked like a deathless God as he faced him.
Odysseus told him, the words with a feathery swiftness,
"Father, surely one of the Gods born to be always
made your form and face much better to look at."

A Need for the
Old Strength
Wise Laertes promptly answered by praying,
"Fatherly Zeus, Athene, Apollo, if only
I felt that strength when I mastered Nerikon's well-built
fort on the mainland's coast and ruled Kephallenians!
My son, if only I felt so yesterday too in our own house!
My shoulders clapped in armor, standing beside you   380
battling suitors, I would have loosened a number
of knees in our hall. The heart would have gladdened
        inside you."
So the two of them spoke that way with each other.

The Lord Has
Come Home!
The slaves had now stopped working: dinner was ready.
All in order, they took their seats or a tall chair.
Their hands went out to the food as Dolios came in,

their old helper, with all six sons of the old man,
tired from fieldwork. Their mother had gone to call them—
the old Sicilian woman—she fed them and fondly
cared for the old one now that age overtook him.   390
They saw Odysseus, they knew the man in their own hearts
and stood amazed in the big room. However Odysseus
promptly spoke to Dolios, telling him mildly,
"Sit down to your food, old man. Let no one be awe-struck.
We've wanted our own hands on this bread for a long time
waiting here in this room, expecting you always!"

He spoke that way but Dolios ran at him stretching
both his hands out, taking Odysseus's right hand
and kissing his wrist. His words had a feathery swiftness,
"Dear man, you've come back home to those with such
            longing!   400
We thought we'd never see you—the Gods must have
            brought you.
I hail you, I wish you well, may Gods make you happy.
Tell me this other truth, help me to know well:
♦ does mind-full Penelopeia know it for certain,
your coming home right here? Do we send her a message?"

An answer came from Odysseus, full of his own plans:
"Old man, she knows it already. Why should you bother?"

Soon as he'd spoken the old man sat on a well-shined
chair and the sons of Dolios welcomed famous
Odysseus, taking his hands and talking the same way.   410
Then they took their seats by Dolios, their father.
They all busied themselves with food in the big room.

Mounting Pain   But Rumor, the Messenger, raced through all of the city
and Anger   with news of a hateful doom, the deaths of the suitors.
Soon as they heard, people gathered from all sides
moaning and crying in front of Odysseus's palace.
They hauled the dead from his house and buried the bodies.
Corpses from other towns were sent to their own homes,
laid on fast-running ships to be ferried by sailors.

Then they thronged the assembly place with their anguished   420
hearts. After they'd all gathered, crowding together,

the man who stood up first to speak was Eupeithes.
A boundless grief lay on his heart for his dear son
Antinoos, struck down first by godlike Odysseus.
He wept for him now as he spoke to the gathering saying,
"My friends, what great crimes this man has aimed at
    Akhaians!
He led off plenty of brave men to Troy on his black ships,
 ◆ then lost the hollow ships and lost the last of the good men.
Now he's come home and killed the best Kephallenians.
Come on then, before he sails in a hurry for Pulos   430
or God-bright Elis, where people are ruled by Epeians,
let's go or plainly appear shameful forever.
Such disgace will be known by men in the future
unless we punish those who slaughtered our brothers
and sons. Life would bring no joy to my own breast.
I'd sooner die, go among those who are rotting.
Instead let's move, or they'll cross the sea and outrun us."

<table>
<tr><td>Better Counsel</td><td>

He'd spoken in tears, pity grasping all the Akhaians,
but Medon came to them now and the God-gifted singer—
sleep had let them go from Odysseus's great hall.   440
They stood in the center, surprise fastened on each man
as Medon spoke to the crowd like a sensible person.
"Listen, you men of Ithaka! Surely Odysseus
planned no work that countered the will of the deathless
Gods for I saw an ambrosial God myself with Odysseus,
standing close by. Strongly resembling Mentor,
surely a deathless God was in front of Odysseus,
often rousing the man and rushing the great hall
at times to panic the suitors, who fell on each other."
</td></tr>
<tr><td>Stinging
Reproaches</td><td>

He spoke that way, they all were gripped by a dull green   450
fear and a war-chief spoke up next. Old Halitherses,
the son of Mastor, had often seen behind and before them—
this man only. He meant well as he told the assembly,
"Listen now, you Ithakans, here's what I tell you.
This work was born, my friends, of wrongs by
    yourselves here.
You never obeyed me or Mentor, a shepherd of people,
or made your sons put an end to their madness,
their own great crimes. They acted reckless and vicious,
wasting the man's wealth and badly treating his woman,
</td></tr>
</table>

a ruler's wife. They thought he'd never return home.   460
So let things stay. Do as I tell you and don't move
now or someone may draw down harm by his own hand."

Another War   He spoke that way but more than half of them jumped up,
shouting him down. The rest who stayed in their places
loathed his talk in their hearts. Obeying Eupeithes,
many were suddenly dashing off for their weapons.
Soon as the gleaming bronze covered their bodies
they all crammed in a broad space in front of the city.
Eupeithes promptly led them away in his folly.
He thought to avenge the death of his son but he'd never   470
come back home himself. He'd go to his own doom.

Help from ◆ Now Athene spoke to Zeus, the son of Kronos.
the Gods   "Our Father, son of Kronos, highest of rulers,
Tell me, I ask, what thoughts are hiding inside you.
Would you arouse more war, pain and the fearsome
noise of battle? Or set down friendship on both sides?"

Stormcloud-gathering Zeus answered by saying,
"Why do you ask me, my child? What are these questions?
Wasn't it you in fact who planned in your own mind
the way Odysseus truly would come for his vengeance?   480
Do as you like. But I'll tell you a way that is likely.
Now that godlike Odysseus has punished the suitors,
men should strongly swear he will rule there always.
Let's you and I make them forget about killings
of sons and brothers. Then they'll care for each other
just as before. Let peace and plenty be ample."

His talk encouraged Athene, anxious already
to leap out swiftly and down from the heights of Olumpos.

The Threat of   The longing for honey-minded food in the farmhouse had
Battle   ended.
Long-suffering, godlike Odysseus spoke first.   490
"Let someone go out and see if men are approaching."

A son of Dolios went out the way he was ordered.
He stood on the threshold, saw a crowd as it came on

and told Odysseus—words with a feathery swiftness—
"They're coming closer, let's arm ourselves in a hurry."

He stopped and they all stood up to put on their armor:
the six who were sons of Dolios, Odysseus's three men,
Dolios too and Laertes donning their armor,
gray as they were, old men forced to be fighters.
Soon as the gleaming bronze covered their bodies,   500
they opened the doors and left with Odysseus out front.

A Family
Fighting
Side by SideAthene, the daughter of Zeus, came to them close by,
both in her voice and body looking like Mentor.
Long-suffering, godlike Odysseus, glad to have seen her,
spoke to his own dear son Telemakhos quickly:
"Learn this much, Telemakhos, now that you've entered
a battle yourself that chooses the bravest of fighters,
not to shame the line of your Fathers who've outdone
all of the earth's men before in prowess and courage."

Telemakhos promptly gave him a sensible answer.   510
"Watch if you like, dear Father: mine is a spirit
that won't disgrace your bloodline the way you describe it."

And soon as he'd spoken Laertes joyfully called out:
"Dear Gods, how this day is making me happy—
my son and grandson rival each other in prowess!"

The First
ThrowGlow-eyed Athene stood up close to him saying,
"Son of Arkeisios, dearer by far than of all my war-friends,
pray to our Father Zeus and his glow-eyed daughter
then swiftly poise your long-shafted weapon and throw it."

♦ Pallas Athene paused and breathed in him great strength.   520
Having prayed to the Goddess, the daughter of great Zeus,
he poised the long-shadowing spear and he threw it,
striking Eupeithes. The bronze cheek of his helmet
failed to stop it, the brazen weapon was right through,
the man fell down heavily, armor rattling around him.

Fierce but
Short FightingThe well-known son and Odysseus drove at their front lines,
stabbing men with two-edged spears or a sword-thrust.

They soon would have killed them all and stopped their
    return home
had not Athene, the daughter of Zeus who carries the great
    shield,
called out loudly and held back all of the people: 530
"End this battle, Ithakans! War is too grueling.
Without more bloodshed now you should part in a hurry."

Athene had spoken: they all were gripped by a dull green
fear and weapons flew from their panicky fingers,
falling to earth in heaps when the Goddess had called out.
They turned and ran to the city, longing for more life.
When long-suffering, godlike Odysseus cried out
savagely and swooped on them fast as a high-diving eagle,
the son of Kronos hurled sulphurous lightning
that fell close to the glow-eyed child of that powerful Father.   540
Glow-eyed Athene told Odysseus promptly,
"Son of Laertes, nourished by Zeus, wily Odysseus,
stop now. End this war involving your whole land.
Don't anger Zeus, the son of Kronos, watching from
    far off."

A Long Peace   When Athene spoke he obeyed, heartily glad to.
Willed   So she made peace, a lasting agreement on both sides—
by the Gods   Pallas Athene, daughter of Zeus who carries the great
    shield,
both in her voice and body looking like Mentor.

Notes
Richard P. Martin

1.1 *The man.* Like other epics, the *Odyssey* starts with the poet identifying his theme in the very first word of the composition—here "man" (*andra*). The epithet *polutropos* (literally, "of many turnings") is translated as "resourceful," but its sense carries over into the phrase "wandering widely" since Odysseus is marked by both his mental twists and turns (his cunning) and the physical battering to which he has been subjected, to and fro across many seas. The hero's intelligence wins out; recklessness and transgression—like that of Odysseus's unfortunate crew—lead to destruction.

1.1 *my Muse.* Daughters of Zeus and Memory (*Mnêmosunê*)—and patron goddesses of poetry, dance, and music (which owes them its name)—the Muses were regularly addressed at the start of ancient Greek compositions. As eternal divinities, they were thought to have witnessed all the events of the past, and therefore a poet could ask them for accurate information, almost as if accessing a database, but subject to the wish of the Muse for the exact entry-point to the past (see line 10: "start in your own place"). At the beginning of both the *Iliad* and the *Odyssey*, a single goddess is invoked. Elsewhere in Homer, they are sometimes addressed as a group (as in *Il.* 2.484), but all nine are named, within early Greek poetry, only in Hesiod's *Theogony*, a poem roughly contemporary with the *Odyssey*. In that miniature epic, telling of Zeus's rise to power, the poet depicts himself as literally inspired ("breathed into") by the Muses and told to sing of the origins of the gods. The assignment of genres to the care of an individual Muse (tragedy to Melpomene, lyric poetry to Erato, history to Clio, etc.) was a later ancient invention. It is difficult to tell to what extent the invocation of the Muse was a performer's fiction—a way of asserting a privileged status and relation to the gods—or a belief deeply held by poets and their audiences. In any event, the convention became standard in later Classical epics and imitations of them.

1.24 *some where the God Huperion sets.* The motif of like groups or places being located at the world's extremes is common in myths worldwide. The phenomenon is referred to as *coincidentia oppositorum* ("coming together of opposites") and is common in the *Odyssey*, where it is reinforced by the archaic Greek geographical belief that the world was disc-shaped and surrounded by a cosmic river, Okeanos. The Greek word *Aithiops*, which gives us "Ethiopians," means "fiery-faced." Apparently it refers to peoples of North Africa, whose darker complexion was explained as the result of their living in regions closer to the sun.

1.30 *Orestes had killed him.* The tale of the family of Agamemnon, leader of the Greeks against Troy, forms a constant counterpoint in the *Odyssey* to that of Odysseus and his family. Agamemnon's position as king of the richest realm naturally placed him at the head of the expedition; also, it was his brother Menelaos's wife, Helen, who had been seduced and led off by the Trojan prince Paris. According to a story not mentioned in Homer, but looming large in later tragic drama, Agamemnon's own wife, Klutaimnestre, took the lead in murdering him after his triumphal return from Troy. In the *Oresteia* trilogy by Aeschylus (458 B.C.), she justifies her act as compensation for the loss of their daughter, Iphigeneia, slain by Agamemnon as an offering to Artemis when that goddess caused the departing Greek fleet to be delayed at Aulis. In the *Odyssey*, Klutaimnestre is a sort of anti-Penelopeia, the image of a faithless wife. But her adulterous lover Aigisthos (Agamemnon's first cousin) is given more of the credit for planning the death of the king. The mention of Orestes, the king's avenging son, will be repeated twice in the early part of the poem (1.298–300 and 3.197–200), when Telemakhos, son of Odysseus, is urged by his elders to make a name for himself. Of course, the analogy has a flaw: the suitors of Penelopeia have not been successful, like Aigisthos, in winning over the queen's affection; Odysseus has not been proven dead; and Telemakhos has no clear basis for revenge. His dawning realization of his unique situation will mark the growth of the young son of Odysseus.

1.91 *the suitors*. Athene casually introduces the suitors into the narrative, as if the audience has already heard about them, although this is the first reference in the poem. Such details make us aware that Homeric poetry was performed for listeners deeply imbued with poetic traditions of all types, who had heard many versions of any given tale. They also well illustrate the allusive and strategic art of the poet. Information is relayed by degrees, usually by the characters themselves, and usually only when it makes an effective rhetorical point. Only gradually will we learn that there are 108 suitors, from Ithaka and surrounding islands; that they have forced the employees of Odysseus's household, from court bard to serving maids, to do their will; and that they were deceived for three years by Penelopeia's ruse of unweaving nightly the handiwork she told them she must finish before she could remarry. The characters of two in particular (Eurumakhos and Antinoos) will be sketched more fully, while the mass of suitors remains largely anonymous.

1.105 *Mentes*. The gods often assume human disguise as they go about their missions on earth. This disguise is significant because the name of the lord of the Taphians means "reminder" (as does the name Mentor, another of Athene's roles, and the word from which the English noun comes). The root on which Mentes is built occurs also in "strength" (*menos*) as well as "memory" (*mnêmosunê*)—precisely the qualities Athene has promised to impart to Telemakhos. The collocation of strength and memory is interesting in itself: *menos* appears to be the special will to survive that comes from recalling kin and obligations.

1.189 *the old war-chief*. One of the many difficulties for understanding the social and political situation on Ithaka is the status of Laertes, father of Odysseus. If his son is absent, why is he not king? Was he ever? If so, how did Odysseus assume the throne before leaving? And why does Laertes seem to live in poverty far from the palace? Apart from the rather cavalier manner in which Homeric poetry mixes together historical or social details (see Introduction, "History and the *Odyssey*"), this characterization must generally reflect the poet's desire to make Laertes powerless and pitiable—and therefore render the return of his son all the more joyous and eventful.

1.215 *My Mother tells me*. The theme of paternity opens and closes the poem. In book 24, the last person to be reunited with Odysseus is his own father Laertes. The slight tone of doubt in the words of Telemakhos here reminds the audience that the return of Odysseus is not just a story of his own heroic success and reestablishment within a proper social sphere. It is also the means to confirm his son's identity. Until then,

Telemakhos, as the child of an absent father, often manifests the mixture of shyness and overcompensating behavior associated with that status.

1.291 *Raise a mound.* Telemakhos is to construct a cenotaph for the presumed-dead Odysseus and arrange his mother's new marriage. The following advice—to kill the suitors—assumes that even if Penelopeia were to acquire a second husband they would still be a problem. It may be that the model tale of Orestes, constantly held up to Telemakhos as an example, has led Athene/Mentes to make an analogy (suitors = Aigisthos; see line 43) that is otherwise unlikely.

1.337 *Phemios, many other songs.* This passage and a stretch of book 8 concerning Demodokos are the primary Homeric depictions of poets at work. The bard is a singer, who accompanies himself on a stringed instrument (the *phorminx*) that resembles a lyre. His repertoire apparently includes any number of tales of heroes and gods, so that an audience (Penelopeia here) can request its preferred songs. The notion that songs are "charming" was taken literally: the power of human performance in Homer is implicitly like that of the Sirens or the Muses, able to exert a fascination on its audience. Since Phemios has been performing during the entire conversation between Telemakhos and Athene, it seems that he also provides a sort of background music to the feasts of the suitors. Of course, they in particular want to hear the stories of how the other Greek heroes came home, because that song-cycle pointedly cannot speak of Odysseus, whose fate at this stage is unknown, and whom they would prefer to obliterate from bardic memory. Telemakhos's spirited speech to his mother sounds like a serious anticensorship plea, but we should probably not take this at face value. His defense of the newest poetry is appropriate for his youth, yet the poem has already pointed out his own inexperience, and his remark about ruling the house (line 359) is obviously an empty boast.

1.412 *sensible answer.* A regular adjective describing Telemakhos is "sensible, prudent" (*pepnumenos*). In the Greek, the word applies to the youth, not the reply; the translator has made the slight adjustment here for emphasis. The growing subtlety and awareness on the part of Telemakhos, even in the first book of the poem, is marked not only by the recurrent epithet but by his way of revealing to the dangerous suitors here only half the truth concerning Athene's visit. His new and mature stature makes an interesting juxtaposition with the final scene of the book (lines 425–44), where Telemakhos seems to revert to being a child, put to bed by his nurse.

2.7 *to assembly.* This Ithakan institution resembles a council of nobles, similar to the elite gatherings of Greek commanders in the *Iliad*, yet in a village setting. The ruling house—here represented by Telemakhos—apparently has the right to call its meetings, but not exclusively (see lines 28–29). There is no hint that the gathering has voting rights or any independent power of action, although a general assembly (*ekklêsia*) where individuals had free speech was to become the hallmark of Athenian democracy after the late sixth century B.C. Much as we may wish to, it is unwise to use this passage as a source for political history. Not only is the date of the poem's composition unknown (see Introduction, "Poem and Poet"); the assembly and its procedures may be an archaism, the Homeric poet's way of imagining institutions well before his time, perhaps tinged with details of his own era.

2.20 *his last meal.* This is one of the few details in the narrative that give outside confirmation of the tale Odysseus tells in books 9 through 12. Most of what we learn about his encounters with the Kuklops and other strange hosts comes only in the hero's personal, perhaps exaggerated, narration. The split among the sons of Aiguptios (one son a suitor, another a crew member, two farmers) suggests workers at three levels of social activity: kingship (as the winning suitor will be Penelopeia's consort), war (with Odysseus at Troy), and agriculture. The French comparative mythologist Georges Dumézil (see Bibliography) has argued that such a "trifunctional" social configuration, seen in ancient Roman, Greek, Indic, Iranian, and Celtic civilizations, goes back to the early Indo-European cultural period (ca. 3000 B.C.) before these groups of people speaking related languages spread to their later historical homelands.

2.77 *pressing my own case.* Ancient Greek legal systems, even in the Classical period (500–300 B.C.), had no public prosecutors or lawyers. The necessity to recover one's own goods, preferably by persuasion, meant eloquence was prized, and eventually in the fifth century B.C., formally taught as rhetoric. The system was also dependent on a highly developed sense of shame: wrongdoers would not want to be denounced publicly. Early Greece has been called a "shame culture" as opposed to a "guilt culture" because its ethical, religious, and legal institutions seem to emphasize proper behavior in public rather than an internalized sense of sin. In such an environment, getting caught in the wrong is worse than the actual deed. Certain traits of Odysseus's behavior—his lies and tricks, for example—have to be evaluated in this light.

2.80 *throwing the scepter.* This scene inevitably recalls the passage in book 1 of the *Iliad* (lines 233–45) where another young warrior, Akhilleus, histrionically throws down the scepter (the sign of the right to speak in assembly) with an oath that he will not fight for the Greeks since he has been deprived of his rightful war-prize. Akhilleus makes a powerful speech, full of high rhetoric, and refrains from crying. If an audience did know both passages, the differences between the *Iliad* scene and this one are as significant as the resemblances: Telemakhos is clearly less mature and less rhetorically creative. If one poet was *not* responsible for composing both the *Iliad* and the *Odyssey*, it is nevertheless not necessary to suppose that an *Odyssey* poet copied an Iliadic scene or vice versa. Rather, the composers of either poem might have drawn independently on a conventional gesture and its description in the irrecoverably lost poetic tradition.

2.104 *So every day at the huge loom.* The story of the web is told in pieces throughout the poem in recollections by various characters (here, by the most hateful of the suitors, Antinoos; later by Penelopeia herself). If not for the traitorous serving women, the rather obtuse suitors would never have caught on to the trick, it seems. The motif of weaving is connected in this poem with female intelligence and cunning. Both Kalupso and Kirke, the divine nymphs, work the loom. Athene, the goddess of craft, is also the crafty weaver of plans and ruses. The trick of Laertes' shroud, woven and unwoven, not only characterizes the wife of Odysseus from the start as being his equal in strategic intelligence. Antinoos takes it as an aspect of what puts this woman above the famous wives of past heroes (lines 119–21). The image also harmonizes with an essential ambiguity on Ithaka: is Odysseus alive or dead? Penelopeia, even after she ceases to weave and undo her work, retains the mental habit of going back and forth between these options.

2.135 *fearsome Avengers.* The Erinus, or Furies, were horrific female divinities who hounded anyone guilty of crimes against kin. Often, they carried out the final curse of the victim. They originated at the beginning of the world, from drops of blood that fell to earth when Kronos castrated his father, Ouranos. In the *Eumenides* of Aeschylus (458 B.C.), Orestes is pursued relentlessly by the Furies roused by his revenge killing of Klutaimnestre, his mother. As Telemakhos has explicitly been compared to Orestes already in book 1, his mention of these avenging spirits is significant, in drawing attention to the contrast in fates: he will not hurt his mother, just as she will remain faithful to his father.

2.159 *reading the dark signs.* Greeks believed in omens, whether from animal behavior (especially that of birds), celestial phenomena like eclipses, dream visions, the appearance of entrails after animal sacrifice, or overheard voices. Yet no fixed meanings were attached to particular signs. Interpreters, like the seer Halitherses, made their own readings through a sort of analogy—sometimes seemingly inexact—with the current situation they faced. Although we hear that Zeus himself sent the eagles (his favored bird), their unusual flight and fight provide no obvious clue for the resulting interpretation, that Odysseus is on the verge of a vengeful return. The refusal of an arrogant character (here, Eurumakhos) to heed a prophet foreshadows his eventual punishment, a motif later exploited by Sophocles in his tragedies *Oedipus the King* (ca. 424 B.C.) and *Antigone* (ca. 440 B.C.).

2.234 *kind as a father.* In the analogy by Mentor, Odysseus is the "father" of his people, who fail, for their part, to pay him respect. Telemakhos, by implication, is the only good son. The comparison of king to father made sense especially in a palace-centered economy, as in the Minoan or Mycenaean periods (see Introduction, "History and the *Odyssey*"), where the prosperity of one man ensured that of the entire community, and his failure or death diminished all. The problem, in Mentor's view, stems from a communal loss of memory. In the terms of the *Odyssey*, this represents a rejection of the very function of poetry, to keep the past alive.

2.260 *Telemakhos walked apart.* Here is another touch reminiscent of Akhilleus in the *Iliad*, who paces the beach (*Il.*1.350) while calling on his sea-nymph mother Thetis for aid. Athene responds here, both a mother figure (given her gender and the *Iliad* resonances) and a father figure (since she appears in the guise of Mentor, described at line 226 as entrusted with the house of Odysseus). Her words stress the almost mystical link between Telemakhos and Odysseus, whose power (*menos*) will enable the son to succeed, provided Telemakhos can act like his absent father.

2.329 *poisons.* Ephure, a town in western Greece, was mentioned by Athene/Mentes at 1.259 as the place where Odysseus had once unsuccessfully sought poison for his bronze-tipped arrows. The anonymous suitor who speaks these lines may imply that Telemakhos shares what was viewed as a less-than-honorable propensity for chemical warfare. The technique of quoting several remarks at a time from unspecified sources is used by the poet to voice crowd reactions.

2.362 *words with a feathery swiftness.* The common Homeric phrase *epea pteroenta*, which introduces commands or polite requests, has been interpreted since ancient times as either "winged words" (like birds) or "words like arrows" (with feather-fletched ends). McCrorie perfectly captures both possibilities in this translation.

2.382 *thought of a new plan.* The goddess Athene essentially takes over the narrative plotting of the poet, bringing about in short order the manning of the ship, the suitors' sleep, the summoning of Telemakhos, embarkation, and a following wind. It is not accidental that weaving—the domain of Athene—was also a metaphor for poetic craft in ancient Greek. Storytelling, like that by the poet or Odysseus, requires the careful combination of various strands back and forth through time.

2.424 *hoisting the fir-wood mast.* This passage describing a ship setting off is a frequently recurring type-scene in the *Odyssey*. Such blocks of repeated lines make it easier for oral poets to compose while performing, but also lend a reassuring sense of proper and efficient behavior. The rhythm of Homeric epic flows from the switching between such familiar scenes and speeches that usually embody new, plot-advancing information. Type-scenes, finally, create the impression of a world governed by everyday rituals—eating, dressing, hosting, preparing for sleep—that are natural and noble in their simplicity.

3.5 *Men were offering.* The sacrifice scene that Telemakhos and his crew encounter at Pulos is the most elaborate and detailed of any in Homeric epic. The distribution and numbers—one bull for each assembly of 500—recall the systems in place throughout Greece in historical times, according to which social hierarchy and solidarity are maintained through the distribution of sacrificial meats at citywide feasts. Within each group, standing could be marked by the awarding of the best parts of the animal to the citizens with most prestige. For the poetic purposes of this epic, the harmonious, centrally organized feasting at Pulos provides a stark contrast to the suitors' selfish slaughter of Odysseus's flocks and herds. This may be the first truly functioning society that Telemakhos has ever seen.

3.23 *I'm not yet trained.* An important aspect of the education of Telemakhos in the first part of the poem, his growing rhetorical ability, is emphasized each time he makes a speech. The "close-packed speaking together" to which he refers represents the rhetorical ideal of densely argued and persuasively fluent speech—the very essence of Nestor's own speech style. The word used for "speaking" is *muthoi,* plural of the word *muthos,* from which English "myth" is derived. Originally, this word designated a particular sort of speech: public, authoritative, usually performed at length, with full attention to detail (see Martin, 1989, in the Bibliography). From this type of personal, assertive speech-act, common in assemblies, and often based on genealogical or heroic precedents, the word came to cover fictions about the past—often self-serving "myths."

3.34 *they all came crowding.* Here is another contrast with the situation on Ithaka; only Telemakhos of all the diners bothered to greet Athene/Mentes in 1.118. The emphasis here on the well-behaved Peisistratos ("he who persuades the army"), a son of Nestor, may be related to the later history of the epic. It is known that an Athenian tyrant of the same name, who traced his family origins to Pulos, had a role in organizing Homeric recitations in the later sixth century B.C. He may have influenced poets to compose episodes that placed his putative ancestors in a good light.

3.54 *Promptly she prayed.* The irony is not just that a god in disguise prays to a god, nor that Athene will fulfill her own prayer (line 62) but in the pair involved. Athene and Poseidon, in many traditional stories, are rivals. The tale of their contest to see who would name the city of Athens was well known. (Athene won when her gift of the olive-tree was favored over Poseidon's spring of water.) And in the *Odyssey*, we have heard from the start that Athene's actions to retrieve Odysseus depend on Poseidon's temporary absence from the Olumpian scene. Odysseus has been pursued by the sea-god ever since he blinded Poseidon's son, the Kuklops Poluphemos. Now the son of Odysseus offers homage to his father's nemesis. Further ironies emerge in this episode when we learn below of the wrath of Athene.

3.92 *approach your knees.* The ritualized gesture for suppliants either on the battlefield or in such encounters as these was to grasp, with one hand, the knees of the person being asked for favors and, with the other, the beard. Some scholars believe that points of the body (chin, head, knee) were thought to contain nodes of power in ancient thought. On the practical level, such a gesture immobilizes the one beseeched. Apparently, a purely verbal reference to the action would often serve the purpose. Telemakhos here assumes the position of suppliant that his father will enact several times on his return home.

3.112 *Antilokhos.* An early epic poem, the *Aethiopis* (now lost except for a brief plot summary in a later author), told how this young man was slain by the Ethiopian warrior Memnon at Troy, as he was trying to rescue his father Nestor from a tight spot in the battle. Akhilleus in revenge killed Memnon, the son of the goddess Dawn. The parallel story of Akhilleus's slaying of Hektor in revenge for the death of his friend Patroklos may have been modeled on an early oral version of the Antilokhos story.

3.135 *rage of the glow-eyed Goddess.* It emerges that the first attempts at homecoming from Troy were complicated by Athene and Zeus, who had been angered by the sacrilegious behavior of some Greeks during the last hours of their sack of the city. Typically, the gods' actions to punish mortals are aided by the humans' own mistakes. There is a "double motivation" for bad things to happen. In this case, the quarrel between Agamemnon and his brother Menelaos is explicitly the result of Athene's rage (line 136). Because the human emotions have been manipulated by the divine, mere human solutions cannot help. Even if Agamemnon stayed to make more sacrifices he could not have appeased her (line 146).

3.170 *north of Khios.* The choice of routes opposes a shorter sail, starting north of the large island of Khios off the Asia Minor coast, but without a safe haven along the way, to a longer sail south of Khios and then through the islands of the Cyclades, with plenty of harbors should need arise. Nestor and his followers risk the first option and land safely at the southern tip of Euboia, Geraistos (line 177).

3.189 *son of Akhilleus.* The reference here is to Neoptolemos, who took on the command of the Murmidon contingent from Thessaly after the death of his father at Troy. Akhilleus in the underworld asks Odysseus for news of this son and bounds away in joy when he is told of the young man's excellence in fighting and speaking (11.510–37).

3.190 *Philoktetes.* Although Nestor does not mention it, this warrior had been left to die by his fellow Greeks on an island off the coast of Troy because his festering wound from a snake-bite stank and his cries of pain disrupted the besieging army. Odysseus, in the company of Neoptolemos, brought him back to Troy at the end of the war when it became clear that only the great bow of Herakles, which had been passed down to Philoktetes, could ensure the destruction of the city. The tragedy *Philoktetes* by Sophocles paints Odysseus as a conniving and cynical rhetorician who, on their joint mission, manipulates his innocent and heroic younger companion, Neoptolemos, and even tries to get the bow while abandoning its owner. We need not assume that this version was current earlier in the tradition; if it was, Nestor's mention of the hero to the son of Odysseus would be an impolitic slip. In fact, from another lost epic, the *Little Iliad*, it appears that Odysseus first brought Neoptolemos to Troy from the island of Skuros after the return of Philoktetes.

3.221 *openly friendly.* When the *Iliad* describes divine aid to warriors in the battle before Troy, gods are usually in disguise. Akhilleus is warned by Athene (book 1) and Diomedes gets direct instruction from her (book 5); Odysseus does not seem particularly favored, although Diomedes (*Il.* 23.782) notes that Athene "stands beside and aids Odysseus, as before, like a mother."

3.251 *Was Menelaos away.* For the tale of Agamemnon's murder to be convincing, his brother must not have been available to ward off death. In the next book we hear from Menelaos himself the cause for his absence. Here, the extended telling of the violent death of Agamemnon serves once more to focus the audience on the similarities as well as crucial differences between the situation in which Telemakhos finds himself and that of the dead hero's son Orestes. The story has already achieved mythic status, but could present a dangerously inexact precedent if the son of Odysseus is unwary.

3.267 *A poet was close by.* Why choose a poet to keep an eye on Klutaimnestre? It may be that we glimpse an archaic role for poetry, as keeper of civic order through the public praise of just people and blame for wrongdoers. Such a social function for poetry is attested for ancient Sparte (see Plutarch, *Life of Lykourgos*) and seems to underly the genre of *iambos* (blame, satire, and invective verse) as practiced by archaic poets like Archilochus and Hipponax (seventh and sixth centuries B.C.). Comparative evidence from modern Africa and medieval Ireland suggests such a controlling role as well.

3.287 *Maleia's / heights.* This is the same dangerous cape at the southeast of the Peloponnese where Odysseus by his own account was blown off course to the land of the Lotos-eaters (9.81).

3.313 *don't wander far.* What began as an implicit exhortation to act like Orestes (see lines 197–200) ends with the suggestion to avoid acting like Menelaos. The parallel is so inexact that we may wonder whether the poet intends to characterize Nestor as declining in intellectual powers. For neither Menelaos nor Agamemnon ultimately stayed away from home on purpose, nor was Menelaos's wealth ever threatened. Indeed, as we shall see in the next book, his haul of goods from Egypt and elsewhere has enriched him enormously.

3.378 *Tritogeneia.* Meaning either "third-born" or "truly born" this epithet, exclusively applied to Athene, is obscure in origin but must allude to her birth from Zeus and her consequent role as the legitimate executor of his plans. Her departure in bird form recalls the similar scene in book 1 (lines 319–23) that first made Telemakhos aware that he had been speaking to a goddess. Nestor makes the epiphany more public and overtly connects it to Athene's protection of Odysseus, thus furthering the theme of "paternity disclosed." As Telemakhos comes more to resemble his father, Odysseus comes closer to home.

3.394 *Aigis.* The Aigis is a magical goat-skin, resembling a tasseled shield, with which

Zeus (and sometimes Athene) protects one side and terrifies the other in the midst of battle—hence the English phrase "under the aegis of."

3.446 *heifer's / hairs.* The cutting off of a heifer's hairs and throwing them in a fire is a symbolic act dedicating the animal to the god and indicating a life is about to depart. In the realm of Greek religious ritual it is connected with the gesture of cutting human hair at marked moments (initiation, marriage, lament for the dead). The passage as a whole is a greatly expanded instance of the recurrent type-scene of sacrifice and meal preparation. In this context, it might carry resonances of initiation ceremonies for Telemakhos, now coming of age, which could explain the poetic urge to make it so extended.

4.5 *son of Akhilleus.* The reference is to Neoptolemos, whose safe homecoming was mentioned by Nestor in 3.189. The unusual double wedding with which this book begins makes a structural parallel with book 3, which began with a community feast. It might also remind the audience that Telemakhos himself is of an age to marry.

4.11 *Megapenthes.* The name means "great grief" and must refer to the emotional state of the father, Menelaos, after Helen left him. Although a son out of wedlock by a slave woman, the young man apparently receives all the privileges of the royal house and marries well.

4.64 *hardly be low-born.* Homeric epic embodies aristocratic values as regards breeding. Menelaos assumes that because Telemakhos and Peisistratos are handsome they must be sons of kings—hardly a democratic notion.

4.81 *wandered often and suffered.* These phrases (and those at lines 267–68) recall the poem's description of Odysseus's journeys (1.1–4). Menelaos, however, undertook his voyages to the lands east and south for the purpose of gain, unlike Odysseus, whose wanderings were not intentional. Of the peoples and places listed, only the Eremboi are obscure (and were even to ancient scholars). The others would have been known to Greeks at least as early as the seventh century B.C.

4.107 *Odysseus worked.* Menelaos brings up the name without any prompting from Telemakhos, in contrast to the encounter with Nestor in the previous book, and even mentions the name of the youth who is seated before him. In a gesture that will be echoed by Odysseus among the Phaiakians, the young man covers his face with his purple cloak to hide his tears.

4.122 *resembling Artemis.* This is ironic, if we think of Artemis as the virgin goddess, since Helen has been married at least three times (to Menelaos among the Greeks, then to Paris and Deiphobos among the Trojans). Also, her rich accessories and the indoor domestic setting contrast with the woods and mountains favored by the goddess. The Egyptian origin of her staff and basket hint at the larger story of Helen's stay in that country. In a non-Homeric version (but one that may have been known to audiences), Helen never went to Troy. Instead, she was whisked away to Egypt, where she spent the duration of the war while Greeks and Trojans battled over a fake Helen, a phantom *eidôlon* created by Here. The story was told by Stesichorus (sixth century B.C.) and later dramatized in Euripides' *Helen.* In the epic version, Helen was delayed with her husband in Egypt by lack of favoring winds on their way back from Troy.

4.145 *my own shame.* Throughout this episode, Helen blames herself for deserting her husband. Whether or not she is sincere, the rhetoric fits with what she says several times in the *Iliad* (3.180, 404; 6.344, 356).

4.188 *son of the Dawn-Goddess.* The reference is to Memnon. See note to 3.112. The mention of Dawn a few lines later (194–95) increases the pathos of this brief scene, as one can imagine Peisistratos being reminded of the death of Antilokhos at each day's sunrise.

4.220 *a drug in the wine.* Helen's uncanny abilities have already been hinted at when she recognizes Telemakhos without prompting (line 143), in contrast to her husband's bluff lack of awareness. They will gain more prominence in the story to come about her trickery at Troy (lines 274–79). Her adeptness at drug administration parallels the skills of Kirke, although the poet stresses that Helen's Egyptian imports are "quite useful and helpful." The anesthetic effect of this potion, which can even counter the pain of watching violence against kin, seems intended to erase the sad memories just evoked rather than to prepare the guests for more war stories.

4.232 *Paieon's the Healer.* Later a title for Apollo in his healing role, this was originally a separate divinity, possibly of Mycenaean date, whose function was doctoring. The name is related to *paian*, a song of thanks and praise used in rituals of healing and purification (cf. the English "paean").

4.239 *relish a story.* In her own story, Helen pictures herself as a loyal Greek, who once aided Odysseus when he slipped into Troy as a spy. The (lost) epic *Little Iliad* attributed to the poet Lesches is said to have included an episode like this as a preliminary to Odysseus's stealing of the Palladium (a sacred statue of Athene, without which Troy would be vulnerable). Noticeably, Helen assigns herself a key role in her own narration. She also uses it to testify to her abiding regret while at Troy (lines 260–64). The details (Odysseus in disguise, recognition by a woman who washes him) will be repeated in the scene in book 19 in which the nurse Eurukleia, bathing the beggar/Odysseus, notices his identifying scar.

4.271 *I'll tell you a task.* Her husband's story counterpoints Helen's, as Menelaos recounts how she nearly betrayed the men within the Trojan Horse through a ventriloquism trick. Only the resolve of Odysseus kept his companions from calling out when Helen imitated their wives' voices. The action of Helen has overtones of choral lamentation as practiced by women at funerals, except Helen here imitates all the voices. All told, Helen emerges as a dangerously clever beauty—and a useful one. Because he is, through her, a son-in-law of Zeus, Menelaos will spend eternity in the paradise of the Elusian Fields (see lines 563–69). Although the opposing stories told by Helen and Menelaos indicate some degree of domestic tension and unresolved animosity, the couple retire amicably to bed (line 305).

4.343 *Philomeleides wrestling.* This is an episode otherwise unmentioned in the epics, but perhaps known to the audience. A later ancient source adds that this local king challenged all newcomers to wrestling and was put to death by Odysseus and Diomedes, who then made his tomb a place of refuge for strangers to the island. Lesbos (later home of the sixth-century lyric poets Sappho and Alcaeus) is located off the coast south of Troy.

4.351 *Gods kept me in Egypt.* Menelaos tells what he learned from an encounter with the shape-shifting Old Man of the Sea, Proteus. In details his story resembles some adventures of Odysseus: a goddess taking pity (Athene in book 1); a meeting with a helpful female (see Nausikaa in book 6 and Leukothee in book 5); instruction on how to approach the helper's parent (book 6); a crew afflicted with hunger (cf. the Island of the Sun in book 12); and a difficult path to obtain information from a prophet (cf. book 11, Teiresias). The motif of divine anger appeased by sacrifice telescopes two aspects of the stories about Odysseus, who is pursued by Poseidon but will eventually erect a shrine to the god (as Teiresias commands).

4.496 *Only two.* An ancient epic that no longer survives, the *Nostoi*, apparently related the tales of the warriors here mentioned. Aias (the "lesser" Ajax) the son of Oileus tried to rape Kassandre at Athene's altar during the sack of Troy and so incurred her wrath. Ironically, it is Poseidon who ultimately kills him for his hubristic boasts. Agamemnon's fate has been brought up already by Zeus, Mentes, and Nestor. But, in typical Homeric fashion, new information is provided each time. We now learn details about the trap set by Aigisthos and the pitiable death at a feast. The stories Menelaos transmits from Proteus are not just background exposition, but have thematic relevance for the tale of Odysseus. Aias was drowned because "grand in his folly" he angered Poseidon; Odysseus, on the other hand, will survive because he keeps his cool intelligence under control. Agamemnon was murdered by his wife's new lover; Odysseus, by contrast, will triumph because his wife remains true. In short, Odysseus will overcome the combined dangers, on sea and land, that individually destroyed these two former comrades.

4.551 *the third man.* Telemakhos finally receives the information he has sought, although how current it is he cannot know. The audience, meanwhile, recognizes in the words of Proteus precisely the situation with which the poem began (1.13–15). The poet through such harmonizing of narrative with character speech, sometimes separated by long stretches of verse, leaves the impression that he sings the truth about a cohesive, actual world of events.

4.563 *Elusian / Fields.* An alternative to the house of Aides (see book 11), this pleasant land seems reserved for favorites or relations of the gods. Other versions in Greek myth of the same ideal place, the White Island or the Isles of the Blessed, become afterlife homes for Akhilleus, Memnon, and at least some of the other heroes who fought at Thebes or Troy, as well as for Helen and Medea. It is clearly not the equivalent of heaven as a reward for good behavior. Yet Rhadamanthus (brother of the Kretan king Minos) is there, a man known from other sources as a judge over the dead, so that some distinctions may be made for admission to this pacific spot.

4.601 *I can't take horses.* Telemakhos shows yet another sign of maturity in his sensible refusal of what would be a useless, though expensive, gift and his polite excuse that he must not keep his crew waiting. The description of Ithaka emphasizes its human scale, a contrast to the nearly divine dwelling and extensive lands of Menelaos at Sparte. The stunning wine-bowl that Menelaos substitutes for his original offer is Phoenician ware, and an appropriate item for royal gift-exchanges. A number of examples of similar imported workmanship have been found at Greek sites, indicating that the circulation of such goods was more than poetic conceit. There is a mythical touch, on the other hand, in the notion that this and all truly exceptional metalwork in Homer descends from Hephaistos the smith.

4.625 *Suitors meanwhile.* The shift in scene is rare within the space of one book of Homeric poetry. Here, it is done with cinematic dissolve effect, as we move from a feast in the palace at Sparte to the unruly feasting of the suitors in Ithaka.

4.653 *I saw Mentor.* Another ironic moment, as Noemon ("The Clever One") does a mental double-take. Perhaps he saw Mentor, or a god who looked like Mentor; but if so, Mentor, seen recently on Ithaka, was supposed to have gone to Pulos. Part of the appeal of the *Odyssey* is its attention to wry humor and to such vignettes.

4.677 *Medon the herald told her.* The novelistic technique, overheard conversation, has been employed once before in this book (line 76). Its use here enables the poet to intensify the air of crisis by making the audience aware of the suitors' plan to kill Telemakhos and then of his mother's frightened reaction. Her subsequent speech to the serving women (line 722ff.) is marked by several conventions found in laments, including praise of the (presumed) deceased and rebuke for those who failed to prevent the disaster.

4.762 *Hear me.* Penelopeia's prayer takes the conventional form "if ever . . . then now," as she reminds Athene of Odysseus's previous sacrificial offerings in her honor. Mortal relations with the gods in Greek religion pivot on such contractual arrangements in which past favors are exchanged for present help. As in Roman religion, the principle governing prayer and sacrifice can be expressed in the formula *do ut des* ("I give in order that you give").

4.796 *She made a figure.* The phantasm or *eidôlon* of Penelopeia's sister acts like other god-sent dreams in epic, to deliver messages and reassure the recipient. The further refusal of the image to answer Penelopeia's questions about Odysseus reminds us of the dodges and shifts by Proteus before his revelations. Having declined "to be windy" (line 837) the *eidôlon*, oddly enough, then flies off to join "a night-wind's breath" (line 839).

5.1 *by lordly Tithonos.* Dawn's mortal lover, a brother of Priam of Troy, was made immortal by the gods after his abduction by her, but continued to age until he shriveled up, as she forgot to beg that he be eternally young. At the stage of the relationship described in this opening line, Tithonos is apparently still desirable. But this cautionary exemplum about the harm that goddesses cause their lovers would have been known to an ancient audience. A version of it appears in the roughly contemporary *Hymn to Aphrodite*. It is completely appropriate to the situation of Odysseus with Kalupso in book 5—and the line is uniquely used here in the poem.

5.5 *Athene recalled and counted.* This conversation on Olumpos between Zeus and Athene recalls their earlier meeting as the *Odyssey* began. Critics in the nineteenth century wanted to cut one or the other scene. But important new points are in fact made in this repetition of the council motif. First, Athene elevates the fate of Odysseus into a test case for human behavior in time to come: if the just king is forgotten, why should any future king be kind? Second, the reply of Zeus takes into account what Athene has accomplished in the meantime, between books 1 and 5. By inspiring Telemakhos to take action, to sail to find news of his father, she has prompted his enemies, the suitors, to conspire in attempting his murder. Zeus knows his daughter's cunning mind. He refers to this sequence of events as if it were an entrapment devised to make Odysseus's eventual killing of the suitors all the more defensible. Of course, it is not beyond the Homeric gods to act this way, as combination prosecutors, advocates, and undercover provocateurs. It is part of their paradoxically "human" divine nature.

5.43 *Splendor of Argos.* "Argeiphontês" is one of the many obscure epithets of Hermes. Another interpretation of the word is "Slayer of Argos." In the first case, Argos is the territory of the eastern Peloponnese, or the city-state by that name, and the second part of the compound adjective is derived from *phainein*, "shine." In the second, Argos is the name of a divine herdsman with one hundred eyes, charged with guarding Io, the paramour of Zeus, after she was turned into a heifer by a jealous Here. Argos was lulled to sleep and slain by Hermes, working for Zeus; Here placed his eyes in the tail of her favorite bird, the peacock.

5.93 *filled with ambrosia.* Nectar is the drink and ambrosia the food of the gods. The latter means literally "immortality" while the former might have signified "going past death" according to some linguists. The gods, so much like humans in other ways, do not have blood in their veins but a clear substance called *ikhôr.* A Greek folk belief that red meat made red blood might underlie the notion. In later texts (such as Aristophanes' play *Birds*), the gods are depicted as dependent on the savory smoke of burnt offerings, an idea that may explain Hermes' remark at line 101 concerning a dearth of towns that could provide sacrifices.

5.121 *chose her Orion.* Like the Tithonos story (see 5.1 above), here is an example for mortals of the dangers of getting too close to goddesses. In one version, Artemis, jealous that Dawn had Orion (a half-mortal son of Poseidon) as lover, shot him with her arrows. He was thereafter elevated to be a constellation. Not much is known of Iasion, whose intercourse with Demeter is reminiscent of agricultural fertility ritual. He played some role in the mysteries of the goddess at Eleusis near Athens. Significantly, Kalupso fails to grasp the force of her own tales and instead of seeing what message they contain for a mortal, views these events only as indications of divine jealousy.

5.153 *a pleasure / no longer.* Kalupso, a nymph, is one of the innumerable lesser divinities inhabiting the Greek landscape. A Greek audience would have heard ominous overtones in the nymph's very name, since a nearly identical word, with one slight pitch variation, means "I will hide" or "I will bury." Ancient (and modern) Greek superstition holds that contact with nymphs can make men crazy—a condition called "nympholepsy." When we first see Odysseus in the poem, he has been living for seven years with Kalupso on her island, unwilling to accept her offer of immortality, yet unable to sail home. Odysseus, although he could choose not to die, wants only to go back to Ithaka. To the nymph's mind, his yearning to choose pain and mortality instead of her is senseless. Yet Odysseus is simply choosing the defining features of what it is to be human. Perhaps he also remembers the unfortunate fates of other men who got involved with goddesses (see above). Even when Kalupso has finally given him a way to leave, Odysseus suspects a divine trick (lines 173–79).

5.185 *Stux's water.* The underworld river, with a name related to the word for "hate," Stux was also the supreme oath witness for gods. In other sources, the name is that of a divinity, daughter of Okeanos, the cosmic river. The *Theogony* of Hesiod (contemporary with the *Odyssey*) says that gods who violate this oath must go one year without nectar and ambrosia and endure nine years of exile from Mount Olumpus.

5.195 *He sat in the chair.* A subtle poetic indication of the affinity between trickster god and cunning human hero. Later in the poem (19.397–98) we learn that Hermes taught the art of thievery to Autolukos, the maternal grandfather of Odysseus. At the same time, the two types of food laid out here—immortal for the nymph, and human for the "death-bound" Odysseus—draw attention to the gulf between the man and the gods.

5.243 *he cut down trees.* Craftiness and craftsmanship are related aspects of the "cunning intelligence" (*mêtis*) attributed constantly to this hero by his regular epithet *polumêtis*. His excellent survival skills might raise questions about why he has not already crafted a boat to escape Kalupso's island. Has she up to this time hidden the required bronze tools? The construction involved is more like that of a ship than a raft (as the simile also implies), since Odysseus fits together wooden planks rather than lashing together timber.

5.272 *watching the Pleiades.* This is the only Homeric reference to navigation by stars. Greeks used Ursa Major (the Great Bear, or Wagon) as a guide, while Phoenician sailors relied for orientation toward the north on the more accurate Ursa Minor. The general direction taken by Odysseus here is easterly. The islands of Kalupso, Kirke, and the Kuklops are vaguely positioned, generically described, and probably meant to be fantasy locations. This has not stopped scholars and adventurers from making claims about the geography of the *Odyssey*, according to which his various ports of call range from Corfu to Malta to the Hebrides. The craze for pinning down and rationalizing myth in this way had begun already in later antiquity.

5.283 *Solumoi Mountains.* These mountains were located in Lycia, a region of what is now southwest Turkey. The gods are credited with supernatural powers of sight.

5.306 *Danaans.* This is one of three commonly used names for the Greeks in Homeric epic, the others being Akhaians (see line 311) and Argives. No special distinctions can be detected among the terms. In this storm scene, famously imitated by the Roman poet Virgil (*Aeneid* 1.94–141), Odysseus expresses the crux of his dilemma: death at sea means loss of any public glory, whereas death in battle could be observed and commemorated, leading to a place for the deceased in epic verse.

5.321 *his clothes.* A suspicious person, as Odysseus seems to be (cf. lines 174–76 and 357), might conjecture that this was Kalupso's intent in giving Odysseus fine clothes; or it could be that her divine unawareness of human realities (like drowning) is once more hinted at. The episode at this point revolves around whether Odysseus should abandon the (male) clothing given by one goddess in exchange for the (female) veil of another. Changes of clothes and even transvestism at Greek transition rituals (such as initiations) are well known symbolic markers.

5.333 *Ino.* One of the daughters of the mortal Kadmos of Thebes, her story would have been well known. Because she acted as nursemaid for the infant Dionusos, Ino and her husband Athamas were driven mad by Here, and she leapt into the sea at Corinth with her child Melikertes (Honey-cutter). The gods transformed her and she was renamed "White Goddess" (Leukothee). Apparently a divinity that protected sailors, the goddess was worshiped in temples throughout Greece. Her role here recalls the magical female helpmate of many folktales.

5.394 *As welcome a sight.* A densely meaningful simile in which roles seem reversed. In reality, Odysseus is the father whose safety has been uppermost in the mind of his child. Yet here he is implicitly compared to the children who welcome a father's return to health after a dangerous illness. The view of solid land is thus focalized, emotionally, through the view of someone like Telemakhos rather than Odysseus—an artful way of reminding us of the subject of the last four books. Such reverse similes occur with increasing frequency as the poem proceeds.

5.422 *Amphitrite*. Amphitrite was a daughter of the sea-god Nereus and a wife of Poseidon; her name is sometimes used simply as a synonym for "sea."

5.437 *foresight*. This gift of Athene (who is after all daughter of Mêtis, "cunning intelligence") consists in using indirection and counterintuitive action. In this case, swimming away from the shore and diagonally outward saves Odysseus.

5.474 *So he pondered*. A recurrent type-scene in both the *Iliad* and the *Odyssey*, particularly associated with Odysseus, this dilemma soliloquy, often addressed to the character's "spirit," externalizes the narrative choices that the poet himself has in his repertoire. By convention, the second option mentioned is chosen as "the better."

5.477 *olive and wild thorn*. The combination of cultivated and natural vegetation might be taken to symbolize the dual character of Odysseus, who is, until his return, somewhere between the wild and the tame, raw and cooked, beast and man. His likeness to a lion (as he meets Nausikaa in book 6) and his clinging to the ram in the Kuklops's cave reiterate this impression, imagistically. The eventual return to civilization, home, and long-desired hearth is foreshadowed in the comparison of the sleeping Odysseus to a firebrand (line 488).

6.5 *close to the overprevailing Kuklops*. The initial proximity of the Phaiakians to the Kuklops seems like an inessential detail until we hear Odysseus's story in book 9 of his encounter with the same "overprevailing" clan. Whether or not he knows this bit of local history, it helps his chances of befriending the Phaiakians when he makes them believe that he and they have a common enemy.

6.9 *He walled their city*. These typical tasks of the founder of a colony would have been familiar, as Greek city-states in the eighth century B.C. had begun a rapid overseas expansion into areas as far west as Marseilles and as far east as the Black Sea.

6.11 *Aides' / house*. Aides' house is more familiar as the house of Hades, god of the underworld. The Greek word was thought to be related to an adjective meaning "unseen" (cf. the English "hell" from a root meaning "covered over").

6.25 *so careless*. Out of all the possible ways of introducing us to Nausikaa, the poet chose to show her neglecting the dirty laundry lying around her room. It is one of the naturalistic details in this poem that rings familiar: even in Homeric times, teenagers had messy rooms. But the topic of clothing has wider social ramifications. As Athene (in dream form) tells the girl, she'll soon be married, and people expect to see a well-dressed wedding party. This vignette brilliantly sets the mood for the episode to follow. Since we know that Nausikaa is just ripe for marriage, though no suitor is specified, her encounter with Odysseus, who washes up near the laundry pools, takes on overtones of erotic potential.

6.57 *My dear Dad*. The Greek uses a term (*pappa*) similar in tone. Critics even in later antiquity complained that a princess would not do laundry, let alone drive her own cart (based on their notions of royal privileges). More interesting is the characterization. Nausikaa disguises her motives for going to the washing-place, saying her father and brothers need clean clothes, and thereby stressing present familial obligation, whereas the real prompting of Athene's call stressed the potential connection to a new family, by way of marriage. The moment is charged with the erotic overtones of the latter possibility when she meets Odysseus, whom several will subsequently identify as a good choice for husband. In another artful touch, the poet shows how the girl's father sees through her mild deception and "sensed it all."

6.102 *looking like Artemis.* The huntress goddess, daughter of Leto (see line 106), was also the divinity who presided over the initiation of girls into womanhood. At shrine sites such as Brauron, east of Athens, young girls regularly spent months in service to the goddess. Their activities, as represented in surviving vase paintings, statues, and inscriptions, included athletic competitions and organized choral dancing. The scene here, with competition (in washing, no less), ball-playing, and group leader Nausikaa, inevitably calls to mind the ritual institutions of Artemis. Teugeton is the mountain-range near Sparte and Erumanthos is in Arcadia, in the center of the Peloponnese.

6.130 *like a mountain lion.* In light of the previous simile, the comparison of Odysseus to a lion makes an interesting contrast. Although we might view him as a beastly threat to the virginal girl on the beach, his likeness to the lion implies through image that Nausikaa (who is like Artemis the huntress) will have a sort of power over him. Naked and helpless, lion-like Odysseus ironically at this juncture is in the hands of a young woman.

6.149 *I clasp your knees.* The supplication gesture is purely in words, since we have just heard that he refrains from touching the girl in order not to alarm her. Odysseus's subsequent speech is a model of decorum and rhetorical art. Not only does he open the practical question of her divine or human status; he takes the opportunity to elaborate this into a flattering compliment to the girl's beauty. In addition, he delicately broaches the topic of her engagement and makes clear his own status as a veteran warrior and leader of men. Soon, with the help of Athene, he will appear to Nausikaa as the ideal type of husband (line 244ff.).

6.181–82 *closeness of two good / minds.* In Greek one noun expresses the concept: *homophrosunê* (literally, "like-mindedness"). This general statement applies perfectly to the case of Odysseus and his thoughtful wife Penelopeia, who will together prove a "sting" to their rivals. Such an explicit praise of marriage as the meeting of true minds is rarely found in ancient literature.

6.273 *Their talk is disgraceful.* Nausikaa's worries about rumor fit the evidence from archaic Greece concerning the social effect of praise and blame. The poetry of this period called *iambos* (from which "iambic" meter is named) comprises stylized expressions of blame, invective, and abuse. Marriage and engagement feature among the topics of *iambos* attributed to Archilochus of Paros (seventh century B.C.). The jealous commentary of the sailors, as Nausikaa imagines it, focuses on the way in which she is thought to prefer another man instead of her island suitors—surely another reminder of the situation of Penelopeia back on Ithaka. At the same time, Nausikaa uses this imagined conversation to express indirectly the wish that someone like Odysseus could be her husband. Her father (7.313–15) explicitly wishes for the hero as son-in-law.

6.305 *my Mother.* Arete, the queen, appears to have power even over the king on Skherie.

This has been taken as a relic of an earlier cultural stage of matriarchy, with the mythical Phaiakians preserving a system that a few scholars believe may have preceded the patriarchal social structures of archaic Greece. Hard evidence of matriarchy (apart from myths) is lacking, however, for any stage of Greek civilization. Arete's prominence here is more likely due to the narrator's desire to juxtapose her situation with that of Penelopeia, and to motivate the long Catalogue of Women passage in the upcoming underworld description of book 11, for which Arete will be in the audience.

7.56 *Nausithoos first.* Athene, posing as a young girl, provides the background to the royal house. That the great-grandfather of the current king once ruled the Giants is surprising, as these were commonly depicted as the enemies of the Olumpian gods. It is also worth noting that the Phaiakian house traces its roots to Poseidon, the god whom Odysseus will describe to them as his personal nemesis. That he can persuade the god's descendants to help him may be as much a matter of his own charm and rhetorical ability as it is of Phaiakian hospitality.

7.74 *she settles quarrels.* In other passages, this is an ability attributed to kings in assemblies. The *Theogony* of Hesiod (roughly contemporary with Homeric poetry) mentions the resolution of disputes as one of the tasks that an ideal ruler carries out.

7.80 *she came to Marathon.* Marathon is the site of the famous battle in which Greek forces led by the Athenians defeated a Persian invading force in 490 B.C. It is perhaps significant that the ruler Peisistratos, who played a role in organizing the festival recitation of Homeric poetry, returned to Athens from one of his several times of exile in the mid-sixth century B.C. via this town on the east coast of Attica, in which he had a body of supporters. His family seems to have traced its origin to the son of Nestor who bore the same name as the late tyrant (see book 3). The house of Erekhtheus, a mythical early king of Athens, was marked by a temple on the acropolis of the city. The latest building commemorating him on the spot—the "Erekhtheum" of 435 B.C.—is still largely intact.

7.105 *weave at looms.* The king's workforce recalls the economic setup of the great palatial centers of early Greece (1600–1200 B.C.) at Knosos on Krete and Thebes and Pulos on the mainland. Inscribed clay tablets from this period, in a prealphabetic writing system (called "Linear B"), were discovered in early-twentieth-century excavations at the palace sites and decoded only after 1952. They show evidence of large-scale woolworking as well as other domestic industries. Even the existence of cloth soaked with oil (apparently for waterproofing) has been confirmed by these earliest Greek documents. Such widespread expertise at the loom further marks Skherie as a place friendly to the craft-goddess Athene, and thus a suitable refuge for her favorite, Odysseus.

7.153 *in some ashes.* Odysseus had taken the position of a suppliant, humbling himself by sitting in the ashes. At the same time, his place at the hearth makes a claim on the royal couple's attention because it is the sacred center of the household, dedicated to the goddess Hestia, and a symbol of social and religious obligations toward strangers.

7.197 *the somber Spinners.* The Fates (Moirai) defined an individual's life through their cloth-working: Lakhesis (Apportioner) set the length, as of a thread; Klotho (Spinner) extended it; Atropos (Without a Turn) cut it off. The Greek world-picture at times placed the Fates above the power of Zeus, but at other times gave them a complementary or subordinate role. Often the degree of tragic emotion demanded by a particular narrative colored the individual author's precise depiction of these forces.

7.234 *she knew the handsome tunic and mantle.* Recognizing the clothes her daughter gave Odysseus, the queen wastes no time in asking pointed questions of her guest. As at Sparte, where Helen readily divined the identity of Telemakhos, the female member of the royal pair appears to be the more observant. The echoing of this motif provides yet another link-up between father and son as they make their separate journeys toward one another.

7.262–63 *a message / from Zeus.* This is a realistic detail. Although the poem's audience knows the message came from Zeus via Hermes, it also knows that Odysseus was not privy to the information. Odysseus could therefore also entertain the idea that Kalupso simply changed her mind. The rest of his recollection in this book matches closely what we have heard from the narrator and thus reinforces our confidence in both hero and teller as mutually supporting witnesses.

7.321 *farther away than Euboia.* The ancient audience would hear this with some amusement and wonder, since Euboia, a large island bordering the mainland to the east, was centrally located in the Greek world and an important departure point for those going to Asia Minor or the Cycladic islands. In the mirror-like fantasy world of the far-off Phaiakians, what is close to most Greeks represents an immense distance. The presence of the mythical judge Rhadamanthus and of Tituos there makes the island a multiform of the Isles of the Blessed or Elusium, happy otherworlds that Greek myth located at the edge of the known world (and which one would never dream of reaching in a single day's sail). This interesting small detail thus reveals a poet capable of imagining the relativity of cultural myths and values.

8.44 *Demodokos.* The bard's name (meaning "welcomed-by-the-people") signals his central role in the community. His "gift" of song is explained (line 64) as a compensation for his blindness. Since ancient times, audiences have understood Demodokos to be a portrait of Homer himself, who was traditionally represented as without sight. There are problems with taking this equation too literally: for one thing, we see Demodokos sing only short compositions (three in all)—nothing like the massive length of the *Odyssey* itself, which would have lasted approximately twenty-four hours even if performed at a fairly rapid rate. A combination of time periods may underlie the portrait of the singer of tales. Like Phemios, the Ithakan singer, he is apparently supported by an elite patron in a palace setting, as would be likely in the high Mycenaean period (1600–1200 B.C.). But his name indicates a status more akin to that of itinerant poets as known from later Greece and depicted in various ancient *Lives* of Homer (post-fifth century B.C.). The poet of the *Odyssey* may have resembled the latter while portraying in his poem an attractive fantasy about the former, the tenured palace jobs once available to bards.

8.76 *They had quarreled.* This scene captures the praise from the bardlike hero Odysseus for a fellow tale-teller. It also clues us in to an otherwise latent motif, that of a past conflict between Akhilleus (the hero of the *Iliad*) and Odysseus. The incident is not attested in any other source. Odysseus and Akhilleus once exchanged harsh words at the start of the expedition to Troy. It appears that Agamemnon had sought the divine guidance of Apollo at his shrine in Delphi (Putho, line 81) and was told, in typically ambiguous fashion, that Troy was to fall after the "best of the Akhaians" quarreled. Interpreting as the significant event this minor squabble between his two subordinate commanders, Agamemnon was glad, not realizing that his own disastrous struggle with Akhilleus was what the god foretold. In book 9 of the *Iliad*, we see hints of a traditional rivalry between the heroes of the two major Homeric epics; similar hints emerge in the underworld scene of the *Odyssey* (book 11).

8.111 *Akroneus rose.* The Phaiakians bear names that reflect their seamanship. In the order they occur here, these are Bowsprit, Swift-sea, Oar-driver, Sailor, Stern-man, Shore-man, Rower, Open-sea, Bow-man, Runner, Embarker, Sea-girt, son of Many-ships and grandson of Shipwright, and Broad-sea, son of Ship-caster.

8.147 *So long as a man is alive.* The high value set on athletic competition parallels the rise of international festivals in the eighth to sixth centuries B.C. featuring sporting events at centers such as Olumpia, Delphi, Nemea, and Athens. The elaborate poetry of Pindar (ca. 518–438 B.C.), who was commissioned by victors to praise their success, crystalizes this attitude, according to which athletics was the main alternative to war when it came to winning fame in the Greek world. That Odysseus views the games as less serious matters suggests a social consciousness similar to that expressed by later poets (such as Xenophanes, sixth century B.C.) who questioned the adulation for athletes at the expense of civic virtue. Eurualos's insult—calling Odysseus a cargo trader—sounds like the denigration of merchants voiced by some aristocratic factions in the Greek archaic age.

8.215 *about polished bows.* The first hint of his identity comes from Odysseus at this point in connection with his favored weapon. Now the Phaiakians will know that their guest is a Trojan War veteran and expert bowman. So central was this manner of attack to the character of Odysseus that his son was called "Telemakhos"—"Far-fighter"—in commemoration of the archer's role, which was to fight from the rear in battle formation. The skill of Odysseus at shooting arrows will figure most prominently in his final victory over the suitors. Philoktetes (line 219), the only better bowman, was abandoned by the Greeks soon after they reached Troy, because his festering wound from a snake-bite and cries of pain disturbed their rites. Troy was fated to be taken with his bow, which once belonged to Herakles. The story of Odysseus's devious plan to retrieve it is told in Sophocles' *Philoktetes.*

8.266 *a delightful / song.* At a break in athletic contests, the bard plays and sings to accompany some expert young dancers who perform before the all-male audience. His subject is the illicit love between the war-god Ares and Aphrodite, wife of the divine smith Hephaistos. It is a story of *mêtis*—the highly prized "cunning intelligence" of the Greeks—winning against might. Although lame and slow, Hephaistos is so skilled at his craft that he can fashion invisible chains to ensnare the adulterous couple in bed. The tale's bawdy treatment of a faithless wife counterpoints the larger narrative about Penelopeia, while the victory of *mêtis* described here foreshadows Odysseus's eventual success against the suitors, as well as Penelopeia's skill at crafting another type of disappearing web.

8.352 *how could I bind you.* This may be an early reference to something resembling the later legal institution of bail bond. Hephaistos's concern may allude to the watery nature of the god. The typical legal recourse of binding an offender and bringing him to justice would not work if Ares defaulted and the slippery Poseidon was left to go pay the security for him, by offering his own body.

8.363 *Paphos.* Paphos was a city on the island of Kupros famous for its shrines to the goddess of love. It is the setting for several famous myths connected with her, such as that of Pygmalion, the sculptor whose prayers Aphrodite answered when she made a beautiful statue he was obsessed with turn into a real woman.

8.392 *clean mantle and tunic.* When Odysseus reached Skherie, the land of the Phaiakians, his reentry to civilized life was marked by Nausikaa's compassionate act of lending him her brothers' clothes. Though his identity is still unknown to the girl's royal parents, Odysseus has shown such rare decorum that they treat him as a special guest. His wardrobe benefits, with the addition of thirteen new cloaks and tunics, gifts of the king and local nobles. Clothing in Homer often comes with stories about its origins. Therefore, as well as marking the new status of Odysseus, these gifts of the Phaiakians are surely meant to advertise their own grandiose hospitality. The hero is bound to transmit their fame, whenever someone later asks him where he obtained such beautiful outfits. The bronze sword from Eurualos (symbol of the youth's apology) and the golden goblet of Alkinoos will play a similar commemorative role.

8.448 *a crafty knot.* Such an unusual detail provides a sense of depth and verisimilitude, assuring the audience in advance that the adventures Odysseus is about to relate really occurred. His motive for quickly doing as Arete suggests will become clear when we hear later of how his crew once undid an easier knot tying up a bag of winds, with disastrous results.

8.475 *carving a slab.* Odysseus lavishly praises the bard again, honors him by presenting him the best cut of roast pork, and commissions a song-performance. He calls for a famous story in which Odysseus himself had a major role, the building of the Trojan Horse. In return, he promises to spread the bard's fame if the tale is told well. In the appreciative comments here, we see the value that Homeric characters place on truth and realism in narrative. These are precisely the qualities that the outer narrative, the *Odyssey* itself, foregrounds for its own listeners, even in its most fantastic episodes.

8.518 *Deiphobos's house.* After the death of Paris in the last year of the war, this Trojan noble took Helen as bride. Sprung from their hiding place in the Horse, Odysseus and Menelaos—Helen's true husband—head first for the place where they might recover the woman for whose sake they had fought so long. The remarkable simile that follows (lines 523–30) compares Odysseus himself, as he weeps hearing the story, to a woman captured in war. This is not the only time the hero becomes assimilated to a long-suffering female figure. His reunion with Penelopeia in book 23 features another "reverse-gender" comparison. Through such subtle poetic overtones, Odysseus and his wife are brought ever closer, at least in the audience's minds, as the poem progresses.

8.580 *so a song would arise.* Here a poet's theological perspective is put into the mouth of the Phaiakian king: the Trojan War was divinely arranged to provide entertainment for later generations. As with the gift of song-making given to Demodokos in compensation for blindness, there is a sense that the beautiful heritage of epic poetry, arising from strife and ruin, somehow redeems and transforms the suffering of the past. For the Phaiakians, the story about Odysseus is as distant as any enjoyable fiction. But for the hero himself, the poet's rendition causes something like a flashback to combat. Significantly, it is Odysseus's tears—not martial or athletic prowess—that lead to revealing his identity.

9.25 *My island is lower.* This description has puzzled readers since antiquity, as a traveler finds Ithaka to be just as high as nearby islands and certainly farther *east*—that is, *closer* to "Dawn and the Sun-God" (line 26) than Same (modern Kephalonia). The objections, of course, assume that the Homeric Ithaka is the same as the island today called Ithaki or Thiaki; a few scholars have played with the idea that ancient Ithaka was in fact the modern Leukada or Kephalonia. (Doulikhion, in line 24, has never been identified.) Two considerations may help reconcile poetic description with reality. First, Ithaka lies off the northeast coast of the much larger Kephalonia, and its working harbors are in fact farther north than those on the big island. Thus, when one sails from the Peloponnese (the path intended by Odysseus and actually taken by Telemakhos), the port seems farther off and "well out to sea." If "Dawn and the Sun-God" is a combination expressing "southeast" rather than simply "east," the line is even more accurate. Second, we should take the description as expressing poetic character more than sailors' directions. Odysseus himself "lies apart" from any group, and often lies low; he is "rough" (line 27), but ultimately good for his young man, Telemakhos. Island matches king.

9.40 *Ismaros.* Ismaros was a town in Thrace. We are not yet in mythical territory. The Kikones were allies of the Trojans, so that Odysseus's piracy could be taken as intentional harassment of the enemy. The casual summary of killing, looting, and stealing women, however, is disturbing and reveals yet another side of the warrior. The failure of the crew to obey Odysseus rather than see to their own pleasures will be repeated several times in the adventures, culminating in their eating of the sun-god's cattle.

9.81 *from Kuthereia, rounding Maleia.* The point of Maleia, at the tip of the easternmost promontory of the Peloponnese, was notoriously difficult for sailors to round. Ideally, Odysseus would have approached Kuthereia, an island to the southwest of the point and then sailed northwest, skirting the mainland. After this location, all the places he lands lie in mythical territory. The Lotos-eaters' land (line 84) might represent a region of North Africa; the location of the Kuklops is even more vague.

9.84 *their food is a flower.* The various strange peoples Odysseus encounters are marked by un-Greek cuisine, whether narcotic plants or human flesh. The lotos may have been a poppy. His desire to find out what "bread-eating" people live in the area (line 89) expresses the Greek norm: civilized folk raise grain crops, which implies use of domestic animals, sacrifice, and the proper rituals toward the gods. The Kuklops have crops but no agricultural labor (line 109) and thus no notion of work and suffering—fundamental to Greek ideas about what mortal life entails.

9.112 *They don't make laws.* The essentials of Greek life are defined by this list of what the Kuklops lack. Civic activity—assemblies, taking counsel—is seen as an advance on rough individualism, and a sign of caring for one another. The island of wild goats that Odysseus goes on to describe (line 116ff.) further crystalizes the differences. Kuklops have no ships or interest in colonizing fertile territory.

9.174 *to find and test those people.* Odysseus in the course of his journeys poses a test for the social groups he encounters, prompting either just behavior—epitomized by hospitality—or its opposite. This role continues when he reaches Ithaka in disguise and experiences the injustice of the suitors. As in many Greek and Roman myths, the unknown stranger, who is sometimes a god in disguise, can inflict punishment on those who fail to welcome him. The tales thus reinforce an essential ethical system, based on the mutual justice of *xenia* ("guest-friendship"), through which strangers are treated as potential future hosts and vice-versa. Zeus, the God of guests (line 270), oversaw the correct working of this reciprocity.

9.229 *I wanted to see the man.* Often, it is the intellectual curiosity of Odysseus that lands the crew in trouble. The choice here—whether to steal or participate in a potential guest-gift exchange—contrasts two modes of life (piracy versus aristocratic economy) and two kinds of character (trickster versus forthright hero). His crew does not even consider the first alternative. As the episode unfolds, Odysseus will be seen to switch tactics in order to survive.

9.283 *The Earth-Shaker Poseidon.* The audience has known since the start of the poem (1.68) that the sea-god fathered this Kuklops, but Odysseus is unaware of the fact. The Giant's disdain of Zeus (line 275) can be related to his confidence in his own ancestry, as son of Zeus's brother. Immediately on hearing that Poseidon has battered the Greeks, the Kuklops undertakes to finish the job (line 287ff.), without any provocation. His sudden and barbaric cannibalism makes an eerie contrast with his meticulous cheese- and milk-making rituals throughout the scene.

9.353 *wine.* Even though the Kuklops seems to know about wine (line 358), he prefers milk, nor does Odysseus cut this drink with the usual proportion of twenty parts water (see line 209)—taking into account the Giant's bulk.

9.366 *My name is No-one.* Apart from setting up the punchline at the end of the episode (line 408), this stratagem also expresses the trickster-hero's ability to blend into the landscape, reducing himself to nothing (as he will in his beggar disguise later, in Ithaka). It comes halfway between the revelation that he is a Greek, one of famous Agamemnon's men (line 263), and the full (in retrospect, foolish) declaration of his identity to the Kuklops (line 504). The Greek for "No-one" is *ou tis*, which in certain syntactical constructions changes to *mê tis*—a near homonym for the noun *mêtis*, "cunning intelligence." Allegorical interpreters who read the *Odyssey* as a story of self-discovery mark this speech as a significant turning point in the hero's quest, the moment when confrontation with vast danger forces him to realize both his smallness and the extent of his resourcefulness.

9.384 *like a man with a drill-bit.* The careful poetic presentation of the stabbing of the eye includes the detail that a green olive-wood stake has taken on a red glow (line 379). Folklorists, who have compared this episode with dozens of other attestations of the same motif worldwide, note that in almost all others, the stake is iron and thus naturally reddens. But the *Odyssey* dwells on the hero's ability to transform nature. The further poetic resonances of the olive-tree in the poem are also relevant; it is associated with survival and with the goddess Athene, patron of the hero. Recall especially the sheltering tree at the end of book 5, under which Odysseus sleeps (like an ember under ashes), and the olive-tree construction of his marriage bed (book 23). As if to emphasize the admirable know-how of the Greeks, the similes clustering around this stabbing refer to ship-construction and bronze-working. Thus, the subduing of the

Kuklops, on another level, represents a sense of Greek pride in the conquest of nature through technology.

9.447 *My dear ram.* This speech increases the suspense while adding a sympathetic touch, as the Kuklops projects onto his favorite animal what he thinks the ram must feel. Ironically, No-one is clinging to the underside of the ram even as the Kuklops laments that he cannot find his enemy. Our temporary feeling for the giant shepherd may be tempered by the final wish he makes, to console himself by spattering Odysseus's brains.

9.501 *Again I answered.* Despite his crew's warning, Odysseus risks destruction by taunting the Kuklops once more. From being No-one a short time before, he now emerges as the proud son of Laertes. But his urge to reveal his name and address—the natural heroic boast of a Greek fighting on the battlefield—in this post–Trojan War world only gets him into further trouble. The Kuklops can now direct his father's wrath against a specific target, when he curses Odysseus to either die en route or arrive home alone.

9.509 *Télemos.* The name literally means "Far, son of Wide." Although we might wonder why the Kuklops ever needed a seer, the detail provides a convenient way to express the ironic contrast between what was predicted—injury at the hands of a handsome, strong hero—and the ultimate arrival of the "no-good runt" Odysseus. The structural technique of ending an episode with mention of a prophecy and its fulfillment has already been seen at the end of book 8 (line 564ff.), when Alkinoos alluded to the old man Nausithoos's foretelling of Poseidon's anger against the Phaiakians.

10.7 *wives to his own sons.* The inbred nature of this family parallels the Kuklops' social arrangements, with the un-Greek nature of the system expressed in terms of excessive self-reliance and a perverse individualism that does without connection to other clans or families.

10.51 *whether to leap from the ship.* Odysseus, in narrating his fleeting thoughts of suicide, does not say what brought him to the decision to "dumbly bear it all" and live, any more than he has ever said what motivates him to go home. This self-characterization fits with the image of a laconic hero, cunning when it comes to revealing his own mind. By contrast, he is able to relate what his crew said to one another, although he was asleep when they opened the bag of winds (lines 34–45)—as if he knows intimately the minds of others.

10.72 *worst of the living.* The sudden shift in attitude, compared with his previous generosity, is appropriate for a god of the ever-shifting winds. Aiolos interprets as fate (being hated by the Gods) what was in fact human choice and accident (the crew's resentful behavior). Throughout Homeric poetry, as in later Greek thought generally, the two explanations of events intertwine: the "will of the gods" often is another way of viewing outcomes that are of purely mortal origin.

10.86 *the paths of night and day.* This may reflect ancient knowledge about the shortness of summer nights in far northern climes, such as Scandinavia. Typically, Odysseus reacts to the scene with a practical, even profit-oriented thought. Just as he realized one could colonize the goat island near the Kuklops, so he notes that a man might double his wages in such latitudes as that of the Laistrugonians. These people present a number of similarities to the Kuklops of the previous book: gigantic and cannibalistic, they too hurl mountaintops to smash enemy ships. On the other hand, they have wooden constructions, a citadel, a king, and a palace, and the royal family has a normal-looking daughter (line 106). The motif of encountering a young princess at her tasks, near water, and being taken by her to the palace, inevitably recalls the meeting of Odysseus himself with Nausikaa. Is the hero elaborating his tale to the Phaiakians with half-fictionalized details from his recent experience on their island?

10.135 *Aiaie.* The name sounds like a Greek interjection of woe, *aiai*, found in later tragedies. The brother of Kirke, Aietes (line 137), lived in another land by this name, located on the east coast of the Black Sea and known to Greeks as the home of his daughter, the witchlike Medea, with whom Ieson eloped when he journeyed there to retrieve the Golden Fleece (see the *Argonautica* of Apollonius of Rhodius, third century B.C.). Like her niece, Kirke, too, has hints of the sorceress, such as knowledge of baneful drugs (lines 236–37).

10.212 *Mountain wolves and lions.* Odysseus subtly blends in his narration details that he could only have learned later, even though he tells the tale suspensefully stage by stage, with a minimum of background exposition. Although he does not make it plain, the possibility remains open that the stag he had shot just before was either one of the drugged animals of the nymph, or worse, a transformed human (see line 433). In a lighter vein: the simile in line 217 provides the earliest reference in literature to the institution of the doggy-bag.

10.226 *a great loom.* Kirke, Kalupso, and Penelopeia are all presented as expert weavers. Skill with cloth production was also a sign of cunning intelligence (*mêtis*), and it is no accident that Athene's sphere of influence includes being patron of such crafts as weaving and ship-building.

10.292 *this helpful plant.* Odysseus has not yet learned what happened to his crew members, as Eurulokhos, the leader of the expedition inland, noticed only that the men had vanished once inside Kirke's house. Hermes fills Odysseus in and provides him with a protective plant, called *molu* in the language of the gods. (We do not learn the human word for the plant, which, from its description, some have argued was garlic.) Several times in Homeric poetry, more often in the *Iliad*, the gods' terms for various objects are juxtaposed with human words. After analysis, the divine words most often prove to be items of high poetic diction.

10.350 *born of surrounding groves.* In ancient Greek belief, nymphs inhabited mountains, rivers, springs, and certain trees. According to some sources, the life spans of tree-nymphs were related to the length of time the trees lived.

10.410 *The way young calves.* Through the simile, the men who had *not* been transformed appear as animals, just after the ones who actually *were* have been turned back into humans. Odysseus becomes, once more, a female figure (the mother of calves, in the simile) and then something like the embodiment of his island, for the men welcome him as they would "the city and land of their fathers."

10.472 *Remember the land.* In contrast to his later years on the island of Kalupso, when he wanted to leave but could not, Odysseus has to be reminded to continue his voyage. The roles are also reversed from the usual scenario, in which Odysseus must call the crew back to duty (as in the land of the Lotos-eaters). The ultimate danger is that the hero will forget his goal. Coming soon after the description of Eurulokhos's angry refusal to obey Odysseus, these lines indicate a growing uneasiness among the crew, which will later lead to full-blown disobedience.

10.491 *Aides' household.* More familiar as Hades, the name of the god of the underworld was thought to mean "the Unseen One." His wife, Persephoneia (or Persephone), was abducted by him when she was a young maiden. The story of the grief this caused her mother, the goddess Demeter, and of the bargain that allowed her daughter to revisit the land above for part of each year, is told in the early Greek *Hymn to Demeter.* Teiresies, as the prophet of Thebes, confronted Oedipus, his king, with his unwitting crimes of parricide and incest (see the tragedy of Sophocles, *Oedipus the King*). In other myths, he was said to have been changed once into a woman, then back again, and thus knew all that either sex could. That only he of all the dead retains consciousness indicates the depth of his intelligence and the special regard in which he was held.

10.511 *deep Okeanos.* Imagined as a river encircling the known world (hence the English "ocean"), this fed all the other rivers of the world. The streams in the underworld have fearsome names: Stux (Hatred); Kokutos (Bewailed); Akheron (Groaning); Puriphlegethon (Fire-Burning).

10.518 *libations.* The practices described were performed at Greek gravesites at set times to commemorate the deceased and "feed" the spirit, so as to prevent it from being angered. The sacrifice of a black ram and ewe matches the rites performed at the graves of those thought to be heroes. As a form of communication with the dead, Odysseus's actions will prove to be successful: the ghosts of the departed will gather around to drink the blood from the pit he has made. But Teiresies in book 11 oddly enough never does give the explicit sailing directions that Kirke mentions here.

11.8 *Goddess who spoke like a woman.* The adjective *audêessa*, "having a human voice," has been applied several times to Kirke and Kalupso in the poem. It draws attention to the prophetic qualities these divinities share, for when a god takes on a human voice or disguise it is usually to warn or direct mortals. Poised at the beginning of the descent to the underworld, this brief description of Kirke reminds us that Odysseus's goal is to obtain knowledge from the ghost of the Theban seer Teiresies.

11.14 *Kimmerian people.* Later Greek tradition placed this people in the Crimea. Already in antiquity there were disputes about their true location, as well as the spelling and meaning of the name. Here, the poet uses them essentially as a marker of the farthest reaches of the flat earth (perhaps to the north, given their constant "haze and cloud"). Note that there is no actual descent to an underworld, unlike similar scenes in Virgil's *Aeneid* or the Babylonian *Gilgamesh.*

11.51 *my war-friend, Elpenor.* At the end of the previous episode, this companion had fallen from the roof of Kirke's house after a drunken sleep. Instantaneously, his spirit came to the land of the dead, while Odysseus was still sailing there. His pleas that the Greeks bury him properly reflect the ancient belief that spirits of the dead could not rest until their survivors had performed the necessary funeral rituals. In later stories, such spirits were said to linger on the far side of the river Stux, unable to take Kharon's ferry across until care had been taken of their bodies.

11.105 *if only you check your spirits.* Teiresies poses as the final challenge to self-control the cattle of the sun-god. From the first few verses of the *Odyssey*, the audience already knows that the crew will fail this test. The further foreshadowing here readies us for the second half of the poem, Odysseus's lone return to Ithaka that will end in the total slaughter of the suitors. More surprising are the seer's detailed instructions (line 121ff.) about the ultimate journey the hero must take. Folklorists have found parallels in mariners' tales from many regions for the story of a sailor who retires to a place that is as far from the sea as one can travel. Here, the spot will be recognizable when the inhabitants mistake the sailor's oar for an agricultural implement. The image of Odysseus's reconciliation, the shrine he will build to his foe Poseidon, not accidentally matches the way a sailor's own tomb would look (compare the request of Elpenor at line 77). Although this passage predicts a gentle death "from the salt sea," another popular epic, the *Telegony* (now lost except for a plot summary) recounted the hero's death at the hands of Telegonos, an illegitimate son by Kirke. This happened on the shore of Ithaka, when the son, invading the island, unknowingly attacked his own father, and stabbed him with the spine of a sea-turtle (thus causing a death "from the sea").

11.181 *Your wife has waited.* For the first time, Odysseus hears news of his immediate family, including his faithful Penelopeia, son Telemakhos, and father Laertes. His father's behavior speaks of deep depression, an affecting vignette as wrenching as his mother's claim that she died from missing him. Apparently, Antikleia did not live long enough to learn of the suitors' occupation. Her account of Telemakhos presents some chronological problems, as her description of his social life makes him sound older than he would have been at her death. But the poetic intent may be to parallel the upcoming story Odysseus tells to the spirit of Akhilleus about that hero's successful son.

11.224 *back to your wife and tell her.* With these words, Antikleia makes way for the so-called Catalogue of Women. Her phrasing seems to indicate that the parade of famous females has an educational value for women alive. We need to remember that Arete, the powerful queen, and Nausikaa, her daughter, are prominent among the Phaiakian listeners to this tale. Odysseus chooses to begin his narration by telling about the famous *women* he met because he wants to please the women in his own audience. At the same time, it could be that the poet of the *Odyssey* here plays to a mixed audience of his own.

11.235 *Turo.* Turo was the grandmother of Nestor, who can thus trace his ancestry to Poseidon. Aiolos in line 237 is not the same as the wind-god. Aison (line 259) was the father of Ieson, who was sent to fetch the Golden Fleece by his uncle, Pelies (line 254).

11.260 *Antiope.* Like Turo, Antiope was a woman connected with the great heroes and city-founders of an earlier generation. Amphion and Zethos, her sons, were said to have constructed the walls of Thebes by magically moving stones through their music-making. Homeric epic carefully avoids mention of such more exotic mythical motifs when it comes to stories of heroic saga.

11.266 *Alkmene.* Zeus came to her in the guise of her own husband Amphitruon shortly before the warrior returned from battle and rejoined his wife. The double intercourse produced twins: Herakles the son of Zeus and Iphiklos the son of the mortal husband.

11.269 *Megare.* First in a series of wives of Herakles, in some versions she was killed by her husband in a fit of madness sent by a jealous Here. Such unflattering or tragic details are often not mentioned by Homeric epic.

11.271 *Epikaste.* Epikaste is a variation on the better known name for his mother, Jocasta (as in Sophocles' drama *Oedipus the King*, ca. 424 B.C.). This brief description of the infamous deeds apparently assumes that Oidipus continued to rule at Thebes after his mother's death. There is no mention of his self-blinding or exile.

11.287 *Pero.* Pero is singled out perhaps because the story of courtship and hardship offers some parallels to the tale of Penelopeia. The fuller version of this elliptical story will be told in 15.225–56.

11.298 *Lede* (also spelled Leda). She was taken by Zeus in the form of a swan and bore Helen and Klutaimnestre—two women deeply involved in the Trojan saga but not alluded to here. Kastor and Poludeukes are also called the Dioskuroi "Zeus sons" (in Latin, Castor and Pollux, the Gemini). After Kastor was killed in combat, the pair were given alternate mortality, each one coming alive every other day.

11.310 *Orion.* Orion was a mythical hunter who was made into a constellation after being killed by Artemis, the divine huntress (see lines 572–75 below). The gigantic youths Otos and Ephialtes, who planned to put Mount Pelion, in the region of Thessaly, atop Mount Ossa in order to scale Olumpos, were a continuing example of hubris punished.

11.321 *Phaidre.* She and Ariadne were both daughters of Minos, at least in later legend. Theseus, the hero of Athens, either forgot or abandoned Ariadne after benefiting from her aid to escape from the labyrinth on Krete. He took Phaidre as wife years later; an unrequited passion for her stepson Hippolutos led her to hang herself.

11.321 *Prokris.* Prokris, an Athenian princess, was married to Kephalos, who once tested her fidelity by seducing her in disguise, and later accidentally killed her with his javelin.

11.326 *Klumene.* Klumene is an obscure figure, perhaps wife of the hero Phulakos.

11.326 *Maira.* Maira was a nymph devoted to Artemis, who slew her after the girl broke a vow of chastity.

11.326 *Eriphule.* Eriphule was the wife of Amphiaraos. She was bribed by Poluneikes the son of Oedipus to persuade her husband to join his war against Thebes.

11.328 *I cannot name them all.* When he breaks off abruptly and announces it is time for bed, Odysseus is urged by the audience to continue and shift to the story of Greek heroes he met in the underworld. Because his decision to resume comes immediately after the royal listeners promise more gifts (lines 336–53), it is reasonable to imagine that the trickster Odysseus has held the most interesting portion of his heroic tale in reserve precisely to create audience demand. The practice occurs in actual song-sessions in other oral traditions. This is one more reminder that the familiar *Odyssey* adventure stories all occur in a one-night-only command performance by Odysseus in the king's court. Like many a singer, he could embellish and time his adventures to suit his rapt audience.

11.409 *Aigisthos caused my death.* Aigisthos was the cousin of Agamemnon and Menelaos, a son of Thuestes, whose brother Atreus, during a vendetta, once served him his own children as a meal. Aigisthos survived and took vengeance by seducing Klutaimnestre, Agamemnon's wife, while the latter was at Troy. The adulterous couple then plotted the chieftain's murder, killing also Kassandre, the Trojan princess and prophetess whom Agamemnon had brought home as a captive. Agamemnon, in his advice not to trust a woman, nevertheless makes an exception regarding Penelopeia, who is described as the polar opposite of his own treacherous spouse (lines 445–46).

11.461 *My godlike Orestes.* Although neither Agamemnon nor Odysseus knows it, the son returned from his foster home to take vengeance for his father's death by killing his mother and her lover Aigisthos. The story has been alluded to several times in the early part of the poem by those wishing to persuade Telemakhos to take action against the suitors.

11.543 *the ghost of Aias* (also spelled Ajax). The tale told in the play *Ajax* by Sophocles and other versions has this warrior, second only to Akhilleus, driven to temporary insanity after losing the contest for the glorious armor of the dead hero. Believing that Odysseus and the sons of Atreus had cheated him, he attacked their tents at night, but Athene deflected his rage onto some nearby flocks. Aias, after coming to his senses, killed himself out of shame. He refuses to speak to Odysseus out of continuing resentment.

11.568 *Minos.* The Kretan king was said to have communicated regularly with his father Zeus in constructing the laws for his people. He thus became a symbol of just dealing. Tituos (line 576) by contrast was famous for his injustice, having attempted to rape Leto, the mother of Apollo and Artemis. The following examples of bad behavior were known for stealing the gods' food (Tantalos) and gossiping about Zeus's love affairs (Sisuphos); "sin" in this context means offenses against divinities, rather than failure to adhere to a moral code.

11.602 *a phantom.* Since Greeks believed Herakles had been taken up to be with the gods on Olumpos after his fiery death on Mount Oita, the poet is careful to say that his spirit is not really in the underworld. But his presence, even in phantom form, makes a good story, as he was the only other hero to journey to Aides' house and return successfully.

11.634 *Gorgo.* A monstrous figure meant to terrify one into silence. In later sources, a woman named Medusa, one of three Gorgo sisters, is decapitated by the hero Perseus before she can turn him to stone with her baleful stare. Why Persephoneia, queen of the underworld, would send the head to Odysseus is unclear. It may perhaps be a polite way of saying that there is no more to say.

12.14 *stele.* A stele is a standing stone for marking a gravesite. Many inscribed stones from the sixth century B.C. and later still survive. Alphabetic writing was known in Greece in the eighth century B.C., the earliest period to which the poems can be dated on other grounds, but the Homeric poems never make indisputable reference to writing of any kind. If this particular stele bore an inscription, the poet has omitted the fact. The epics also tend toward archaizing, suppressing references to more recent technologies and events in the interest of recreating the world of the twelfth century B.C.

12.39 *Seirenes.* The Sirens are never said to lure men to their deaths, nor is shipwreck involved: passers-by are drawn into the danger of staying forever through their own desire to hear the voices of these divine singers. Neither are they represented in the poem as bird-women, in contrast to the early Greek artistic tradition, which often portrays Sirens and Sphinxes (similar enigmatic singers). The meadow (line 45) is a common symbol for the typical place of sexual seduction in Greek poetry. It may be that the Sirens were a Near Eastern importation, from cultures in which they were known as goddesses of death.

12.60 *Amphitrite.* Amphitrite was the wife of Poseidon. The *Plangktai,* or Clashing Rocks, also figured prominently in the stories of Ieson's journey to find the Golden Fleece. Some scholars have seen in the voyages of Odysseus a poetic attempt to include and outdo earlier Argonaut traditions. At line 70, the poem makes explicit reference to the ship of Ieson (line 72), the *Argo,* as the only vessel to have made it through the moving rocks.

12.81 *Erebos.* Erebos is the dark; it is also another name for the west.

12.85 *Skulla.* The name is related to a word for puppy and both may derive from a verb meaning "to tear, rip up." Like most terrors of Greek myth, this being is conceived of as female. She acts like a giant squid that half hides in an opening in the rock face.

12.104 *Kharubdis.* Another female monster, she is indistinguishable from the whirlpool she creates. The choice is between losing the entire ship and its crew to her, or having six men be snatched up for each of Skulla's six mouths, on the other side of the narrow strait.

12.132 *Nymphs.* The nymphs have appropriate names: Lampetie is "shining" (origin of the English "lamp"); Phaethousa is "illuminating"; Huperion, another name for the sun-god, means "he who goes above"; Neaira, their mother, simply means "youthful."

12.184 *Here, well-known Odysseus.* The content of the Siren-song appeals directly to the hero's sense of self-worth: it is nothing less than his own story, since they sing about the Trojan War, which he was able to conclude by his ruse of the Horse. The statement that their performance will be a source of both knowledge and pleasure makes an apt summary of the goals of most Greek poetry of the archaic and Classical periods: its instructional value for audiences is always stressed. Some have seen in the topic they choose to sing a reference to *Iliad* traditions, in which case Odysseus, by resisting their lure and still hearing the song, goes that tradition one better, just as he has surpassed Akhilleus by getting both fame and a homecoming.

12.223 *I never told them.* Odysseus, trickster and master mariner, has made a strategic decision in keeping secret that which he knows about the fate of his crew. In later Greek literature, especially in tragic dramas such as the *Philoctetes* and *Ajax* of Sophocles, the secretive and deceptive tendencies of Odysseus make him a less than admirable character, even an emblem of amoral action. In Homer, however, there is no hint that his concealments are wrong.

12.338 *honeyed sleep.* At key moments, as when his crew opened the bag of winds, Odysseus falls asleep. Structurally within the *Odyssey,* this motif plays the same role as the absence of a god: compare the way in which the plot was put in motion in book 1 when Poseidon is away with the Ethiopians, or Hephaistos's absence as part of the adultery story of book 8. Presence and consciousness, within the *Odyssey,* are important partners. That this connection is deep within the culture, not just the poetry, may be reflected in the etymological connection between the word for consciousness or mind (*noos*) and the word for safe return to one's home (*nostos*). Odysseus, in enacting the latter, also embodies the former.

12.357 *tender greens.* The sacrifice to which the mutinous Eurulokhos leads the crew is marked out as irregular by several details. In proper ritual terms, barley was placed before the sacrificial animals and scattered on their heads; here, they must make do with leaves (which are properly used in very different rituals). Wine, too, is lacking (line 362), so the men use water. Finally, the victims *belong* to a god already, and so are hardly in the proper realm for devoting *to* the gods. In sum, this meal represents an antisacrifice. The horrid crawling of hides and mooing of the meat (lines 395–96) vividly express the inversion.

12.383 *light up the dead.* The gods work like powerful factional politicians, threatening to withdraw their favors from the other gods if their wishes are not met. The sun-god's promise to descend to the house of Aides means that crops will not grow on earth (see the stress in line 386 on "grain-giving farmland"). Without crops, there is no sacrifice, and the gods ultimately lose the worship of mortals. In this regard, the threat is exactly that made by the grain-goddess Demeter against the other Olumpians when her daughter Persephoneia was abducted by the lord of the underworld. As then, Zeus gives in to the wishes of the offended party.

12.439 *a man stands up.* The poet's choice of similes sometimes relies on the juxtaposition of crisis, once-only moments in the narrative with orderly, regularly recurring moments from normal life. To express the length of time Odysseus clung to the tree looming over the abyss, a snapshot of civic life is given. The image of a judge arising at dusk recalls the role of archaic kings in resolving disputes. Psychologically, the technique is precisely apt, since those who have survived crises most often report that their minds, at the times of keenest danger, went back to the events of everyday living. The image curiously brings to mind the description by Odysseus's mother of the way in which Telemakhos dines, like a judge (11.186). Perhaps flashing through the hero's mind is the memory of his son, and this is voiced by his later narration—after all, the simile is part of Odysseus's own poetic retelling of events.

13.13–14 *a cauldron / and large tripod.* The Phaiakians are to provide Odysseus with a swift and safe return to his own island after loading him with fantastic gifts. These include the sort of valuable items that we know were actually exchanged among aristocrats in the Greek archaic period (ca. 800–500 B.C.). Some of the items, such as bronze cauldrons, were in addition frequently dedicated to the gods at prestigious sanctuaries like Delphi and Olumpia, where Greeks from every city-state could see them displayed and hear about their donors. There is an overlap in this scene between two other cultural scenarios: that of gifting a bard for his performance and that of endowing an honored guest. For the Phaiakians, Odysseus has acted both roles. There may be a further hint, to a contemporary external audience, that good narrators—like Odysseus in the poem and the actual poet who is performing—are worth rewarding well.

13.103 *a charming cave.* Archaeologists have found many caves throughout Greece with dedications to the goat-god Pan and to the nymphs. One such site, with dedicatory objects, was discovered on Ithaka in the 1930s by members of the British School at Athens. The elaborate description offered here may reflect local knowledge of a religious site. In later antiquity, this passage was subjected to detailed allegorical interpretation by the Neo-Platonic philosopher Porphyry (ca. A.D. 232–306), who saw the cave as an image of the universe, with nymphs representing souls and men as bodies.

13.125–26 *Poseidon / recalled the threats.* Thanks to the advocacy of Athene, her favorite hero, Odysseus, has made it home. But now the clash of divine interests comes to a crisis point. It emerges that just treatment of Odysseus by the gods hinges on their own very *human* concerns, like the craving for honor. To Poseidon's complaint that he loses status because people do not see Odysseus suffering enough, Zeus responds with smooth reassurances. Poseidon cautiously avoids further direct attacks on Odysseus. Instead, he vents his anger and saves face at the same time by quite literally petrifying the Phaiakians, turning their ship to stone. Underlying such depictions of divine deal-making in Homeric epic one can discern a serious attempt on the part of Greeks to explain why bad things happen to good people. The shaping of justice in such a world depends on theological assumptions: that there is more than one powerful god, and that the gods act like honor-obsessed Greek heroes.

13.194 *everything looked quite strange.* Dropped off in the night on an island he does not yet know, Odysseus suspects that his Phaiakian escorts misled him (lines 209–12). Typ-ically practical-minded, he sets out to count his possessions to see whether he has been robbed. Athene, disguised as a young shepherd, comes along to reveal the name of his latest landfall—Ithaka. The idealized natural abundance she describes (lines 244–47) fits the mood of the narrative at this precise moment—to the eyes of Odysseus, there can be no richer, more lovely place. The one feature regularly noted as lacking on Ithaka—room for horses—marks out its king as somehow different from aristocratic, horse-breeding mainlanders. Like the island, Odysseus is more humble.

13.255 *his brain was a wizard's.* Even at the moment he lands back on Ithaka, after twenty years, the wily Odysseus still makes up protective fictions. To the young shepherd (actually Athene), he describes himself as a Trojan War veteran and fugitive murderer of a son of Idomeneus (known from the *Iliad* as a wartime companion of the hero). Some details recall the adventures he has just been through. The "shepherd" in reply (lines 291–310) not only reveals her identity but also aptly expresses her frank admira-tion for the *mêtis* (cunning intelligence) that Odysseus possesses, so much like her own. There is, in fact, a touch of one-upsmanship in her reminder that even Odysseus could not penetrate her disguise this time. A significant aspect of cunning emerges in the plan she begins to weave: namely, temporary passivity in the face of suffering, a quiet endurance that hoodwinks the enemy and pays off in the end.

13.325–26 *no, it's some other / land.* After Athene reveals herself, the wary hero continues to keep up his guard, questioning whether this unfamiliar-looking island is in fact his home. His caution—a function of his *mêtis*—seems to make the goddess value him more. Theirs, unlike other pairings in Greek myth, can never be a love relationship (as Athene is forever virgin, a *parthenos*). But in its intimacy, this encounter comes close. Goddess and hero are intellectual equals, two of a kind. As Athene compliments Odysseus and asserts her unwavering confidence, she has to address the awkward fact that she was absent for the past ten years of his wanderings. The explanation that she could not fight Poseidon rings somewhat false (since *mêtis* normally beats force). There could be here, as at several other points in the poem, a hint that Athene has been antagonistic to Odysseus, precisely because his *mêtis* equals hers.

13.397 *I'll make you unknown.* Odysseus must remain incognito, at least until he deter-mines the loyalty of his family and former supporters. Under the guidance of his patroness Athene, Odysseus will make his way, first, to the hut of his aged retainer, the swineherd Eumaios. His question about his son—whether Telemakhos, too, should "suffer pain while others devour his resources"—shows an awareness that his son's fate echoes and depends on his own. Athene's reply reminds the audience that the entire plot has been her devising and that Telemakhos, thanks to her, will win fame by his own voyage to the mainland.

14.6 *a handsome place.* The descriptions of the palaces of Menelaos, Aiolos, and Alkinoos, and the homes of Kirke and Kalupso, have all highlighted their status as near divinities. We might have expected, by contrast, that the humble keeper of Odysseus's hogs would live in a hovel, but instead he has built a solid and comfortable homestead. His natural nobility and good breeding become apparent as the poem progresses; in fact, he turns out to be a king's son, kidnapped when young. The rituals of hospitality are meticulously observed by him, all the more meaningfully since he has so little to give. His regular epithet *dios* ("shining; glorious; godlike"), otherwise reserved for heroes, points to the regard in which he is held by his master and his important role in the story of the return. That the *Odyssey* can produce sympathy for such characters, in spite of their low social standing, is a mark of its broad humanity.

14.56 *My guest.* His words to Odysseus perfectly sum up the religious reasons for guest-friendship. Yet there is irony as well in this short speech: if the man he is hosting, Odysseus, had only stayed home, Eumaios would not be living in such reduced circumstances. The hero's absence has disrupted the whole social order, leading to the suitors' notorious abuses—the opposite of the kind swineherd's heartfelt hospitality.

14.100 *twelve herds of cattle.* This full listing of the master's stock in herds and cattle, followed by the information about the suitors' depredations, calls to mind the cattle of the sun-god incident (book 12). Just as Helios, the sun-god, punished those who stole and slaughtered his oxen, so Odysseus, like an avenging divinity, will bring the unruly suitors to ruin.

14.161 *this very month.* This is the first in a series of increasingly specific and insistent prophecies in the second half of the poem. Ironically, the prophecy has already been fulfilled and comes from Odysseus himself. The time between the waning and waxing of moons seems to have coincided with a local festival of Apollo, the archer-god, an appropriate emblem for Odysseus as avenger.

14.182 *Arkeisios's bloodline.* Arkeisios was the father of an only son, Laertes, who was father in turn of one son, Odysseus. Telemakhos is the latest of the line.

14.199 *broad island of Krete.* Odysseus tells a tale of hard luck, describing how he spent years as an insatiably roving warrior from Krete, then went off to the Trojan War, and ended up kidnapped and shipwrecked. In another version of this tale, told to the suitors, he adds the detail that he was nearly enslaved on Kupros. Penelopeia hears from him yet another version, in which the beggar (her husband in disguise) pretends to have welcomed Odysseus years ago on Krete. The localization of these tales is significant, because it is probable that already audiences knew the traditional saying "All Kretans are liars." It is as if Odysseus, by claiming to come from that island, advertises the fictionality of his biographical digressions. At the same time, a subtle narrative joke has been constructed for the poet's own audience: after hearing Odysseus narrate his own adventure story for a good stretch of the poem (books 9 through 12), we are now made to see that the hero can lie expertly when he wants to. Why should we believe any of his tales? But then again, even the Muses, goddesses of poetic craft, are credited by early Greek poetry with this skill. In Hesiod's *Theogony*, a poem about the origins of the world, the Muses pay the poet a divine visit and inform him, "We know how to tell many falsehoods like true things, and also know how to tell the truth—when we want to." It is not accidental that the first of these Hesiodic lines from the Muses' declaration is used by the Homeric poet in book 19 to describe Odysseus's storytelling. Not only is the hero like the poet; he is like the poet's divine source of inspiration, a font of inventions.

14.263 *ravaged handsome fields.* The incident and description recall Odysseus's own raid on the Kikones of Thrace (9.39–61). In this fiction, however, he represents himself as a suppliant of the enemy king. Gestures of submission on the battlefield—a strategy he says Zeus inspired—caused the Egyptian king to pity him and take him under protection. In addition, the local nobles gave him gifts over the next seven years. As he sketches this ideal reception from his past, Odysseus in this speech probably hints that his hard-up present state deserves similar treatment. Every speech in the *Odyssey* depends on the poetic context for its full resonance. When Odysseus, in his beggar's disguise, tells this fictionalized life story to Eumaios, the swineherd, we should suspect that the details are not accidental. In this case, they bring up the topic once more of guest-friendship (*xenia*).

14.288 *a man arrived from Phoinikia.* The unflattering picture Odysseus paints in this speech of these seagoing traders contrasts with the helpful role he assigns them in other, later tales he tells. Eumaios, we will soon learn, was kidnapped by Phoinikians. Odysseus, as his former master, no doubt knows this detail already and therefore wins the sympathy of his audience by making the Phoinikians the villains within his story.

14.308 *like cormorants.* This detail and several of the following match the final shipwreck of Odysseus's crew, as he narrated it in 12.417ff.

14.316 *Thesprotians.* Thesprotia was Greek territory on the northwestern coast of the mainland, to the north of Ithaka and its neighboring islands. The scenario Odysseus describes—a royal child who finds him shipwrecked and leads him to the palace of a kindly king—copies the reality of his stay on Skherie among the Phaiakians.

14.327 *Dodone.* Dodone was a sanctuary dedicated to Zeus, in far northern Greek territory, near the city of Ioannina in Epiros, at which a sacred oak produced oracular responses through the rustling of its leaves. Priests of Zeus interpreted the oracles. The fictionalized version corresponds to Odysseus's journey to the underworld to seek advice for his homecoming from Teiresies the seer. Odysseus cleverly represents himself as having heard of Odysseus's trip to this site; such a visit may actually have figured within an alternative telling of the *Odyssey*, in some now lost version. Once again, the detail of near-kidnapping (line 340ff.) is meant to resonate with Eumaios's own experience.

14.379 *a man from Aitolia.* Remarkably, the tale we have just heard Odysseus make up has been anticipated by another traveling beggar. This gives the impression that the hero in crafting his fictions is borrowing from a common store of motifs—connection with Krete and Idomeneus, accumulation of great wealth—already circulating about himself.

14.469 *the time we set up an ambush.* The beggar tells this story about Odysseus in order to ask indirectly for a cloak for himself in the present time. The recollection that he narrates, about a winter ambush at Troy, summons up Odysseus as an ingenious, sympathetic commander, who invents a military mission just to keep one of his men warm. As with tricksters in many folk traditions worldwide, Odysseus thereby brings about the useful distribution and recycling of basic material goods. The irony here is that the trickster's *present* ingenuity in begging a cloak relies on telling a story about a trickster's *past* deed involving clothes. At lines 131–32 Eumaios had slyly hinted about being aware that beggars made up stories to get favors from Penelopeia. He has also shown an unwillingness to be hoodwinked himself. Whether he finally has been conned, or simply appreciates a good tale, Eumaios relents and gives Odysseus a warm cloak—but only for the night. It will be Odysseus's own son who will eventually clothe the beggar—an intriguing role reversal.

15.1 *broad Lakedaimon.* Athene goes to Sparta, in which we last saw Telemakhos at the palace of Menelaos in book 4. The juxtaposition of the arrival of Odysseus (book 13) and the departure of his son forces the audience to remark how similar the two are in thoughtfulness and strategic intelligence, even though they have been separated for twenty years. Athene's warning that the mother of Telemakhos might marry and then forget about him puts Penelopeia's character in a different light. From what the audience has already heard, this outcome appears unlikely, but enough doubt is cast here that we are sure to pay closer attention to her words and actions in the following books.

15.75 *stay till I load your car.* The artful juxtaposition of scenes of guest-friendship, from book 14 to book 15, also gives us the sense of aristocratic continuity—sons inherit their fathers' friends; they gain their own wealth and reputation by maintaining such contacts. Ironically, in the case of Telemakhos, it is the imagined *loss* of his father Odysseus that has brought him into the circle of adult exchange relationships. In the view of the hearty and voluble husband of Helen, Telemakhos is now in a position to acquire excellent goods by making the circuit of guest-friends and accepting gifts all along the tour (lines 82–85). Though Telemakhos declines it, the offer gives a glimpse of the economic and social importance attached to this key Greek institution. The silver wine-bowl, a gift to Menelaos by a Phoinikian king (lines 117–18), and the robe woven by Helen (lines 126–27), will adorn Telemakhos's own palace and bride when he comes to his full station in life.

15.160 *a bird flew by.* Omens from the flights of birds were common in all periods of Greek religion, but seem to have been subject to flexible interpretations by ordinary individuals. In this Greeks acted unlike the Romans with their elaborate science of augury and its strictly prescribed meanings, to be explained only by skilled professional priests. Menelaos delays in performing his interpretation of the sign (an eagle carrying off a goose) but the keen-witted Helen, as she had in book 4, anticipates him. Her interpretation relies on a contrast between far-off (eagle's nest, Odysseus's wanderings) and home (domestic goose), and reads the movement between these spaces as symbolic of the warrior's return.

15.201 *I must be home.* This exchange provides fine touches of characterization of both Telemakhos and Nestor. The young man knows he will be delayed by the old warrior's generous hospitality, so seeks to avoid the trip back to Pulos. And the old man's son worries that Nestor will get angry and ride halfway back to Sparta to buttonhole Telemakhos. Through such brief sketches the poet manages to round out and enliven the figures in his narrative.

15.225 *Melampous.* "Black-foot," a famous seer, is alluded to in the Catalogue of Women (ll. 292) in connection with his role in the wooing of Nestor's sister, Pero. He tried to steal the herds of Phulakos in order to provide his brother Bias with the bride-price demanded by Neleus. Captured by the herds' owner, he was imprisoned in a house where woodworms were telling one another that the beams were nearly eaten. Through his ability to hear them, Melampous warned of the fall of the roof, impressed his captor, and won release, with the cows as a further gift (for curing the impotence of Phulakos). The Erinus (line 234) is the Fury, who usually pursued those guilty of crimes against the members of the extended family. Why she is mentioned here remains obscure.

15.242 *and fathered Antiphates.* The list of descendants includes seers famous in the myth of the Seven Against Thebes, Amphiaraos and his son Alkmaion. Eriphule, wife of Amphiaraos, was given a golden necklace by Poluneikes so she would persuade her husband to go to war on his behalf. Mantios ("Seer") is the ultimate ancestor of Theoklumenos, who approaches Telemakhos at his departure, an outlaw from his native Argos (a region of the eastern Peloponnese).

15.364 *Ktimene.* Only here do we learn of the sister of Odysseus, who otherwise plays no role in the poem. The other information that Eumaios provides confirms what Odysseus's mother personally related to him in the underworld. The close relationship of Eumaios to the royal family means that he is almost a foster brother to Odysseus and a father figure for Telemakhos.

15.384 *your people's town.* The options listed are the main ways in which a person might be sold into bondage: as one taken in war or the victim of pirate slave-traders. Slavery, which supported the Greek economy from earliest antiquity, was not based on race. Other Greeks, foreigners, captives, or debtors might end up working for middle-class or wealthy masters.

15.403 *Surie.* Not Syria, but an island (probably modern Syros), in the Cyclades, between mainland Greece and western Asia Minor.

15.404 *Ortugie.* Ortugie was identified with Delos, the small islet sacred to Apollo, east of Syros.

15.455 *trading a whole year.* The Phoinikians were well known as the Mediterranean's most daring and active traders from the eleventh century B.C. on. From their home ports, in what is now southern Lebanon, they sailed as far west as Gibraltar, establishing trading-posts and transporting textiles, purple dye, and metalwork. The Greeks traced the alphabet to them, a tradition that modern scholarship confirms. Some critics suggest that Homer's seafaring Phaiakians were modeled on, and got their name from, the Phoinikians.

15.525 *on his right side.* The right side is the lucky side, in Greek bird-signs. Theoklumenos takes the opportunity to make what might be a flattering interpretation, asserting that his host and his family will retain the kingship of Ithaka. Unlike the reading done by Helen of a similar bird-sign in the previous book, this features no point-by-point symbolism—simply an equation of the stronger bird with the power of rulers.

16.17 *A loving father.* This is an ironic foreshadowing that also expresses the close relationship between the swineherd and Telemakhos. The simile suggests a double focus: a father welcomes home a son gone for ten years (just as Laertes might have welcomed Odysseus immediately after the ten-year-long Trojan War) and the father has agonized over his son (just as Odysseus has thought often of Telemakhos). These parallels and resonances make an implicit bond between the hero and his grown son, both now coming home, even before they are reunited later in the scene. In another artful touch, it is Eumaios, the surrogate father, who goes on to chide Telemakhos, like a parent, for the young man's supposed preference for staying in town with the suitors (lines 27–29).

16.62 *He claims the broad island.* In this bare-bones version of Odysseus's fictional tale, Eumaios does not repeat the flattering details that his guest supplied the previous night—how he is supposed to be of royal blood, a Trojan War veteran, and once wealthy (all of which are of course, in another context, true). Instead, he describes Odysseus as almost a runaway slave. The shrewd old man thus shows that he has hardly at all been taken in by the stories of the beggar.

16.112 *a sensible answer.* Odysseus, in his outburst, strategically sought to test his son's feelings about the situation and obtain information about the goings-on in his own house. Nowhere had there been a mention up until now of maltreatment of "women and handmaids" (line 108). But rather than taking this as a slip on the poet's part, attributing knowledge to Odysseus that he could not have, we should view the remark as simultaneously foreshadowing and characterization: the homecoming hero can only imagine the worst. His son's vigorous reply makes clear that he would fight the suitors even now, if reinforcements were available. As it is, the Odyssean line comprises a series of only sons (a further emblem of the hero's solitary character) and Telemakhos has no brothers to aid him.

16.162 *The dogs and Odysseus.* The poet pays particular attention to the reactions of animals in this episode. The fierce country dogs barked at Odysseus when he first approached, until he made a submissive gesture; they greeted Telemakhos warmly; and now they sense the advent of Athene. (Later, Odysseus's own hound will recognize him.) Odysseus is closer to animals in his keen awareness of the presence of the gods and his fierce reaction to humans he does not like. His heart "barks" (20.13–16) when he sees the shamelessness of the suitors' women companions.

16.172 *touched by the golden wand.* Odysseus experiences a series of recognitions as he works his way back into the heart of his home. A boyhood scar, a secret bed, trees in an orchard—all will serve as signs of his identity to people close to him. In the case of his son a miraculous change of clothing plays a role in the recognition, as part and symbol of a larger transformation. Thanks to Athene's rejuvenating powers, Odysseus goes from old beggar to vigorous king at a touch of a magic wand. This is the moment to which previous dressing and changing scenes have been leading: the hero has his status back. Telemakhos, however, insists that only a god could accomplish such a quick change of looks. The repeated reassurances by Odysseus that he is really only human (lines 187–189, 202–4) become themselves the ultimate token of his fatherhood: generation, growth, and decline do not matter to the gods.

16.246 *their count.* This is the first full reckoning of the number of the suitors; the total is 108 men, not counting their support staff. If the relative numbers represent the size of the suitors' homelands, "Doulikhion"—the location of which is still undetermined— might have been the large promontory of Leukada, east of Ithaka. (The poem refers to it as an island, however—see line 397—which it is now but was not in antiquity.)

16.363 *Antinoos.* The meanest suitor (his name means "antimind" or "anticonscious-ness"), he would have been gladdest to see Telemakhos ambushed. The failed attempt, as he points out, only makes the crisis worse, since the king's son now has more reason to rouse up the islanders against his would-be assailants. Another ambush must be planned. By giving voice to the suitors and their plots in this way, the poet increases the suspense and quickens the pace of the narrative, while preparing the audience for the death of such unsympathetic figures. That one suitor, Amphinomos, is more restrained in his approach (lines 394–405) complicates the rationale behind the final slaughter.

16.417 *reviled him.* Penelopeia has been seen previously in her mourning or humbly following her son's command. Her pointed words to Antinoos reveal other aspects of this complex woman: rhetorical ability, historical awareness, pride, and courage. As her husband comes closer to home, the feisty and intelligent queen whom he first took as his bride begins to emerge. It is easy to imagine her as first cousin to the high-spirited (and dangerous) Helen and Klutaimnestre.

17.37 *looking like Artemis.* Penelopeia is poised between two goddesses, one the virgin huntress, the other goddess of love. The brief, double comparison captures an ambi-guity about her future in the plot: is she to marry one of the suitors, or remain mourning for her husband?

17.151 *Godlike Theoklumenos spoke.* The seer's name means "hearing the god" and his words carry authority, given his prophetic ancestry. His comment at this point goes beyond what he told Telemakhos on embarking. The urgency and specificity added to the prophecy—that Odysseus is on Ithaka even as they speak—will increase the ten-sion during the interview between the beggar and Penelopeia, since it may well be that the old man is the warrior come home.

17.172 *Medon.* As herald, his role was to announce sacrifices, and thus, major meals; it seems that originally such *kêrukes* were official singers at the rituals. The central civic nature of sacrifice required an authority figure to announce who would receive which portion of the animal—the major way in which social and professional groups were to be distinguished in everyday life. By working only for the suitors, Medon seems to have abandoned any wider social role, or to have shrunk and collapsed the broader society of Ithaka down to the size of one family, at the unruly household of his employers.

17.205–6 *a well-built / fountain.* On Ithaka, the nymphs are associated with two important places—a cave near the harbor, where Odysseus stores his goods when he first arrives home, and an ancient, tree-shaded spring of cold water, constructed by Ithakos, the distant and obscure hero for whom the island was named. At this fountain near the town, wayfarers made their small offerings to the local divinities of the waters. It appears that Odysseus, according to his swineherd, had in the past regularly made larger sacrifices to the nymphs. True to the quid pro quo principle of Greek religion, the swineherd can ask for divine aid now by reminding the nymphs of what they formerly received. Ironically, he prays while in the presence of Odysseus, whose iden-tity is still hidden from the other Ithakans, such as the surly goat-herd, Melantheus, who accosts him here.

17.291 *a dog lying nearby.* The hound's name, Argos ("Flash"), makes a sad contrast with his present condition. Just as the growth of his son offers a tangible marker of how long Odysseus has been away, so the dog's debility embodies twenty years of neglect—a symbol for the decline of the whole household. His outward appearance matches the ragged look of his master in beggar's guise. One of the most pathetic moments in the poem is this recognition scene, which Odysseus, in order to save his cover, must pretend is not happening. The dog's death, unseen by his old master, surely was meant to milk a tear from the audience.

17.384 *A prophet, a healer.* The list gives a glimpse of social conditions in a postpalatial economy, where wandering experts are summoned from a distance, instead of being employed on site by local kings. Healer and prophet could be the same; Apollo is an example of the combination. On the other hand, poets could compare their craft to carpentry, in an old metaphor for fitting together a composition. The inclusion of singers with the other professions named may hint at the true status of the Homeric poet. Instead of resembling Phemios, the Ithakan palace bard whose music floats through this episode, the epic performer more likely circulated from town to town or frequented regional festivals where bards competed.

17.412 *Having tested Akhaians.* The purpose of Odysseus's begging goes beyond gathering information. Like a representative of Zeus, the patron of strangers, he probes the crowd to find out who is generous and who is stingy. This function is later made explicit (line 482ff.), when younger suitors remind Antinoos that gods roam the earth in human form to check on mortal behavior. The formal curse Odysseus makes against the churlish Antinoos (lines 475–76) will, of course, come true.

17.443 *to Kupros.* The rest of the details jibe with Odysseus's original story to Eumaios, but he substitutes this far-off island as his most recent stop, perhaps to throw the suitors off the scent. From other brief mentions (e.g., 16.427), it is clear that Thesprotia (his last stop in the earlier version of his tale) was among regions familiar to Odysseus and allied with the Ithakans even before his journey to Troy. Bringing up the name could have alerted his enemies.

17.494 *So may Apollo.* Penelopeia's wish corresponds to her husband's curse against Antinoos. Having uttered it, she might well think later, once Odysseus has shot the suitors, that a god came down to the palace in person to carry out this revenge. Her disbelieving response to her nurse says as much (23.63–64). Penelopeia's immediate reaction—to summon the injured beggar so as to ask him about Odysseus—may also have been anticipated by the hero when he chose to upbraid Antinoos. The not-unexpected abuse that results becomes the quickest way for Odysseus to gain his wife's company.

17.518 *stare at a poet.* We have already seen Odysseus acting the part of the bardlike storyteller in books 9 through 12, all of which are in his own voice. Now Eumaios confirms the effect that this man can have on an audience. The comment is also a reflection (by the poet) about the high value of his own art of Homeric song: this medium can literally enchant the listener. The activities of the Muses, the Sirens, and the bard are thus united in their magical powers.

17.541 *Telemakhos sneezed loudly.* Like the flight of birds, this sudden event can be taken as an omen. The content of the previous speech is thereby endorsed as about to come true. What was hypothetical in Penelopeia's remarks (see lines 539–40) has now been transformed into a near certainty. Part of the complex artistry of these episodes arises from the triangulation of opinion, feeling, prophecy, and reaction, with Odysseus, Telemakhos, and Penelopeia each shaping a part of the plot, and often predicting or praying for certain outcomes.

17.570 *wait until sunset.* Odysseus has observed the continual presence of the suitors and also the housemaids, whom he may already suspect of sympathizing with the enemy. His strategic decision to delay the interview with the queen has also been taken by some critics to imply that he will attempt to reveal his identity to her during their evening meeting. Already his wife takes the delay as a sign of the stranger's cleverness (line 586) and her suspicion may grow that he is none other than Odysseus.

18.6 *Iros.* The nickname plays on the name of the divine messenger and goddess of the rainbow, Iris. The unfortunate beggar's real name, Arnaios, means something like "Lamb-man" and the fact that his mother, rather than father, named him indicates he was most likely illegitimate. The apparently digressive episode of the spat between Iros and Odysseus allows for suspense to build further. It also recalls the hero's intolerance for bullying (as in the encounter with Euryalos among the Phaiakians, book 8), and sets up a satisfying knock-down fight. Finally, the structure of the event might remind us of the long-ago quarrel between the "best of the Akhaians," Odysseus and Akhilleus, at a banquet, alluded to in Demodokos's song. Just as Agamemnon's joy at that event (8.78) was later reversed, so here Antinoos's delight can soon be expected to turn to sorrow.

18.85 *King Ekhetos.* The king is a mythical bogey-man, it appears, whose name means "Grabber" and whose methods suit the title.

18.129 *Listen and take heed.* Victor in the fight, and jokingly honored by the suitors, Odysseus, in the character of wise veteran, takes the opportunity to sermonize about the unavoidable justice of the gods. The speech embodies an archaic Greek worldview, one that can be seen as well in the poetry of Hesiod, Aeschylus, and the lyric poets. In its essentials, this view holds that humans are helplessly dependent on the whim of the gods for success, failure, or the mental attitudes they hold from one day to the next; that hope and optimism are delusive; that greed, arrogance, and injustice will inevitably be punished; and that humble acceptance of divine will is best. The message is underlined by the poet's added detail, that even Amphinomos, a suitor who has seemed less bad than others, will die at the final reckoning.

18.161 *She'd make herself esteemed.* In one of the most puzzling passages in the poem, it is unclear whether Penelopeia knows that her husband is the beggar in the hall and wishes to make him see her act; wants to marry another now, to flirt with the suitors, or to extract from them more gifts; or desires to force Telemakhos to proclaim his maturity through her chiding—thus enabling her to marry again (see lines 269–70). Some combination of these motives may be at work. Or it may be that the poet means to depict a whim on the queen's part (and therefore notes the "silly laugh" with which Penelopeia speaks to her maid). She refuses to make herself up with cosmetics, but Athene beautifies her anyway. And she expresses the wish to die a gentle death even as she has acted as if either a new wedding or longed-for husband is near. If we are confused and intrigued by her behavior, those who see her have their own conclusions:

the suitor Eurumakhos takes the chance to flatter her, perhaps thinking she is on the verge of choosing him; Telemakhos treats her with cool rationality; and Odysseus happily assumes she is adding to his wealth by extorting more courting gifts.

18.259 *Ah my woman.* The farther the poem progresses in time, the more we learn about the past history of Odysseus and his family. This is an emotionally apt time for Penelopeia to reveal her husband's parting instructions. The maturing process of Telemakhos can now be seen as a key to whether his mother will wed. (Thus the foregrounding of the son's adventures in books 1 through 4 makes more sense.) While lamenting her approaching remarriage, the queen takes the opportunity to pile blame on the suitors for their backward way of courting. And her audience gets the point, sending their servants off to provide her with heaps of clothes and jewelry.

18.321 *Melantho.* Her brother, the similarly named Melanthios ("Blackened"), has already accosted Odysseus (book 17). The further motif here, of an ungrateful young person raised in the house, makes a contrast with the story of Eumaios and recalls what Penelopeia has revealed about Antinoos's upbringing. Melantho's terror at Odysseus's violent verbal response can only please an audience. Naturally, given what we hear about her relations with Eurumakhos (line 325), that suitor now takes the opportunity to mock Odysseus and to aim a footstool at him.

18.410 *biting their lips.* Telemakhos has gained full rhetorical ability with the assurance that the suitors' doom is closing in. In recognition of his forcefulness, Amphinomos backs up the young man's commands and disperses the unruly revelers.

19.33 *Pallas Athene.* The impressive display of god-sent light also plays on the notion, evident in the Greek, that "justice" (*dikê*) is a form of display, of "pointing out" (from the verb *deiknumi*). The "way of the Gods" (line 43) is literally illuminated for mortals who collaborate with them. Odysseus's calm assurance that the divinity is at work characterizes him as the tried and true hero, in contrast to the anxious awe of his son at this miraculous light.

19.96 *Eurunome.* Like Melantho, she seems to be working in the hall all through the conversation between husband and wife. If there is to be a recognition scene, Odysseus is surely aware of disloyal onlookers like Melantho, and will avoid showing his identity. We can expect a form of coded communication between the couple as a result. On the other hand, it could be that Penelopeia (as the majority of critics still maintains) only has suspicions and is not yet aware that her husband is seated before her.

19.109 *faultless king's.* Those in favor of a coded communication here argue that Odysseus's indirect reply, with an elaborate praise and reference to kingship, is a way of pointing to his own true character. He is the king whose presence in the land will lead to renewal.

19.138 *The shroud came first.* In proof of her loyalty to her husband, Penelopeia recounts her famous ruse. Like the cunning Athene, she is renowned for her expertise at handicraft—specifically, weaving. This skill, emblematic of the good wife in Greek culture, enabled her to buy time and save herself from remarrying. She did so by a doubly cunning device: weaving alone involves craft, but unweaving—a contrary, seemingly useless act—turns out to be even craftier. And when the suitors after three years discovered the ruse, Penelopeia's cunning rhetoric continued to put them off. A significant detail is that Penelopeia claimed to be weaving a shroud for Laertes: in other words, completion of the cloth would be a sign of impending death. Symbolically, this fatal image applies to Penelopeia's own situation, for finishing the shroud would mean she has to give up hope that her first husband is alive, and take another. The further signs she mentions—her son's maturity, her parents' urging, and the suitors' impatience—heighten the sense of crisis.

19.163 *not from storied oak.* This proverb apparently alludes to archaic beliefs that some humans (as well as nymphs) could come from features of the landscape or the earth itself.

19.172 *Krete's a lovely land.* As the center of pre-Greek high culture in the area, this large island had already by Homeric times established a reputation for ancient traditional beliefs and a large, mixed population. Akhaians may designate Mycenaean-age Greek settlers while "Kretans from old times" seems to refer to pre-Greek inhabitants (the so-called Minoans). The "three clear strains" of the Dorians were the traditional three tribal groups into which this more recent set of Greek-speaking settlers divided. Pelasgians were thought to be another group of pre-Greek inhabitants, whose identity remains unknown. Knosos, now a major tourist site, has been excavated by the British since 1900; it was the site of a vast palace complex connected with the stories of the labyrinth and of mythical King Minos (hence "Minoan" was the name given by discoverer Arthur Evans to the civilization).

19.183 *Aithon.* After boasting of a prestigious genealogy, going back to Zeus, Odysseus calls himself "Blazing" (an epithet applied to both fire and hunger). The name of his true island, Ithaka, probably comes from the same root.

19.188 *Amnisos.* Another pre-Greek site from the Minoan age (ca. 1600 B.C.) on Krete. Eileithuie was a goddess of childbirth worshiped there.

19.215 *testing you closely.* A match for her cunning husband, Penelopeia wants proof that the stranger has in fact hosted Odysseus some years ago. She thus provides the opportunity for Odysseus to recount in exquisite detail the very clothing he was wearing twenty years before, as also the look of the trusty companion he had with him. If she at this point realizes that only Odysseus himself would know such signs, Penelopeia does an expert job of concealing her recognition, even going so far as to assert that she will never again see her husband (line 257ff.).

19.271 *The man's close by.* The beggar's insistence might be taken as a signal that "close by" means "here" and the reference to the Thesprotians—where he himself has just come from—could prompt the equation of beggar and hero. Odysseus even reveals his own recent adventures with the Phaiakians, imputing them to the "Odysseus" who is to come. His mention of the matchless schemes of the trickster might, finally, be meant as reassurance to his wife that he is now in control.

19.346 *an older handmaid.* Rejecting Penelopeia's offer of a more comfortable bed, he accepts the idea of a footbath, but only if given by a hard-worn woman. The choosing of Eurukleia by the queen is made with explicit acknowledgment that this maid had been Odysseus's nurse. Penelopeia's comments (line 358ff.) on the likeness of the beggar to her husband, in terms of his projected aging, at least heighten the suspense, if they are not already a signal that she knows he is Odysseus. The nurse's apostrophe at line 363 to her (supposedly absent) master pours on more irony.

19.390 *thinking 'the scar.'* It is difficult to imagine that the man who plans every move simply forgot that his mark of identity could be discovered in this manner. As with the rest of the scene, motivations remain intriguingly obscure. Did Odysseus intend that his old nurse recognize him? Or did Penelopeia select her for the job of footwashing knowing that this might reveal who the stranger is? Like a trapdoor in the narrative, the mention of the scar triggers a long flashback to explain how Odysseus came to bear this mark, in the course of which we learn the familial roots of his cunning and the significance of the hero's name.

19.394 *Parnesos.* Parnesos was the well-known mountain behind Apollo's temple at Delphi. The *Hymn to Hermes* (ca. sixth century B.C.), which tells the story of the cooperation and exchange between Apollo and his newborn half brother Hermes, may be a clue to the connection of Autolukos ("Real Wolf") and this locale. Hermes, god of communication, trade, and thievery, possesses the sort of cunning intelligence that is a necessary complement (in Greek terms) to the authoritative power of Zeus and his older son Apollo. As we hear at this point the maternal grandfather of Odysseus and the one who actually named him learned the arts of "swearing and stealing" directly from Hermes. By swearing, the poet means the art of making *false* oaths: so Odysseus's skillful tale-telling runs in the family. The translator faithfully preserves what is a pun in the original Greek—the similarity between the verb form "being the object of anger" (*odussamenos*) and the name Odysseus. In the terms of the poem, the hero is "at odds" with gods and mortals, yet survives despite (or because of) this antipathy.

19.452 *Odysseus caught him.* The boar-hunt at his grandfather's marked the young man's first kill, an important, almost Faulknerian, initiatory moment. It is significant for our appreciation of Odysseus's character that the childhood naming scene is telescoped in this flashback with the vignette of coming of age, over both of which the Hermes-figure, Autolukos presides. A further interesting detail: the thicket from which the boar lunges (lines 439–43) is described exactly as was the shelter that kept Odysseus safe on Skherie just after his final shipwreck (5.478–85), hinting at a link between heroic identity (a scar from his first boar) and ultimate survival (salvation by concealment).

19.479 *shifted her thoughts.* The queen fails to notice the flurry of activity. In a simpler epic, the scar would have led to outright recognition and the reunion of the long-separated couple. The *Odyssey* poet's sense of realistic detail and consistency of character, however, demands that all precautions be taken and all steps described before the final resolution. Odysseus still needs the element of surprise to overcome 108 men: letting his nurse tell Penelopeia now would risk spreading the news, especially if other maidservants, like the disloyal Melantho, are still in the vicinity. Gagging and threatening the old woman, Odysseus resembles the man who once engineered the successful Trojan Horse ambush by muzzling the companion who would cry out (see 4.287–88).

19.518 *Pandareos's daughter.* Aedon (her name means "nightingale"), daughter of the king of Krete, married Zethos, king of Thebes, but was jealous that her new sister-in-law Niobe had more children. Attempting to kill one of them at night, she mistakenly slew her own son, Itus (or Itulos), and was transformed into a bird. The myth explains the bird's mournful song. (It did not bother the Greeks that it is actually the male nightingale that sings.) Although Penelopeia makes this comparison to express her own variability (cf. lines 521 and 524), the theme of a son's (potential) death is also relevant to what Telemakhos has just gone through. It is psychologically apt that he weighs on the mother's mind, as it is characteristic that she projects onto her *son* (her own?) desire that she marry and go off (line 533ff.).

19.535 *explain it.* Penelopeia might invite his interpretation simply because she has already noticed the beggar's cleverness, or, if she suspects his identity, might be fishing for further confirmation through his response to her enigmatic dream. As critics have noted, the symbolism is actually interpreted within the dream itself: the eagle that killed her geese announces that he is her husband (line 549). We need not assume that her grief at the death of the geese indicates unconscious desire for the suitors' presence, as her mourning for them occurs in the dream *before* the explanation. Odysseus asserts the truth of the internal explanation, but Penelopeia (line 560ff.), either uncertain or still concealing her real intuitions, resorts to another mythic allusion, the gates of horn and ivory, in denying truth to her dream. Etymological puns connect "ivory" (*elephas*) with "deceive" (*elephairomai*) and "horn" (*keras*) with "fulfill" (*kraino*). Those who think the entire interview has been a coded communication point out that it is precisely now, after Odysseus's reassuring "interpretation" asserting his own presence back in Ithaka, that Penelopeia decides on the marriage-test, the contest with the arrows and axes (lines 572–78).

20.14 *the way a dog will growl.* In the similes that follow we hear echoes of recent scenes in the narrative, much in the way that dreams reconfigure the real events of the day. The protective dog recalls Argos, the aged hound of Odysseus, while the stomach packed with blood (lines 25–26) brings to mind the beggar's reward for defeating Iros (18.44–45). Such poetic touches create the sense that narrator and hero are working within the same frame of reference, or even that the narrator is like the hero (just as Odysseus was like the narrator, for books 9 through 12).

20.30 *Athene came to him.* Odysseus agonizes about how to kill the 108 suitors who boss around his servants, have their way with the housemaids, and eat up all his livelihood. In the midst of his doubt and anxiety, the goddess Athene appears to him, in a remarkably beautiful epiphany all the more noteworthy for its depiction of the tender, protective care of a goddess for a mortal, a moment that would not be out of place in the devotional literature of medieval Christianity. Yet Athene, bringer of light, is here promising her hero something more than religious comfort. The virgin goddess will see to it that Odysseus and his small band of retainers execute a merciless slaughter.

20.66 *Pandareos's daughters.* This is the same king mentioned in 19.518; in another version, his three daughters (Aedon, Merope, and Kleothera) were swept away because their father had offended the gods. The point of the allusion seems to lie in its emotional resonance: Penelopeia's own experiences have meant she can identify both with the loneliness of the orphaned girls (now) and their good fortune (as when she was with Odysseus). In addition, her impending remarriage strikes her as worse than death, and the thought of young girls spirited away before their weddings is, in a paradoxical way, consoling. The motif as death-as-marriage (or the inverse) structures the myth of Persephone and occurs throughout Greek tragedy.

20.303 *upbraiding Ktesippos.* This is the third time within a few episodes that a suitor has aimed an object at Odysseus, but the only time Telemakhos has responded with such a threat. The growing confidence of the young man emerges in his speech. Looking back on his life, Telemakhos remarks on his previous inability to fight, then asserts he is now ready to die, repeating exactly what Odysseus, still unrecognized, had said to him earlier (16.106–11).

20.346 *to laugh wildly.* The bizarre, divinely induced laughter signals the loss of control and imminent destruction of the guilty. If good order goes with justice in the early Greek worldview, then men whose laughs are like tears of mourning and whose food is bloodied and inedible are the image of chaos. Theoklumenos, the seer who has traveled with Telemakhos, sees into the future within the space of the same banquet room, where these men will die.

21.14 *Iphitos, Eurutos's son.* The flashback is thematically relevant in the context of guest-friendship and its abuse. Upon meeting in Messene (a region southwest of Sparte), Odysseus and this doomed hero had exchanged gifts of weaponry, as might be expected among aristocratic warriors. Later, Iphitos was murdered by Herakles, although a guest in the latter's house. In a variation on the theme, Odysseus will slay uninvited and abusive "guests" in his own house with the very gift of Iphitos. Symbolically, at least, the earlier victim has revenge.

21.42 *she came to the storeroom.* Penelopeia's great strength lies in her powerful memory. In this, she resembles the poet himself, a link that perhaps explains the narrator's sympathy for the character. As she prepares for the marriage-contest that will decide her fate, the wife of Odysseus ventures into the storeroom to bring out his great bow. The sight and feel of it unleash overwhelming memories. Nor are we the only ones to sense her fine imagination in this vignette. Penelopeia herself seems to recognize her susceptibility to the past, and tells the suitors that even after a new marriage she will still dream of her old home (lines 78–79). Making her assertion all the more powerful is the poet's technique here. The solid, finely carved dark interior of the storeroom has been depicted with the painterly care of a Dutch master, making tangible the house Penelopeia will lose and the enduring love it had sheltered.

21.123 *He'd never seen them.* The uncanny knowledge that Telemakhos has about how to set up the feat matches his inborn ability to accomplish his father's feat of stringing the bow. For there is little doubt that he would have, had not Odysseus prevented it (line 129). The insistence on the continuity of heroic virtue gives rise to the interesting paradox that the only one worthy of winning Penelopeia in the contest of strength is her own son (as inheritor of his father's skills). The Homeric poet leaves to the tellers of Oedipus myths any exploration of this theme, however. In pretending to be incapable, Telemakhos resembles his father all the more, disguising his true strength and purpose until the time is ripe.

21.186 *Antinoos held off.* Counterpointing the hints of impending doom (lines 98–100, 153–54) is the crescendo effect of the trial of the bow, with the stronger and better known leaders of the suitors reserved for the last. Just at the point where the poet might have turned to their attempt, he moves to the revelation of Odysseus to his servants (lines 207–25), thus cementing alliances for the final battle and allowing the hero to orchestrate the total destruction.

21.259 *Who'd bend a bow.* Although it seems a shooting contest would be entirely appropriate for a feast-day of Apollo, the archer-god, Antinoos uses the festivity as an excuse to delay the final test of his own strength, apparently shaken at the failure of Eurumakhos. The mention of the god underlines the significance of Odysseus's action: his role will match Apollo's, just as his vengeance recalls that of the sun-god, Helios.

21.295 *Wine once crazed.* Dramatic irony arises from what we sense will be the fate of the speaker. Antinoos cites as a mythic exemplum for keeping order at a feast the well-known story of the Lapiths, a human clan whose king was Pirithoos (a companion of Theseus) and the Kentaurs, the hybrid horse-men of Thessaly in northeastern Greece. At the wedding of Pirithoos, the Kentaur Eurution tried to steal the bride; the resulting battle left many of his fellows dead. The story was represented as a human victory over forces of disorder, most prominently on the pediment of the temple of Zeus at Olumpia. In this sculptural group (large fragments of which survive) the central figure, an upright Apollo, effortlessly wards off the attacking beast-men. In the *Odyssey* passage, Antinoos, intent on taking the king's woman, unwittingly plays the Kentaur figure while Odysseus will assume the ordering function of Apollo.

21.350 *go to your room.* Penelopeia has insisted that the beggar get the bow, leading the audience once more to suspect that this chance for Odysseus to participate in the contest was prearranged. If so, the reaction of Telemakhos might be a cover: he does not want to make his mother's role obvious. At the same time, his words are appropriate, given the leaps in confidence that he has been making since Athene's intervention in his life. The nearly identical wording of lines 352-53 and 1.358-59 forces the reminiscence of his earlier command to his mother, when she had wanted Phemios the bard to stop singing. As that episode marked the start of Telemakhos's growth trajectory, so this signals the completion.

21.406 *as a man skilled with a lyre.* Among the Phaiakians, it was the bard's last song, about the fall of Troy, that finally led Odysseus to reveal his own identity. When he returns home to Ithaka soon thereafter, it is once again a marked association with song and music that spotlights Odysseus. When Odysseus tries his hand at stringing the great bow, in the poet's resonant simile system the master bowman becomes a musician; the sound of the bowstring itself is described in terms of bird-song. Through the power of condensed metaphors, the double abilities of Odysseus—master performer and unerring marksman—become united. The picture makes sense within the Homeric worldview, where words themselves are "winged" or "feathered" like arrows. Rhetoric, song, and bowmanship—all spring from Odysseus's cunning intelligence.

22.8 *Antinoos first.* The moment of revelation has arrived. Odysseus begins his revenge by shooting down the loudest, meanest suitor. As the others scatter in panic, Odysseus pronounces their death sentence. But why must *all* the suitors be slain? Odysseus mentions three offenses: theft of his goods, forced sex with his housemaids, and the courting of Penelopeia while he was alive. Eurumakhos, the most reasonable suitor, fails to propitiate Odysseus with a promise of restitution (lines 55-59), because these offenses have so deeply threatened the hero's home and honor. The scene recalls a key point in the *Iliad*, when the chief hero, Akhilleus, dismisses the lavish gifts of Agamemnon, who has dishonored him. In both cases, symbolic capital, a warrior's reputation and ability to defend his possessions, far outweighs material compensation. Unbound by modern legal or ethical notions, Odyssean justice recognizes nearly unlimited revenge. This is the most troubling dimension of the poem. As it turns out, Zeus and Athene will have to intervene to stop the vendetta that this slaughter ignites.

22.88 *Death-mist promptly flowed.* This and other phrases in the scene narrating wounds and death are identical to formulas used in the *Iliad* to describe the battle between Greeks and Trojans. Poetically, Odysseus's revenge is the equivalent of an international war, one that also happened to have been fought over a woman, the cousin of Penelopeia—Helen.

22.154 *I made the mistake.* Yet another sign of the young man's maturity, this claiming of responsibility does not prompt a rebuke from his father, an equally telling detail of characterization. As if the two have already dismissed the incident, violent punishment of the goat-herd Melanthios, who has ransacked the unlocked storeroom for weapons, is left to the other servants to carry out.

22.237 *She wanted to test the vigor.* Just as Odysseus himself has been engaged, in a somewhat different mode, testing the suitors and servants, his patroness withdraws in order to leave a challenge for him. The attitude is quintessentially Greek: the gods bring out the excellence of mortals not by pampering them but by posing difficulties that they must overcome by drawing on all their inner resources. Athene's metamorphosis into bird form recalls the conclusion of her initial visit as Mentes to Telemakhos (1.320).

22.318 *I was their soothsayer.* Until he utters this line, Leiodes may have had a chance at obtaining his plea for mercy. But Odysseus now assumes either that the man foresaw his own arrival and tried to avert it, or was a fraud, seeking easy employment from the suitors. Like bards, seers are depicted either as traveling about or working for patrons in palaces. Their persons were not sacrosanct.

22.344 *respect me, have pity.* Like the soothsayer, the bard might be suspected of abetting the enemy, but Phemios defends himself by claiming that the suitors forced him to sing for them. His further defense—that he is divinely inspired yet taught himself— has been thought by some critics to contain a contradiction. But in the context, it can imply that his full emotional art (the divine inspiration) comes into play only when he sings for his own master, and that in that case he does not borrow another's generic phrases for his poems but sings the praises of Odysseus, "as though for a god," based on personal knowledge of his patron. This flattering approach, with its promise of continuing poetic fame for his master, seems to work. Of course Odysseus, himself an expert storyteller, can appreciate the bardic art. A similar personal connection leads Telemakhos to spare the herald Medon (line 357).

22.412 *Rejoicing over men.* The ferocity of Odysseus's revenge is tempered by his rebuke of Eurukleia. Treating the suitors as a threat to civil life, and therefore more than personal opponents, he also colors his own action as that of an instrument of the gods, who must inevitably punish such brash and hubristic arrogance.

22.468 *broad-winged thrushes.* Like the dead suitors, who were compared to a pile of gasping fish (line 384ff.), their paramours are made less than human by this simile treating them as victims of another sort of snare. Furthermore, the comparison to creatures that will become food naturalizes the killing, making it seem a necessity for survival. In each simile, the skill of the captors, fishermen or bird-catchers, is contrasted with the helplessness of the doomed prey, but we are not therefore meant to feel sorry for either group. The involuntary twitching of the hanged girls is noted clinically, as if the victims are beneath sympathy. The brutal treatment of Melanthios makes a similarly grim and chill finale.

23.15 *Why do you fool me.* Throughout the poem, Penelopeia has been depicted as cautious; her regular epithet is "thought-full" or "intelligent." She distrusts dreams, oracles, and beggars, even one as apparently convincing as Odysseus in book 19. At this moment when an audience wants her to rush to her husband, the poet has Penelopeia maintain her resistance, a realistic touch that speaks volumes about character. At the same time, the mention of how sweet her sleep has been (line 16) hints that she realizes, at least unconsciously, that the twenty years of anxiety have ended.

23.51 *with sulfur.* The purging with sulfur is an important detail, since the only other mention of this cleansing element in the poem comes in the line describing the smell that filled the air immediately after Zeus's thunderbolt blasted the ship and impious crew of Odysseus (12.417; cf. 14.307, Odysseus's lie). The poetic analogy between his own disobedient men and the disrespectful suitors once again elevates the hero to the position of a vengeful god.

23.85 *mulling a great deal.* The suspense moves to a new level, as Penelopeia now seems to contemplate not whether the man before her is Odysseus but whether he is the same, emotionally, as the man who departed two decades before. In the triangular arrangement of wife, husband, and son, all on stage at last, each plays the role we have come to expect: Penelopeia immovable, Telemakhos impatient, and Odysseus indifferent to what others think.

23.136 *it's a wedding.* This is ironic, since the local people expect a marriage to one of the suitors, whereas a remarriage of sorts has just happened between the long-separated pair. The comments reported (lines 149–51) from anonymous passers-by confirm the intensity of the critical observation with which Penelopeia has struggled all along, and recall again the key role of constantly shifting praise or blame in structuring this archaic society.

23.181 *to test her man.* The tables are turned on the man who has been testing others all along. By coolly ordering what she knows is an impossibility—that the rooted bed be moved—Penelopeia elicits the proof she has been wanting. This is more than just the recognition of shared secret signs. The deep emotion behind Odysseus's response shows that he still values their marriage, as symbolized by the olive-tree bed he so carefully crafted. His identity as a maker and shaper (whether of plans or objects) is thus finally brought together with his identity as husband, harmoniously fitted to the exactly right wife.

23.218 *Helen of Argos.* By alluding to her cousin's predicament, Penelopeia points to the power of public opinion in keeping order. If Helen had imagined she would have to come back home, her behavior would have been different; just so, if Penelopeia had trusted a visitor (like Paris) she might have remarried (either a false Odysseus or a suitor) and ended up equally embarrassed. A clearer point comes from her neat summing up of the entire Trojan saga—the separation of the Ithakan couple arose from Helen's abandonment of her own husband.

23.233–34 *a welcome / sight to a swimmer.* Odysseus has been the actual shipwrecked swimmer, but the simile makes Penelopeia the person who escapes a sea of trouble to find solid land—in this case, a stability and strength represented by her husband. The comparison echoes and reverses the episode of Odysseus's desperate swim to land at Skherie, where the young woman Nausikaa represented safety.

23.310 *He told her how.* Prompted by his wife, Odysseus has already mentioned his next trip, the journey inland to appease Poseidon. Now he offers a brief digest of all the major episodes we have heard him tell in books 9 through 12, including the sojourns with Kirke and Kalupso. The length of time he spent with the former goes unmentioned, as does the exact detail of his relation with the latter, while Odysseus mentions the danger of both and his resistance.

23.357 *get some back by looting.* The poet offers us a glimpse into early economic and legal procedure. Raiding and counter-raiding made up a large part of the process for increasing one's stock of goods and animals, and played an important role in the training of young warriors. Cattle were the common currency of exchange, with goods and even women or slaves being valued in terms of the number of cows they were worth. By "Akhaians" Odysseus most likely refers to his fellow islanders who owe him for supporting or not stopping the suitors' depredations.

24.1 *from Mount Kullene.* Mount Kullene was the favorite haunt of Hermes, in the wilds of Arcadia in central Greece. Hermes' wand (called the *kerukeion*) makes him resemble a herald, who can pass across borders to bring messages. His further functions as a god of exchange, of thievery, of communication, and of herding all revolve around his ability to move easily throughout the universe.

24.11 *Leukas Rock.* Leukas Rock was not Leukada, the promontory near Ithaka, but a mythical "White Rock" marking the boundaries of consciousness, near the cosmic river Okeanos.

24.16 *Antilokhos.* Antilokhos was the son of Nestor who died while trying to rescue his father in the battle outside Troy (see 4.202).

24.37 *You died at Troy.* The *Iliad*, concentrated on one episode late in the war, ends before the death and burial of its protagonist, Akhilleus. The *Odyssey* manages to complete the story, providing a view of the great warrior's funeral through this retrospective conversation in the underworld. The chorus of mourning nymphs, led by his divine mother Thetis, and the presence of all nine Muses as lamenters, mark the cosmic importance of this finale to the greatest Greek saga. At the same time, the event now fades into the past, a topic for reminiscences, in contrast to the living fame of Odysseus, which the suitors' ghosts will transmit even to the dead.

24.119 *We barely prevailed.* This is a possible allusion to the reluctance of Odysseus when he was asked to join the Trojan expeditionary force. Other sources relate that he feigned madness to avoid going to war, until a ruse by Palamedes, who accompanied Agamemnon and Menelaos, forced Odysseus to show his sanity. Although pretending to plow a field crazily, he nevertheless swerved to avoid hitting his infant son, whom Palamedes placed in the way. Agamemnon's reference to the recruiting trip, even more than the previous conversation, takes us back further into the early part of the saga.

24.123 *I'll tell you myself.* Amphimedon is of course a biased witness, one of the men who courted the queen and paid for it with his life. In his partial view, Penelopeia secretly planned the killing (line 127), in the same way she deceived the suitors for three years with her ruse of the shroud. Telemakhos was also in on the plot (line 153), as was "one of the Gods" (line 182). The opportunity for the enemy to tell his story recalls Homeric technique in the *Iliad*, in which both sides get equal treatment from the poet and sympathy from the audience. The skewed summary in this speech, however, contrasts with the truthful sketch of the voyages given by Odysseus in book 23. Nor do we feel sympathy for Amphimedon, even as he complains he was duped.

24.192 *Happy son of Laertes.* Instead of answering the dead suitor directly, Agamemnon apostrophizes his former companion Odysseus, praising him for his good luck and good sense. The poet thus builds into the narrative an overarching comment on the power of women, and gives it authority and perspective by placing it in the mouth of Agamemnon, who should know. The artful ring composition returns us to the story of this hero, killed by his wife Klutaimnestre (daughter of Tundareos) on homecoming, the tale that opened the *Odyssey*. The murdered king contrasts the reputations of two archetypal wives, his own and that of Odysseus. The song of praise that will forever commemorate Penelopeia (lines 197–98) is of course the very poem in which he speaks, the *Odyssey*.

24.221 *to test his father.* Some critics have found this further probing by the hero to be unnecessary and distasteful. Since antiquity, when some Homeric scholars of the third century B.C. declared the entire last book of the poem to be an addition, readers have sought to find ways to justify an earlier ending of the *Odyssey*, one that would privilege the reunion of husband and wife as the proper conclusion to the epic. Ancient critics suggested 23.296 as the "end" of the poem, but it is unclear whether the Greek word used meant absolute finish or just a denouement. Against supporters of a shorter *Odyssey* it might be argued that the hero is not fully restored to his status as king, son, husband, and father until he rejoins his own father, Laertes. The further episode about the incipient vendetta by the suitors' relatives is in keeping with the *Odyssey*'s generally practical outlook. And the hero's urge to keep on testing his kin matches the trajectory of his character thus far: incessant wariness and disguise are as much identifying marks as his scar. His testing thus tells his father it is really Odysseus home at last.

24.304 *I'm from Alubas.* This place and the names that follow are meant to echo other words. Odysseus jokingly identifies himself as "In the Fight" (*Eperitos*) from "Wanderland" (*Alubas*), the son of "Unsparing" (*Alpheidas*) who is in turn "Son of much pain" or "of much gain" (*Polupemon*). Sikanie is Sicily, a real location. Unable to maintain his façade when his father finally breaks down, Odysseus then identifies himself by the scar and by the shared inheritance of the land—the trees and vines his father gave him.

24.404 *know it for certain.* Dolios does not know that Penelopeia has been rejoined to her husband. Much worse—if this is meant to be the same Dolios named earlier (17.212) as the father of the disloyal Melanthios and Melantho—he has apparently not yet learned that his children have been put to death by Odysseus's servants at his command.

24.428 *lost the hollow ships.* Odysseus has not given his explanation yet to the townspeople or other islanders who sent their sons with him to Troy. In the paradoxical situation of the lone survivor, information about the loss of the crew must rest on the testimony of a man whose experience was, by definition, ultimately separate from that of the rest. Only his word remains to persuade others about the disobedience of his men or the disasters they underwent. The realistic speech, like the vendetta preparations, reminds us of the local political consequences of war.

24.472 *Athene spoke to Zeus.* The poem ends as it began, with a conversation between the chief goddess and her father. Since this situation results from Athene's original plea on behalf of Odysseus, Zeus lets her decide, though he urges her to end the whole business with amnesty. The resolution by divine intervention—the prototype of tragic drama's deus ex machina endings—particularly resonates with the local history of Athens, where the Furies (Erinus) pursuing Orestes for his kin-murder were appeased thanks to the action of Athene (a process dramatized in Aeschylus's *Eumenides,* 458 B.C.).

24.520 *Pallas Athene paused.* As the scene unfolds, four major Greek beliefs are reasserted. First, the gods when prayed to can fill one with preternatural strength: so it happens with the weak and aged Laertes before he casts his spear. Second, peace among humans depends on cooperation with the will of the gods. Third, self-control—the primary virtue of the thoughtful Odysseus—is what enables one to end vendettas and follow the gods' will. And fourth—perhaps less obvious to us—the gods' action is a function of memory and mindfulness. The name Mentor—the human disguise taken by Athene once more—actually means "he who calls to mind." It gives English a word for instructor and guide. Yet in the terms of the *Odyssey,* a greater theology is at work: human mindfulness, divine reminders, and the poet's mastery of memory all collaborate to keep mortals humane and alive.

Names in the *Odyssey*

This translation continues a strong trend that began in the twentieth century to revive the original spelling and pronunciation of Homer's proper names. Given that the *Odyssey* was originally performed aloud, the musical flavor of those names undoubtedly contributed to the epic singer's effectiveness. But later Latinizations and Anglicizations of the names often took their sounds a long way from the rugged strength of the Greek. Homer's *Kuklops*, for example, a name for the race of Giants of whom Poluphemos is a member, evolved strangely into our "Cyclops." In Homer's day it sounded harsher and stronger, rather like ĸooĸ-lohps. This pronunciation guide aims to restore a good deal of Homer's music with W. Sidney Allen's *Vox Graeca*, the standard treatment of ancient Greek pronunciation, in mind.

Some names of course have complicated the picture. Homer's *Penelopeia* does not appear in this book as "Penelope" but as PAY-neh-law-PEY-uh, a name that often ends its line as a beautiful dactyl-trochee combination. Later redactors, however, placed an accent mark, or diacritic, on the third syllable: pay-neh-LAW-pey-uh. Which is the better guide, these marks or the meter as described above? Often the two do not conflict. But (1) since scholars continue to puzzle over the exact significance and origin of the diacritics, (2) since our knowledge of the meter is now quite extensive, and (3) since I cannot imagine, as a poet and translator, that Homer's meter played a minor role in performance, the entries here give the nod in most cases to the metrical pronunciation. Furthermore, whenever an old diacritic falls on the last syllable, as in the River ahl-phey-AWSS (*Alpheios*), I've moved the accent to another syllable to help the word sound like English (rather than French): ahl-P(H)AY-awss. Admittedly some new forms of the old misspellings will take getting used to. For Homer's death-god, for example, this translation does not use the traditional "Hades" (presumably HEY-deez) but rather Homeric *Aides*, pronounced AI-dayss.

By dint of hard tradition or unusually difficult pronunciation in the English, some names have not been restored. "Odysseus" is not respelled *Odusseus*. The name probably sounded like aw-DOOSS-(eh)ooss in Mycenaean times and perhaps a future translator will return to that form. The upsilon in the second syllable certainly became a troublesome letter in this and other nouns. During the centuries following Homeric Greek it became a rounded front vowel like the French *u* in *plume*; it was eventually spelled in English with a *y*. The problem of course is that *y* in modern English can be pronounced *ee*, *ih*, or *ai*, as in "Cyclops." Some entries below, therefore, have both the traditional Anglicized form (generally used in this book) and the Homeric word. The entry "Thrace or Threke" is an example; so is "Nymphs or Numphai." Often the two words are quite close to each other in spelling and pronunciation. In addition, the group or adjective form of some nouns remains the simpler, Anglicized version. *Aithiopes*, somewhat ungainly in English, became the usual "Ethiopians." Instead of "living in Oikhalie" (in 8.224), this text reads "Oikhalian."

Still, the vast majority of entries here include a suggested spelling and pronunciation approximating Homer's. (A few exceptions demanded special care, like *Aiguptos*, which in Homer can mean "Egypt" or "the Nile.") Entries also include the name's first appearance in the epic, where readers will generally learn something about the subject. Names used by Homer to refer to more than one character are designated as (a), (b), and so forth. Parentheses around a letter indicate a muting of that sound. Homeric chi, phi, and theta do not correspond exactly to modern English *ch, k, f,* or *th*; *Khios,* for example, should sound rather like k(H)EE-awss, where the (H), though not fully articulated, has the effect of softening the k, as in German *licht*. *Phoibos,* still another name for *Helios / Apollon /* the Sun-God, should sound like P(H)OI-bawss, where the (H) has the effect of making the plosive, you might say, somewhat more plosive—less like the *p* in *map* and more like the strong *p* in *power.* Parentheses around vowels also indicate a muting, as with Homer's diphthongs. The form *eu* (epsilon plus upsilon) in *Akhilleus* probably sounded, according to Allen, less like the *ew* in our *few* and more like a quickly voiced eh-oo, the former slightly muted; thus, uh-k(H)ILL-(eh)ooss. The restored name becomes easy enough to say after a few tries. And it's certainly closer to Homer's language than the older "Achilles," pronounced by my younger brother in his teens—following good English rules—to rime with BAT-chills. (We chuckled at the mistake and concocted a new epithet: cold enough, Ach-ills becomes the a-CHOO-er.) To avoid this tendency I've changed all the old English *ch* spellings for Homeric chi to *kh*.

A final note on the capitalization: Homer's divinities were certainly "Gods" (not lowercase "gods") to his characters, just as Jesus of Nazareth is God, not "god," to his followers. The oldest Greek texts offer no objection, of course, being entirely in capitals. Where godhead is associated with lesser figures, as with *Ker*, I've also capitalized: "the Powers of Death." Parents belonging to the speaker at hand are also capitalized: "I saw the mother of Oidipus," Odysseus tells us, back from the land of the dead (in 11.271) and (in 11.84) "The ghost of my dead Mother came" as well.

Adreste, 4.123: ah-DRESS-tay

Agamemnon, 1.30: uh-guh-MEM-nohn

Agelaos, 20.321: uh-geh-LAH-awss (the g as in *guard*)

Aiai, 9.32: AI-ai

Aiaie, 10.135: ai-AI-ay

Aiakos, 11.471: AI-uh-kawss

Aias, 3.109: AI-ahss

Aides, 3.410: AI-dayss

Aietes, 10.137: ai-AY-tayss

Aigai, 5.381: AI-gai

Aigis, 3.394: AI-giss (the g as in *guard*)

Aigisthos, 1.29: ai-GISS-t(h)awss

Aiguptios, 2.15: ai-GOOP-tee-awss

Aiolia, 10.1: ai-AW-lee-uh

Aiolos, 10.1: AI-aw-lawss

Aison, 11.259: AI-sohn

Aithon, 19.183: AI-t(h)ohn

Aitolia or Aitolos, 14.379: ai-TOHL-awss

Akastos, 14.336: uh-KAHSS-tawss

Akhaia and Akhaians, 1.90: uh-k(H)AI-uh, uh-k(H)AI-uns

Akheron, 10.514: uh-KEH-rohn

Akhilleus, 3.106: uh-k(H)ILL-(eh)ooss

Akroneus, 8.111: uh-KRAW-n(eh)ooss

Aktor, 23.228: AHK-tawr

Alektor, 4.10: uh-LEK-tohr

Alkandre, 4.125: ahl-KAHN-dray

Alkinoos, 6.12: uhl-KIH-naw-awss

Alkippe, 4.124: uhl-KIP-peh

Alkmaion, 15.248: ahlk-MAI-ohn

Alkmene, 2.120: ahlk-MAY-nay

Aloeus, 11.305: uhl-oh-EY-ooss

Alpheidas, 24.305: ahl-PHEY-duss

Alpheios, 3.489: ahl-P(H)AY-awss

Alubas or Alubantos, 24.304: uh-LOO-bahss,
    uh-loo-BAHN-tawss

Amnisos, 19.188: ahm-NEE-sawss

Amphialos, 8.114: ahm-P(H)IH-aw-lawss

Amphiaraos, 15.244: ahm-p(h)ee-uh-RAH-
    awss

Amphimedon, 22.242: ahm-PHIH-meh-dohn

Amphinomos, 16.351: ahm-P(H)IH-naw-
    mawss

Amphion, (a) 11.262 and (b) 11.283: AHM-
    p(h)ee-ohn

Amphithea, 19.416: ahm-p(h)i-T(H)AY-uh

Amphitrite, 3.91: ahm-p(h)ih-TREE-tay

Amphitruon, 11.266: ahm-p(h)ee-TROO-ohn

Amuthaon, 11.259: uh-moo-T(H)AH-ohn

Anabesineos, 8.113: AH-nuh-bay-SIH-
    neh-ohss

Andraimon, 14.499: ahn-DRAI-mohn

Ankhialos, (a) 1.180 and (b) 8.112:
    ahn-K(H)IH-uh-lawss

Antikleia, 11.85: ahn-tih-KLAY-uh

Antiklos, 4.286: AHN-tih-klawss

Antilokhos, 3.112: ahn-TEE-law-k(h)awss

Antinoos, 1.383: ahn-TIH-naw-awss

Antiope, 11.260: ahn-tih-AW-pay

Antiphates, (a) 10.106 and (b) 15.242: ahn-
    tih-P(H)AH-tayss

Antiphos, 2.19: AHN-tih-p(h)awss

Apeire, 7.9: uh-PAY-ray

Aphrodite, 4.14: ah-p(h)raw-DEE-tay

Apollo. *See* Phoibos Apollo

Ares, 3.109: AH-rayss

Arete, 7.54: uh-RAY-tay

Arethousa, 13.408: uh-reh-T(H)OO-sah

Aretios, 16.395: ah-RAY-tee-awss

Aretos, 3.414: ah-RAY-tawss

Argive or Argeios, 1.61: AHR-gaiv, Ahr-GAY-
    awss

Argo, 12.70: AHR-go

Argos, (a) 1.344 and (b) 17.292: AHR-gawss

Ariadne, 11.321: uh-rih-AHD-nay

Arkeisios, 4.755: ahr-KAY-see-awss

Arnaios, 18.5: ahr-NAI-awss

Artakie, 10.107: ahr-TAH-kee-ay

Artemis, 5.123: AHR-teh-miss

Arubas, 15.426: uh-ROO-bahss

Asopos, 11.260: ah-SOH-pawss

Asphalion, 4.216: ahss-p(h)uh-LEE-ohn

Asteris, 4.846: AHSS-teh-riss

Athene, 1.44: ah-T(H)AY-nay

Athens or Athenai, 3.278: uh-T(H)AY-nai

Atlas, 1.52: AHT-luss

Atreus, 1.40: AH-tr(eh)ooss

Autolukos, 11.85: ow-TAW-loo-kawss

Autonoe, 18.182: ow-taw-NAW-ay

Avenger(s) or Erinus, 2.135: eh-REE-nooss

Boethous, 4.31: baw-AY-t(h)aw-ooss

Bootes, 5.272: baw-OH-tayss

Damastor, 20.321: duh-MAHSS-tohr

Danaans or Danaoi, 1.350: duh-NAH-ans,
    duh-NAH-oy

Dawn or Eos, 2.1: AY-ohss

Deiphobos, 4.276: day-IH-p(h)aw-bawss

Delos, 6.162: DAY-lawss

Demeter, 5.125: day-MAY-tayr

Demodokos, 8.44: day-MAW-daw-kawss

Demoptolemos, 22.243: DAY-mawp-TAW-
    leh-mawss

Deukelion, 19.180: (deh)oo-KAH-lih-ohn

Die, 11.325: DEE-ay

Diokles, 3.488: dih-aw-klayss

Diomedes, 3.181: dih-aw-MAY-dayss

Dionusos, 11.325: dih-aw-NOO-sawss

Dmetor, 17.443: duh-MAY-tohr

Dodone, 14.327: doh-DOH-nay

Dolios, 4.735: daw-LEE-awss

Dorians or Doriees, 19.177: doh-rih-EH-ess

Doulikhion, 1.246: doo-LIH-k(h)ih-awn

Dumas, 6.22: DOO-mahss

Dusk or Hesper, 8.29: HESS-pair

Egypt or Aiguptos or Nile, 3.300: ai-GOOP-
    tawss

Eidothee, 4.366: ey-daw-T(H)EH-ay

Eileithuie, 19.188: EY-ley-t(h)-oo-EE-ay

Ekheneos, 7.155: eh-k(h)eh-NAY-awss

Ekhephron, 3.413: eh-K(H)EH-p(h)rohn

Ekhetos, 18.85: EH-k(h)eh-tawss

Elatos, 22.267: eh-LAH-tawss

Elatreus, 8.111: eh-LAH-tr(eh)ooss

Elis, 4.635: AY-liss

Elpenor, 10.552: el-PAY-nohr

Elusian (Fields), 4.563: ay-LOO-see-ahn

Enipeus, 11.238: eh-NEE-p(eh)ooss

Epeians, 13.275: eh-PAY-uhns

Epeios, 8.493: eh-PEY-awss

Eperitos, 24.306: eh-PAY-rih-tawss

Ephialtes, 11.308: eh-p(h)ee-AHL-tayss

Ephure, 1.259: eh-P(H)OOR-ay

Epikaste, 11.271: eh-pih-KAHSS-tay

Erebos, 10.528: EH-reh-bawss

Erekhtheus, 7.81: eh-REK(H)-t(h)(eh)ooss

Eremboi, 4.84: eh-REM-boy

Eretmeus, 8.112: eh-RET-m(eh)ooss

Eriphule, 11.326: eh-rih-P(H)OO-lay

Erumanthos, 6.103: eh(oo)-roo-MAHN-
t(h)awss

Eteoneus, 4.21: eh-teh-OH-n(eh)ooss

Ethiopians or Aithiopes, 1.22: ai-T(H)IH-
aw-payss

Euanthes, 9.197: eh (oo)-AHN-t(h)ayss

Euboia, 3.174: eh (oo)-BOI-uh

Euenor, 2.242: (eh)oo-AY-nohr

Eumaios, 14.55: eh(oo)-MAI-awss

Eumelos, 4.798 : eh(oo)-MAY-lawss

Eupeithes, 1.383: eh(oo)-PEY-t(h)ayss

Euruades, 22.266: (eh)oo-roo-AH-dayss

Eurualos, 8.115: eh(oo)-ROO-uh-lawss

Eurubates, 19.247: (eh)oo-roo-BAH-tayss

Eurudamas, 18.297: (eh)oo-ROO-dah-muss

Eurudike, 3.452: eh(oo)-roo-DEE-kay

Eurukleia, 1.428: eh(oo)-roo-KLAY-uh

Eurulokhos, 10.232: eh(oo)-ROO-law-k(h)awss

Eurumakhos, 1.399: eh(oo)-ROO-muh-
k(h)awss

Eurumedon, 7.58: eh(oo)-roo-MEH-dohn

Eurumedousa, 7.8: eh(oo)-roo-meh-DOO-suh

Eurumos, 9.509: EH(oo)-roo-moss

Eurunome, 17.495: (eh)oo-ROO-naw-may

Eurunomos, 2.21: eh(oo)-ROO-naw-mawss

Eurupulos, 11.520: eh(oo)-ROO-poo-lawss

Eurution, 21.295: (EH)oo-roo-TEE-ohn

Eurutos, 8.224: EH(oo)-roo-tawss

Gaia, 7.325: GAI-uh

Geraistos, 3.177: geh-RAISS-tawss (the *g* as in
guard)

Gerenians or Gerenos, 3.68: geh-RAY-nawss
(the *g* as in *guard*)

Giants or Gigantes, 7.59: GEE-gahn-tayss
(both *g*s hard)

Gorgo, 11.634: GAWR-goh

Gortun, 3.294: GAWR-toon

Graces or Kharites, 6.19: K(H)AH-rih-tess

Great Bear. *See* Wagon

Gurai, 4.501: GOO-rai

Halios, 8.119: HUH-lih-awss

Halitherses, 2.157: huh-lih-T(H)AIR-sayss

Hebe, 11.603: HAY-bay

Helen or Helene, 4.13: heh-LEH-nay

Helios or Eelios, 1.8: HAY-lih-awss

Hellas, 1.344: HELL-uhss

Hellespont, 24.82: HELL-ess-pawnt

Hephaistos, 4.617: hay-P(H)AISS-tawss

Herakles, 8.224: HAY-rah-klayss

Here, 4.513: HAY-ray

Hermes, 1.38: HAIR-mayss

Hermione, 4.14: hair-mih-AW-nay

Hippodameia, 18.182: HIP-paw-duh-MEY-uh

Hippotes, 10.2: HIP-paw-tess

Hulakos, 14.203: HOO-luh-kawss

Hupereia, 6.4: hoo-peh-REY-uh

Huperesie, 15.255: HOO-peh-ray-SEE-ay

Huperion, 1.9: hoo-peh-REE-ohn

Iaolkos, 11.256: ih-uh-OHL-kawss

Iardanos, 3.292: i-AHR-duh-nawss

Iasion, 5.126: ih-AH-sih-ohn

Iasos, 11.283: EE-uh-sawss

Idomeneus, 3.191: ih-daw-MEN-(eh)ooss

Ieson, 12.72: ih-AY-sohn

Ikarios, 1.329: ee-KAH-rih-awss

Ikmalios, 19.57: ik-MAH-lih-awss

Ilion or Troy, 14.71: IH-lih-awn

Ilos, 1.259: IH-lawss

Ino, 5.333: IH-noh

Iphiklos, 11.290: ih-P(H)IH-klawss

Iphimedeia, 11.305: IH-p(h)ih-meh-DEY-uh

Iphitos, 21.14: IH-p(h)ih-tawss

Iphthime, 4.797: ih-P(H)T(H)EE-may

Iros, 18.6: IH-rawss

Ismaros, 9.40: ISS-muh-rawss

Ithaka or Ithake, 1.18: IH-t(h)uh-kay

Ithakos, 17.207: IH-t(h)uh-kawss

Itulos, 19.522: IH-too-lawss

Kadmeians, 11.276: kahd-MEY-uns

Kadmos, 5.333: KAHD-mawss

Kalupso, 1.14: kuh-LOOPS-oh

Kassandre, 11.422: kah-SAHN-dray

Kastor, (a) 11.300 and (b) 14.203: KAHSS-tohr

Kaukones, 3.367: KOW-koh-ness

Kentaur, 21.295: KEN-towr

Kephallenians or Kephallenes, 20.210: keh-p(h)ahl-LAY-ness

Keteians or Keteioi, 11.521: KAY-tey-oy

Khalkis (River), 15.295: K(H)AHL-kiss

Kharubdis, 12.104: k(h)uh-ROOB-diss

Khios, 3.170: K(H)EE-awss

Khloris, 11.281: K(H)loh-riss

Khromios, 11.286: k(h)raw-MEE-awss

Kikones, 9.39: KIH-kaw-ness

Kimmerians or Kimmerioi, 11.14: kim-MEH-rih-oy

Kirke, 8.448: KEER-kay

Kleitos, 15.249: KLEY-tawss

Klumene, 11.326: kloo-MEN-ay

Klumenos, 3.452: KLOO-meh-nawss

Klutaimnestre, 3.266: kloo-taim-NAY-stray

Klutios, 15.540: KLOO-tih-awss

Klutoneos, 8.119: kloo-TAW-nay-awss

Knosos, 19.178: KNOH-sawss

Kokutos, 10.513: koh-KOO-tawss

Korakos (Rock), 13.408: KAW-ruh-kawss

Krataiin, 12.124: krah-TAI-in

Kreion, 11.269: KREY-ohn

Krete, 3.192: KRAY-tay

Kretheus, 11.237: KRAY-t(h)eh-ooss

Kronos, 1.45: KRAW-nawss

Krounoi (springs), 15.295: KROO-noy

Ktesios, 15.413: (K)TAY-sih-awss

Ktesippos, 20.288: kuh-tay-SIP-pawss

Ktimene, 15.364: k(t)ih-MEN-ay

Kudonians or Kudones, 3.292: koo-DOH-ness

Kuklops, 1.69: KOOK-lohps

Kullene, 24.1: kool-LAY-nay

Kupros, 4.83: KOO-prawss

Kuthereia, 8.288: koo-t(h)eh-REY-uh

Laerkes, 3.425: lah-AIR-kayss

Laertes, 1.188: lah-AIR-tayss

Laistrugonians or Laistrugonie, 10.82: LAISS-troo-gaw-NIH-ay

Lakedaimon, 3.326: Lah-keh-DAI-mohn

Lamos, 10.81: LAH-mawss

Lampetie, 12:132: luhm-peh-TEE-ay

Lampon, 23.245: LAHM-pohn

Laodamas, 7.170: LAH-aw-DUH-muss

Lapiths or Lapithai, 21.297: lah-PEE-t(h)ai

Lede, 11.298: LAY-day

Lemnos, 8.283: LEN-nawss

Leiodes, 21.144: ley-OH-dayss

Leiokritos, 2.242: ley-OH-krih-tawss

Lesbos, 3.169: LESS-bawss

Leto, 6.106: LAY-toh

Leukas (Rock), 24.11: L(EH)OO-kuhss

Leukothee, 5.334: L(EH)OO-kaw-T(H)EH-ay

Libya or Libue, 4.85: lih-BOO-ay

Lotos-eaters, 9.84: LOH-tawss

Maia, 14.436: MAI-uh

Maira, 11.326: MAI-ruh

Maleia, 3.287: muh-LEY-uh

Mantios, 15.242: MAHN-tih-awss

Marathon, 7.80: MAH-ruh-t(h)ohn

Maron, 9.197: MAH-rohn

Mastor, 2.158: MAHSS-tohr

Medon, 4.677: MEH-dohn

Megapenthes, 4.11: meh-guh-PEN-t(h)ayss

Megare, 11.269: meh-GAH-ray

Melampous, 11.292: meh-LAHM-pooss

Melantheus or Melanthios, 17.212: meh-LAHN-t(h)eh-ooss

Melanthos, 18.321: meh-LAHN-thoh

Memnon, 11.522: MEM-nohn

Menelaos, 1.285: meh-neh-LAH-awss

Menoitios, 24.77: meh-NOY-tih-awss

Mentes, 1.105: MEN-tayss

Mentor, 2.225: MEN-tohr

Mermeros, 1.259: MAIR-mair-awss

Mesaulios, 14.449: meh-SOW-lih-awss

Messene, 21.15: mehs-SAY-nay

Mimas, 3.172: MEE-mahss

Minos, 11.322: MIH-nohss

Minuans or Minuai, 11.284: mih-NOO-ai

Moulios, 18.424: MOO-lih-awss

Mukenai, 3.305: moo-KAY-nai

Mukene, 2.120: moo-KAY-nay

Murmidons or Murmidones, 3:188: moor-mih-DAW-nes

Muse or Mousa, 1.1: MOO-sah

Naubolos, 8.116: NOW-baw-lawss

Nausikaa, 6.17: NOW-see-KAH-uh

Nausithoos, 6.7: now-SEE-t(h)aw-awss

Nauteus, 8.112: NOW-t(eh)ooss

Neaira, 12.133: neh-AI-rah

Neias and Neiades, 13.104: NAY-uhss and NAY-uh-dess

Neion, 1.186: NEY-awn

Neleus, 3.4: NAY-l(eh)ooss

Neoptolemos, 11.506: neh-awp-TAW-leh-mawss

Nerikon, 24.377: NAY-rih-kawn

Neriton, 9.21: NAY-rih-tawn

Neritos, 17.207: NAY-rih-tawss

Nestor, 1.284: NESS-tohr

Nisos, 16.395: NEE-sawss

Noemon, 2.386: naw-AY-mohn

No-one or Outis, 9.366: oo-tiss

Northwind or Borees, 5.296: baw-REH-ayss

Nymphs or Numphai, 6.105: NOOM-p(h)ai

Ocean or Okeanos, 4.568: oh-keh-UH-nawss

Odysseus or Odusseus, 1.21: aw-DOOSS-(eh)-ooss

Ogugie, 1.85: Oh-goo-GEE-ay (the *g* as in *guard*)

Oidipus, 11.271: OY-dih-pooss

Oikhalian or Oikhalie, 8.224: oy-k(h)uh-LIH-ay

Oikleies, 15.243: oy-KLEY-ayss

Oinops, 21.144: OI-nawps

Okuolos, 8.111: oh-KOO-uh-lawss

Olumpos, 1.27: aw-LOOM-pawss

Onetor, 3.282: aw-NAY-tohr

Ops, 1.429: OHPS

Orestes, 1.30: aw-RESS-tayss

Orion, 5.121: oh-REE-ohn

Orkhomenos, 11.284: or-K(H)AW-men-awss

Ormenos, 15.414: OR-men-awss

Ortilokhos or Orsilokhos, 3.489: or-TIH-law-k(h)awss

Ortugie, 5.124: or-too-GEE-ay (the *g* as in *guard*)

Ossa, 11.316: AWS-sah

Otos, 11.308: OH-tawss

Paieon, 4.232: pai-AY-ohn

Pallas, 1.125: PAHL-luhss

Pandareos, 20.66: pahn-DAH-reh-awss

Panopeus, 11.581: puh-NAW-p(eh)ooss

Paphos, 8.363: PAH-p(h)awss

Parnesos, 19.394: pahr-NAY-sawss

Patroklos, 3.110: PAH-traw-klawss

Peiraios, 15.539: PEY-rai-awss

Peirithoos, 11.631: pey-REE-t(h)aw-awss

Peisandros, 18.299: pey-SAHN-drawss

Peisenor, (a) 1.429 and (b) 2.38: pey-SAY-nohr

Peisistratos, 3.36: pey-SISS-truh-tawss

Pelasgians or Pelasgoi, 19.177: peh-LAHSS-goi

Peleus, 8.75: PAY-l(eh)ooss

Pelies, 11.254: peh-LEE-ayss

Pelion, 11.316: PAY-lih-awn

Penelopeia, 1.223: PAY-neh-law-PAY-uh

Periboia, 7.57: peh-RIH-boy-uh

Periklumenos, 11.286: peh-rih-KLOO-men-awss

Perimedes, 11.23: peh-rih-MAY-dayss

Pero, 11.287: PAY-roh

Perse, 10.139: PEHR-say

Persephoneia, 10.491: PAIR-seh-p(h)aw-NEY-uh

Perseus, 3.414: PEHR-s(eh)ooss

Phaethon, 23.245: P(H)AH-eh-t(h)ohn

Phaethousa, 12.132: p(h)ah-eh-T(H)OO-suh

Phaiakians or Phaiekes, 5.35: P(H)AI-
ay-kess

Phaidimos, 4.617: P(H)AI-dih-mawss

Phaidre, 11.321: P(H)AI-dray

Phaistos, 3.296: P(H)AI-stawss

Pharos, 4.355: P(H)AH-rawss

Pheai, 15.297: P(H)EH-ai

Pheidon, 14.316: P(H)EY-dohn

Phemios, 1.154: P(H)AY-mih-awss

Pherai, 3.488: P(H)EH-rai

Pheres, 11.259: P(H)EH-rayss

Philoitios, 20.185: p(h)ih-LOY-tih-awss

Philoktetes, 3.190: p(h)ih-lawk-TAY-tayss

Philomeleides, 4.343: P(H)IH-law-may-LEY-
dayss

Phoibos Apollo, 3.279: P(H)OY-bawss
uh-PAWL-oh

Phoinikian or Phoinikes, 4.83: p(h)oy-
NEE-kess

Phorkus, 1.72: P(H)AWR-kooss

Phronios, 2.387: P(H)RAW-nih-awss

Phrontis, 3.282: P(H)RAWN-tiss

Phthie, 11.496: p(h)t(h)EE-ay

Phulake, 11.289: p(h)oo-LAH-kay

Phulakos, 15.231: P(H)OO-luh-kawss

Phulo, 4.125: P(H)OO-loh

Pierie, 5.50: pee-eh-REE-ay

Pirithoos, 21.298: pih-REE-t(h)aw-awss

Plangktai, 12.61: PLAHNK-tai

Pleiades, 5.270: PLAY-uh-dess

Poias, 3.190: POY-uhss

Polites, 10.224: paw-LEE-tayss

Polubos, (a) 1.399, (b) 4.126, (c) 8.373, and
(d) 22.244: PAW-loo-bawss

Poludamna, 4.228: paw-loo-DAHM-nuh

Poludeukes, 11.300: paw-loo-D(EH)OO-kayss

Polukaste, 3.464: paw-loo-KAHSS-tay

Poluktor, 17.207: paw-LOOK-tohr

Poluneos, 8.114: paw-LOO-nay-awss

Polupemon, 24.305: paw-loo-PAY-mohn

Polupheides, 15.249: paw-loo-P(H)EY-dayss

Poluphemos, 1.70: paw-loo-P(H)AY-mawss

Polutherses, 22.287: paw-loo-THAIR-sayss

Ponteus, 8.113: PAWN-t(eh)ooss

Pontonoos, 7.179: pawn-TAW-naw-awss

Poseidon or Poseidaon, 1.20: paw-sey-
DAH-ohn

Pramneia, 10.235: prahm-NEY-uh

Priam or Priamos, 3.108: PREE-uh-mawss

Prokris, 11.321: PRAWK-riss

Proreus, 8.113: PROH-r(eh)ooss

Proteus, 4.365: PROH-t(eh)ooss

Prumneus, 8.112: PROOM-n(eh)ooss

Psurie, 3.171: puh-SOO-REE-ay

Pulos, 1.93: POO-lawss

Puriphlegethon, 10.514: POO-rih-p(h)leh-GEH-
t(h)ohn (the g as in *guard*)

Putho, 8.81: POO-t(h)oh

Rhadamanthus, 4.564: r(h)uh-DUH-mahn-
t(h)ooss

Rheithron, 1.186: R(H)EY-t(h)rawn

Rhexenor, 7.63: r(h)ayx-AY-nohr

Salmoneus, 11.236: sahl-MOH-n(eh)ooss

Same or Samos, 1.246: SAH-may or SAH-
mawss

Samos, 4.671: SAH-mawss

Seirenes, 12.39: sey-RAY-nayss

Sicily or Sikanie or Sikelie, 20.383: sih-
kuh-NEE-ay or sih-keh-LEE-ay

Sidon, 4.84: SEE-dohn

Sinties, 8.294: SIN-tih-ess

Sisuphos, 11.593: SEE-soo-p(h)awss

Skherie, 5.34: sk(h)eh-RIH-ay

Skulla, 12.85: SKOOL-luh

Skuros, 11.509: SKOO-rawss

Solumoi, 5.283: SAW-loo-moy

Sounion, 3.278: SOO-nih-awn

Southeasterly or Euros, 5.295:
(EH)OO-rawss

Southwind or Notos, 3.295: NAW-tawss

Sparte, 1.93: SPAHR-tay

Spinners or Klothes, 7.197: KLOH-t(h)ess

Stratios, 3.413: STRAH-tih-awss

Stux, 5.185: STOOX

Surie, 15.403: SOO-REE-ay

Tantalos, 11.582: TAHN-tuh-lawss

Taphians or Taphoi, 1.105: TAH-p(h)oi

Taphos, 1.417: TAH-p(h)awss

Teiresies, 10.492: tey-REH-see-ayss

Tekton, 8.114: TEK-tohn

Telamon, 11.543: TEH-luh-mohn

Telemakhos, 1.113: tay-LEH-muh-k(h)awss

Telemos, 9.509: TAY-leh-mawss

Telephos, 11.519: TAY-leh-p(h)awss

Telepulos, 10.82: tay-LEH-poo-lawss

Temese, 1.184: teh-MEH-say

Tenedos, 3.159: TEH-neh-dawss

Terpis, 22.329: TAIR-pis

Teugeton, 6.103: tay-oo-geh-tawn (the *g* as in *guard*)

Thebes or Thebai, 4.127: T(H)AY-bai

Themis, 2.68: T(H)EH-miss

Theoklumenos, 15.257: t(h)eh-aw-KLOO-meh-naws

Theseus, 11.322: T(H)AY-s(eh)ooss

Thesprotians or Thesprotoi, 14.316: t(h)ess-PROH-toy

Thetis, 24.91: T(H)AY-tiss

Thoas, 14.499: T(H)AW-ahss

Thon, 4.228: T(H)OHN

Thoon, 8.113: T(H)AW-ohn

Thoosa, 1.71: t(h)aw-OH-suh

Thrace or Threke, 8.361: T(H)RAY-kay

Thrasumedes, 3.39: thrah-soo-MAY-dayss

Thrinakie, 11.106: t(h)ree-nuh-KEE-ay

Thuestes, 4.517: t(h)oo-ESS-tayss

Tithonos, 5.1: tih-T(H)OH-nawss

Tituos, 7.324: TIH-too-awss

Tritogeneia, 3.378: TREE-taw-geh-NEY-uh (the *g* as in *guard*)

Trojans or Troes, 1.237: TROH-ess

Troy or Troie, 1.2: TROY-ay

Tudeos, 3.167: TOO-deh-awss

Tundareos, 11.298: toon-DUH-reh-awss

Turo, 2.120: TOO-roh

Unfailing or Atrutone, 4.762: ah-TROO-toh-nay

Wagon or Great Bear, Amaxa or Arktos, 5.273: AH-mux-uh or AHRK-tos

Westwind or Zephuros, 2.421: ZDEH-p(h)oo-rawss

Zakunthos, 1.246: zdah-KOON-t(h)awss

Zethos, 11.262: ZDAY-t(h)awss

Zeus, 1.10: ZD(EH)OOSS

Bibliography
Richard P. Martin

Athanassakis, Apostolos. *Hesiod: Theogony, Works and Days, Shield* (Baltimore, 1983).

———. *The Homeric Hymns* (Baltimore, 1976).

Austin, Norman. *Archery at the Dark of the Moon* (Berkeley, 1975).

Butler, Samuel. *The Authoress of the Odyssey* (2d ed., London, 1922).

Clarke, Howard. *The Art of the Odyssey* (Englewood Cliffs, N.J., 1967).

———. *Homer's Readers: A Historical Introduction to the Iliad and the Odyssey* (London, 1981).

Clarke, Howard, ed. *Twentieth-Century Interpretations of the Odyssey* (Englewood Cliffs, N.J., 1985).

Clay, Jenny Strauss. *The Wrath of Athena* (Princeton, 1984).

Cohen, Beth, ed. *The Distaff Side: Representing the Female in Homer's Odyssey* (New York, 1995).

Doherty, Lillian. *Siren Songs: Gender, Audiences, and Narrators in the Odyssey* (Ann Arbor, 1996).

Dougherty, Carol. *The Raft of Odysseus: The Ethnographic Imagination of Homer's Odyssey* (New York, 2001).

Dumézil, Georges. *The Destiny of the Warrior.* Trans. A. Hiltebeitel (Chicago, 1970).

Felson-Rubin, Nancy. *Regarding Penelope: From Character to Poetics* (Princeton, 1994).

Finley, John, Jr. *Homer's Odyssey* (Cambridge, Mass., 1978).

Finley, Moses. *The World of Odysseus* (2d rev. ed., London, 1977).

Foley, John Miles. *Immanent Art: From Structure to Meaning in Traditional Oral Epic* (Bloomington, Ind., 1991).

———. *Oral-Formulaic Theory and Research: An Introduction and Annotated Bibliography* (New York, 1985).

———. *Traditional Oral Epic: The Odyssey, Beowulf, and the Serbo-Croatian Return Song* (Berkeley, 1993).

Griffin, Jasper. *Homer on Life and Death* (Oxford, 1980).

Heubeck, A., S. West, and J. B. Hainsworth, eds. *A Commentary on Homer's Odyssey.* 3 vols. (Oxford, 1988–90).

Katz, Marilyn A. *Penelope's Renown: Meaning and Indeterminancy in the Odyssey* (Princeton, 1991).

Lord, Albert. *Epic Singers and Oral Tradition* (Ithaca, N.Y., 1991).

———. *The Singer of Tales.* (2d ed., Cambridge, Mass., 2000).

Malkin, Irad. *The Returns of Odysseus: Colonization and Ethnicity* (Berkeley, 1998).

Martin, Richard. *The Language of Heroes: Speech and Performance in the Iliad* (Ithaca, N.Y., 1989).

———. *Myths of the Ancient Greeks* (New York, 2003).

Moulton, Carroll. *Similes in the Homeric Poems* (Göttingen, 1977).

Myres, J. L. *Homer and His Critics* (London, 1958).

Nagy, Gregory. *The Best of the Achaeans: Concepts of the Hero in Archaic Greek Poetry* (2d ed., Baltimore, 1999).

——. *Plato's Rhapsody and Homer's Music: The Poetics of the Panathenaic Festival in Classical Athens* (Washington, D.C., 2002).

——. *Poetry as Performance: Homer and Beyond* (Cambridge, 1996).

Olson, S. D. *Blood and Iron: Stories and Storytelling in Homer's Odyssey* (Leiden, 1995).

Packard, D. W., and T. Meyers. *A Bibliography of Homeric Scholarship 1930–1970* (Malibu, 1974).

Page, Denys. *Folktales in Homer's Odyssey* (Cambridge, Mass., 1973).

Peradotto, John. *Man in the Middle Voice: Name and Narration in the Odyssey* (Princeton, 1990).

Powell, Barry, and Ian Morris, eds. *A New Companion to Homer* (Leiden, 1997).

Pucci, Pietro. *The Song of the Sirens: Essays on Homer* (Lanham, Md., 1998).

Reece, S. *The Stranger's Welcome: Oral Theory and the Aesthetics of the Homeric Hospitality Scene* (Ann Arbor, 1993).

Reynolds, Dwight. *Heroic Poets, Poetic Heroes: The Ethnography of Performance in an Arabic Oral Epic Tradition* (Ithaca, N.Y., 1995).

Schein, Seth, ed. *Reading the Odyssey* (Princeton, 1995).

Segal, Charles. *Singers, Heroes and Gods in the Odyssey* (Ithaca, N.Y., 1994).

Stanford, W. B. *The Ulysses Theme: A Study in the Adaptability of a Traditional Hero* (2d ed., Oxford, 1963).

Taylor, Charles H., Jr., ed. *Essays on the "Odyssey"* (Bloomington, Ind., 1963).

Van Wees, H. *Status Warriors: War, Violence, and Society in Homer and History* (Amsterdam, 1992).

Wood, Michael. *In Search of the Trojan War* (New York, 1985).